GEO-ECONOMICS IN SOUTH ASIAN ENVIRONMENT

GEO-ECONOMICS IN SOUTH ASIAN ENVIRONMENT

Editors

Rakesh Kumar
University of Delhi, India

Harjit Singh
Symboisis International (Deemed University), India

NEW JERSEY · LONDON · SINGAPORE · BEIJING · SHANGHAI · TAIPEI · CHENNAI

Published by

World Scientific Publishing Co. Pte. Ltd.
5 Toh Tuck Link, Singapore 596224
USA office: 27 Warren Street, Suite 401-402, Hackensack, NJ 07601
UK office: 57 Shelton Street, Covent Garden, London WC2H 9HE

Library of Congress Control Number: 2024032505

British Library Cataloguing-in-Publication Data
A catalogue record for this book is available from the British Library.

GEO-ECONOMICS IN SOUTH ASIAN ENVIRONMENT

Copyright © 2025 by World Scientific Publishing Co. Pte. Ltd.

All rights reserved. This book, or parts thereof, may not be reproduced in any form or by any means, electronic or mechanical, including photocopying, recording or any information storage and retrieval system now known or to be invented, without written permission from the publisher.

For photocopying of material in this volume, please pay a copying fee through the Copyright Clearance Center, Inc., 222 Rosewood Drive, Danvers, MA 01923, USA. In this case permission to photocopy is not required from the publisher.

ISBN 978-981-12-9838-7 (hardcover)
ISBN 978-981-12-9839-4 (ebook for institutions)
ISBN 978-981-12-9840-0 (ebook for individuals)

For any available supplementary material, please visit
https://www.worldscientific.com/worldscibooks/10.1142/13990#t=suppl

Desk Editors: Nambirajan Karuppiah/Kura Sunaina

Typeset by Stallion Press
Email: enquiries@stallionpress.com

Printed in Singapore

© 2025 World Scientific Publishing Company
https://doi.org/10.1142/9789811298394_fmatter

Preface

The term 'Geo-economics' highlights the potential economic dividends owed to a particular region. This book highlights the potential areas for dividends which South Asia as a region offers to the regional countries owing to shared cultural, social, religious, and geographical connectedness. Drawing on empirical research, this book has the potential to bridge the gap between the current intra-regional state of economic and political affairs in South Asia and, therefore, proposes new dimensions in trade and economic cooperation in a wider perspective focusing on all segments of the economy. The rich collections of chapters not only enrich the understanding of the reasons behind the low level of regional trade and economic cooperation in South Asia but also offer new insight into the facts to adopt and apply progressive regional trade policy in the fast-changing business environment amid evolving geopolitics in the region.

The disruption in international trade due to the lockdown in the leading trade partners from the external markets, COVID-19 has offered the South Asian countries to look into inward policy towards regional markets. If man-made barriers and perceived threats are overcome, this book presents a strong case for potential gains in trade and economic cooperation in South Asia amid the evolving geo-economics in the post pandemic era.

Detailed and insightful, this book is intended primarily for researchers and students of international trade, public foreign policy, finance, international relations, and South Asian studies, and for policymakers from South Asia and beyond to adopt and apply progressive policy in the South Asia region. This book enriches the skills and understanding of the readers through a variety of means. Hence, this book offers the following advantages to the readers:

- It provides an in-depth analysis of a variety of issues related to evolving geopolitics and potential challenges and opportunities in regional trade and economic cooperation in South Asia.
- It highlights the role of common cultural, linguistic, and historical heritage, which can harmonise the tense geopolitics in the region.
- It fills the gaps in our understanding between the actual and perceived reasons behind the low level of regional trade and economic cooperation in South Asia.
- It highlights the evolving geopolitics in South Asia.
- It highlights the feasibility of rail and road connectivity across South Asia.

The title of this book is structured around the potential challenges and opportunities which South Asia as a region offers to the countries located therein. Chapter 1 of this book enlists the potential areas where South Asian countries have vast opportunities to realise mutual gains through dialogue and cooperation. The rest of this book is divided into five parts. All the five parts attempt to showcase the geo-economics aspects of the South Asian region in various areas. Part I of this book, which comprises three chapters, highlights the economic dividends arising out of religious and other forms of tourism in the region. Chapter 2 outlines the shared cultural, social, and religious heritage in South Asia. It shows how tourism is becoming a promising tool for promoting people-to-people contacts. Chapter 3 applies a rigorous econometric model to examine the impact of tourism on the growth rates of South Asian countries. Chapter 4 highlights the potential of tourism which South Asia offers to the people having Buddhist faith in the region.

Part II of this book posits the trade disruption and divergence due to perceived and actual security threats in the region. Hence, Part II focuses on the most important aspects in South Asia which serves as the root cause of all the regional problems. This part includes four chapters in all. Chapter 5 examines the potential security threats and how India can provide security concerns to the other countries in the region if some sort of regional peace treaty is restored. Chapter 6 examines the root cause of low intraregional trade. It is the political argument over the economic considerations which governs the trading relations in the region, states the chapter.

Chapter 7 enlists the man-made trade barriers which are responsible for trade divergence in the region. Chapter 8 attempts to highlight the debt crisis in the two largest economies in the South Asian region due to heavy spending on military and defence equipment.

Part III of this book empirically examines the preferred trade model in South Asia and comprises four chapters. Chapter 9 attempts to show empirically a bilateral trade model due to tense geopolitical relations in the region for the fast and quick recovery of the economy amid the COVID-19 pandemic. Chapter 10 stresses the well-structured regional trade agreements for the mutual gains of the member countries. Further, Chapter 11 attempts to show the role of India in building a trade network in services in the South Asia region for mutual benefits. Chapter 12 enlists the governance-related reasons which tend to act as challenges to South Asia as a unified geographical unit.

Part IV, which includes three chapters, highlights the potential benefits of rail and road connectivity for the transportation of goods and services in the region. For example, Chapter 13 shows the trade disruptions owing to supply chains in South Asia amid the pandemic. Strong connectivity through rail and road offers multidimensional benefits to neighbouring countries during the crisis hours, such as COVID-19 pandemic. In addition, Chapter 14 highlights the potential economic benefits arising out of production networks in South Asia. Further, Chapter 15 enlists the policy challenges and lessons in the way forward of rail and road connectivity in the South Asian region.

Part V, which includes three chapters, attempts to show the resilience of South Asian countries during pre and post COVID-19 pandemic. For example, Chapter 16 examines the financial and economic crisis which South Asian countries witnessed during the COVID-19 disruption. Chapter 17 attempts to showcase the role of economic diplomacy in building diplomatic relations during the pandemic. Lastly, Chapter 18 proposes an econometric model to examine how the population and skill set of the population are helpful in attracting foreign direct investment in the countries.

The authors are solely responsible for the contents of the papers compiled in this book. The publisher or editors do not take any responsibility for the same in any manner. Errors, if any, are purely unintentional and readers are requested to communicate such errors to the editors or publishers to avoid discrepancies in future.

About the Editors

Rakesh Kumar is currently working in the capacity of Associate Professor in the Department of Management Studies, Deen Dayal Upadhyaya College (University of Delhi), New Delhi, India. He holds an M.A. (Economics) from Kurukshetra University, an MBA (Finance) from MDU Rohtak, and a Ph.D. (Finance) from FMS, University of Delhi. His doctoral research explores the risk and returns trade-off, the effect of diversification of risk in the Indian stock market by utilising the Capital Asset Pricing Model, and spillovers of regional trade partnerships on the economic welfare of the people.

He has demonstrated research publications that explore the impact of trade relations on financial and trade integration while focusing on the South Asia region, and the impact of international exogenous factors on the volatility of stock markets. He has published more than 25 research papers in high-impact factor international journals in the field of international finance and economics. He has presented more than 20 papers at national and international conferences in India and foreign countries like France, Spain, Russia, and Kazakhstan. Emerald Publishing UK has conferred him a Highly Commended Research award for publishing papers in the field of financial economics.

 **Harjit Singh**, a regular contributor to national and international journals, is a Professor of Finance at Symbiosis Centre for Management Studies, Noida, India, and Symbiosis International University, Pune, India. He has over two decades of rich experience in teaching, research, and consultancy. He has travelled extensively in and outside India to conduct workshops, seminars, MDPs, and FDPs. He has written several textbooks, study materials, edited books, and case studies with internationally reputed publication houses. His research areas are fintech, business restructuring, blockchain, international economics, corporate governance, and ChatGPT. He is also the reviewer for Inderscience, Emerald, Taylor & Francis, Springer, etc.

Acknowledgements

In the preparation of this book, we have received encouragement and support from various quarters. We would like to express our deep appreciation and gratitude to all the authors who have contributed their chapters. We also acknowledge the deep gratitude to all the reviewers for their valuable and insightful comments for the improvement of all the chapters.

Finally, we would be failing in our duty if we do not acknowledge the support and encouragement which we have received from our publisher World Scientific Publishing, Singapore.

Contents

Preface		v
About the Editors		ix
Acknowledgements		xi
Chapter 1	Geo-Economics in the South Asian Environment: An Introduction *Rakesh Kumar and Harjit Singh*	1
Part I	People to People Contact: Role of Tourism	21
Chapter 2	Paradigm Shift of Religious Tourism in South Asia *Shikha Misra*	23
Chapter 3	Feasibility of Tourism in South Asian Economies: An Econometric Analysis *Nilendu Chatterjee and Tonmoy Chatterjee*	47
Chapter 4	Buddhist Religious Circuit: A Connect to India, Nepal, Sri Lanka, Bhutan and Myanmar *Yogieta S. Mehra, Monika Bansal, and Vidhan Garg*	65

Part II	Trade Disruption Amid Perceived versus Realistic Security Threats	83
Chapter 5	The Interface between Economics and Security: Defence Industry for a Resurgent India *Raghbendra Jha and Ashok Sharma*	85
Chapter 6	Conflicts and the Politicisation of Trade: Implications for Economic Cooperation in South Asia *Zahid Shahab Ahmed and Muhammad Jahanzaib*	115
Chapter 7	Implications of Trade Barriers and Their Effect on South Asian Countries *Deepika Dhingra, Rahul Mehriya, Hardik Sharma, and Abhishek Kumar Singh*	133
Chapter 8	External Debt Distress in Pakistan and India *Shahida Wizarat*	149
Part III	Bilateralism versus Multilateralism: Potential Trade Model in South Asia	163
Chapter 9	Regional Geopolitics and Economic Fallout of COVID-19: Policy Options for India *Rakesh Kumar*	165
Chapter 10	Institutional Setup and Export Performance: Evidence from South Asia *Suadat Hussain Wani and Effat Yasmin*	183
Chapter 11	Can India's Export of Services Build Economic Partnerships in South Asia? *Sagnik Bagchi*	201
Chapter 12	Challenges for Regionalism in South Asia: The Role of Institutions and Human Development *Rashmi Arora*	227

Part IV	**Rail and Road Connectivity: Scope for Regional Production Networks**	**245**
Chapter 13	**Trade Disruption and Shifting Trends in Trade Partners amid the Pandemic: A Case Study of South Asia** *Mojtaba Hajian Heidary*	**247**
Chapter 14	**Supply Chain Network in South Asia** *Karuna Chauhan and Surender Kumar*	**267**
Chapter 15	**Enhancing Rail and Road Connectivity in South Asia: Challenges and Prospects** *Manoj Chaudhary and Harjit Singh*	**277**
Part V	**Resilient South Asian Economies amid Global Pandemic**	**293**
Chapter 16	**Financial Crises in South Asia Caused by COVID-19 Disruption** *Muhammad Nadir Shabbir, Kainat Iftikhar, and Tanveer Bagh*	**295**
Chapter 17	**South Asia: A Case for Economic Diplomacy in Pre- and Post-Pandemic** *Jitin Gambhir and Ranu Kumar*	**313**
Chapter 18	**Population Dynamics, Skill Heterogeneity and Globalisation: A General Equilibrium Analysis** *Sushobhan Mahata, Rohan Kanti Khan, Riddhi Sil, Utsa Kar, and Purbita Nag*	**327**
Index		351

Chapter 1

Geo-Economics in the South Asian Environment: An Introduction

Rakesh Kumar*,‡ and Harjit Singh†,§

Deen Dayal Upadhyaya College, University of Delhi, New Delhi, India

†*Symbiosis Centre for Management Studies, Symbiosis International University, Pune, India*

‡*saini_rakeshindia@yahoo.co.in*
§*harjit.singh@scmsnoida.ac.in*

Abstract

South Asia is the least integrated region in spite of shared cultural, linguistic, and historical heritage. The intra-regional trade is under 5% which is substantially lower as compared to other regional trade blocs. The deeper trade ties between the countries from the region could not evolve so far because of political differences at the regional level and other man-made barriers. Hence, the pre- and post-effects of COVID-19 have offered new lessons to South Asian countries to re-examine the existing regional policies. If trade barriers are overcome, intra-regional trade tend to expand manifold for mutual gains. Similarly, the pandemic has forced the South Asian countries to actively work on inward policies at the regional level to meet the potential challenges which tend to emerge due to pandemic and other geopolitical reasons. India, being the largest country in the region, has the responsibility to engage the South Asian countries in a wider perspective.

Keywords: Trade; economic cooperation, South Asia, pandemic, tourism.

1. Introduction

South Asian countries comprising India, Pakistan, Bangladesh, Sri Lanka, Nepal, Bhutan, Maldives and Afghanistan is home to over 1.90 billion people, making up 25% of the world population. It is found to be the least integrated region worldwide economically and politically, while South Asia is linguistically, culturally, socially and historically a highly integrated region. The intra-regional trade is only 5% despite the region being well-connected geographically. The intra-regional capital flows in the South Asian region are much more limited than inter-regional trade. Deeper intra-regional trade ties could not evolve due to human-made trade barriers and mutual trust deficit owing to actual and perceived threats on the national security. All the countries from the region could not overcome their common problems such as low per capita income, low infrastructure, low social services and high poverty rates despite possessing rich natural resources and high potential for regional trade. All the South Asian countries stand at lower social and economic benchmarks when compared to the rest of the world as shown in Tables 1 and 2.

Table 1. Key economic indicators.

	1990	1995	2000	2005	2010	2022
GDP per capita (current US$)						
India	363.96	370.10	438.86	707.01	1345.77	2388.62
Pakistan	371.57	493.66	533.86	711.47	1040.14	1596.66
Sri Lanka	463.51	714.07	869.50	1250.00	2808.55	3354.38
Bangladesh	297.57	319.61	405.60	484.16	757.67	2688.30
Nepal	184.92	197.31	223.71	309.31	589.17	1336.55
Bhutan	515.30	550.66	722.83	1201.43	2194.13	NA
GDP growth rate (annual %)						
India	5.53	7.57	3.84	7.92	8.50	7.00
Pakistan	4.46	4.96	4.26	6.52	1.61	6.19

Table 1. (*Continued*)

	1990	1995	2000	2005	2010	2022
Sri Lanka	6.40	5.50	6.00	6.24	8.02	−7.82
Bangladesh	5.62	5.12	5.29	6.54	5.57	7.10
Nepal	4.64	3.47	6.20	3.48	4.82	5.61
Bhutan	10.38	7.07	3.36	7.29	11.95	NA
Trade to GDP ratio (%)						
India	15.51	22.87	26.90	42.00	49.26	49.37
Pakistan	35.03	36.13	25.36	32.15	32.87	32.32
Sri Lanka	68.24	81.64	88.64	73.60	NA	46.52
Bangladesh	18.97	28.21	29.32	34.40	37.80	33.78
Nepal	32.19	59.49	55.71	44.06	45.98	49.40
Bhutan	61.22	83.88	80.35	105.52	115.92	NA
Foreign direct investment, net inflows (% of GDP)						
India	0.07	0.59	0.77	0.89	1.64	1.48
Pakistan	0.61	1.19	0.38	1.83	1.14	0.36
Sri Lanka	0.54	0.43	1.06	1.12	0.81	1.21
Bangladesh	0.01	0.00	0.53	1.17	1.07	0.34
Nepal	0.16	0.00	−0.01	0.03	0.55	0.16
Bhutan	0.56	0.02	NA	0.78	4.86	NA
GCF to GDP ratio (%)						
India	27.34	29.15	25.68	37.43	39.79	31.16
Pakistan	18.94	18.55	17.58	17.72	15.80	15.14
Sri Lanka	22.21	25.73	28.04	26.83	NA	34.39
Bangladesh	16.46	19.12	23.81	25.83	26.25	32.05
Nepal	18.13	25.20	24.31	26.45	38.27	37.42
Bhutan	27.86	44.72	50.34	54.04	63.21	NA
Domestic Saving to GDP (%)						
India	21.64	25.76	24.31	32.26	34.27	28.96
Pakistan	13.48	15.83	16.45	14.19	9.97	3.76
Sri Lanka	17.71	16.52	18.01	17.90	NA	30.84
Bangladesh	15.91	13.13	20.02	21.06	20.81	25.22
Nepal	6.99	15.66	15.17	11.56	11.45	5.77
Bhutan	18.34	35.31	27.32	23.81	34.24	NA

Source: World Development Indicators (2023) and Asian Development Bank Database, https://aric.adb.org/integrationindicators.

Table 2. Key social indicators.

	1990	2000	2010	2022
Population (in million), total				
India	870.45	1059.63	1240.61	1417.17
Pakistan	115.41	154.37	194.45	235.82
Sri Lanka	17.20	18.78	20.67	22.18
Bangladesh	107.15	129.19	148.39	171.19
Nepal	19.62	24.56	27.16	30.55
Bhutan	0.56	0.59	0.71	0.78
Unemployment, total (% of total labour force) (modelled ILO estimate)				
India	NA	7.77	8.32	7.33
Pakistan	NA	0.61	0.65	6.42
Sri Lanka	NA	7.74	4.78	6.71
Bangladesh	NA	3.27	3.38	4.70
Nepal	NA	10.60	10.55	11.12
Bhutan	NA	1.63	3.32	3.60
Labour force participation rate, total (% of total population ages 15+) (modelled ILO estimate)				
India	54.21	57.20	54.73	49.49
Pakistan	49.35	50.41	51.00	52.75
Sri Lanka	61.45	55.57	53.29	50.90
Bangladesh	58.27	58.28	57.28	58.75
Nepal	41.43	41.29	40.19	40.05
Bhutan	71.12	69.89	68.15	61.87
Mortality rate, infant (per 1,000 live births)				
India	88.80	66.70	45.10	NA
Pakistan	106.90	84.80	70.20	NA
Sri Lanka	19.40	14.20	9.60	NA
Bangladesh	101.00	63.10	38.90	NA
Nepal	96.40	58.70	36.60	NA
Bhutan	88.90	57.40	34.10	NA
Human development index				
India	0.434	0.491	0.575	0.633*
Pakistan	0.400	0.441	0.505	0.544*
Sri Lanka	0.636	0.688	0.737	0.782*
Bangladesh	0.397	0.485	0.553	0.661*
Nepal	0.399	0.467	0.543	0.602*
Bhutan	NA	NA	0.581	0.666*

Note: * indicates data for the year 2021.

As a first step towards promoting regional cooperation, seven South Asian countries (India, Pakistan, Bangladesh, Sri Lanka, Nepal, Bhutan, and Maldives) formed the South Asian Association of Regional Cooperation (SAARC) way back in 1985. Further, SAARC countries agreed to create South Asia Free Trade Agreements (SAFTA) in January 2004, which finally became operational from January 2006. This arrangement has been argued to be favourable for the least developed countries (LDCs) in the region. As of now, intra-regional trade in South Asia stands under 5%. Since 2016, no SAARC meeting has been convened after the cancellation of the 19th SAARC meeting scheduled to be held in Pakistan. It was cancelled after the boycott of the meeting by India on the grounds of terrorist attacks on its military establishment (see Kumar, 2021). Against the expectation, the SAARC could not realise its main objective due to prevailing trust deficit and other prominent reasons such as terrorism.

The regional trade of India, which is the largest economy in the region, is under 4%. Despite being the largest economies in the region, India and Pakistan have witnessed low trade relations in the last decades. The conflicting relations between the two countries caused by unresolved territorial disputes and proxy war through terrorism deeply govern the geopolitics in South Asia (see Ashraf *et al.*, 2017; Akram, 2020; Kumar, 2020). Because of these reasons, the deeper trade ties between the countries from the region have not been evolved so far. At the multilateral level, the dialogue process received serious setbacks after the cancellation of the 19th SAARC summit supposed to be held in Pakistan. The track record of trade in South Asia posits that it is the political argument that drives trade between the two countries instead of economic consideration.

The outbreak of COVID-19 pandemic at end of 2019 in the Wuhan, China, shocked the whole world with far-reaching socio-economic consequences for all the South Asian countries. The World Bank Report on South Asia Economic Focus (2021) highlighted that all the countries from the region witnessed lower investment flows, disruption in supply chains and reported substantial increase in debt during the pandemic. The largest trade partners from the extra-regional markets like the United States, East Asia and European countries were under strict lockdown for a long period, which further had severe consequences for the South Asian countries, the report adds. Hence, the economic fallout due to COVID-19 was believed to be disastrous with far-reaching socio-economic consequences for South Asian countries owing to their economic, social and demographic conditions. India, Pakistan and Bangladesh were believed to be the most affected countries in the region due to high population size and density.

The top trading partners from the external markets like China, the United States, Japan and South Korea, including the European countries such as Germany, France, UK and Spain were under extensive lockdown to contain the disease. All the economic activities including imports and exports were under suspension as a part of the lockdown. All mentioned eight countries are the top trade partners for all South Asian countries, which serve as the destinations of over 30% of total exports and are the sources of 35% of total imports (see Chapter 9). Hence, the pre- and post-effect of COVID-19 have offered new lessons to South Asian countries to re-examine the existing regional policies. Hence, the pandemic has forced them to actively work on inward policies at the regional level to meet the potential challenges which tend to emerge due to pandemics and other geopolitical reasons. India, being the largest country in the region, has the responsibility to engage the South Asian countries in a wider perspective. Besides, India is centrally located in the Indian sub-continent, hence can act as a bridge for the easy transportation of goods between the countries from the region through rail and road connectivity.

India accounts for the largest share in the export and import of goods and services in the total trade volume of the South Asia region with the rest of the world. As per World Development Indicators (2023), India accounts for the largest Gross Domestic Product (GDP) share in the total GDP of South Asia, and it is rising over the years, whereas the GDP share of the other countries from the region have been declining during the last decades. As per the World Development Report on South Asia (2023) estimates, South Asia is expected to grow at just under 6%, which is a faster growth rate than any other developing region worldwide. However, the South Asian outlook represents a slowdown from pre-pandemic averages due to weak financial systems and fiscal positions. In India, which accounts for the bulk of the region's economy, growth is expected to remain robust at 6.3% in FY23/24. Maldives is expected to grow by 6.5% in 2023, while Nepal is expected to rebound to 3.9% due to a strong revival in tourism in both countries. In Bangladesh, growth will slow to 5.6% in FY23/24, while Pakistan and Sri Lanka will grow at only 1.7% respectively during FY23/24 due to the weakening of currencies caused by financial crisis, the report adds.

The policy implications of this book should be viewed in the context of developing deeper economic cooperation between the South Asian countries both regionally and globally. It should be pursued by unlocking regional sources of growth like promotion of regional trade and capital flows with the objective of long-term gain. The financial and trade integration should be viewed as an opportunity to correct the regional economic growth imbalances.

2. Intra, and Inter-Regional Trade Linkages

As per the World Development Indicators (WDI), India, Pakistan, Sri Lanka and Bangladesh are the largest economies in the South Asian region. The four countries account for the largest share in trade and GDP from the region. At the regional level, the economic cooperation among the South Asian countries is found to be very low. For example, Kumar (2021) reports that the intra-regional trade of South Asia stands at only 5%, which is substantially low as compared to the other trade blocs worldwide. The study reports that trade is heavily oriented towards extra-regional markets. The possible reasons are restricted regional trade policies and high political differences.

The Asian Development database (2023) makes the following observations: (1) India and Pakistan are net exporters to the region, while Bangladesh, Sri Lanka, Nepal and Bhutan are net importers from the region. (2) India accounts for the largest trade volume in South Asia followed by Bangladesh. The trade volume of India has increased from US$656.50 million with a 1.57% trade share during 1990 to US$21,957 million with a 3.41% trade share during 2020. (3) Bhutan accounts for the largest trade share in South Asia. The trade share (trade volume) of Bhutan has increased from 9.70% (US$8.32 million) during 1990 to 91.81% (US$2646 million) during 2020 followed by Nepal. The trade share (trade volume) of Nepal has increased from 11.88% (US$94.80 million) to 63.54% (US$7186 million) during the same period. (4) It is found that all the South Asian countries have witnessed expanded trade volume especially after the implementation of SAFTA in the region.

The evolving geopolitics at the regional and global level also led the South Asian countries to change their conventional trade partners to new ones from the extra-regional markets. For example, ASEAN+3 (26.73%) is the major trade partner of South Asia followed by Middle East

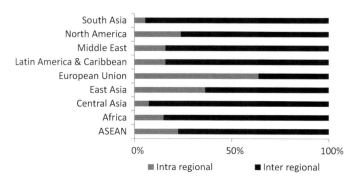

Figure 1. Intra and inter-regional trade of major trading blocs in 2017.
Source: Asian Development Bank Database, https://aric.adb.org/integrationindicators.

(22.41%) and East Asia (17.97%) in 2020, collectively accounting for more than 55% trade share of the region (see Asian Development Bank Database, 2023). At the country level, top trade partners are different and directions of trade of sample countries vary over time. As of now, the top three trade partners of India account for more than 53% of total trade. The trade partners are East Asia (trade share has increased from 12.54% in 1990 to 21.43% in 2020) followed by the Middle East (trade share has increased from 13.41% in 1990 to 18.87% in 2020) and Europe (however trade share has decreased from 32.25% in 1990 to 17.03% in 2020). The European Union, which was the largest trade partner of India in 1990, has been replaced by East Asia and Middle East over the years (see Kumar, 2023a).

When intra-regional trade in South Asia is compared with the other trading blocs, it is found that the intra-regional trade of South Asia stands only at 5.64%, much lower than East Asia (36.35%), ASEAN (22.49%), Latin America and Caribbean (15.94%), North America (23.88%) and European Union (63.87%) as shown in Figure 1. Despite being the largest economy, India's trade with its neighbours, for example, is under 5% of its total trade.

3. South Asia: Potential Geo-Economic Areas

3.1. *People to people contact: Role of tourism*

In the present globalised world, tourism has proved to be a potential tool for the growth of different segments of the economy such as accommodation, communication, health, environmental aspects and other businesses (see Chapter 3). Hence tourism industry has become one of the prime factors for the overall development of countries, especially for small economies. The development of the tourism industry generates social and economic dividends for the country such as development of transport facilities, hotels and hospitality facilities, recreational values, environmental standard, political stability and enhances the much-needed social tolerance among the people (see Chapter 3; Petrescu, 2011). For example, Chapter 3 shows that tourism is one such aspect that requires various facilities to work together in order to have a successful impact on the growth of the nation.

Law and order, which are dependent on security and political stability, is the pre-requite for determining the shape and volume of tourism in the country. It is the political and security that has a positive moderation effect on the relationship between international remittances and international tourism development. Among others, political stability, violence and terrorism are important factors that international tourists consider while deciding the destination to visit for touring purposes. As of now the tourism industry has been one of the fastest growing as well as the basic source of livelihood in several parts in the world (Shahzad *et al.*, 2017).

The impact of COVID-19 has proved disastrous for the hospitability and the tourism industry. The tourism industry witnessed job loss of 50 million worldwide as per estimates of the World Tour and Travel Council Report. The outbreak of the pandemic has severely affected the demand for and supply of travel, as per the report of the UN World Tourism Organisation. International tourists have decelerated between 20% and 30% in 2020, which translates into a loss of between US$30 and US$50 billion in spending by international visitors, the report adds. As per the World Tour and Travel Council Report (2022), prior to the pandemic, travel and tourism created one in five new jobs across the world during 2014–2019, and 10.3% of all jobs (334 million). Tourism contributed 10.4% to the global GDP (US$ 10 trillion) in 2019. The international visitor spend amounted to US$ 1.9 trillion in 2019, the report adds. In 2022, the travel and tourism sector contributed 7.6% to global GDP, which is an increase of 22% from 2021 and only 23% below 2019 levels. In 2022, there were 22 million new jobs, representing a 7.9% increase on 2021. Due to tourism, international visitor spending rose by 81.9% in 2022 (see World Tour & Travel Council Report, 2022).

The South Asian countries belong to the Indian sub-continent have common historical, linguistic and cultural heritage since ancient times,

Table 3. Religious demographics in South Asia.

Country	Religious demographics
Afghanistan	Islam (99%), Hinduism, Sikhism and Christianity (1%)
Bangladesh	Islam (90%), Hinduism (9%), Buddhism (0.6%), Christianity (0.3%), Others (0.1%)
Bhutan	Buddhism (75%), Hinduism (25%)
India	Hinduism (79.5%), Islam (14.5%), Christianity (2.3%), Sikhism (1.7%), Buddhism (0.7%), Jainism (0.4%), Others (0.9%)
Maldives	Sunni Islam (100%)
Nepal	Hinduism (82%), Buddhism (9.0%), Islam (4.4%), Kirat (3.1%), Christianity (1.4%), Others (0.8%)
Pakistan	Islam (96.28%), Hinduism (2%), Christianity (1.59%), Ahmaddiyya (0.22%)
Sri Lanka	Buddhism (70.19%), Hinduism (12.61%), Islam (9.71%), Christianity (7.45%)

Source: World Atlas.

which also translates into reasonable religious and social linkages as shown in Table 3. People having common faiths are living across the South Asian countries. Hence, religious tourism has the potential to transform the local economies of these countries. The concept of religious tourism covers religious travels and tours for joining religious celebrations, gatherings, meetings, seminars and festivals at different places (see Chapter 4). It also includes travel for the purpose of offering prayers to the deities. This region has been the birthplace of Hinduism, Buddhism, Sikhism and Jainism while communities such as Islam, Christianity, Zoroastrianism (called Parsees in India, Bangladesh and Pakistan) besides a few other minority faiths have either migrated to this area or they have converted from some other religious faith over the years.

A holy trip to Sri Harminder Sahib, Amritsar in India or Nankana Sahib in Pakistan attracts the people of Sikhism from the sub-continent. Similarly, a trip to 12 Shakti Peeths or 51 Siddh Peeths, Char Dham Yatra, which includes Badrinath, Dwarka, Jagannath and Rameswaram, and 12 Jyotirlingams across India attracts the people of the Hindu faith on a large scale. Similarly, cities like Haridwar, Rishikesh, Varanshi, Madurai (Meenakshi temple), Thiruvananthapuram (Padmanabhaswamy Temple), Kathmandu (Pashupatinath temple), among others, are must-visit destinations for Hindus (see Chapters 1 and 4). While the religious sites located across the South Asian continent such as, India (Bodh Gaya, Sarnath, Vaishali, Rajgir), Nepal (Lumbini, Muktinath Temple, Boudhanath temple, Kopan Monastery, and Tango Monastery), Bhutan (Bumthang, Jakar, Paro) and Sri Lanka (Abhayagiriya, Dambulla, and Ruwanwelisaya temples) are must-visit places for people practising Buddhism. Similarly, famous mosques and dargahs located in various cities in India (Deoband, Delhi, Ajmer, Agra, Lucknow), in Pakistan like Badshahi mosque, Faisal Mosque, Data Darbar among the others, are famous places for Muslims for religious tourism (see Chapters 1 and 4).

As of now, religious tourism is largely restricted and confined to the domestic people of that country. For example, there is limited access to travel outside the country in the sub-continent for religious tourism purposes. Religious tourism has the great potential to transform the local economies of these countries if it is promoted and liberalised. For mutual gain, there is a need of the hour to develop policies for a 'common tourist visa' to visit all these countries on the lines of the Schengen Visa for religious tourism (see Chapters 2 and 4).

3.2. *Trade disruption amid perceived vs. realistic security threats*

A large economic literature supports the argument in favour of pro-trade policies for the mutual gains of the partner countries. International trade involving the transfer of innovations and technology enhances the technical edge of the country. It provides high opportunities for the exploitation of resources of the country. International trade promotes the human skills and technological base of a country through the importation of innovations (see Belloumi, 2014). The neoclassical growth theories posit that a country with a higher degree of economic openness tends to grow at a faster rate because of technology absorption than that of a country with a lower degree of openness.

In South Asia, non-economic factors determine the course of trade instead of economic dividends. The troubled track record between India and Pakistan over the years is one of the primary reasons for the low level of economic cooperation among the South Asian countries. There are many occasions when bilateral tensions have led to closure of borders hampering the smooth movement of goods and people. On many occasions, high political tensions led to the suspension of bilateral or regional agreements that aim to promote economic cooperation through free trade agreements (see Chapter 6). Among the others, the human-made barriers such as trade barriers, subsidies, intellectual property rights, non-tariff barriers, exchange rate manipulation and bilateral trade agreements are also acting as an obstacle in the free flow of goods and services (see Chapter 7).

Since independence, both India and Pakistan have witnessed a track record of trust deficit and tense political relations due to actual and perceived military threats from each other. Both countries have fought three major open wars in the past in 1947–48, 1965, 1971 and one small-scale territorial armed conflict at Kargil in 1999. Besides, there is frequent bombardment on the territories of each other. Because of these external threats, both Pakistan and India are heavily spending on armed imports beyond their limits. India was the world's largest importer of major arms and accounted for 14% of global arms imports. During 2016–20, India was the second largest arms importer just behind Saudi Arabia (see Chapter 5). If we see the military spending in terms of ratio to GDP, both India and Pakistan are spending extremely high on military and military equipment, even more than that of combined expenditure on education and health of the two countries. To meet the military requirements, India is spending over 2.66% of GDP, while Pakistan is spending over 3.83% of GDP on the military (see Chapter 8).

If threats on the part of national security are overcome by the way of formation of some common peace treaty, South Asia has vast economic potential to offer in terms of economic dividends to the people living there. However, the existing conflicts continue to dominate the regional space. South Asia as a region is exposed to new geopolitical dynamics in the shape of the Taliban's takeover in Afghanistan and China's Belt and Road Initiative (BRI) (see Chapters 5 and 6). These are some common challenges where leadership of South Asian countries need to look into to unlock mutual gains for their people. Research from the Asian Development Bank (2023) suggests that with the removal of trade barriers and improved connectivity, intra-regional trade in South Asia could be on the order of billions of dollars (approximately US$100 billion) per annum, almost doubling the current figures.

3.3. *Bilateralism vs. multilateralism: Potential trade model in South Asia*

Until the early 1990s, all the South Asian countries were closed economies with low international trade volume coupled with high tariff and non-tariff barriers and regressive foreign investment policy. It is only after the signing of the World Trade Organization (WTO) during the 1990s that they started to align with the world economy after introducing moderate to major reforms which were initiated on the policy part of foreign trade and investment. At the regional level, deeper trade ties could not develop over the years. It is only India which serves as major source for international trade of Nepal and Bhutan. As of now, India is a source of over 61% of total trade for Nepal. Similarly, India is the source of 81% of total trade for Bhutan while the trade between India and Pakistan, which are the largest economies in the region, is under suspension. Similarly, the small consumer base of Sri Lanka and the Maldives, and terrorism in Afghanistan are the main problems among the others that offer limited opportunities (see Chapter 9).

Given the geopolitical circumstances, what is the preferred trade model in the South Asia region? Many empirical studies support the argument in favour of a bilateral trade model. For example, the study of Bandara and Yu (2003) finds that India will realise the maximum economic welfare from SAFTA, while small countries will gain marginally. Further, the study of Siriwardana and Yang (2007) and Taguchi and Rubasinghe (2019) support the bilateralism over multilateralism trade model for greater economic benefits in South Asia. Their arguments are based on the potential threats to national security and the disproportionate size of the economy among others.

A sound body of literature supports the arguments in favour of the multilateral trade model for South Asia for higher economic gains (see Perera, 2009; Kher, 2012; Hye et al., 2013; Kumar, 2020). Their arguments are based on the fact that trade complementarities exist in South Asia because of wide diverse trade compositions. For example, a recent study by Kaur et al. (2020) highlights that Pakistan and Sri Lanka have a competitive advantage in Transport Services, while India has a competitive advantage in Computer and Information Services and Other Business Services. Similarly, Maldives and Nepal have competitiveness in travel-based services and Bangladesh in Public Services.

Hence, the existence of trade complementarities offers vast opportunities for all the South Asian countries for mutual gain. This argument is supported by their existing trade composition to and from South Asia. For example, Table 4 shows the product shares (%) of exports and imports for the top five sectoral products of major South Asian countries to/from countries in the South Asian region. This shows the percentage

Table 4. Export & import composition.

Product exports	Share (%)	Product imports	Shares (%)
India's exports and imports to/from South Asia			
1. Textile and clothing	18.05	1. Vegetables	21.65
2. Fuels	14.69	2. Textiles and clothing	21.57
3. Transportation	13.18	3. Transportation	13.43
4. Metals	11.19	4. Metals	10.43
5. Chemicals	10.87	5. Food Products	6.31
Bangladesh's exports and imports to/from South Asia			
1. Textile and clothing	61.54	1. Textile and Clothing	39.06
2. Vegetables	5.96	2. Vegetables	15.0
3. Metals	5.14	3. Chemicals	8.79
4. Chemicals	4.73	4. Mechanical and Electrical	8.71
5. Food products	4.17	5. Transportation	8.69
Pakistan's exports and imports to/from South Asia			
1. Vegetables	29.43	1. Chemicals	27.94
2. Textiles and clothing	26.93	2. Textile and clothing	24.64
3. Food products	11.02	3. Vegetables	17.23
4. Minerals	8.66	4. Plastic and rubber	7.78
5. Chemicals	6.02	5. Mach. and Elect.	5.16
Sri Lanka's exports and imports to/from South Asia			
1. Vegetables	19.43	1. Fuels	16.71
2. Textile and clothing	13.53	2. Textile and clothing	15.14
3. Fuels	9.37	3. Vegetables	10.79
4. Food products	9.31	4. Transportation	10.68
5. Mechanical and electrical	8.40	5. Chemicals	10.16
Nepal's exports and imports to/from South Asia			
1. Textile and clothing	27.03	1. Fuels	21.63
2. Vegetables	23.02	2. Metals	17.61
3. Food products	17.71	3. Mechanical and Electrical	10.68
4. Metals	15.12	4. Vegetables	10.40
5. Chemicals	8.35	5. Transportation	10.01

Table 4. (Continued)

Product exports	Share (%)	Product imports	Shares (%)
Bhutan's exports and imports to/from South Asia			
1. Metals	33.81	1. Fuels	22.91
2. Fuels	33.52	2. Metals	22.15
3. Minerals	11.50	3. Mechanical and Electrical	10.63
4. Chemicals	5.87	4. Vegetables	8.51
5. Vegetables	5.36	5. Woods	4.67

Source: Data is compiled from World Integrated Trade Solution as maintained by World Bank.

shares of product exports (imports) to the total exports (imports) of the respective countries. Some observations can be made from trade pattern as shown in Table 4: (1) Textile and clothing, chemicals and vegetables are the common items in the export and import baskets for all the sample countries. (2) India stands as the top exporter and importer of Transportation Goods, while Bangladesh, Sri Lanka and Nepal are the major importers. (3) Bangladesh and Pakistan are the top exporter and top importer of Textile and Clothing products in the region. (4) For India, Nepal and Bhutan, metal comes in the top list for imports and exports. (5) Vegetable is the top item in the export and import baskets among the others for all South Asian countries except India, which is an importer. (6) India, Sri Lanka and Bhutan export fuels in the region, while Nepal, Sri Lanka and Bhutan import the same from the region. (7) Bhutan is the top importer and exporter of metal and fuel items, among others. (8) Mechanical and electrical items top the import list for Bangladesh, Pakistan, Nepal and Bhutan.

In Chapters 9–12, authors apply empirical methods in studying the role of Regional Trade Agreements (RTA) and institutional setup while focusing on the role of institutions in making regional integration a success. Their study supports the RTAs as they positively contribute to export promotion between countries. This highlights the importance of trade liberalisation in the member countries to increase the pace of economic development in the long run. Similarly, the results provide strong support for the role of institutional setup in partner countries.

In the last decades, India has made tremendous progress in the services economy. As of now, services contribute more that 50% to the total GDP in India. While India's export share of services has been lower than its South Asian neighbours, import of services occupies a significant portion in the import basket of the South Asian countries. If trade is liberalised in South Asia, in the service categories of Transport, Travel, Telecommunications and Information Services, Financial Services and Personal Cultural and Recreation Services, India faces a high demand from its South Asian neighbours (see Chapter 11).

3.4. Rail and road connectivity: Scope for regional production networks

The unlocking of vast economic potential in South Asia requires well-integrated and coordinated trade networks between the countries therein. Regional trade offers mutual benefits to the partner countries in terms of the building of production networks, easy access of raw materials, economical transportation and easy adaptability of products due to shared social and cultural systems. Because of these reasons, various trade blocs have come into existence in the last decades to meet the domestic and regional requirements of goods and services. Some of the noted trade blocs like the North America Free Trade Agreement (NAFTA) formed in 1994 and the ASEAN Free Trade Area (AFTA) formed in 1992. These trade blocs consider the member countries at parity irrespective of economic size, hence works on the sole objective to ease the conduct of business through exports and imports.

The supply chain network in South Asia faces significant challenges. Despite being well-connected geographically, South Asian countries are the least connected through roads and railways. Trust deficit due to concerns of national security has led these countries to close their borders hampering the easy movement of goods and materials and people. Heavily guarded boarders between the South Asian countries have made it almost impossible for the businessmen, retailers, distributors and other stakeholders to explore the new markets for their products and services.

There is enormous potential for growth and development through the exploitation of resources and building of trade networks. For South Asia, the strategic location, expanding middle class and high opportunities for innovation provide a strong ground for building of supply chain networks to become a global hub for trade and commerce. Hence, collaboration between various stakeholders is crucial to address the potential challenges for unlocking the region's full potential for shared gain (see Chapters 13–15).

3.5. *Resilient South Asian economies amid global pandemic*

Over the years, South Asian countries have emerged as resilient economies from internal and external shocks. Historically, South Asia as a region has been unstable politically, socially and economically since the disintegration of the Indian sub-continent. A Troubled track record of armed conflicts between India and Pakistan, continuous political instability in Afghanistan since 1980s and military takeovers of central governments in Pakistan and Bangladesh on many occasions make this region unstable both politically and militarily. Similarly, the social tensions between the communities caused by communal riots on many occasions in India, Pakistan and Bangladesh have also rendered this region as socially unstable.

Unexpectedly, South Asian countries recovered from the global pandemic within a short span of time because of short-term social aid and macroeconomic strategies by the respective governments to enhance economic activity. Health care initiatives like vaccinations were implemented on a large scale for quick recovery of the economy in South Asian countries in response to the pandemic (see Chapter 16). Besides, income and cash transfers, assistance for the health sector, wage support programmes and food grain distributions through the public distribution system have all been used as fiscal stimulus to aid the poor and marginalised sections of society. The World Development Report on South Asia (2023) highlights that South Asia will have a slower post-pandemic growth rate of 5.6% during the years 2024 and 2025 due to tightening of fiscal and monetary policies and reduced global demand due to rising oil prices in the international market. Government debt in South Asian countries averaged 86% of GDP in 2022, hence there is high risk of defaults, especially in Pakistan and Sri Lanka.

COVID-19 has offered important lessons to South Asian countries for combating unforeseen disasters. Among others, the economic diplomacy emerges as a crucial tool to revitalise economies, foster international cooperation and build new blocs. Following the pandemic, nations are looking for strategies to rebuild their economies and spur economic expansion. Short-term social aid in terms of distribution of direct cash and food grains to the marginalised sections and expansion of health care were implemented in South Asian countries in response to the pandemic to mitigate the direct impact of the pandemic on the marginalised sections of society (see Chapters 16 and 17).

References

Akram, H. W. (2020). Trade within South Asia: Unrealistic expectations. *South Asia Research*, *40*(3), 1–16.

Ashraf, T., Nasrudin, M., and Akhir, M. (2017). Revisiting SAARC: A perspective from Pakistan. *South Asian Studies, 32*(2), 335–350.

Asian Development Bank. (2023). *Asian Economic Integration Report 2023*. http://dx.doi.org/10.22617/TCS230031-2.

Bandara, S. J. and W. Yu (2003). How desirable is the South Asian free trade area? A quantitative economic assessment. *The World Economy*, *26*(9), 293–1323.

Belloumi, M. (2014). The relationship between trade, FDI and economic growth in Tunisia: An application of the autoregressive distributed lag model. *Economic Systems*, *38*(2), 269–287.

Economic Impact Reports, World Travel and Tourism Council. (2022). https://wttc.org/.

Hasan, M. A., Abdullah, Hashmi, M. A., and Sajid, A. (2022). International remittance and international tourism development in South Asia: The moderating role of political stability. *Journal of Economic Impact, 4*(3), 177–187.

Hye, Q. M. A., Wizarat S., and Lau W. Y. (2013). Trade-led growth hypothesis: An empirical analysis of South Asian countries. *Economic Modelling, 35*, 654–660.

Kathuria, S. (2018). A glass half full: The promise of regional trade in South Asia. *South Asia Development Forum*. World Bank, Washington, DC.

Kaur, S., Khorana, S., and Kaur, M. (2020). Is there any potential in service trade of South Asia? *Foreign Trade Review*, *55*(3), 402–417.

Kher, P. (2012). Political economy of regional integration in South Asia. UNCTAD, Background Paper No. RVC 5, Geneva.

Kumar, R. (2020). India & South Asia: Geopolitics, regional trade and economic growth spillovers. *Journal of International Trade & Economic Development*, *29*(1), 4569–4588.

Kumar, R. (2021). South Asia: Multilateral trade agreements and untapped regional trade integration. *International Journal of Finance & Economics*, *26*(2), 2891–2903.

Kumar, R. (2023a). Policy challenges and testing the scope for regional trade integration - A case of South Asia. *Journal of Economic and Administrative Sciences* (ahead of print). https://doi.org/10.1108/JEAS-12-2021-0263.

Kumar, R. (2023b). India-ASEAN economic engagement: Challenges and new lessons for trade integration. In Dadwal, S., Kumar, P., Verma, R., and Singh (Eds.) *Opportunities and Challenges of Business 5.0 in Emerging Markets* (pp. 212–226). IGI Global Publishing, USA.

Perera, M. S. S. (2009). The South Asian free trade area: An analysis of policy options for Sri Lanka. *Journal of Economic Integration*, *24*(3), 530–562.

Petrescu, R. M. (2011). The involvement of the public and private sector–elements with influence on travel & tourism demand during the crisis period. *Tourism and Hospitality Management*, *17*(2), 217–230.

Shahzad, S. J. H., Shahbaz, M., Ferrer, R., and Kumar, R. R. (2017). Tourism-led growth hypothesis in the top ten tourist destinations: New evidence using the quantile-on-quantile approach. *Tourism Management*, *60*, 223–232.

Siriwardana, M. and Yang. J. (2007). Effects of proposed free trade agreement between India and Bangladesh. *South Asian Economic Journal*, *8*(1), 21–38.

Taguchi, H. and Rubasinghe D. C. I. (2019). Trade impacts of South Asian free trade agreements in Sri Lanka. *South Asia Economic Journal, 20*(1), 1–18.

World Atlas. https://www.worldatlas.com/articles/religious-composition-of-the-countries-of-south-asia.html.

World Bank Database. (2022). http://databank.worldbank.org/data/source/worlddevelopment-indicators.

World Bank Report on South Asia Economic Focus. (2021). https://www.world-bank.org/.

World Development Report on South Asia. (2023). https://www.worldbank.org/en/region/sar/publication/south-asia-development-update.

World Integrated Trade Solution, World Bank. https://wits.worldbank.org.

Part I

People to People Contact: Role of Tourism

Chapter 2

Paradigm Shift of Religious Tourism in South Asia

Shikha Misra

Tourism Management, Department of History of Art,
Faculty of Arts Banaras Hindu University,
Varanasi, India

shikhamisra@bhu.ac.in

Abstract

This chapter engages in a discussion of the existing status of religious tourism in South Asia and explores the new paradigms that are evolving to provide a more wholesome and personalisation experience to the tourists visiting the region. There is a significant shift in the interests of tourists from monumental tourism to religious, spiritual and experiential tourism worldwide. The author has come to understand that religious tourism has been upgrading, transforming and adding new components to create better communitas for the religious tourist and increasing the footfall and night stays at religious destinations. Some of the newly added components are use of artificial intelligence to create a personal experience, better infrastructure and superstructures, improved connectivity to the destinations and sites, risk mitigation to minimise human and financial losses and handling the crisis situations by increasing the involvement of stakeholders and by providing regular security drills to them. Change in the temple governance and better backward linkages to make paraphernalia a more pro-poor activity are also two major changes resulting in faster decision-making and availability of better financial resources. This chapter considers religious tourism beyond the continuum of tourism, religious tourism and pilgrimage. It has drawn on a multidisciplinary approach and also provides details on the developments and innovations being applied at religious destinations in the South Asian region, primarily during the last 10 years.

Keywords: Religious tourism, temple governance, risk mitigation, information technology (IT), artificial intelligence (AI), robotics, pro-poor, social media, communita, South Asia.

1. Introduction

The South Asia region comprises eight countries: Afghanistan, Bangladesh, Bhutan, India, Maldives, Nepal, Pakistan and Sri Lanka. These countries have also come under the umbrella of SAARC (South Asian Association for Regional Cooperation) nations as they have created this regional mutual cooperation group, and the region is also known as the Indian subcontinent.

Pakistan and Afghanistan have been suffering from political instability for many decades, and therefore tourism of any sort at a particular time to these countries is entirely dependent on the prevailing safety and security conditions in those countries during a particular time. Hasan *et al.* (2022) concluded that political security has a positive moderation effect on the relationship between international remittances and international tourism development (Hasan *et al.*, 2022). There are few other researches in the recent past, which concluded that political stability, violence and terrorism are important factors that international tourists consider while deciding on the destination to visit (Chawdhury, 2016; Neumayer, 2004; Khan *et al.*, 2020; Llorca-Vivero, 2008; Saha and Yap, 2013). As cited in Hasan *et al.* (2020), the South Asian region has been facing more challenges, such as inflation, high unemployment, low productivity and hence balance of payment issues too. This all results in approximately 75% of the international remittance being spent on basic needs and only 25% of it being saved and invested by individuals (Hasan *et al.*, 2022).

1.1. *Religious tourism*

The concept of religious tourism covers religious travels and tours for joining religious celebrations, gatherings, meetings, seminars and festivals at different places. It also includes travel for the purpose of offering prayers to the deities. Theologians do not appreciate the use of the word 'religious tourism' as they believe that 'religion' and 'tourism' do not go hand in hand; still the business of 'religious tourism' has shown a significant growth and diversity worldwide in the past few years (Sharpley, 2009). Here it is worth mentioning that both religious and nonreligious tourists participate in religious activities during their trips. Religious tourism encompasses 'a range of spiritual sites and associated services, which are visited for both secular and religious reasons' (Raj *et al.*, 2015).

Early religious tourism was based on ritual processes and experiences. MacCannell concluded that sightseeing of religious sites is a kind of ritualistic respect from the tourist to the host community as they absorb a part of host culture during the process (MacCannell, 1976). Turner and Turner also observed that every tourist is a half pilgrim (religion neutral) and every pilgrim is a half tourist (Turner and Turner, 1978). Smith completely reversed this concept. On the basis of motivation to travel and experience, he placed tourists and pilgrims on two opposite extremes on the continuum of travel (Smith, 1992). Cohen, in his classification of tourists, argued that neither of these opposing findings is universally correct. He proposed that tourists want different experiences and modes of experiences during different times (Cohen, 1979).

The study of religious tourism involves a multidisciplinary approach as it has attracted scholars from varied disciplines such as sociology, history, theology, archaeology, culture, heritage, religion, marketing, business studies, dance, drama, music and handicrafts. As per the Annual Report 2022–2023 of the Ministry of Tourism (MoT), Government of India, in the financial year (FY) 2022–2023, with 6.19 million foreign tourist arrivals (FTAs) and with 677.63 million domestic tourists, the total number of tourists in India stood at 683.82 million approximately. Although tourism grew manifold, the mention of the percentage of growth is irrelevant here as tourism had still been recovering from the global pandemic (SARS-CoV-2 virus infection that causes COVID-19 disease) resulting in subsequent global lockdowns (in the years 2019 and 2020 and in few parts of the world in the years 2021, 2022 and even 2023 too in a few parts of South China) and with almost nil touristic mobility around the world.

1.2. Organisation of religious tourism

Pilgrims move in either large group tours organised by national and state tourism boards, in small groups organised by small travel agencies, or independently on their own. The Third type of tourist is the largest in number. As cited in Murat Yesil, religious tourism has been a steady source of income for the local economy. It is because faith-based travellers are committed travellers and save for their travel in advance. Hence, though economic crisis of any magnitude affects the tourism industry, it does not proportionately affect the religious tourism part of it (Yesil, 2013). As cited in Kim *et al.* (2019), United Nations World Tourism Organization (UNWTO) also identified in 2017 that religious tourism is one of the important factors in economic and cultural development of the areas that have religious characteristics (Kim *et al.*, 2019).

1.3. Objectives

This chapter primarily focuses on the major factors that have been driving changes in religious tourism during recent times in South Asian countries. The objectives are as follows:

(i) To analyse the potential of religious tourism in South Asia.
(ii) To explore the factors that facilitate religious tourism in South Asia.
(iii) To assess the role that international South Asian regional associations have been playing to enhance transnational tourism in the region.
(iv) To explore the paradigm shift in religious tourism post COVID-19 pandemic.
(v) To suggest steps to be taken by South Asian countries to enable cross-border religious tourism.

1.4. Post COVID-19 pandemic recovery

The COVID-19 pandemic, which led to lesser tourist mobility, also gave opportunity to the governments to come up with major developments in different sectors and religious tourism was no different from it. Here onwards, this chapter focuses on the developments that have been taking place in the religious tourism industry of South Asia that have shaped religious tourism as a niche market in recent times. For the convenience of understanding by the readers, these details have been discussed under different subheads.

Tourism contributed more than US$3 billion to the economy together in Bhutan, Bangladesh, India, Nepal and Sri Lanka and less than US$1–2 billion together in Afghanistan, Maldives and Pakistan, which are respectively 9.8% and 8.9% of their total GDP. Tourism also generated 184.4 million (9.9%) and 7.5 million (9.9%) of the total new jobs in the respective above-mentioned areas (World Travel and Tourism Council, 2023).

2. Religious Structure and Religious Tourism Economies in South Asia

The South Asian region has been the birth place of some of the major faiths of the world like Hinduism, Buddhism, Sikhism and Jainism, while communities belonging to Islam, Christianity, Zoroastrianism (called Parsees in India, Bangladesh and Pakistan) and a few other minority faiths have either migrated to this area or converted from some other faiths which were prevalent in the region. The religious constitution of South Asia is given in Table 1.

Religious tourism has both economic (direct income by stake holders, revenues and taxes collected by governments, money generated by unorganised sector, employment generation) and non-economic (cultural sustainability, infrastructure development, resilience in society, increase in imagery appeal of the religious place, creation of opportunities for exchange of opinions and global relationships) multiplier effects. Although it is largely beneficial for the destination, it also causes harm to these places by negatively affecting religious and cultural genuineness. Furthermore, substance abuse damages the piousness of the place and local youth develop a mindset that since tourists are bringing money, so tourists' culture is superior to their own, resulting in the dilution of local values, culture, heritage, pluralist community and uniqueness of a saleable product from a business viewpoint per se. Excessive use of natural resources, construction of infrastructure and superstructures cause deforestation and may also cause ethical and cultural clashes, which are a few more negative impacts of religious tourism at a destination.

Table 1. Religious structure and religious tourism.

S. No.	Country/faith	Hindu	Buddhist	Islam	Christian	Jain	Sikh	Others
1.	Afghanistan (2009)	—	—	99.7%	—	—	—	0.3%
2.	Bangladesh (2022)	7.95%	0.61%	91.04%	0.30%	—	—	0.12%
3.	Bhutan (2005)	22.1%	75.3%	—	—	—	—	2.6%
4.	India (2011)	79.8%	0.7%	14.2%	2.3%	0.4%	1.7%	0.9%
5.	Maldives	—	—	Sunni Muslim (official)	—	—	—	—
6.	Nepal (2021)	81.2%	8.2%	5.1%	1.8%	—	—	3.2% (Kirat) 0.5% (Others)
7.	Pakistan (2020)			96.5% (Muslim official)				3.5% (Christian and Hindu also included)
8.	Sri Lanka (2012)	12.6%	70.2% (Buddhist official)	9.7%	7.4%	—	—	0.05%

Source: Data retrieved from the official websites of Central Intelligence Agency (Government of the United State of America) (CIA), Population & Housing Census 2022 (Preliminary Report) (Bangladesh Bureau of Statistics, 2022), Press Information Bureau (Government of India) (National Informatics Centre, 2023).

There are big economic markets which have been flourishing around the religious sites. Religious tourism plays a major role in shaping the economy of countries like Saudi Arabia, Vatican City and India (Iliev, 2020). Meditating at a Buddhist monastery in Bangkok, Thailand, volunteer tourism in Tibet and India, a visit to the Batu Cave temples or masjid Negara in Malaysia, Shwedagon Pagoda in Myanmar, a holy trip to Harminder Sahib, Amritsar in India or Nankana Sahib in Pakistan, a trip to 12 Shakti Peeths or 51 Siddh Peeths, Char Dham Yatra or 12 Jyotirlingams trip in India and a trip to St. Francis Xavier church in Goa, India or The Basilica de San Martin in Batagas, Philippines are all examples of religious visits to places belonging to different faiths in Asia.

Bhutan is altogether a different type of destination for religious tourism as it believes in the holistic development of spirituality by preserving its culture and environment by being socially equitable and by promoting good governance and good health.

India being a centre for home-grown religions and faiths like Buddhism, Sikhism, Hinduism and Jainism is a highly favoured destination for spiritual and religious tourism (Haq and Medhekar, 2020).

Cross-border tourists visiting Nepal via India for religious and spiritual tourism is a very common phenomenon. Bhairahawa–Nautanwa/Sunauli check post at the international border between India and Nepal is the largest checkpoint for the third country tourists who visit Nepal via India. Most of these tourists go to Nepal to visit Lumbini. In 2017, the count of foreign tourist visitors (FTVs) who crossed this border to visit Lumbini outnumbered the foreign tourists who visited Lumbini by crossing any other land entry points to Nepal. Every year, millions of Hindu and Buddhist tourists from South Asia visit Bagmati river, Pashupatinath temple and meditation camps that are organised in Nepal. The birth place of Buddha, i.e. Lumbini, is also situated in Nepal.

For a better comprehension, the chapter has been further divided into sections. Each section deals with a particular area in which major developments related to religious tourism have been taking place in South Asia.

3. Religious Tourism of Minority Faiths in South Asia

Minority faiths that are prevalent in South Asia are Jainism (0.4% in India and a minority in the rest of South Asia), Buddhism (dominant religion in

Bhutan and Sri Lanka and a minority in the rest of South Asia) and Sikhism (1.7% in India and a minority in the rest of South Asia) (WorldAtlas, 2018). Jainism predominantly exists in India; hence, its shrines and pilgrimage are also more in India only and finding a Jain temple that has a significant role in tourism in the rest of South Asia is a rarity. Shravanbelagola at Hassan district in Karnataka and Ranakpur and Dilwara temples in Rajasthan, India, Sri Adinath 1008 Digambar Jain temple in Kathmandu, Nepal, are a few of the main Jain worshipping sites. Shri Digambar Jain Chaitalaya and Ahinsa Kendra, Katunayake, Sri Lanka, are two of the big Jain temples outside India. According to *The Hindu*, there is almost no population of Jains in Pakistan (Suhasini Haidar, 2022) though a few Jain shrines in a dilapidated condition may be found in that country. The story of Afghanistan is also no different from that of Pakistan. Bhutanese society mainly practices tantric Mahayana Buddhism and Jains are almost negligible in number in that country.

Buddhism, a faith like Jainism, also started from India. Hence, we find more Buddhist temples only in India. Emperor Ashoka from Maurya Dynasty (321–185 BCE) in India played a significant role in taking Buddhism outside India to its neighbouring countries, starting from 250 BCE. Later on, it spread in South and South-East Asia by traders from India, China and Sri Lanka. Today, one of the largest population of Buddhists (approximately 30 million) can be found in Sri Lanka (CENGAGE, 2019). Most of these Buddhists are Sinhalese. The main Buddhist sites in South Asia are Lumbini (Nepal), Bodh Gaya, Sarnath and Kushi Nagar (India), and Dambulla Cave Temple (UNESCO World Heritage Site), Pidurangala Royal Cave Temple and Mihintale temple (Sri Lanka). Sri Lanka has been suffering from insurgency of Tamil rebels for the last 35 years except for a brief time in 2009 after the death of the supreme leader of the Tamil separatist group, Liberation Tigers of Tamil Eelam (LTTE), Velupillai Prabhakaran. There were 981,928 Buddhists in Bangladesh in 2013 (NationMaster.com, 2023) but the researcher could not find any major Buddhist site in Bangladesh. Buddhism was persisting in Maldives before the arrival of Islam. Some of the recent excavations in Maldives prove that there were Buddhist shrines existing there (Mikkelsen, 2000) though Maldives is an official Sunni Muslim country at present.

On the 550th Prakash Parv (birth anniversary) of Guru Nanak Dev on 9 November 2019, the Kartarpur Corridor was opened between India and Pakistan. Kartarpur is the final resting place of Guru Nanak Dev, the founder of Sikhism. It was closed during the pandemic and reopened on 17 November 2021. To facilitate the Indian pilgrims visiting Kartarpur, the Government of India and the Government of Pakistan have agreed that the pilgrims (day visitors who have to return on the same day) don't need a visa and only an Electronic Travel Authorization (ETA) will suffice (Bureau of Immigration, Ministry of Home Affairs). India has the largest Sikh population in South Asia and as of December 2022, a total of 0.13 million Indian pilgrims have visited the site (Tribune News Service, 2022). Important Sikhism Gurudwaras in Bangladesh are Gurudwara Guru Nanak and Sangat Tola both in Dhakha.

4. Resource Development Schemes in Religious Destinations

As per a report published in the *Hindustan Times*, religious tourism destinations in India earned INR 1345.43 billion and 1433 million domestic tourists visited these places in FY 2022–2023 (HT Correspondent, 2023). Different surveys done on the basis of parameters such as tourist arrivals, total income and infrastructure development report different top religious tourism destinations in India, but a few of them appear in all the lists, which in random order are Vaishno Devi and Amarnath Cave (Katra and Anantnag districts of Jammu and Kashmir respectively), Ayodhya and Varanasi (both in Uttar Pradesh), Somnath and Dwarka (both in Gujarat), Rameshwaram and Madurai (both in Tamil Nadu), Harmandir Sahib (aka Golden temple, Amritsar, Punjab), Tirupati (Andhra Pradesh), Puri Jagannath Temple (Odisha), Sree Padmanabhaswamy Temple (Thiruvananthapuram, Kerala) and Badrinath and Kedarnath (both in Uttarakhand).

Religious tourism is largely pro-poor tourism as the stakeholders and paraphernalia involved in it (e.g. flower sellers, prasad makers, cooks, sellers, small vendors selling religious products like idols, framed pictures of Gods, candles, incense sticks, auspicious symbols and providing services near pilgrim sites) are mostly produced and sold by unskilled marginal communities. Crowdsourcing from locals for expertise in art, culture, handicrafts, cuisines and other resources is common. The Indian government has identified places for implementation of the schemes that have these indigenous resources and potential for offering world-class religious tourism experiences to the visitors. These schemes are time-bound and streamline all resources through other union and state-level projects for the development of identified places on public–private partnership (PPP) basis.

The Ministry of Tourism, Government of India (GoI), has realised that the development of domestic tourism is highly dependent on religious tourism. Therefore, it is based on current tourist footfall and the possibility of future potential of development of touristic resources, facilities and infrastructure; so the government has launched many schemes for the integrated development of the identified and selected religious cities in a sustainable manner and for the revival of infrastructure for enriching the religious site's holistic religious tourism experience.

Most of these schemes were launched and have been operational since 2014–15 when funds were allocated in the union budget. Initially, heritage and pilgrimage city-related development schemes were kept separately by the government, but with the passage of time, it realised that these two are highly connected and hence from October 2017 onwards, the Government of India has merged these two types of tourism schemes together. Some of these schemes are HRIDAY (Heritage City Development and Augmentation Yojana by the Ministry of Urban Development), spiritual enhancement drive — PRASHAD (National Mission on Pilgrimage Rejuvenation and Spiritual, Heritage Augmentation Drive by the Ministry of Tourism) and development of smart cities. Governments have realised the direct and multiplier effects of religious tourism such as the religious site's economic development and its potential for employment generation, and have developed these schemes on a PPP model in collaboration with the World Bank.

Earlier PRASHAD (community-based development scheme) and HRIDAY schemes had been operational in 12 cities. Besides these, the Ministry of Tourism has also launched schemes to develop thematic circuits. These circuits are the Buddhist Circuit (Transnational — India and Nepal), Coastal Circuit, Desert Circuit, Eco Circuit, Heritage Circuit, Himalayan Circuit, Krishna Circuit, North East Circuit, Ramayana Circuit, Rural Circuit, Spiritual Circuit, Sufi Circuit, Tirthankar Circuit, Tribal Circuit and Wildlife Circuit. The Ministry of Tourism is planning to extend Ramayana circuit to Janakpuri, Nepal. In these 15 circuits, six circuits deal with different faiths. Under the PRASHAD scheme, the Government of India developed a Global Information System (GIS) based interactive and intelligent portal and mobile application for the users. It is a permission-based portal, so keeps a tap on the footfall at the destination by sharing the location with the app and website. These schemes are output-oriented and the parameters to check the progress are very much quantitative in nature, some of which are increase in tourist traffic, employment generation, increased awareness and skill development programmes. These schemes are operated largely on a PPP model.

Little corporate funding has also been channeled toward these identified places through corporate social responsibility (CSR) initiatives and donations from non-resident Indians (NRIs) (Namami Gange scheme to clean the Ganges River). For example, there were approximately 1700 diesel or petrol engine-fuelled boats in the river Ganges in Varanasi. In FY 2021, through an initiative to float 500 'green boats' on the Ganges river, the Gas Authority of India Ltd. (GAIL) donated INR 210 million under the CSR initiative to Varanasi Municipal Corporation (VMC) to upgrade these boats to compressed natural gas (CNG) engine fitted ones.

The boatmen were also made stakeholders in this project and so a nominal amount was charged from them. CNG emits 7–11% lesser greenhouse gases than diesel or petrol engines and creates lesser sound pollution too. CNG being lesser in price than diesel and petrol has also helped boatmen in reducing their operational costs. GAIL also established the very first floating CNG filling station of India at the Namo Ghat (erstwhile Khidkiya Ghat) on the Ganges river for the refuelling of these boats in Varanasi. VMC further plans to fit all the 1700 boats with CNG kits. After the completion of the project, the Ganges river will be the river on which the most number of CNG-fitted boats will ferry in the world. As of 22 July 2022, 500 boats have been converted to CNG kit fitted ones.

4.1. *Infrastructure development*

The Government of India is paying ample attention to connectivity to religious places through city road network development, information dissemination, development of new tourist information centres, provision of clean and clear drinking water, proper sanitation facilities, establishment and development of tourist police, better internet connectivity, clearing of encroachment and widening the passages, development of facilities, building of entertainment and shopping centres, among others. Besides these infrastructure development processes, community sensitisation and soft skills among first-line service providers (e.g. manual rickshaw pullers, auto-rickshaw and taxi drivers, boatmen, pandas and small unorganised vendors at the sites) are another threshold point where religious sites were lagging behind earlier. The governments in South Asian countries have now been regularly organising programmes like a drivers' training programme, different types of tourist facilitator certification programmes, boatmen/policemen/tourist police training programmes and community sensitisation through flash plays. These all create a heightened communitas, which further gets deeply influenced by the new spatiality and enhances the quality of religious tourism experience of the tourists.

5. Use of Social Media to Connect Better with the Devotees

Social media is different from other communication tools used by the religious destination management organisations as most of the content available on them is developed by the people visiting the destination themselves, sometimes even during their real-time visits themselves. A major revolution in social media usage happened in 1997 by the introduction of blogging and vlogging. Wikipedia, launched in 2000, and WordPress, released in 2004, have made blogging a more serious affair. Nowadays Facebook, YouTube, X (erstwhile Twitter), Instagram, Pinterest, LinkedIn and MySpace are some of the widely used and accessible global social networking sites. Most of the religious sites and destinations around the world have become part of these social networking sites. For example, the Facebook page of Pashupatinath temple, Nepal.

The best way to influence a person to visit a destination is through word of mouth and word of mouse (WOMs). The positive textual content on Twitter and Facebook, images on Instagram and videos in YouTube are universally accepted sources of information by the tourists during their decision-making process. LinkedIn is more used by sellers for B2B sale. Social media buzzes into its users quickly and if its algorithms, user search history and interests are utilised by the destination management organisations (DMOs) timely and wisely, then it can be used to build long-term trust. Nowadays, social media is being used at every stage of planning, that is, before, during and after travel. But there is a catch; people value opinion of unknown people on social media more than that of influencers and their own friends and relatives. Since social media is not a controlled medium, it is imperative for the religious sites to develop a strategy to manage its harmful effects before it causes any serious damage to the image of the destination (Yesil, 2013).

5.1. *Use of artificial intelligence (AI) and robotics*

Religious tourism site management organisations and tour operators have now been using artificial intelligence (AI) to provide more of a personal experience to the pilgrims. People who cannot travel to faraway religious places can now offer their prayers and perform religious ceremonies online through chatbots. For example, a chatbot prepared by Tel Aviv University to offer Jewish prayer in Hebrew with a virtual rabbi.

Another such example is Quranic Arabic Corpus Mecca, which helps people to read and understand the hymns of the Quran (both these places are not in South Asia). Virtual priests and *pujaris* (priests) in Hinduism and Imams in Islam are available in a significant number to help devotees perform rituals, offer prayers and answer the queries asked by them.

The Vatican City has also made an app 'Sindr', which is available in the South Asian market too to help the Catholic Christians to confess their sins with a chatbot. Several temples in India have introduced robot priests to perform daily rituals and also to bless the devotees. Some of these robots can communicate in four languages as these are equipped with AI.

Mecca (not in South Asia) has also been using AI and robots to reply to pilgrims' queries. Though use of AI represents a new height of scientific innovation, its use is also causing a lot of ethical, moral and religious concerns among the host communities, priests and devotees as religion has always been following a very pious and highly human-centric approach and uses of such technologies may bring bad omens to their users. The Irinjadappilly Sri Krishna Temple in Thrissur in Kerala has replaced a real elephant with a life-sized 'animatronic temple elephant' to perform rituals by devotees in a 'cruelty-free manner'. It is a gift by the animal-friendly group People for the Ethical Treatment of Animals (PETA) to the temple.

Many of the above-mentioned innovations have not taken place in South Asia, but these are consumed and are also available to be sold in South Asian markets. All developments are aimed at reaching the last person in the supply chain. Besides these, a few others are the availability of online booking for personalised artis, Mahamritunjaya puja, virtual tours to religious sites and temples and other more complicated and rarely available religious resources.

6. Temple Governance

In India, religious tourism is deeply associated with deities and the rituals related to these deities are generally performed at temples and/or in their premises. Temples are broadly represented by a premise and its possessions. The deity of the temple is considered to be the owner of the temple. As per a report published in the *Times of India* (an Indian newspaper), on 12 April 2023, the six richest temples in India are as given in Table 2.

Earlier in India, temples were managed and governed by local communities. The devotees of the temple used to donate to the temple in the form of cash, jewellery, eatable items, clothes, artefacts, immovable properties and social services. These endowments were used by temples for the benefit and well-being of society by developing gaushalas (shelter homes for stray cows), community schools, community colleges, dharmshalas (a local name used for an economical inn type of an accommodation facility provided to pilgrims) and organising *bhandaras* (community feeding organised for the poor sections of society without any charges). Temples in North India were plundered by many invaders who usually came from the Middle East, but South Indian temples being geographically located at a safe distance from the North-Western Indian borders remained secured and their wealth also could not be plundered. But in the 19th century, their wealth started attracting the East India Company, which took charge of them to control their wealth.

In 1817, the East India Company, which was a corporate profit-making organisation, passed the Madras Regulation Act to bring all the temples of India under its control. In simple words, the impact of this act was that temples came under the control of the Company and though the small temples were allowed to retain their income to cope with their expenditures. Large temples were required to share approximately 14% of their income with the Company. The Company was using this money to repair and maintain public buildings and spaces and also to take custody and dispose of escheats. This siphoned off a huge sum of the income of the temples. Before this act, the temples were either having patronage from the rulers or large temples were providing resources to the smaller temples in their nearby areas. The Company and then the British Government controlling India that followed did not provide any funds to the small temples with little or very little incomes. This resulted in the poor financial state of all the temples irrespective of their sizes and incomes and finally led to their deterioration. Some temples eventually

Table 2. Temple Governance: some cases.

S. No.	Temple	Location	State	Income/net worth
1	Shree Padmanabhaswamy temple	Thiruvananthapuram	Kerala	INR 1200 billion
2	Tirumala Venkateswara temple	Tirupati	Andhra Pradesh	INR 14.50 billion
3	Siddhivinayak temple	Mumbai	Maharashtra	INR 0.48 billion to 1.25 billion
4	Sai Baba temple	Shirdi	Maharashtra	INR 18 billion, 380 kg gold, 4428 kg silver, and also a large amount of US dollars and British pounds
5	Harmandir Sahib (Golden temple)	Amritsar	Punjab	INR 5 billion, 400 kg gold mounted on the upper floors of the temple
6	Vaishno Devi temple	Jammu	Jammu and Kashmir	INR 5 billion p.a., 120 kg gold

Source: *Times of India*, 12 April 2023.

went into a dilapidated condition as the management of these temples did not have enough resources to sustain them.

Recently, there have been a few discussions in the government, communities and temple managements to provide autonomy to the temples so as to govern their incomes to manage their daily activities. These discussions have suggested that the government should play only administrative role of 'enabling the temples' and not 'controlling the temples'. This new system should be the least intrusive and seamless. The larger temples should provide financial and professional support to the smaller temples in their area. While mutt and denomination temples will continue to be operated in the same manner as they are, hereditary temples will need to be evaluated for their performance and financial leakages. If any discrepancy in following the laws is detected, then these temples may be handed over to the committees constituted by empowered local people and a few administrators. Still in these temples, the inheritor will play a primary role during functions and performance of traditional spiritual, religious and ritual activities.

An annual social audit needs to be conducted in all the temples by an Oversight Committee. The overall ecosystem and temple finances should be managed in such a way that big temples are self-sustaining and can further support small temples in the surroundings, which survive on their sustenance (Ramesh, 2020). These amendments in temple governance will give liberty to the temples, will provide them with more financial resources and temples will be able to establish better connectivity with their devotees (because of having more autonomy to take decisions). Temples will also be in a better position to use their resources for their development and maintenance. The wealthier status of larger temples will also help smaller nearby temples in the latter's sustenance, resulting in a higher footfall and better and faster decision-making.

6.1. *Post-pandemic risk mitigation and disaster management at religious places*

The COVID-19 pandemic has caused a disruption in the volume of visitors to religious places. Religious sites are required to change their operating procedures to fit into the post-pandemic psyche of their visitors like hygiene, social distancing and a higher inclination towards spirituality. These sites also need cohesive efforts in their entire supply chain to be more resilient towards such disasters and continue making money through some efforts.

A few researches conducted on the spread of COVID-19 due to religious gatherings discussed the disruption and disempowerment that COVID-19 caused. The Tablighi Jamaat community is a widely known Islamic community with a significant presence in South Asia. It organises its religious gatherings known as Islamic Ijtima to spread its faith and practices in India, Pakistan, Indonesia and Malaysia, which attracts more than two million devotees across the globe, where the devotees gain Islamic knowledge and learn its ways of life. Restrictions imposed by the Indonesian government on such mass gatherings during COVID-19 in 2020 and on its rituals resulted in Tablighi Jamaat taking a stand that COVID-19 is anti-Islam and not life-threatening. Later on, the community was forced to amend their worshipping and proselytisation procedures so that they are safer and the spread of the disease can be avoided. The community further consented to comply with the Indonesian government's restrictions and made changes in the religious gathering methods from large groups to targeting individuals and family members. In spite of being a hardcore orthodox organisation, they also started using social media for their religious purposes (Hamdi, 2022).

Besides Tablighi Jamaat, Hizbut Tahriri and Wahabi groups were also a few other communities which drew the attention of researchers as the virus spread widely through their large communal gatherings. Shincheonji Church in Daegu in South Korea is also one such community which does not accept illness as a reason for someone's absence from the service. It continued its services even after the spread of COVID-19. Later on, they complied with the rules by the governments and closed their churches during the pandemic (Paula Hancocks and Yoonjung Seo, 2020).

The COVID-19 pandemic has increased the dependence of our businesses on virtual connectivity with the source markets. Before the pandemic, very few of our religious places like Vaishno Devi were prepared and were equipped with the required information technology (IT) and human resources to get connected with their devotees. They largely followed a human-centric approach and were dependent on a continuous flow of devotees 'in person' to sustain itself. Post pandemic, many temples, such as the Kashi Vishwanath temple, Salasar Balaji temple, Shree Mahakaleshwar temple, Shree Dwarkadhish temple and Ambaji temple, have developed virtual arti and darshan facilities.

A few spiritual gurus such as Sri Sri Ravi Shankar and Sadhguru also provide virtual connectivity to their followers for various religious events. These virtual platforms also facilitate the individualised bookings of arti and also prasadam and *bhabhoot* (auspicious ashes) delivery by Indian Postal services. This is a welcome facility for devotees who are staying at faraway places, senior citizens, physically challenged and differently abled.

The pandemic also brought a very significant change in the attitude and behaviour of people at the religious sites due to restrictions on travel and darshans. People realised that the almighty is not present outside but is somewhere in them only. This made people look inward, turn spiritual and has controlled their behaviour at the religious sites. This also drew their attention towards yoga and other alternative practices requiring self-discipline and sound temperament.

The pandemic also gave a good opportunity to the religious destinations to equip and prepare government and quasi-government organisations, such as the national and state disaster relief forces, state police and state tourism police and volunteering organisations active during disasters (NGOs and religious organisations), to handle crisis situations. Besides these organisations, the role of every player in the religious tourism supply chain like service providers at the religious sites, vendors who sell paraphernalia used for rituals, tour operators, local/state/national government, all have to play a very crucial role, which should be decided in advance, communicated and reinforced by providing training and refresher courses from time to time to the stakeholders involved in the religious site. The role of the host community during the disaster should also be ascertained, streamlined and communicated through community sensitisation programmes. Altogether, this holistic approach will be aimed at minimising the loss of human lives, maintaining health, safety and security of the affected and to smooth the flow of logistics during the crisis.

Religious tourism sites are also vulnerable to frequent floods (e.g. Uttarakhand and Himachal Pradesh in India, heavy flood in Bhutan in 2018, floods in Bagmati river in Kathmandu and Nepal in August 2023), landslides (e.g. Vaishno Devi and Yamunotri, India and Kathmandu, Nepal), cloud bursts (e.g. Amarnath shrine, Uttarakhand in India), heavy rains (Kedarnath, Sabarimala in India), earthquakes (e.g. Mansarovar in Tibet and Chhoti Char Dham yatra in India), stampedes and terrorist attacks (Nasheed attack in 2021 and extremist attack on 21 June 2022 in a yoga event in Maldives). Every year, the United Nations Alliance of Civilizations (UNAOC) comes out with statements on the number of attacks that had taken place every month on the religious sites around the world and condemns these attacks.

In response to COVID-19, UNICEF and its partner organisations have also prepared a multi-religious-faith action programme. It is called the Religions for Peace and Joint Learning Initiative, which has been put to operation in South Asian countries. It engages religious leaders to educate, prepare and guide the communities to honour the health guidelines issued by health authorities during the pandemic while performing burials, performing rituals and mass gatherings (Sandhu and Sandhu, 2020).

7. Opening of International Borders and Mutual Cooperations

In 2003, by the initiative of the Asian Development Bank (ADB), a sub-regional group in South Asia emerged as SASEC, (South Asia Sub-Regional Economic Cooperation), which included India, Bhutan, Nepal and Bangladesh with tourism as its priority business. In their initial first three meetings between 2003 and 2005, they decided that there should be a sub-regional tourism development plan (TDP), which should be incorporating tourism development plans in these four countries. They also decided to undertake the thematic development of tourism frameworks in future. They decided on two common themes: ecotourism based on natural and cultural heritage and Buddhist circuits. TDP focuses on making tourism pro-poor, branding of SASEC's products, joint marketing, development of a more competitive tourism industry with better links with neighbouring countries and to also reposition the sub-region as a tourist-friendly area. It introduced seven sub-regional programmes and 23 projects of approximately $25 million with an estimated returns of 35% (Tourism Recourse Consultants Ltd., New Zealand in Association with Metcon Consultants PTE Ltd., Nepal, 2004).

Nowadays, SASEC brings seven countries together (India, Bhutan, Nepal, Bangladesh, Maldives, Sri Lanka and also Myanmar (not a South Asian country)) and its priority sectors include transport and tourism along with the development of the private sector too (Asian Development Bank, 2023). Except for Pakistan and Afghanistan, all South Asian countries are now part of it. This group has identified six international corridors that are used for trade and transportation. The group has decided to lower the physical and procedural constraints by simplifying visa processes and lower cross-border movements to facilitate tourism. The Asian Development Bank (ADB) is also assisting Maldives in preparing its 5th tourism master plan, which will increase the collaboration between the neighbouring SASEC countries, especially Sri Lanka. It is also planning 'maritime tourism' through sub-regional cooperation. Three circuits, which are in priority are, the Buddhist circuit, medical tourism circuits and sea cruise tourism circuits. Nepal is upgrading its Tribhuvan International Airport and Gautam Buddha Airport and Maldives is constructing bridges, airport runways and maritime infrastructure, and better hinterland connectivity to decrease the cost of reaching there under SASEC tourism infrastructure projects.

A note on a land border crossing agreement signed in May 2018 between India and Myanmar is noteworthy as the purpose of this agreement is to facilitate cross-border ties between people on both sides. India, Myanmar and Thailand have also agreed upon developing a 'trilateral highway' that will start from Manipur and will up to Thailand. This will also facilitate the road connectivity among the South Asian countries that share their land borders with each other. To further provide land access to the tourists, Thailand and Malaysia already provide access to third-country tourists crossing land borders between them. In April 2017, the finance ministers of The South Asia Sub-Regional Economic Cooperation (SASEC) met in in New Delhi and signed a vision statement, which necessitates the positioning of SASEC with seamless borders, joint marketing efforts and standardisation of services to facilitate joint development of tourism products and position the entire SASEC region as one tourism product. For these joint efforts, SASEC realised that Hinduism and Buddhism could be the common areas of touristic interest (Bhonsale, 2019).

The Bay of Bengal Initiative for Multi-Sectoral Technical and Economic Cooperation (BIMSTEC) is also focusing on developing a conducive ecosystem by common branding for tourism products with joint efforts for common standardisation, training and joint promotion programmes. Thailand, Myanmar, Bhutan and Sri Lanka, the four Buddhist majority BIMSTEC countries, are already engaged in cooperation to promote the tourism sector. India and Nepal have also mutually agreed upon developing Kushinagar–Lumbini railway connectivity. It will be crucial for the development of an International Buddhist Circuit (Bhonsale, 2019).

All these efforts combine and create a heightened future joy, belongingness, commonality of purpose, sense of communitas and diminishes the external geographical, financial, social and educational differences that the pilgrims experience at their origin. These help in providing the tourists with the very spiritual motive for visiting a religious place and heighten their satisfaction level by bringing in an internal positive change in them, which they take back with themselves.

8. Conclusions and Recommendations

Governments come out with advisories during crisis situations regularly. Here it is recommended that the government not just issue advisories only during crisis situations but also during the spread of seasonal diseases (like conjunctivitis, influenza infection, viral fevers, malaria, cholera, which are either contagious or spread during different seasons). The governments should also release advisories and standard operating procedures (SOPs). This will make the host population as well as religious tourists aware of the precautions and available treatments with contact details, if they contact an infection. This procedure should also be followed by the need for local governments and local phone numbers and addresses to be updated more promptly to curtail the diseases at the earliest. There is a dire need to also have an action plan in the same proportion as the unpredictable nature of disasters and their aftereffects. These measures need to be categorised as proactive and reactive sets and the stakeholders involved in both these sets have to be clearly identified separately. This will smooth the chain of disaster management process.

All these eight countries are marked by several common cultural elements. Hence, there is a need to develop policies for a 'common tourist visa' to visit all these countries like the Schengen Visa, though common currency may be entirely ruled out as a few areas are also severely affected by terrorism.

Here the readers need to understand clearly that though for intellectual human resources, big markets, economical human resources and natural resources, the world is looking towards South Asia very optimistically. But out of the 'three largest political land masses' here, which are

India (Bharat), Pakistan and Afghanistan, two of these countries are severely impacted by terrorism and are extremely politically volatile. Hence, India (which is also the largest economy here) has an opportunity to outshine others in the region and make a global mark.

References

Asian Development Bank. (2023, September 1). South Asia Subregional Economic Cooperation (SASEC) initiative. Retrieved September 1, 2023, from Asian Development Bank: https://aric.adb.org/initiative/south-asia-subregional-economic-cooperation-initiative.

Bangladesh Bureau of Statistics. (2022). Publications. Retrieved August 16, 2023, from Population and Housing Commission, Government of the People's Republic of Bangladesh: https://sid.portal.gov.bd/sites/default/files/files/sid.portal.gov.bd/publications/01ad1ffe_cfef_4811_af97_594b6c64d7c3/PHC_Preliminary_Report_(English)_August_2022.pdf.

Bhonsale, M. (2019). Religious tourism as soft power: Strengthening India's outreach to Southeast Asia. Observer Research Foundation, New Delhi.

Bureau of Immigration, Ministry of Home Affairs. (n.d.). Pilgrimage to Sri Kartarpur Sahib. Retrieved August 9, 2023, from Ministry of Home Affairs, Government of India: https://prakashpurb550.mha.gov.in/kpr/.

Cengage. (2019). Buddhist in South Asia. Retrieved August 5, 2023, from Encyclopedia.com: https://www.encyclopedia.com/humanities/encyclopedias-almanacs-transcripts-and-maps/buddhists-south-asia#:~:text=Buddhists%20in%20South%20Asia%20number,of%20the%20island%20nation's%20population.

Chawdhury, J. (2016). Political instability a major obstacle to economic growth in Bangladesh. Centria University of Applied Sciences, Talonpojankatu, Kokkola, Finland.

CIA. (n.d.). University library international and area studies library. Retrieved August 16, 2023, from Central Intelligence Agency: cia.gov/the-world-factbook/field/religions/.

Cohen, E. (1979). A phenomenology of tourist experience. *Sociology*, *3*(2), 179–201.

Hamdi, S. (2022). Covid-19, social stigma and changing religious practice in Tablighi Jamaat communities in Lombok, Indonesia. *International Journal of Disaster Risk Reduction*, 76.

Haq, F. and Medhekar, A. (2020). The rise of spiritual tourism in South Asia as business internationalisation. *The Rise of Spiritual Tourism in South Asia*, 52–78.

Hasan, M. A., Abdullah, Hashmi, M. A., and Sajid, A. (2022). International remittance and international tourism development in South Asia: The moderating role of political stability. *Journal of Economic Impact*, *4*(3), 177–187.

HT Correspondent. (2023, March 21). Places of religious tourism earned ₹1,34,543 crore in 2022, reveals govt data. *Hindustan Times* (India).

Iliev, D. (2020, December). The evolution of religious tourism: Concept, segmentation and development of new identities. *Journal of Hospitality and Tourism Management*, 131–140.

Khan, A., Bibi, S., Ardito, L., Lyu, J., Hayat, H., and Arif, A. M. (2020). Revisiting the dynamics of tourism, economic growth, and environmental pollutants in the emerging economies — Sustainable tourism policy implications. *Sustainability*, *12*(6).

Kim, B., Kim, S., and King, B. (2019). Religious tourism studies: Evolution, progress, and future prospects. *Tourism Recreation Research*, *45*(2), 185–203.

Llorca-Vivero, R. (2008). Terrorism and international tourism: New evidence. *Defence and Peace Economics*, *19*(2), 169–188.

MacCannell, D. (1976). *The Tourist: A New Theory of the Leisure Class*. Schocken Books, New York.

Mikkelsen, P. E. (2000). *Archaeological Excavations of a Monastery at Kaashidhoo*. National Centre for Linguistic and Historical Research, Maldives.

National Informatics Centre. (2023, August 16). Print release. Retrieved August 16, 2023, from Press Information Bureau: pib.gov.in/newsite/printrelease.aspx?relid=126326#:~:text=total%20Population%20in%202011%20is,Stated%200.29%20crores%20(0.2%25).

NationMaster.com. (2023). Bangladeshi religion stat. Retrieved August 7, 2023, from NationMaster: https://www.nationmaster.com/country-info/profiles/Bangladesh/Religion.

Neumayer, E. (2004). The impact of political violence on tourism — dynamic econometric estimation in a cross-national panel. *Journal of Conflict Resolution*, *48*(2), 259–281.

Paula Hancocks and Yoonjung Seo. (2020, February 27). How novel coronavirus spread through the Shincheonji religious group in South Korea. Retrieved July 8, 2023, from CNN: https://edition.cnn.com/2020/02/26/asia/shincheonji-south-korea-hnk-intl/index.html.

Raj, R., Griffin, K., and Blackwell, R. (2015). Motivations for religious tourism, pilgrimage, festivals and events. In Raj, R. and Griffin, K. (Eds.) *Religious Tourism and Pilgrimage Management: An International Perspective* (pp. 103–117). CAB International, Wallingford.

Ramesh, G. (2020, September). Governance and management of temples: A framework. IIM Bangalore, Bengaluru, Karnataka, India.

Saha, S. and Yap, G. (2013). The moderation effects of political instability and terrorism on tourism development: A cross-country panel analysis. *Journal of Travel Research*, *53*(4), 509–521.

Sandhu, S. V. and Sandhu, H. S. (2020). Role of religious practices in the spread and mitigation of COVID-19. *Annals of the National Academy of Medical Sciences*, *56*(4), 235–238.

Sharpley, R. (2009). Tourism, religion and spirituality. In Jamal, T. and Robinson, M. (Eds.) *The SAGE Handbook of Tourism Studies* (pp. 161–171). Sage Publications Ltd., London.

Smith, V. L. (1992). Introduction: The quest in guest. *Annals of Tourism Research*, *19*(1), 1–17.

Suhasini Haidar. (2022, March 2). Jain group seeks Centre's nod to travel to Pakistan. Retrieved August 7, 2023, from The Hindu: https://www.thehindu.com/news/national/jain-community-appeals-to-mha-for-permission-to-visit-restored-shrines-in-pakistan/article65184492.ece.

Tourism Resource Consultants Ltd., New Zealand in Association with Metcon Consultants Pte Ltd., Nepal. (2004, December 1). South Asia subregional economic cooperation tourism development plan. Retrieved September 1, 2023, from Asian Development Bank: https://www.adb.org/sites/default/files/publication/27954/tdp-final.pdf.

Tribune News Service. (2022, December 16). 1.3 lakh pilgrims visited Kartarpur Corridor. Retrieved August 9, 2023, from The Tribune: https://www.tribuneindia.com/news/nation/1-3-lakh-pilgrims-visited-kartarpur-corridor-461392.

Turner, V. and Turner, E. (1978). *Image and Pilgrimage in Christian Culture*. Columbia University Press, New York.

World Travel and Tourism Council. (2023, March). Travel and tourism: Economic impact 2022. Retrieved August 31, 2023, from World Travel & Tourism Council: https://wttc.org/Portals/0/Documents/EIR/EIR%202023/EIR2023-Infographic-Maps-2019.png.

WorldAtlas. (2018, August 16). Religious composition of South Asian countries. Retrieved September 11, 2023, from WorldAtlas: https://www.worldatlas.com/articles/religious-composition-of-the-countries-of-south-asia.html#:~:text=It%20teaches%20harmlessness%20and%20renunciation,%2C%20Afghanistan%2C%20and%20Sri%20Lanka.

Yesil, M. M. (2013). The social media factor in the development and promotion of religious tourism. *Turkish Studies — International Periodical for the Languages, Literature and History of Turkish or Turkic*, *8*(7), 733–744.

Chapter 3

Feasibility of Tourism in South Asian Economies: An Econometric Analysis

Nilendu Chatterjee[*,‡] **and Tonmoy Chatterjee**[†,§]

*Department of Economics, Bankim Sardar College,
South 24 Parganas, West Bengal, India*

†*Department of Economics, Bhairab Ganguly College,
North 24 Parganas, West Bengal, India*

‡*nilubsc87@gmail.com*
§*tonmoychatterjee.economics@gmail.com*

Abstract

All South Asian economies can be considered as emerging in the sense that they have been catching up fast with the developed economies and they have the capabilities of playing major roles in the promotion and establishment of sustainable development. But poor socio-economic conditions coupled with lack of political stability, in a few of these nations, have created hindrances in the growth process. Tourism is one of the sectors that requires various facilities to work together in order to have a successful impact on the growth of the nation. On the other hand, growth of GDP and policies of the governments in many cases have led to the promotion and growth of tourism. Some nations in South

Asia depend heavily upon tourism for survival. Again, there are nations that have capabilities and opportunities to flourish in the tourism sector, given certain aspects are given importance. Which factors are actually influencing tourism and vice-versa that need to be addressed. This analysis should give varying results across nations. In this work, by the help of simultaneous equation modelling, we shall look to address the lacuna in the existing literature for the six nations of South Asia. Such an analysis would be unique as it would help us to understand which factors are actually having an impact on the growth of tourism, also helping us to find the existence of one-way or both-way causal-effect relationship between tourism and GDP. The study ends with important policy recommendations.

Keywords: South Asian economies, tourism industry, simultaneous equation model, causal-effect relationship.

1. Introduction

In the modern world, travel and tourism industry is not only one of the most flourishing ones but it has been one of the distinctive as well as important social phenomena for long. Apart from having a huge impact on business, revenue earning, employment generation and well-being of a considerable segment of population, travel and tourism do have significant impact on the cultural and human negotiations among nations and its people (Narayan *et al.*, 2010). There are certain core aspects of tourism for any nation — these are transport facilities, hotels and hospitality facilities, recreational values, environmental standard, political stability, accessibility to the tourist place and availability of basic amenities, policies of the government and so on (Petrescu, 2011). It is a well-accepted fact that this industry has been one of the fastest growing ones as well as the basic source of livelihood earning in several parts of the world (Shahzad *et al.*, 2017).

In the present globalised world, tourism depends on and covers multiple aspects starting from accommodation to communication to health to environmental aspects to business issues, hence it has become one of the prime aspects for the overall development of tourism destinations and in many cases, for small economies, the overall development of the economy as well (Robaina *et al.*, 2016). If we include all forms of effects of travel and tourism industries, that is, direct effects, indirect effects as well as induced effects, it would accumulate to almost 20% of all employment created worldwide in the last six years prior to the COVID-19 pandemic (Economic Impact Reports, World Travel and Tourism Council, 2022). It is an obvious fact that these values have stumbled to a great extent due to COVID-19 that brought this sector to a complete closedown and the sector is still recovering from that shock of COVID-19 and it is yet to achieve its pre-COVID statistics and growth, even though the catch-up rate has been very fast and it is expected to get back to the pre-COVID growth scenarios very soon (Economic Impact Reports, World Travel and Tourism Council, 2022). The latest factsheet suggests that this sector contributed around 7.5% to the global GDP. In the Asia-Pacific region as well in 2022, a growth rate of over 22% was recorded over 2021, which brings optimism but still falls short of the pre-COVID-2019 values by around 23%. In the year 2022, the sector generated 22 million new employment opportunities, which was around 8% higher than 2021 but almost 11.5% lower than 2019 values. Although both domestic and international tourism registered significant growths in the post-COVID era, international tourism grew manifold faster than its domestic counterpart, registering almost 82% growth in 2022 compared to that of around 21% by domestic tourism but both falling way short than their 2019 figures by over 40% and 14%, respectively (Economic Impact Reports, World Travel and Tourism Council, 2022). Such figures are self-explanatory in the sense that a lot needs to be done at least to get back to the pre-COVID values and then arises the question of progressing further.

If one looks at the eight nations of South Asia, that is, Bangladesh, Bhutan, India, Maldives, Nepal, Sri Lanka, Pakistan and Afghanistan, it becomes clear that these nations together have all of the good tourism destinations — beginning from dense forest to deserts to mountains to seas — yet these nations have not been performing that well in this field, except Maldives. In this analysis, we have kept Afghanistan and Maldives out of our analysis. The rest of the six nations together are known as SAARC economies as well. The reasons for not considering these two nations in our analysis are that there are inconsistent as well as incomplete data series available for Afghanistan who are very much suffering from their own domestic problems for decades now. Moreover, the Maldives is chain of small islands in the Indian Ocean and hence considered as an outlier. There is even no rank assigned to the Maldives by Travel and Tourism Development Index, 2021 of the World Economic

Forum (2021) despite being a very popular tourism destination and very much ahead of other South Asian nations in several aspects of tourism facilities. There are different causes applicable to each of these nations for their 'below potential' performance. For a few nations, it is the domestic violence or cross-nation relationship that have been hampering growth, whereas for others it is poor economic infrastructure or lack of proper initiatives on the part of the governments and private sectors. In this analysis, we have considered six South Asian nations and analysed the economic aspects of their tourism sector.

In developing economies like the South Asian region, the government does have a huge role in developing the infrastructure and policies of the government should ensure peace and legal aspects and ease of doing business in the economy, although it is the private players and initiatives that ensure the growth of this sector by and large (Jenkins and Henry, 1982; Jenkins, 1991; Sharpley and Ussi, 2014). Recent initiatives by governments of these developing nations towards full-fledged development of tourism industry from all aspects apart from paving the way for private players indicate this line of thought. There are several instances of governments of Indian states and the Indian Government itself taking up all aspects of tourism development and developing tourism destinations. There are many such instances in Nepal, Bangladesh and Sri Lanka as well. Looking at the six South Asian economies brings out the fact that direct public spending on travel and tourism has remained at a fairly low level, except in Nepal. Only in Nepal, public spending varied in the range of 5–12% of GDP followed by Sri Lanka where it crossed the 4% level. But in others it hardly reached 3%, with India ranked at last of these six economies.

If anyone inquires into the role of private bodies in the development of this sector, it is understandable that their role is manifold as well as enormous. They not only ensure employment generation by developing individual segments associated with any tourism destination, but they also improve the well-being and uplift the standard of living of the people living in and around those destinations (Wang and Xu, 2011; Banerjee *et al.*, 2015). If one looks at the private direct investment for tourism in the studied economies, it gives again a gloomy scenario. Apart from Nepal, no other nation had that investment level above US$10 million until 2014. India was always in competition with Sri Lanka for the second rank and even slipped into third rank for a few years in the early 2000s. But in the post 2014 period, the investment level increased to a great extent, but only till the devastating COVID-19 set in. In a post-COVID scenario, the world tourism sector is healing and so is the level of investment and participation from the private entities and hence it is yet to achieve the levels of the pre-COVID era from all aspects.

Inter-regional tourism is one such area that depends upon good political relationship among the nations and it plays a good role in developing the cultural harmony among the nations and its people. There are several such places in South Asian nations in which people from other nations visit. One can name the Buddhist religious places in India such as Bodh Gaya and Sarnath and in Sri Lanka such as Sigiriya and Polonnaruwa that people from Japan, China and Korea visit in large numbers. There are several places in Pakistan which are visited by Indian pilgrims and vice versa. Almost 17,000 Indians visited Pakistan in the last five years and from Pakistan over 100,000 tourists visited India since 2016. Likewise, India and Bangladesh also share several places visited by citizens from each nation such as Chittagong and Dhaka in Bangladesh; several places in Kolkata and East India are visited by Bangladeshis. In these six South Asian nations, nearly 20% of total tourism takes place among each other. Even out of the total tourists, almost 65% of the tourists visit India followed by Bangladesh (World Bank, 2020). Apart from religious purposes, health and education are also among the prime reasons for the tourist visits.

The rest of this chapter is going to unfold in the following manner. Section 2 deals with a brief literature survey followed by a few facts and figures related to the development of tourism sector in the six South Asian economies in Section 3. Section 4 discusses the data and methodology to be used in our study, following which Section 5 will analyse the findings of the econometric analysis. Finally, concluding remarks and policy recommendations are made in Section 6.

2. Literature Review

Going though the existing set of literature gives the conception that though there are works on effects of travel and tourism industries, not too many are in existence on the South Asian nations when considered together. Even the existing works are narrative in nature, without investigating any causal-effect relationship or doing econometric testing. This lacuna is the prime source of motivation behind this work. It is a fact that before the 1990s, most of the works on tourism were based on developed economies. As the decade of 1990s witnessed the implementation of globalisation policies across the developing economies along with which a considerable increase in the numbers of foreign tourists and GDP started to occur, only then the studies about tourism on developing economies started to develop.

Mainly, two forms of studies regarding tourism are found in literature — few have focused on analysis at the country-specific level whereas others are based on cross-country analysis with application of panel data. Even though the analysis based on the application of panel data have assumed certain restrictions, country-specific analyses are mostly based on behaviours of the included variables over the years.

Several studies have focused on the first category of work (Durbarry, 2004; Kumar, 2014; Ishikawa and Fukushige, 2007). These studies have focused on individual nations. Examples of panel studies along with empirical testing are also found regarding tourism and growth (Holzner, 2010; Kumar and Kumar, 2013; Narayan et al., 2010). These studies have found long-run one-way association between tourism and economic growth. The opposite also holds, that is, economic growth enhancing the development of tourism (Aslan, 2014). Existence of both-way causal relationship is also observed where both economic growth and tourism have been influential in each other's growth (Durbarry, 2004). As this front of development and growth came along with globalisation post 1990s in the South Asian economies, studies on tourism in this part of the world are descriptive due to lack of available data before 1990. Cooperation between government and private sectors not only reduces the cost of networking but also provides several economies of scale to both bodies. This is excluding the fact that such collaboration is expected to cut down various forms of conflict at various stages of development between the two bodies (Healy, 1997; Dedeurwaerdere, 2005).

It becomes absolutely vivid from the above discussion that development of tourism is indeed an outcome of several complex phenomena involving several bodies and agencies at numerous levels of decision making as well as policy implementation (Chatterjee, 2022). It also becomes evident that for South Asian economies, there is almost no work involving all the nations together and those that inquire the impact of one or more important variables on another important variable of tourism. Most of the works are descriptive and there is no application of econometric techniques. The application of econometric modelling makes the study more forecast oriented, which makes the study attractive. This study looks to fill up that lacuna.

3. Few Facts and Figures

Here, a brief presentation of a few facts and figures are made about some important indicators related to the development of tourism in these six nations. We know that in the present age, tourism is a very complex as well as important phenomenon that involves the development of several related things. A brief description will be made in Section 4.

The basic development of tourism of any nation lies in the numbers of international tourists arriving in that nation and what earning prospects it is generating for them. Depending on these values, the policies of the nation get formulated or the government decides to invest to develop more.

In the following diagrams, a diagrammatic representation is done on four important variables: number of arrivals of tourists (in millions), total earnings from tourism (in US$), total earnings from foreign tourists as a percentage of export as well as a percentage of GDP — for the six South Asian economies under study over the period 2000–2019. We have not considered 2020 since this year was the year of COVID and tourism has been suffering since then to a great extent. Post-COVID data on all tourism-related variables are yet to be available.

Figures 1–4 explain many aspects of tourism in the six South Asian economies over the first two decades of this century with regard to the four important variables considered. Even out of the six economies, there

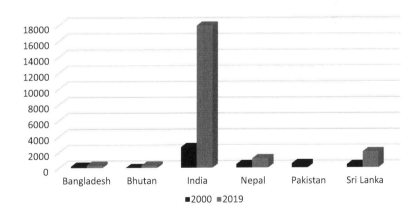

Figure 1. International tourists arrival in South Asian economies (2000–2019).
Source: World Development Indicator.

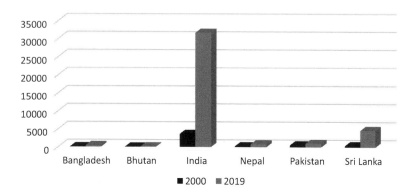

Figure 2. Earnings from international tourism in South Asian economies (2000–2019).
Source: World Development Indicator.

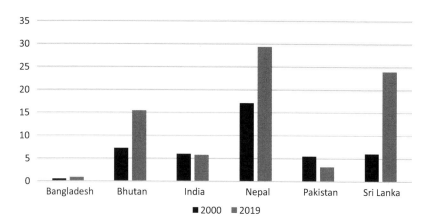

Figure 3. Earnings from international tourism in South Asian economies as a percentage of total export earnings (2000–2019).
Source: World Development Indicator.

are differences in development of tourism. In the case of Bangladesh, all these values are at a very low level till 2015 after which Bangladesh has begun to grow at a good pace. In the case of Bhutan, even though arrival of tourists and earnings from tourism are low compared to other South Asian nations, tourism occupies an important position as far as earnings

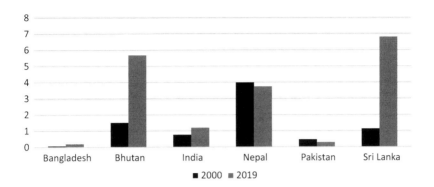

Figure 4. Earnings from international tourism in South Asian economies as a percentage of GDP (2000–2019).

as a percentage of GDP and as a percentage of foreign earnings are concerned. India, quite naturally, occupies the first rank for being the largest South Asian economy, as far as number of arrivals of foreign tourists and earnings from tourism in absolute sense are concerned but relative with export and GDP, the figures are not encouraging. Opposite things can be said about Nepal and Sri Lanka who have been growing in all aspects over the two decades. Pakistan, because of several issues, has failed to show any improvement in tourism, and even decreasing trends have been observed in a few aspects during this period.

4. Data and Methodology

The Travel and Tourism Index is quite a new concept — developed since 2007. But over the years, especially in the post-COVID period, it has taken a new shape. COVID, environmental awareness, health awareness and political stability are dimensions that have now been incorporated in developing the index. Thus, tourism not only encompasses multiple development indicators in one frame but also represents the absolute scenario of development of a nation. The latest index of travel and tourism, developed by the World Economic Forum (2021) (World Travel and Tourism Index, WEF), reveals that it is redesigned and it has now been developed based on five broad indicators — Enabling Environment, Travel and Tourism Policy and Enabling Conditions, Infrastructure, Travel and

Tourism Demand Drivers and Travel and Tourism Sustainability. It is correct that all aspects have impact of different magnitudes on tourism of a nation, even if all of these are equally not significantly important together. The important question which comes up is that are all these aspects equally important? Or, important to which extent? There are also questions about which aspect has influence on what — is it tourism that influences GDP or is it GDP that influences tourism? These questions need to be investigated. It is, by now, well understood that development of tourism is a highly complex phenomenon, with an inter-dependence of several variables. Such a relationship can be captured best by simultaneous equation technique model. This technique helps us to identify which variables are influencing the target variables and to what extent and again whether that dependent variable influences the erstwhile independent variables (Chatterjee and Chatterjee, 2021; Chatterjee and Kundu, 2021). Hence, this technique helps to identify the two-way or multi-way causal-effect association among a set of variables, which is the basic necessity when we are inquiring the effects of different sets of variables on the development of tourism. For the sake of investigating the existence of two-way or multi-way association between tourism-related variables and growth of GDP in these six nations, we have applied simultaneous equations of the following forms:

$$gr(\text{GDP})_{xt} = \theta_0 + \theta_{1x} gr(\text{EFIT})_{xt} + \theta_{2x} gr(\text{MYS})_{xt}$$
$$+ \theta_{3x} gr(\text{CO}_2)_{xt} + \theta_{4x} gr(\text{GFCF})_{xt} + \varepsilon_{xt} \quad (1)$$

$$gr(\text{EFIT})_{xt} = \gamma_0 + \gamma_{1x} gr(\text{GDP})_{xt} + \gamma_{2x} gr(K)_{xt}$$
$$+ \gamma_{3x} gr(\text{OPN})_{xt} + \gamma_{4x} gr(\text{GFCF})_{xt} + \varepsilon_{xt} \quad (2)$$

$$gr(\text{ITA})_{xt} = \beta_0 + \beta_{1x} gr(\text{PMC})_{xt} + \beta_{2x} gr(\text{COR})_{xt}$$
$$+ \beta_{3x} gr(\text{INF})_{xt} + \beta_{4x} gr(\text{PS})_{xt} + \varepsilon_{xt} \quad (3)$$

Here we have used the yearly or annual data of the six nations under study from the World Development Indicator (WDI) for the period 2000–2019. Corruption (COR) data are available since 2005. Here the focus is to check whether growth of GDP is influenced by other tourism-related variables such as growth from Earnings from International Tourism (EFIT) and how far the tourism-related variables (EFIT) and international tourist arrivals (ITA) are influenced by national GDP and other socio-economic variables that encourage or discourage tourism in a nation. Our main focus is to inquire about the connection between GDP and EFIT and other tourism-related variables. For the sake of checking this association, we have used the above-mentioned three simultaneous equations. In these equations, x denotes the total number of cross-sections used in our analysis which is 6. Here t stands for 1, 2, 3, ..., T, that is, the period on which our study is based. The coefficients θ_1, θ_2, θ_3 and θ_4 estimate the effects of growth of Earnings from international tourism (EFIT), mean years of schooling of the people aged above 15 (MYS), Emission of carbon dioxide (CO_2) and gross formation of fixed capital (GFCF) on GDP. These effects are reflected by equation (1). Equation (2) estimates the effects of various aspects that do influence the earnings from international tourism. Hence, γ_1, γ_2, γ_3 and γ_4 estimate the effects of growth of GDP, capital stock (K), trade openness (OPN) and gross fixed capital formation (GFCF) on the growth of earnings from international tourism. In equation (3), we have estimated which aspects are influential in generating demand in the international tourists to visit a nation, that is, which factors influence the growth in the numbers of arrival of international tourists (ITA) — these effects are postulated by the help of β_1, β_2, β_3 and β_4 estimating the effects of person with mobile connection (PMC), level of corruption (COR), inflation rate (INF) and political stability and absence of violence (PS). We have estimated the above simultaneous equation model both for the overall panel and individual cross-section nations.

Applications of Durbin–Wu–Hausman test and Hansen test have been made for the estimation of the simultaneous equation model (Newey, 1985; Smith and Blundell, 1986). Durbin–Wu–Hausman test is an important one since it focuses on the endogeneity aspects of all the three equations under study. This test is also crucial, since it tells whether or not we need the application of instrumental variables because a rejection of null-hypothesis implies the impacts of endogenous regressors on the estimates are meaningful. Hansen test is used to find the appropriate instruments, testing the validity of instruments by means of finding the over-identification restrictions to be imposed. For the sake of flawless estimation procedure, panel unit-root tests are performed. We have applied the four famous panel unit-root tests — LLC test (Levin, Lin and Chu, 2002); IPS test (Im et al., 2003); PP-Fisher chi-square test (Maddala and Wu, 1999) and ADF test of Fisher-type. The generalised method of moments (GMM) has been applied for estimating the three equations of simultaneous equation model. GMM gives more robust outcomes than 2SLS and 3SLS for simultaneous equations. Hence, we have given the results of GMM estimation. Apart from LLC test, all three tests of panel unit-root test assume heterogeneity of coefficients across different cross-sections. Only LLC test assumes homogeneity of coefficients. Significantly enough, we have found all our considered variables follow I (0). Next, we move on to discuss and analyse the findings of our econometric findings.

5. Discussion of Findings

The results obtained from equation (1) are reported in Table 1. The table vividly describes the impacts of different variables on GDP growth in the South Asian economies. Out of the six economies, EFIT has significant impact over GDP in four nations, except Bangladesh and Pakistan. In Bangladesh, earnings from foreign tourists are very low and in Pakistan, perhaps, domestic political violence and instability are the prime causes for such outcome. Apart from that, one can see that schooling, emission

Table 1. GMM estimation results of equation (1).

Nation	Intercept	EFIT	MYS	CO_2	GFCF
India	0.28	0.014*	0.17**	0.21***	0.24***
	(0.84)	(0.08)	(0.04)	(0.00)	(0.00)
Bhutan	0.17**	0.37***	0.041*	0.078	0.41***
	(0.03)	(0.00)	(0.07)	(0.24)	(0.00)
Bangladesh	0.37	0.017	0.12***	0.24***	0.21***
	(0.37)	(0.14)	(0.00)	(0.00)	(0.00)
Nepal	0.24**	0.41***	0.018**	0.011**	0.31***
	(0.06)	(0.00)	(0.05)	(0.04)	(0.00)
Sri Lanka	0.10*	0.47***	0.20***	0.16**	0.28***
	(0.09)	(0.00)	(0.00)	(0.04)	(0.00)
Pakistan	0.09	0.021	0.21*	0.47***	0.81***
	(0.27)	(0.48)	(0.08)	(0.00)	(0.00)

Notes: Hansen test (*p*-value) 14.08 (0.91).
Durbin–Wu–Hausman test (*p*-value) 10.88 (0.00).
Values in the parentheses represent the respective *p*-values.
*,**,*** represent significant at 10%, 5%, and 1% level, respectively.

levels and fixed capital formation or investments do bear a significant impact on GDP, which are quite expected. For Bhutan, CO_2 is insignificant possibly due to the fact that this nation has negligible industrial activities, which keep the emission level very low. However, interestingly enough, overall panel GMM estimation reveals significant impact of all variables on the growth of GDP.

Outcomes of equation (2) are reported in Table 2. These results are even more interesting. It shows how different variables have been affecting the EFIT in these studied economies. In Bangladesh and Pakistan, the growth of GDP casts no role over EFIT, but in the other four nations, it does. The facts that capital stock, openness in international business with the rest of the world and investment or fixed capital formation are immensely important in encouraging tourism and earnings from it have been recognised by our findings and this is true for all the six economies. Hence, it is a two-way causal relationship between EFIT and GDP whose growths have significant influence over each other in four South Asian economies. But in the remaining two nations, these variables have no significant impact over one another.

Table 2. GMM estimation results of equation (2).

Nation	Intercept	GDP	K	OPN	GFCF
India	0.42*	0.14**	0.29***	0.18***	0.19***
	(0.07)	(0.05)	(0.00)	(0.00)	(0.00)
Bhutan	0.38	0.08*	0.14**	0.14*	0.19***
	(0.00)	(0.09)	(0.08)	(0.09)	(0.00)
Bangladesh	0.81**	0.12	0.28**	0.10*	0.14***
	(0.04)	(0.11)	(0.04)	(0.08)	(0.00)
Nepal	0.68***	0.18**	0.36***	0.14***	0.28***
	(0.00)	(0.02)	(0.00)	(0.00)	(0.00)
Sri Lanka	0.11	0.58***	0.48***	0.078*	0.15***
	(0.78)	(0.00)	(0.00)	(0.08)	(0.00)
Pakistan	0.29*	0.21	0.29**	0.37*	0.16**
	(0.08)	(0.88)	(0.03)	(0.09)	(0.05)

Dependent variable: Growth of EFIT

Notes: Hansen test (p-value) 13.88 (0.78).
Durbin–Wu–Hausman Test (p-value) 11.26 (0.00).
Values in the parentheses represent the respective p-values.
*,**,*** represent significant at 10%, 5%, and 1% level, respectively.

Table 3. GMM estimation results of equation (3).

Nation	Dependent variable: Growth of ITA				
	Intercept	PMC	COR	INF	PS
India	0.62	0.51***	−0.10***	−0.28***	−0.11***
	(0.21)	(0.00)	(0.00)	(0.00)	(0.00)
Bhutan	0.08***	0.27**	−0.54**	−0.22***	−0.05
	(0.00)	(0.04)	(0.05)	(0.00)	(0.24)
Bangladesh	0.21	0.25***	−0.31**	−0.09**	−0.28***
	(0.44)	(0.00)	(0.02)	(0.04)	(0.00)
Nepal	0.17***	0.54***	−0.16*	−0.22***	−0.13***
	(0.00)	(0.00)	(0.09)	(0.00)	(0.00)
Sri Lanka	0.18	0.20***	−0.62***	−0.52***	−0.44***
	(0.24)	(0.00)	(0.00)	(0.00)	(0.00)
Pakistan	0.40**	0.42**	−0.59***	−0.14***	−0.31***
	(0.02)	(0.04)	(0.00)	(0.00)	(0.00)

Notes: Hansen test (*p*-value) 12.22 (0.74).
Durbin–Wu–Hausman Test (*p*-value) 10.24 (0.00).
Values in the parentheses represent the respective *p*-values.
*,**,*** represent significant at 10%, 5%, and 1% level, respectively.

The overall panel estimation by application of GMM, once again, reveals significant impact of all variables on the growth of EFIT.

Finally, the results of equation (3) are reported in Table 3, which reveal the impact of different factors that are expected to have a meaningful influence over ITA. The table clearly depicts the importance of spread of modern technology and their use such as mobile connectivity and internet, as very important. A focus on reduction in corruption, general price level and establishing political stability by reducing violence are going to bring more tourists to these nations. Bhutan, for long, has been a peaceful nation without any incidents of violence. Perhaps that is why, for Bhutan, PS is not meaningful. Overall GMM estimation of panel data, however, finds meaningful impact of all variables.

6. Concluding Remarks

This study on six South Asian economies based on the dataset of tourism and its probable influential variables, covering the time period in this century, reveal that tourism has a great potential in these economies given certain factors are taken care of. In four of the six nations, earnings from tourism and GDP have direct influence on one another. Hence it is a two-way causal relationship like that seen in many developed European economies. The fact that emission or pollution has a positive impact on GDP is a bit worrying, that is, there could be a need to focus on using environment-friendly technologies. But in developing nations, such a process generally takes several decades because of poor financial conditions. Investment having a positive impact on GDP and EFIT is meaningful because it focuses on strengthening of infrastructure, which further promotes tourism. The positive impact of capital stock establishes this proposition appropriately. In a globalised world, openness and relationships with the rest of the world do bear meaningful impact on tourism and these economies are no different. Last but not the least, in the modern world, tourists always consider several economic factors before visiting any nation — the geographic position as well as relationship between these nations among themselves and within their own boundaries have always been important factors in the growth of tourism. Perhaps, that is why violence and stability play such an important part in nations like Pakistan and Sri Lanka. Our study finds that spread of technology is crucial as expressed by significant impact of the variable PMC. Nations do need to bring down the level of corruption and control the level of inflation so as to encourage more tourists to visit these economies.

Lastly, one can say that all the six South Asian economies have great prospects in tourism, and it bears direct influence over GDP growth and vice-versa and therefore acts as a source of employment generation along with the fact that a huge part of earnings in nations like Bhutan, Nepal and Sri Lanka come from tourism. Hence, being a hugely environmentally and culturally diversified area, these economies need to invest more in the development of tourism. Populous nations like India, Bangladesh and Pakistan need to consider tourism as an important source of fostering economic growth and development, especially in the post-COVID era where there have been major paradigm changes in the labour market and certainly in the economic systems and given the fact that tourism industry has been reviving itself in the post-COVID era at a fast pace and showing signs of regaining its pre-COVID glory of employment creation, there is a need to follow appropriate measures not only by investing in tourism-related monetary variables but also by creating as well as ensuring tourism-conducive conditions for the social, cultural and environmental scenarios.

References

Aslan, A. (2014). Tourism development and economic growth in the Mediterranean countries: Evidence from panel Granger causality tests. *Current Issues in Tourism*, *17*(4), 363–372.

Banerjee, O., Cicowiez, M., and Gachot, S. (2015). A quantitative framework for assessing public investment in tourism-an application to Haiti. *Tourism Management*, *51*, 157–173.

Chatterjee, N. (2022). Households' willingness to pay for improved water supply system in the dryland areas of West Bengal — an estimation using double-bounded dichotomous-choice model. *Economics Affairs*, *67*(05), 787–795.

Chatterjee, N. and Chatterjee, T. (2021). Effects of labor productivity and growth of manufacturing sector on overall growth of the nation — a panel data analysis of the major economies. In Pal, M. (Ed.) *Productivity Growth in the Manufacturing Sector* (pp. 17–29). Emerald Publisher, Bradford, UK.

Chatterjee, N. and Kundu, D. (2021). Role of FDI in developing the base of knowledge — an analysis of the BRICS nations. In Bhattacharyya, R. (Ed.) *Comparative Advantage in the Knowledge Economy* (pp. 113–126). Emerald Publisher, Bradford, UK.

Dedeurwaerdere, T. (2005). The contribution of network governance to sustainable development (p. 13). *Les seminaires de l'Iddri*. Universite catholique de Louvain, Fonds national de la recherche scientifique, Belgium.

Durbarry, R. (2004). Tourism and economic growth: The case of Mauritius. *Tourism Economics*, *10*(4), 389–401.

Economic Impact Reports, World Travel and Tourism Council. (2022).

Holzner, M. (2010). Tourism and economic development: The beach disease? *Tourism Management*, *32*(4), 922–933.

Im, K. S., Pesaran, M. H., and Shin, Y. (2003). Testing for unit roots in heterogeneous panels. *Journal of Econometrics*, *115*(1), 53–74.

Ishikawa, N. and Fukushige, M. (2007). Who expects the municipalities to take the initiative in tourism development? Residents' attitudes of Amami Oshima Island in Japan. *Tourism Management*, *28*(2), 461–475.

Jenkins, C. L. (1991). Tourism development strategies. *Developing Tourism Destinations*, 61–77.

Jenkins, C. L. and Henry, B. (1982). Government involvement in tourism in developing countries. *Annals of Tourism Research*, *9*(4), 499–521.

Kumar, R. R. (2014). Exploring the nexus between tourism, remittances, and growth in Kenya. *Quality & Quantity*, *48*(3), 1573–1588.

Kumar, R. R. and Kumar, R. (2013). Exploring the developments in urbanization, aid dependency, sectoral shifts and services sector expansion in Fiji: A modern growth perspective. *Global Business and Economics Review*, *15*(4), 371–395.

Levin, A., Lin, C.-F., and Chu, C.-S. J. (2002). Unit-root tests in panel data: Asymptotic and finite-sample properties. *Journal of Econometrics*, *108*(1), 1–24.

Maddala, G. and Wu, S. (1999). A comparative study of unit root tests with panel data and a new simple test. *Oxford Bulletin of Economics & Statistics*, *61*(S1), 631–652.

Narayan, P. K., Narayan, S., Prasad, A., and Prasad, B. C. (2010). Tourism and economic growth: A panel data analysis for Pacific Island countries. *Tourism Economics*, *16*(1), 169–183.

Petrescu, R. M. (2011). The involvement of the public and private sector–Elements with influence on travel & tourism demand during the crisis period. *Tourism and Hospitality Management*, *17*(2), 217–230.

Robaina-Alves, M., Moutinho, V., and Costa, R. (2016). Change in energy-related CO_2 (carbon dioxide) emissions in Portuguese tourism: A decomposition analysis from 2000 to 2008. *Journal of Cleaner Production*, *111*, 520–528.

Shahzad, S. J. H., Shahbaz, M., Ferrer, R., and Kumar, R. R. (2017). Tourism-led growth hypothesis in the top ten tourist destinations: new evidence using the quantile-on-quantile approach. *Tourism Management*, *60*, 223–232.

Sharpley, R. and Ussi, M. (2014). Tourism and governance in small island developing states (SIDS): The case of Zanzibar. *International Journal of Tourism Research*, *16*(1), 87–96.

Wang, C. and Xu, H. (2011). Government intervention in investment by Chinese listed companies that have diversified into tourism. *Tourism Management*, *32*(6), 1371–1380.

Online Sources

World Development Indicators. https://wdi.worldbank.org/.

World Economic Forum. (2021). Travel and Tourism Development Index 2021. https://www.weforum.org/reports/travel-and-tourism-development-index-2021/.

Chapter 4

Buddhist Religious Circuit: A Connect to India, Nepal, Sri Lanka, Bhutan and Myanmar

Yogieta S. Mehra[*,‡], Monika Bansal[*,§], and Vidhan Garg[†,¶]

[*]Department of Management Studies, Deen Dayal Upadhyaya College, University of Delhi, New Delhi, India

[†]Delhi Public School, R. K. Puram, New Delhi, India

[‡]yogieta@ddu.du.ac.in
[§]monikabansal@ddu.du.ac.in
[¶]vidhangarg24@gmail.com

Abstract

For centuries, India has been home to all religions in the world. India and its strong roots in religion has been an attraction for visitors and pilgrims for hundreds of years.

India has always stood on the foundations of its rich culture and its robust democracy. India's influence in South Asia, a strategic area for the nation, stems from the region's long history of cultural exchange. Buddhism is a part of this ancient exchange, and every day there is a procession of pilgrims from South Asian nations to India. Cross-border religious tourism is investigated in this research, which proposes a Buddhist Religious Circuit in South Asia by examining visitorship trends to Buddhist sites in India, Nepal, Sri Lanka, Bhutan and Myanmar.

Keywords: Religious tourism, religious circuit, Buddhist religious circuit.

1. Introduction

Different faiths suggest and describe different approaches to travel and have done so from humankind's earliest days (Vijayanand, 2012). India is home to some of the world's most revered pilgrimage destinations due to the country's long and varied religious heritage. In recent times, we observe that significance of cross-country religious tourism circuits is gaining popularity, which allow visitors to explore multiple religious sites in a single trip. Religious tourism can be understood as a tour planned for reasons based on religion (Rinschede, 1992). Religious tourism is a major economic driver for many countries around the world. In India, for example, religious tourism accounts for an estimated 60–70% of total domestic tourist arrivals. The research on the benefits of religious tourism circuits is still ongoing. However, the evidence to date suggests that religious tourism can be a valuable asset for a country or region. By developing religious tourism circuits in a sustainable way, countries can reap the economic, cultural, social, and environmental benefits of this important form of tourism.

It is well known that the reasons people travel vary from trip to trip, and that even within a single trip, visitors may have different reasons for going. Recent years have seen a renewed interest in religious sites and pilgrimage paths (Digance, 2003), notwithstanding the general trend towards secularisation throughout the globe. A huge possibility exists for the growth of various locations. OMT (2014) estimates that religious tourism has an annual economic impact of between $18 billion and $20 billion, with an estimated 300–330 million people making pilgrimages each year. Terzidou *et al.* (2017) examine the literature on the issue of religion and tourism from a number of different perspectives to better understand the interplay between the two industries. Tourist locations that cater to religious believers are no different from any other kind of destination (Bond *et al.*, 2014), and vice versa. India's soft power projection may be strengthened via the promotion of international peace and harmony through the promotion of Buddhism and tourism.

As per Annual Report of the Ministry of Tourism, Government of India 2022–2023, to promote India as the Buddhist tourist destination, the ministry is taking concrete steps for positioning India as the land of Buddha:

- "India aims to promote and showcase the rich Buddhist Heritage in India and highlight the major destinations visited by Buddha personally across the country."
- Development of Sanchi under Buddhist Circuit–Satna–Rewa–Mandsaur–Dhar in Madhya Pradesh (Sanchi Stupa is one of the oldest Buddhist monuments in the country and is also a UNESCO World Heritage Site).
- Development of Shravasti, Kushinagar and Kapilvastu (Buddha Circuit in Uttar Pradesh).
- "Ministry developed 08 short films of 30 seconds duration each and one mother film of 60 second duration on Bodh Gaya, Sarnath, Kapilvastu, Shravasti, Kushinagar, Vaishali, Rajgir and Sanchi destination. Ministry developed an advertorial brochure on Kushinagar for promoting India as the land of Buddha. Also, thematic brochure on the Buddhist sites in India was redeveloped."
- "With the huge potential to attract more than 500 million vigorous Buddhist communities throughout the world to India," the government of India says, "this religion has the "The Land of Buddha," Buddhist tourism in India, is a high-potential tourism product."

The travel and tourism business (including its direct, indirect and induced effects) is responsible for one-fourth of all new jobs created worldwide (333 million) and 10.3% of global GDP ($9.6 trillion) in 2019 as reported by the World Travel and Tourism Council (WTTC). Meanwhile, the total amount spent by foreign tourists was $1.8 trillion (6.8% of total exports). In 2019, tourism is expected to account for 7% of India's GDP, or INR 15723.3 billion. About 8.4% of India's labour force was engaged in this industry, totalling 40.1 million individuals. Even if just a third of all travellers are motivated by religious motives, the potential economic impact and job creation appears substantial.

2. India's Neighbours

The Kingdom of Bhutan, located in the eastern Himalayas, Druk-Yul, "the land of the thunder dragon," shares its borders with China to the north and India to the south and west. The mountains are quite tall, and there are lush valleys and dense woods. Thimphu serves as the capital of Bhutan, a nation whose government is organised as a democratic monarchy. 70% of the population is Buddhist, 25% is Hindu, and 5% is Muslim.

The Union of Myanmar (once known as Burma, the country of Myanmar (also known as Pyeidaungzu Myanmar Niangangandaw) is located in Southeast Asia, near the Bay of Bengal. It is bordered by Laos and Thailand to the east and by India and Bangladesh to the west. The military has essentially taken over the nation, and the capital of the country is the city of Yangon (formerly Rangoon). Approximately 85% of the population is Buddhist, with the rest being made up of Animists, Muslims, and Christians.

The Kingdom of Nepal, or *Nepal Adhirajya*, is a mountainous, landlocked nation in the Himalayas. It is surrounded by India on three sides and Tibet (China) to the north. The seat of government is in Kathmandu, and King Gyanendra Bir Bikram Shah Dev serves as the country's head of state. The Parliament (Rajya Sabha) is the legislative branch of government, and it consists of 205 representatives (Pratinidhi Sabha). Hinduism (followed by 89% of the population) is the official religion of the state. Buddhism (5%), Islam (3%), and Christianity (2%) also have minority following.

The Democratic Socialist Republic of Sri Lanka, Sri Lanka, about 80 km east of India's southernmost point, across the Palk Strait, is an island also known as Prajathanthrika Samajavadi Janarajaya. Colombo serves as the country's administrative centre, and Ranil Wickramasinghe serves as president. The majority of the population is Buddhist (73%), followed by 15% Hindus, 7% Muslims, and 5% Christians (Figure 1).

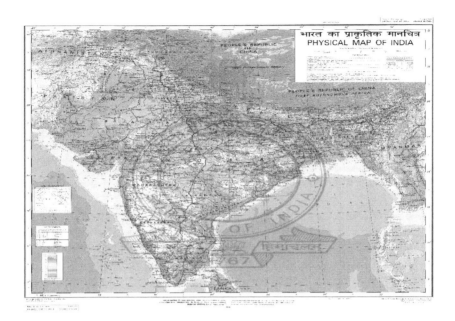

Figure 1. Physical map of India.
Source: Embassy of India, Hague.

3. Objectives

The objectives of this chapter are:

- To understand the meaning of tourist circuits.
- To understand the specific benefits of transnational religious tourism circuits for India.
- To propose a transnational Buddhist Tourist Circuit.

4. What is a Tourist Circuit?

A tourist circuit is a well-defined route with a fixed beginning and an end at two very different far-off places. However, these two places will have a minimum of one more stop in the middle and they are connected with one common theme which could be wildlife, birds, desert, a particular religion or some historical significance. The main condition for these minimum three interconnected places is that they should be far off from each other and should not be a part of the same city, town or village. Only in such a condition are the three interconnected destinations said to be part of a tourist circuit. It is expected that tourists will visit all the three destinations of the particular circuit during their tour. While designing a particular circuit, appropriate care is taken to develop infrastructure and provide rail/road connectivity among all the destinations that are part of the circuit. Development of a particular tourist circuit facilitates travelling of the tourists to all the destinations, which are part of the circuit which benefits them as well as provides a big economic boost to all the destinations that are part of the circuit. Further, it increases the duration of time spent by the tourists. It's useful for boosting both the number of visitors who visit these places and the average duration of their stays.

Thus, the main features of a tourist circuit are:

1. It should have at least three major destinations: This is the most important aspect of a travel route. A complete circuit requires at least three significant endpoints.
2. None of them should exist in the same town, city or village: There shouldn't be any stops along the route that are also in the same city, town or hamlet as the final destination.
3. It should not be separated by a long distance: Each stop along the route has to be far apart for the circuit to work properly. The proximity of these is important.
4. It should have well-defined entry and exit points: There should be a clear starting point for visitors to the circuit and a corresponding ending point from which they may leave.

5. Types of Tourist Circuits

The tourist circuits are of various types, viz., heritage, wildlife, religious, coastal, desert and tribal. As the name suggests, these circuits are connected by a common theme. This facilitates the tourists with a particular area of interest/passion to travel to all the places of their interest in an easy manner. The Government would start special trains which would take the tourists to all the places that are part of the circuit with appropriate stopovers so that the tourists can explore the destinations comfortably without worrying about the connectivity between the places part of the circuit. Some of the tourist circuits popular in India are mentioned below.

5.1. *Heritage tourist circuits*

India's civilisation is more than 500 years old, so modern India is an ideal destination for heritage tourism. The common points of all the destinations that would be part of the heritage circuit would be traditions, languages or monuments of a particular era and of historical significance. When we talk about heritage, we're referring to things like long-standing customs, languages and structures. India has a very rich heritage and we have developed numerous heritage circuits. The cultural continuity and intercultural understanding fostered by heritage tourism circuits are invaluable. The country of India is home to 35 UNESCO World Heritage Sites. The primary goal of these types of cultural circuits is to keep our history and culture alive and to revitalise long-lost traditions. The goal is, essentially, to learn to value the past. An example of a heritage circuit is Varanasi–Khajuraho–Agra. The city of Varanasi has been inhabited from ancient times, making it India's oldest city. Khajoraho is well-known for its sexually explicit architecture in the temple walls, while Agra is home to the iconic Taj Mahal.

5.2. *Wildlife tourist circuits*

Wildlife usually refers to the natural flora and wildlife of a certain area. Witnessing wild creatures in their own environment is a popular part of wildlife tourism. Animals photographers and nature watchers both go to the tourism hotspots that specialise in animal sighting. Countries in Africa and South America, as well as Australia, Canada, India, the Maldives, Indonesia and Sri Lanka, are popular destinations for this kind of travel. Offering wildlife fans trip packages and safaris allows them to get a better look at the animals they love. When tourists travel as part of a particular circuit, it eases their formalities of registering at every place for photography, stay or travel deep in the woods as a single license would work at all the places, which are part of the circuit. The primary goal of these kinds of circuits is to protect animals in their natural habitats. An example of a Wildlife Tourist Circuit is Corbett–Ranthambore–Bharatpur–Bandhavgarh–Kanha. Tigers and jungle safaris are what make this route so popular.

5.3. Religious tourist circuits

Many different faiths and traditions may be found in India. Throughout one's life, there are some religious sites that one must visit. India is a fantastic place to visit if you're interested in visiting a church, temple, monastery or mosque. The spiritual and material benefits of religious tourism may benefit any nation (Vukonic, 2002). Despite Hinduism's overwhelming predominance, other faiths, including Islam, Christianity, Buddhism and even smaller ones like Sikhism, Jainism, Vaishnavism and Judaism all have sizable following in the nation. When planning a trip motivated by religious conviction, many people choose to follow a religious tourism circuit. The main goal of these journeys is to reach holy places of worship. An example of a Religious Tourist Circuit is Lucknow–Shravasti–Kushinagar–Gorakhpur–Varanasi–Bodhgaya–Rajgir Nalanda–Patna. These are main destinations of Buddhist Circuit tour. Here are some specific examples of the benefits of religious tourism circuits:

- Travellers from all over the world go to Spain every year to walk the Camino de Santiago, which commemorates the path that pilgrims have walked to visit the tomb of St. James the Apostle in Santiago de Compostela. Economic activity in the form of billions of euros is predicted to be generated annually by the circuit's massive crowds.
- The 88 temples of Shikoku form the basis of a famous religious tourist circuit in Japan known as the Shikoku Pilgrimage. Millions of spectators go to the circuit year, resulting in billions of yen in economic output.
- Badrinath, Kedarnath, Gangotri and Yamunotri are the four main pilgrimage sites that make up the Char Dham Yatra, one of the most well-known religious tourist circuits in India. It is projected that the circuit's annual attendance of millions of spectators results in billions of dollars in economic activity.

6. Why Trans-National Religious Tourism Circuit for India?

- **Economic benefits:** India may reap substantial economic gains from cross-country religious tourism circuits. Spending on lodging, meals, transportation and mementoes is common among those who visit these routes. Economic growth and new employment opportunities may result from this. The four main Hindu pilgrimage sites of Badrinath, Kedarnath, Gangotri and Yamunotri make up the Char Dham Yatra, a well-known religious tourist circuit. The circuit is visited by millions of people annually and is responsible for billions in economic activity.

- **Cultural preservation:** Travelling religious pilgrimages around India are a great way to spread awareness of the country's rich history and culture. Visitors visiting these routes get an understanding of the background and customs of other faiths. This may aid in fostering an environment where people of all faiths and backgrounds feel included and valued. Some of the most important stops on the Buddhist pilgrimage trail in India include the cities of Bodh Gaya, Sarnath and Kushinagar. These locations are significant to Buddhists all across the globe because they assist to keep Buddhist traditions alive and well.
- **Social benefits:** Travelling religious pilgrimages throughout the nation may strengthen communities and foster tolerance and acceptance. People from various walks of life might be seen conversing with other travellers throughout these corridors. This might help lessen discrimination and build stronger relationships among people. Ajmer Sharif, Delhi, and Madurai are just few of the stops on the Sufi circuit in India. Important for Sufis all around the globe, these locations also foster religious tolerance and conversation.
- **Environmental benefits:** It is possible to minimise negative impacts on the environment while still participating in cross-country religious tourism circuits. Public transit usage, eco-friendly lodging options and trash reduction are all things that may help make a destination more appealing to tourists. This may aid in preventing damage to the environment and guarantee that future generations can experience the joys of interfaith travel. Leh, Manali, and Shimla are just a few of the stops in India's Himalayan circuit. Some of India's most breathtaking scenery may be seen at these locations, and visitors can do so in a responsible manner.
- **Geopolitical benefits:** The circuit has the potential to contribute to regional stability and peace. It's possible that the circuit's ability to bring individuals from diverse nations and cultures together will promote mutual respect and understanding. The potential for this to ease tensions and forestall violence is significant.

7. Buddhist Religious Circuit

There are more than 500 million Buddhists worldwide, making Buddhism one of the world's largest faiths. Originating in India, the religion has now made its way to various countries of Asia such as Nepal, Sri Lanka, Bhutan and Myanmar. Some of the holiest Buddhist sites in the world are located in these nations. In recent years, there has been a growing interest in developing Buddhist travel circuits as these circuits would allow visitors to explore multiple Buddhist sites in a single trip. There are many potential benefits to developing Buddhist travel circuits, including economic, cultural, social and environmental benefits.

8. Why Buddhist Circuit?

India has seven of the eight most important Buddhist sites, yet only around 1% of Buddhists make the trip there. India, the birthplace of Buddhism, has a long and storied history of Buddhist culture. Only Stupas (stone-encased moulds commemorating Buddha's remains), Chaityas (prayer halls) and Viharas (monks' cells) were permitted as part of its push towards austerity. Buddhist Train India will get you near to all these sites so you may have a meaningful spiritual encounter.

Tourists interested in Buddhism might go on a pilgrimage to the holiest locations in the world by following the Buddhist circuit. In the *Mahaparinirvana Sutra*, the Buddha instructs his disciples that visiting his birthplace of Lumbini, the enlightenment site of Bodhgaya, first teaching site of Sarnath, and nirvana site of Kushinagar would bring them merit and a good rebirth. The Ministry of Tourism has proposed a Buddhist circuit that would take visitors from Kapilavastu and Lumbini in Nepal to Shravasti, Sarnath, Kushinagar, Rajgir, Vaishali and Bodhgaya in India. There are some specific geopolitical benefits that could be realised from a Buddhist religious circuit connecting India, Nepal, Sri Lanka, Bhutan and Myanmar. The circuit could help to:

- **Strengthen ties between the countries involved:** People from all around the world would be able to meet and talk to one another at this circuit. This has the potential to improve relations and foster collaboration between the nations on a variety of fronts.
- **Promote regional development:** The racetrack has the potential to stimulate local business and travel. This has the potential to alleviate poverty and raise living conditions in the area.

- **Increase understanding of Buddhism:** Participants will learn about the rich history and culture of Buddhism on this trip. This has the potential to increase public familiarity with Buddhism and its global impact.

Creating Buddhist tourist itineraries might have many positive effects, not only the geopolitical ones mentioned above. Among them are:

- **Increased understanding of Buddhism:** It is possible that Buddhist tourism routes will contribute to a better global knowledge of Buddhism and its significance. One way to achieve this goal is to educate the public about the Buddhist religion and its teachings.
- **Improved cross-cultural understanding:** Buddhist pilgrimages have the potential to foster greater international understanding and friendship. One approach would be to host gatherings at which people of different ethnicities and cultures may mingle and share their experiences.
- **Boost to the tourism industry:** Buddhist pilgrimages have the potential to increase visitor numbers to the area, which in turn would enhance the local economy. The economy of the participating nations may benefit as a result.

There are several ways in which the growth of Buddhist tourist routes might improve the region's economy, security and culture. The area may be made more peaceful, stable and affluent if the required actions are taken to design and develop these circuits so that they can reach their full potential. A total of 76 projects in Jharkhand, Madhya Pradesh, Jammu & Kashmir, Bihar and Gujarat have been approved by the Ministry of Tourism of the Government of India as part of the Swadesh Darshan Scheme (SDS 1.0) for tourism development throughout the nation. The goal of the scheme is to upgrade the existing infrastructure and amenities in these hotspots for tourists.

9. Understanding the Buddhist Circuit

9.1. *Lumbini*

- According to legend, Siddhartha (Buddha) was born at the holy city of Lumbini in Nepal, in 563 BC. It's a major destination for Buddhists from all over the world (Figure 2).

Figure 2. Lumbini.
Source: http://www.irctcbuddhisttrain.com/

9.2. *Kapilavastu*

- Kapilavastu, the capital of the Shakyas situated in Southern Nepal, is the home that Siddhartha shared with his parents and where he stayed until he departed at the age of 29 to seek enlightenment.

9.3. *Shravasti*

- Shravasti, a historic city in Uttar Pradesh on the banks of the Rapti River, served as Kosala's capital. There, the Buddha is said to have meditated for a total of 14 Chaturmasas, or a sacred time of four months. Several ancient Buddhist viharas and stupas may be seen in Shravasti.

9.4. *Sarnath*

- Sarnath (Figure 3), at Sarnath, Uttar Pradesh, at the meeting of the Gomathi and Ganges rivers, the Buddha spoke his first sermon after achieving enlightenment.

Figure 3. Sarnath.
Source: http://www.irctcbuddhisttrain.com/

9.5. *Kushinagar*

- It is widely held that Buddha experienced Parinirvana, or full nirvana, at the city of Kushinagar in the Indian state of Uttar Pradesh.

9.6. *Rajgir*

- As the site of the first Buddhist council, Rajgir has a special place in Buddhist history. Many of Buddha's teachings were likely given here during his 12-year sojourn.

9.7. *Vaishali*

- The second Buddhist council took place at Vaishali in 383 BC, not far from the spot where Buddha delivered his last lecture before his death in 483 BC.

Figure 4. Bodhgaya.
Source: http://www.irctcbuddhisttrain.com/

9.8. *Bodhgaya*

- As the site where Buddha obtained enlightenment beneath the Bodhi tree, Bodhgaya has great religious significance for Buddhists. An official UNESCO World Heritage Site, the Mahabodhi Temple Tree (Figure 4).
- The circuit's goal is to provide world-class facilities to entice Buddhist pilgrims to India, thereby significantly boosting tourism revenue and employment opportunities.

9.9. *Proposed Buddhist circuit — SINBM*

The chapter proposes the first trans-national tourist circuit, the Buddhist circuit, which spans India, Nepal, Sri Lanka, Bhutan and Myanmar. This would attract Buddhist tourists from across the globe by offering them a spiritual journey through these five countries. A common visa would ease the pain of separate bookings and travel arrangements. Development of such a circuit would not only attract people of these five countries but also those across the world.

10. Why Visit Buddha by Trans-National Buddhist Circuit?

All the key locations associated with Buddha's life and teachings would be included on the Transnational Buddhist circuit. The trip could begin from Sri Lanka and cover the popularly called cultural triangle, comprising Anuradhapura, Mihintale, Dambulla, Sigiriya and Kandy. All of them were once home to priceless Buddhist treasures that have withstood the test of time. The second stop would be India, and the first destination in India would be Bodhgaya, where Buddha attained Enlightenment. Both the Iconic Buddha Statue and the Mighty Temples, such as the Mahabodhi Temple, which is a UNESCO World Heritage Site, serve as centres of devotion. The group might then go to Nalanda, known for its internationally renowned university and archaeological museum. Next, you'll go to Sarnath, where you may see the enormous Dhamekh Stupa, India's oldest archaeological monument, the Sarnath Museum, the Ashokan Pillar, and the Ganges Ghat for the sunset Aarti. The next stop would be Lumbini in Nepal where Gautama Buddha was born, and where tourists may pay their respects at the Ashokan Pillar and the Maya Devi Temple. From Nepal, the Buddhist enthusiasts would move to Bhutan and visit, the Tiger's Nest (Paro Taktsang) in Bhutan. Perched on the brink of a 3,120-metre cliff, this renowned monastery provides breathtaking views of the Paro valley below. The Paro Taktsang is revered so highly because of its association with the birthplace of Buddhism.

And then, the final destination in Myanmar. Once the tourists reach Yangon (Capital of Myanmar), they can visit the Reclining Buddha at Chauk Htet Gyi, a popular destination for Buddhist worshippers. Next, they can visit Shwedagon Pagoda, one of Myanmar's most important religious structures and a pilgrimage destination for Buddhists worldwide. Myanmar is home to numerous tourist places with ancient gold-plated pagodas. The Circuit ends at Yangon; however, the tourists may be given the privilege to visit different cities of Buddhist interest if they wish to. The development of this Trans-National Buddhist Circuit SINBM (Sri Lanka, India, Nepal, Bhutan and Myanmar) would usher in a brand-new era in the geopolitical interactions between these states. It's all part of the goal to turn the BIMSTEC area into a "borderless" tourism destination. In the Bangkok Declaration of 6 June 1997, the Bay of Bengal Initiative for Multi-Sectoral Technical and Economic Cooperation (BIMSTEC) was formally established. It is a regional organisation consisting of India, Sri Lanka, Bangladesh, Myanmar, Thailand, Nepal and Bhutan.

11. Recommendations

The following should be done to maximise the benefits of Buddhist tourism itineraries:

- Develop a comprehensive plan for developing Buddhist travel circuits: As part of this strategy, you'll need to choose which landmarks and landmark infrastructure should be included in each circuit.
- Promote Buddhist travel circuits to potential visitors: This may be accomplished using conventional and online media such as newspapers and television.
- Work with local communities to ensure that the development of Buddhist travel circuits benefits them: This involves safeguarding natural resources and providing locals with access to the tourist sector.

References

Bond, N., Packer, J., and Ballantyne, R. (2014). Exploring visitor experiences, activities and benefits at three religious tourism sites. *International Journal of Tourism Research, 17*, 471–481.

Digance, J. (2003). Pilgrimage at contested sites. *Annals of Tourism Research, 30*, 143–159. https://businesseconomics.in/religious-tourism-turns-economic-multiplier-across-globe#:~:text=Economic%20impact%20of%20religious%20tourism%20The%20sector,GDP%20or%20employment%20generation%20seems%20quite%20significant. https://tourism.gov.in/sites/default/files/2023-02/MOT%20Annual%20Report_2022-23_English.pdf.

OMT. (2014). El Primer Congreso Internacional de la OMT sobre Turismo y Peregrinaciones Explora el Nexo Entre el Turismo y las Rutas Espirituales. September 17.

Rinschede, G. (1992). Forms of religious tourism. *Annals of Tourism Research, 19*, 51–67.

Terzidou, M., Scarles, C., and Saunders, M. (2017). Religiousness as tourist performances: A case study of Greek orthodox pilgrimage. *Annals of Tourism Research, 66*, 116–129.

Vijayanand, S. (2012). Socio-economic impacts in pilgrimage tourism. *International Journal of Multidisciplinary Research, 2*(1), 329–343.

Vukonic, B. (2002). Religion, tourism and economics: A convenient symbiosis. *Tourism Recreation Research, 27*(2), 59–64.

Part II

Trade Disruption Amid Perceived versus Realistic Security Threats

Chapter 5

The Interface between Economics and Security: Defence Industry for a Resurgent India

Raghbendra Jha[*,¶] and Ashok Sharma[†,‡,§,||]

[*]*Arndt-Corden Department of Economics, Australia South Asia Research Centre, Crawford School of Public Policy, The Australian National University, Canberra, Australia*

[†]*Australian Defence Force Academy, University of New South Wales Canberra, Canberra, Australia*

[‡]*University of Canberra, Canberra, Australia*

[§]*Australia-India Institute, University of Melbourne, Melbourne, Australia*

[¶]*r.jha@anu.edu.au*
[||]*ashok.sharma@adfa.edu.au*

Abstract

This chapter reviews the sluggishness of manufacturing sector growth in India in a comparative and historical perspective and argues that without accelerated growth in this sector, India's industrial transition will be incomplete. We argue that India faces multi-faceted threats to its security, particularly from China and Pakistan and from the new dispensation in Afghanistan. India has fought open wars with both China and Pakistan and faces further threats from the expansionist tendencies of China in countries in the immediate neighbourhood of India and from frequent terrorist activities directed towards India from Pakistan. India also needs to play a role for the defence of its extended neighbourhood. For all these reasons, India needs a stronger military. The development of the military sector and enhanced arms exports will provide a ready market for expanded defence manufacturing. Thus, India needs a military–industrial complex for augmenting economic growth and enhancing national security.

Keywords: India, defence industry, economy, manufacturing, lead sector, security threat, China and Pakistan, great power, Indo-Pacific.

Since the industrial revolution, no country has become a major economy without becoming an industrial power.

— Lee Kuan Yew, Delivering the 2005, Jawaharlal Nehru Memorial Lecture, New Delhi

Changes happening around the world often become a matter of concern for us. We, as a nation, must keep our guards high during these times of uncertainties and upheavals around the world.... As such, we need to be vigilant at all times.

— Rajnath Singh, India's Minister of Defence, after dedicating an indigenously built Coast Guard ship in a keynote address at Defence Services Staff College in Wellington, Tamil Nadu, 28 August 2021

1. Introduction

There is no gainsaying the fact that India needs both a strong industrial base and a robust defence industry. World Bank data for 2020 reveals that the share of manufacturing in gross domestic product (GDP) was 26% for China and precisely half that (13%) for India. China is India's predominant economic as well as military competitor. Indeed, the shares of manufacturing in GDP are higher than India's for many Association of Southeast Asian Nations (ASEAN) countries. The share of manufacturing in total employment was 27% for China and 25% for India in 2019. In line with differences in the industrial structures in both these countries, manufacturing employment in India is largely in the micro, small and medium enterprises (MSME) whereas manufacturing employment in China is centred largely around medium-sized enterprises. Manufacturing, mining and electricity added together account for the industrial sector. In 2020, industry accounted for 37.8% of China's GDP and 23.2% of India's GDP. Hence, a critical difference between the Indian and Chinese economies is the difference in the shares of the manufacturing sectors in the two countries (Jha and Afrin, 2021).

Concurrently, defence sector manufacturing has been ignored in India and her defence needs have been met largely through imports. Despite its massive size, capability and security concerns, India is among the world's largest importers of arms. A March 2021 report (SIPRI, 2021; Pandit, 2021) indicates that during 2011–2015 India was the world's largest importer of major arms and accounted for 14% of global arms imports. During 2016–2020, India was the second largest arms importer behind Saudi Arabia. During this period, Saudi Arabia accounted for 11% of total arms imports whereas India accounted for 9.5%. However, India faces a very challenging security situation and excessive reliance on imports can be risky. India has fought open battles with Pakistan in 1947–1948, 1965, 1971 and 1999 and Pakistan-sponsored terrorist activity continuously since at least 1999. India has also fought an open war with China in 1962 and has had major skirmishes with its powerful northern neighbour several times since then, most recently in 2020–2021. India's border disputes with China and Pakistan are not settled. Unlike the United States, which has fought most of its wars outside its borders, India has fought all its battles on its border along which there has been a perpetual standoff. Thus, there are strong reasons for India to replenish both its manufacturing and its armaments capacity. Thus, India needs a military–industrial complex (MIC).

We argue that akin to the MIC in the United States in the post-World War II era, India needs a defence industry sector as a leading sector to develop its manufacturing sector and defence preparedness in an increasingly hostile security threat environment. We assess the significance of the domestic defence industry for developing the manufacturing sector in the context of the Modi government's 'Make in India' initiative. The development of the domestic defence industry base will accelerate India's economic growth, generate employment, make India self-reliant, address security concerns, expand strategic engagement and help India's ambition of playing a meaningful role in global leadership. The chapter uses exploratory and analytical methods of research for addressing these concerns.

This chapter is organised as follows. Section 2 develops the economic rationale for expanding India's manufacturing sector base. Section 3 overviews India's security challenges and underscores the need to develop a strong armaments industry. Section 4 explores how the development of the manufacturing sector and the armaments sector could complement each other. Section 5 concludes and suggests policy measures.

2. The Economic Rationale for Augmenting India's Manufacturing Sector

Although recent high economic growth in India has been accompanied by a sharp drop in the share of agriculture in GDP, this has not translated into a sharp rise in the share of manufacturing (Jha and Afrin, 2021). Trends show that the share of manufacturing in GDP has been stagnating in India for quite some time, although prior to British rule in India, the country recorded 25% of world manufacturing output (Jha, 2018; Jha and Afrin, 2021).

Because of the legacies of the past restrictive policies (licence quota raj) India's manufacturing sector has a large informal sector component. Even within organised manufacturing sector, there is a preponderance of MSME sector enterprises, which provide the overwhelming bulk of India's formal sector employment. Figures for the growth of the manufacturing sector are deceptive since domestic value-added in manufacturing represents a diminishing share of manufacturing output (Jha, 2018). There are a few large firms that are basically multinational in character whence the sector overall is characterised by what has been called "the missing middle". The public sector still has a strong dominance in the manufacturing sector. Within this group, there is a strong concentration of profit and, particularly, loss-making enterprises. Furthermore, there is a strong regional concentration of manufacturing activity, particularly of unorganised manufacturing. India's industrial transition can thus be described as incomplete.

Several reasons have been cited for India's incomplete industrial transition. Chief among these are the lack of adequate infrastructural facilities, rigid labour laws that prevent flexibility in labour markets and discourage firms from employing more labour, "missing middle" in Indian manufacturing, restrictive foreign trade policies and a plethora of product market regulations and tax structures.[1] Some of these constraining factors are being eased now.

---

[1] The country's indirect tax structure has been simplified considerably with the enactment of a comprehensive Goods and Services Tax (GST). This tax became operative on 1 July 2017.

On the other hand, China's early industrialisation after the onset of Deng Xiaoping's reforms was impressive. China has had a strong record of manufacturing sector growth fuelled largely by cheap labour and flexible capital and labour markets, market-friendly regulations and strong export orientation. As a result, after years of very high GDP and manufacturing sector growth, wages in China's manufacturing sector are now rising strongly. Indeed, Eurozone International estimates (Aleem, 2017) that Chinese factory wages have nearly trebled over the past decade, are higher than wages in most Latin American countries and are closing in on wages in the weaker Eurozone countries. In comparison, Indian labour is much cheaper and India has the scale and capacity to replace China as the world's leading producer of inexpensive manufactured products.

For India to occupy the low value-added manufacturing production space being vacated by China, it must deal with competition from other countries in South and South-East Asia, which are clamouring for the same production space, although most of them have higher wages than those prevailing in India. In this context, the Economic Survey 2016–2017 of the Government of India says: "Clearly India still has potential comparative advantage in terms of cheaper and more abundant labour. But these are nullified by other factors that render them less competitive than their peers in competitive countries" (Ministry of Finance, 2017, p. 132)

Bangladesh and Vietnam have emerged as tough competitors for India in the apparel sector; Vietnam and Indonesia are emerging as major production and export hubs for leather goods. Other countries in South Asia and South-East Asia are emerging as hubs for cheap electronic production and, hence, exports. Therefore, India's window of opportunity to take advantage of rising wages in China to become a low value-added manufacturing hub is closing quickly. As part of its strategy to boost its manufacturing sector and exports, India should make concrete efforts to integrate into Global Value Chains (GVC), which have been used very effectively by many countries including China and those in South-East Asia to boost manufacturing.

Prominent developmental economists such as Albert Hirschman, Benjamin Higgins and H.W. Singer have conceptualised this in the context of unbalanced growth for economic development. Hirschman believes that deliberate unbalancing of the economy is the best development strategy, and that if the economy is to continue progressing, development policy should manage tensions, disproportions and disequilibrium. Instead of focusing on balanced growth, the primary goal should be to manage the existing imbalances that can be seen in profit and losses. Hence, the sequence leading away from equilibrium is a perfect pattern for development. Inequitable development of different sectors frequently makes way for rapid development. Underdeveloped industries are encouraged to concentrate on encouraging more developed industries (Hirschman, 1958; Hirschman, 1969). Benjamin Higgins propounds "Deliberate unbalancing of the economy, in accordance with a pre-designed strategy is the best way to achieve the economic growth." H.W. Singer observes, "Unbalanced growth is a better development strategy to concentrate available resources on types of investment, which help to make the economic system more elastic, more capable of expansion under the stimulus of expanded market and expanding demand" (Rogers and Gentry, 2019; Higgins, 1954).

The lead sector generates dramatic technological progress in commercial and industrial leading sectors, which serve as a platform for global political leadership (Reuveny and Thompson, 2001). Because of the presence of their leading sectors, the world's leading economies, for example, Britain in the 19th century, experienced robust growth, which enabled them to dominate the global economy.

A parallel view was that of the "big push" propounded first in the 1950s when the newly independent developing countries were looking to quickly attain high rates of economic growth in order to improve living standards. This was put forward first by Rosenstein-Rodan who argued that rapid industrialisation of many sectors of the economy can be profitable for them all even when no individual sector can break even when industrialising alone (Rosenstein-Rodan, 1943, 1961). Kevin *et al.* (1989) explore conditions under which the theory of the big push can lead to rapid industrialisation in a least developed country (LDC). Such a big push is possible in economies in which industrialised firms capture in their profits only a fraction of the total contribution of their investment to the profit of other industrialising firms, thus generating positive spinoffs for each industry's industrialisation (Murphy *et al.*, 1989). However, Easterly (2006) is sceptical of the possibility of the big push. In a related paper, Sachs and Warner (1999) argue that if the theory of the big push is applicable, then resource booms in developing countries should be accompanied by rising per capita incomes, which has not often been observed. However, this may have happened because of Dutch disease effects of resource booms (Pasaribu, 2019). Matsuyama (1992) emphasises the importance of market size and entrepreneurship in the success of the big push, whereas Trindade (2005) stresses the key importance of exports and being open to international trade in ensuring the success of efforts at the big push.

In the present context, the development of MIC would form a key element of unbalanced growth and the contributions that this sector will provide to the rest of the economy suits well the requirements of the big push. Since the size of India's market is large, the defence and armaments sector can potentially provide a committed market. This is because India's internal security and external security environment require a much more pronounced military presence than has hitherto existed if India is to defend itself adequately and fulfil its role as an important bulwark of peace and stability in the Indo-Pacific and beyond. There are strong complementaries between India's national security strategy and industrialisation strategy. Thus, Matsuyama's market size requirement will be fulfilled. India also has considerable entrepreneurship in the area of rocket and missile technology where it has a significant cost advantage. This should also keep India's export options robust and the existing FDI regulations, which allow for 100% foreign investment in defence, would also satisfy some of the other conditions that the extant literature has stipulated to ensure the success of the big push strategy. Thus, the MIC could provide India the "big push" it still needs for attaining high industrial growth.

3. India's Security Challenges, Strategic Outreach and Great Power Ambition

That India needs to develop a defence industrial base is evident given the mismatch between the security threat that India faces and its defence expenditure and capability.

Table 1 indicates the United States, China, India, Russia and the UK (in that order) are the top five spenders on defence.

Table 1. Top five countries in terms of defence expenditure.

Country	GDP/nominal (million $) 2020	Percentage increase in 2019–2020	Defence expenditure (billion $) 2020	Defence % of total GDP 2020
US	21,433,226	4.4	778	3.7
China	14,342,933	1.9	252	1.7
India	2,891,582	2.1	72.9	2.9
Russia	1,692,930	2.5	61.7	4.3
UK	2,826,441	2.9	59.2	2.2

Thus, the United States continues to lead defence expenditure followed by China, India, Russia and the UK. In 2020, the US defence expenditure increased by 4.4% to $778 billion, China by 1.9% to $252 billion, India by 2.1% to $72.9 billion, Russia by 2.5% to 61.7 billion and the UK by 2.9% to 59.2 billion (SIPRI, 2021). India increased spending but not commensurately with its security threat and the growing strategic interest beyond its periphery. Tables 2 and 3 provide historical and comparative information on India's manufacturing sector.

Lemahieu and Leng compute an index of power for the Asia-Pacific region based on a weighted average of eight indicators: (i) economic capability, (ii) military capability, (iii) resilience, (iv) future resources, (v) economic relationships, (vi) defence networks, (vii) diplomatic influence and (viii) cultural influence (Lemahieu and Leng, 2021). The highest possible value for this index is 100. In 2020, the United States with a score of 81.6 was the most powerful country in the region with power trending down. China was the second most powerful with a value of 76.1 for this index. China's power was relatively stable. Japan was at number 3 with an index value of 41, trending downwards. India was at number 4 with an index value of 39.7 (trending down). Russia was at number 5 with an index value of 33.6 trending down and Australia was at number 6 with an index value of 32.4 (trending upwards). Apart from the large gap between the power positions of India and China, India does not yet cross the threshold value of being a major power.

India's defence industry readiness and modernisation must be viewed in the context of its security threat environment. To begin with, India's relationship with Pakistan has been tense and hostile since partition in 1947. This inimical relationship is characterised by three full-fledged wars, one implicit war in Kargil, two major incidences of military stand-offs, continuing low-conflict border skirmishes and military deadlocks. Despite the diplomatic and political initiatives and confidence-building measures to improve the Indo-Pak relationship, attributes such as the memories of violent partition, unresolved complex border disputes, political incompatibility, mutually incompatible positions on nationhood and the lack of substantial trade and business ties between the two countries contribute to the rivalry's persistence (Paul, 2006; Korbel, 1954; Brecher, 1968; Sharma, 2012). Although neither India nor Pakistan as nuclear power nations would fight a conventional or nuclear war, the possibility of war remains. Contrary to the deterrence theory, India and Pakistan's respective military strategies, such as India's Cold Start Doctrine (CSD)

Table 2. Manufacturing as a share of GDP and growth rates: India and select other countries.

Country/country group	Share of manufacturing in GDP (average)					Manufacturing sector growth (average)				
	1970–1979	1980–1989	1990–1999	2000–2009	2010–2015	1970–1979	1980–1989	1990–1999	2000–2009	2010–2015
India	15.23	16.03	15.79	16.13	16.79	4.31	5.77	5.84	7.5	7.13
China[a]	36.75	35.69	32.61	31.91	30.80	11.31	10.60 (10.7)	12.93 (14.7)	11.24	8.86
East Asia and the Pacific (excluding high income)[b]		29.70	26.31	24.74	23.61					
Europe and Central Asia (excluding high income)[c]				17.82	15.22				3.82	3.82
Low and Middle income[d]	26.32	26.33	23.63	22.08	22.04					

Notes: [a]Chinese industry, rather than manufacturing, growth figures are reported. Last figure for share of manufacturing in China's value-added is the average of 2010–2013. Figures in parenthesis indicate an average annual growth rate of manufacturing for Chinese manufacturing in 1980–1990 and 1990–1998, respectively, obtained from UNIDO (2001).
[b]Manufacturing sector growth rate WDI data for these countries are not available for these countries.
[c]Some data are missing for these countries.
[d]WDI data on manufacturing sector growth rates is not available for these countries.
Source: Authors' computation based on data from World Development Indicators 2017.

Table 3. India's manufacturing sector in comparative perspective for 2010.

Country	Manufacturing gross value-added in 2010 ($ billion)	Rank in 1990	Rank in 2000	Rank in 2010	Manufacturing output as percentage of world total in 2010
China	1,923	8	3	1	18.9
United States	1,856	1	1	2	8.2
Japan	1,084	2	2	3	
Germany	614	3	3	4	6.0
Italy	308	4	6	5	3.0
Brazil	282	12	12	6	
Korea	279	13	8	7	
France	268	7	7	8	2.6
UK	231	6	5	9	2.3
India	226	16	13	10	2.2
Russia	209	9	16	11	
Mexico	179	14	9	12	
Indonesia	176	25	10	13	
Spain	170	10	11	14	

Source: Authors' compilation from Twelfth Plan document, Planning Commission of India and other government documents.

and Pakistan's Strategic Equivalence, differing views of Indian and Pakistani strategists about the dangers of war, asymmetrical expectations of how a war would develop and miscalculation arising from ballistic missile defence systems make them vulnerable to war (Sagan, 2004, 2009; Sharma, 2012). India's nuclear programme, which goes beyond the nation's stated policy of credible deterrence and no first use of nuclear weapons to counter security threats from Pakistan's nuclear strategy, keeps the country vulnerable to a war-like situation (Clary and Narang, 2018/2019).

Pakistan's continued inaction in combating the terror network on its soil, as well as its support for cross-border terrorism and border misadventure, is deteriorating India–Pakistan relations. Recently, India has taken a tough stance on Pakistan's border misadventure, as evidenced by the surgical strike in response to the Pulwama terror attack, discrediting Pakistan in international forums for its financial support to terror outfits and failure to crack down on terror networks, and repealing Article 370, which granted Jammu and Kashmir a special status. However, Pakistan's nuclear arsenal continues to expand, with new warheads, delivery systems and a thriving fissile material industry. A review of a large collection of commercial satellite images of Pakistani army garrisons and air force bases reveals what appear to be mobile launchers and underground nuclear power plants. Moreover, Pakistan is developing numerous delivery systems, four plutonium production reactors and expanding uranium enrichment facilities. Its stockpile is expected to grow significantly over the next decade (Kristensen *et al.*, 2018). Pakistan's successful test of a nuclear-capable, submarine-launched cruise missile (SLCM), Babur 3, with a range of 450 km provides it a "credible second strike capability bolstering its nuclear force structure" (Clary and Panda, 2017). Pakistan possesses 160 nuclear warheads, surpassing India's 150 nuclear warheads (SIPRI, 2021).

The failure of the establishment of regular diplomatic dialogue between the two countries perpetuates hostility between the two nations. Peace efforts are stalled since the 2008 Mumbai terror attacks. The Indian government, with its strong political base, frowns on granting concessions or having a soft approach to any of Pakistan's misadventures. It advocates a tough stand on Pakistan and zero tolerance on terrorism as a core principle of the Bharatiya Janata Party (BJP). Pakistan's continued anti-India rhetoric and postures and deepening security partnership with China to contain India continue to dim the long-time peace prospects. With the overwhelming support for the Modi government's surgical strikes and Balakot airstrikes on the line of control (LoC) in 2017 and 2019, any terror incident could lead to war between the two countries.

There is a strong possibility of China joining Pakistan. A comprehensive China–Pakistan All-Weather Friendship, in addition to China's India encircling strategy and growing defence power, adds to India's security concerns. The possibility of future conflict with both China and Pakistan is not mere speculation. India has clashed with both countries. China endorses Pakistan's claim to J&K and continues to block UN resolutions against Pakistan on terrorism, including the resolution designating Masood Azhar as a terrorist (*The Times of India*, 2017). Pakistan backs China's territorial claims to Tibet, Taiwan, Hong Kong and Xinjiang. This trend is visible in recent years in the diplomatic spat between India and the combined efforts of China and Pakistan at international forums, particularly UN, as well as China's use of veto power against India at the UN Security Council. China has in the past stepped in on many instances to block the listing of Pakistani terrorists at the UNSC sanctions committee. China raised the Kashmir issue at the UN Security Council at least three times in 2019 and 2020, calling for discussions after India repealed Article 370 (Krishnan, 2020).

The friendship between China and Pakistan is also visible in their arms trade, military drills and nuclear ties. Since 1963, when the two countries signed a border agreement that divided territory in Pakistan-occupied Kashmir (POK), China has provided Pakistan with missile and nuclear technology. Over the last decade, Pakistan has become China's client state and is the largest recipient of the Chinese arsenal (Gao, 2020).

Both countries have increased their joint military exercises in recent years and target India. The two countries have developed a series of joint exercises spanning navy, army and air force, including the recent "Sea Guardians-2020," the first joint naval exercise featuring anti-submarine and marine rescue training in the north Arabian Sea in January 2020, the Shaheen (Eagle)-IX air drill in Sindh province less than 200 km from the Indian border and joint military exercises in Tibet marking 70 years of their friendship along the Line of Actual Control (LAC), weeks ahead of the first anniversary of the bloody clash in Ladakh's Galwan valley (*The Global Times*, 2020). These military drills, which are intended to improve cooperation, interoperability and mutual trust amid tensions surrounding the common enemy, also send a blunt message to India. During his November 2020 visit to Islamabad, China's defence minister signed a Memorandum of Understanding (MoU) between China and Pakistan aimed at strengthening defence ties between their armies (Aamir, 2020). The China–Pakistan defence cooperation has accentuated amidst the deteriorating China–India relationship, and the deepening India–US comprehensive strategic partnership.

The worst scenario could be both China and Pakistan joining forces to form a hostile alliance against India. Emphasising this concern, Chief of Indian Army Staff, Manoj Mukund Naravane, remarked in January 2021, "There is no doubt that Pakistan, China threat exists not just in theory, but very much on the ground. Their collusive approach against India poses a challenge" (*The Economic Times*, 2021). On 4 March 2021, Chief of Defence Staff Gen Bipin Rawat reiterated the growing China–Pakistan threat, emphasising the importance of studying transformational concepts and being prepared for threats to military primarily from China and Pakistan (*The Indian Express*, 2021).

Despite growing bilateral trade ties (in which India has a large balance of trade deficit), India's relationship with China has been strained since the 1962 Indo-China War. The 2013 border standoff in Ladakh, the 2017 Doklam standoff and the most recent Galwan Valley clash in June 2020 all demonstrate their long-standing tense and managed rivalry. Despite peace talks, this relationship remains marred by fundamental conflicts of interest, border disputes and security quandaries (Raghavan, 2019; Bloomfield, 2021).

Furthermore, China is using multiple strategies including diplomatic manoeuvring, favourable economic aid and investment, port and base construction, and arms sales to encircle India in the Indian Ocean and small island nations. What is concerning is that these commercial ports and bases could be used for military purposes by hostile economically and militarily assertive China next door to India.

China is encircling India through its String of Pearls: a network of military and commercial facilities in the nations along its sea lines of communication, which stretches from the Chinese mainland to Port Sudan in the Horn of Africa. The sea lines run through several major maritime choke points such as the Strait of Mandeb, the Strait of Malacca, the Strait of Hormuz and the Lombok Strait as well as other strategic maritime centres in Pakistan, Sri Lanka, Bangladesh, the Maldives and Somalia. The String of Pearls is now being pursued as part of the larger and more ambitious Belt Road Initiative (BRI), of which the China–Pakistan Economic Corridor (CPEC) is a key component. Through these strategies, China has made inroads into India's South Asian neighbours and the island nations of the Indian Ocean Rim by establishing ports and bases in Pakistan, Sri Lanka, the Maldives, Myanmar, Thailand, Seychelles, Mauritius and a military base in Djibouti. Under CPEC, China's Gwadar Port in Pakistan threatens India from the Arabian Sea. The CPEC passes through the Gilgit–Baltistan region in the POK, which India claims as its integral part, located close to the Siachen Glacier as well as to Ladakh, the current flashpoint between India and China. This has consolidated China's strategic position and can be used to launch an offensive in the event of a Sino-Indian conflict. China's help in the development of the port of Chittagong, in the heart of the Bay of Bengal, and its request to Bangladesh to allow a naval base near Chittagong; the development of a multi-billion-dollar deep sea port by China in Kyaukphyu Port in Myanmar on the coast of Bay of Bengal; China's move to construct a canal in Thailand across the

Isthmus of Kra connecting the South China Sea to the Bay of Bengal, and the Hambantota port in Sri Lanka helps China to consolidate its position in encircling India and give its forces immediate and unfettered access to the Bay of Bengal and Indian Ocean (*The Global Times*, 2018; Chinoy, 2021; Patranobis, 2018). BRI, as a whole, lacks transparency and is geared towards advancing China's interests through "debt trap" financing. The Hambantota port fiasco in Sri Lanka is an example and has exposed China's debt trap financing strategy, which is concerning for India as China (unsuccessfully) pushed for a naval base and requested Sri Lanka to allow one of its nuclear submarine dockings at Hambantota. The commercial rationale of its String of Pearls, CPEC and other projects under BRI around India's periphery do not hold ground and can be used for military purposes during conflict, posing a serious security threat for India.

Some portray China as a benign emerging world power and goods providing nation with an obligation to the Asia-Pacific region's stability, suggesting that China's grand strategy is defensive rather than offensive (Wang, 2016). In his address to the Belt and Road Forum for International Co-operation in Beijing, Xi framed the BRI in terms of "peace and co-operation", "openness and inclusiveness", "mutual learning" and "mutual benefit" (CGTN, 2017). Notwithstanding China's interests and claims of benign power, its posture in the Indian Ocean and its naval presence in these waters is seen by India as a security threat (Brewster, 2018; Lintner, 2019). Since BRI's inception, India has been opposed to it and views it as China's expansionist agenda, an India encircling strategy and China's challenge as a viable alternative to the United States in terms of global leadership. This is concerning for India as China's debt diplomacy is intended to lure India's South Asian neighbours (Mohan 2012).

China has recently emerged as a major player in the defence industry along with the United States, Russia, France and Germany, and a top arms exporter since 2014 (Wezeman *et al.*, 2019). What concerns India is that a significant portion of China's defence products are exported to Pakistan. Between 2007 and 2018, China exported 16.2 billion units of ammunition, mostly to Asia, the Middle East and Africa, with Pakistan topping the list with 6.57 billion units. The majority of China's arms exports are to countries covered by the BRI and India's South Asian neighbours (Shao, 2019).

Developments in Afghanistan have increased India's security concerns. The Taliban has overtly taken a neutral stance on Kashmir, stating that it is an "internal and bilateral" matter between India and Pakistan and has praised India's contribution to Afghanistan's reconstruction efforts, but India's security threat remains. Pakistan has played a key role in the ascension of the Taliban to power in Afghanistan. Major figures in the newly established government in Afghanistan are on terror watch lists of the United States and the United Nations. Pakistan's link with the Taliban goes back to the 1990s, and the Pakistani state, with its strong Islamist motives, has allowed Islamist forces within the Pakistani community and state agencies to grow ties with the Taliban (Behuria, 2007). Despite being at war with the forces of radicalisation and Talibanisation within the country, Pakistan supports peace talks while maintaining ties with the Taliban amid efforts to counter spillover of the Afghan civil war into Pakistani territory. Islamabad's strategic security objectives in Afghanistan continue to mitigate Indian influence.

The evidence of Pakistan's mounting support for Taliban insurgents, its military and intelligence agencies' ties with Taliban leadership and the celebration of the Taliban takeover of Afghanistan by the Lashkar-e-Taeba (LeT) and Jaish-e-Mohammad (JeM) — terror outfits responsible for numerous terror attacks in India — are all concerning for India (Ganguly, 2021). There are genuine concerns about some of the weapons and military equipment left behind by the US forces, as well as trained terrorist cadres from Afghanistan making their way into J&K as a result of ISI's ties to the Taliban and groups active on the state's western border (Ali *et al.*, 2021).

The US exit from Afghanistan and possibility of Pakistan and China cooperating to gain a stronger foothold in Afghanistan will erode India's influence and pose serious security challenges on India's northwestern border. China has been eyeing Afghanistan to pursue its larger geopolitical goals and has been actively collaborating with Afghanistan on the construction of the Peshawar–Kabul motorway which would benefit China's trade in the region as well as the extraction of natural resources in Afghanistan (Grosman, 2021). Afghanistan may have nearly a trillion dollars in extractable rare-earth metals within its mountains (Choi, 2014). A sustained positive China–Taliban engagement may further enable Beijing to make broad economic and security inroads into Afghanistan and Central Asia. China has already engaged Pakistan in its ambitious BRI under the CPEC and will seek to team up with Islamabad to engage or perhaps control Taliban to achieve their economic and strategic goals. All these undermine Indian interests and pose security challenges.

Afghanistan has also become a testing ground for India's ambition of a big power and ability as a security provider, as the region requires India to demonstrate its influence and play a constructive role in the region's stability. India has made significant investments in Afghanistan's reconstruction efforts, including assistance in the development of infrastructure, schools and hospitals. India's $3 billion aid since 2001, the largest regional aid and the fifth largest in the world, and its commitment of approximately 150 projects totalling $80 million for Afghanistan in November 2020, demonstrate New Delhi's stake in the country (Roy, 2020). India is only rational in wanting to be prepared to deal with both countries at the same time, lest its hostility towards either of the two nuclear rivals escalate into a war (Sharma, 2012).

Notwithstanding de-escalation overtures, China's military preparedness along LAC continues to increase, for example, integration of army and air force elements with 10 additional PLA air defence units in its Western Theatre (Tibet and Xinjiang), forming a combined Air Defence Control System (PLAAF) that can potentially control all air defence network assets along the LAC. Furthermore, China–Pakistan joint defence drills in Tibet near LAC include targeting warships, planes, missiles and unmanned aerial vehicles (UAVs), the deployment of Chinese air-defence system of low-to-medium altitude (LY-80) and anti-ship cruise missiles (YJ-81, YJ-82, and C-802) pose serious security risks to India (Banerjee, 2021). Though India has offensive capability against Pakistan, its defence capability is asymmetric when compared to China. India has an advantage in some sectors, but overall remains vulnerable to China, not to mention the joint Chinese–Pakistani force.

India's quest for a rightful place and desire to play a meaningful role in global governance for a secure and stable world also underscore India's need to emphasise the development of arms industry. India's ambition of becoming a great power is driven by a combination of factors including the need for the development to lift millions of people out of poverty, quest for energy and resources for its growing economy, address security challenges, protect its economic and strategic interests and in the tradition of its ancient civilisational glory.

Though achieving great power status has not been an explicit agenda of India since independence in 1947, all the Prime Ministers from Nehru to Modi have expressed India's desire for great power status to play a meaningful role in the global affairs (Colley and Suhas, 2021). The French Indologist Sylvain Levi, on the eve of India's independence, argued that the "indelible imprints" that India has left on "one quarter of the human race" from Siberia to Java and Borneo, and from Oceania to Socotra, over its several millennia long history had given it "the right to reclaim in universal history the *rank* that ignorance has refused her for a long time and to hold her place among the *great nations*." For Nehru, India was one of the four great powers of the postwar and post-colonial international system along with the United States, the Soviet Union and China (Nehru, 1946). Almost half a century later, Prime Minister Atal Behari Vajpayee took the decision to make India a nuclear power with the Pohkran Atomic Test in June 1998 (Vajpayee, 1998), which was nurtured by the self-exceptionalism and belief of civilisational superiority by Indian elites and average Indians alike (Cohen, 2000), the first step towards great power status. Since then, India's political and defence classes have concurred that India must progress to great power status. From the beginning of his prime ministerial campaign in 2013, Modi has been explicit about making India a great power and has often invoked the ancient glory of India to motivate Indians towards progress and glory and engaged the world for India's rightful place in the world (Modi, 2013), and since 2015 India's intent to be a great power became clear (Horimoto, 2017).

India has expanded its strategic reach beyond its region, especially in the Indo-Pacific — the hub of economic activity and great power competition in the twenty-first century (Medcalf, 2020; Ladwig III, 2010; Pardesi, 2015; Brewster, 2012) and a key strategic player in the US-backed Indo-Pacific strategy and a re-emerging great power capable of playing key roles in ensuring a rules-based order and a free, open, prosperous and secure Indo-Pacific. India's strategic outreach in the region began with the Look East Policy in the 1990s and is now being pursued vigorously under the Act East Policy, as evidenced by the frequency of military exercises under bilateral, trilateral, quadrilateral and multilateral security arrangements with major stakeholders in the region, including the United States, France, Japan, Australia and Vietnam. In the face of the emerging strategic challenges posed by a militarily assertive and expansionist China to both India and the Indo-Pacific order, India's commitments and expectations as a re-emerging great power have grown in the region (Bekkevold and Kalyanaraman, 2021; Sharma, 2019; Mohan, 2012; Malik, 2011). A growing economy, as well as the "push factor" of Chinese rivalry and the "pull factor" of the US' rebalancing strategy towards the Indo-Pacific, all contribute to the focus on defence.

India's quest for great power is challenged by China. The India–China great power tussle became visible during the passage of the US–India nuclear deal (strongly opposed by China). Beijing's campaign against India's inclusion in the Nuclear Suppliers Group (NSG) and blocking of India's inclusion in the NSG in 2016 reflecting China's stalwart strategy to undermine India's rise added to the intensification of their competition (Lee *et al.*, 2021; Sharma, 2017; Tellis, 2015). At the strategic level, the emergence of the Indo-Pacific geopolitical construct and the revival of the Quadrilateral security arrangement — United States, India, Japan and Australia — and the United States and advanced industrialised nations' move to fix the over-reliance of global supply chain on China during the COVID-19 outbreak have further intensified India–China great power competition. India is considered as significant in the great power balance, both economically and strategically.

Furthermore, India is seen as a security provider (Medcalf, 2012) and a significant strategic balancer in emerging security concerns arising from China's growing power and assertion in the Indo-Pacific. President Trump's November 2017 articulation on the Indo-Pacific was widely seen as something that would usher in a new (US–China) Cold War. This led to the Indian Prime Minister spelling out the Indian vision of Indo-Pacific as an enabler for a common pursuit of progress and prosperity, which is not directed against any country and based on principled commitment to rule of law.

Though the recent Galwan Valley clash is seen primarily in the context of a long-standing border dispute, the conflict is driven by the India–China strategic rivalry in the Indo-Pacific. China views India as an imperial rival, though not on par, interfering in Tibet and obstructing China's ambition of dominating the Indo-Pacific and eventually the world (Pardesi, 2021). India has emerged as a significant strategic and economic player, and the re-emergence of the Quad and the combined efforts of the like-minded democratic nations to play India a significant role in the Indo-Pacific, requires India to be militarily powerful.

The defence industrial base is significant. Yale historian of international relations, Paul Kennedy, says a credible great power must have a solid defence industry base (Kennedy, 1987). Despite being highly ranked on several major indicators to be considered to have great power status, the larger perception of India's international stature appears to be undermined by a lack of its strategic culture, which is further reflected in inadequate defence industrial base, one of the foremost conventional attributes to measure a country's great power status (Cohen and Gupta, 2012; *The Economist*, 2013). Studies show that defence capability stemming from economic development helped Western democracies to defend their interests and overcome their adversaries during security challenges (Beckley, 2010). India is no exception.

4. India's Defence Sector: Lacking a Clear-Cut and Long-Term Policy for Structural Reforms and Policy Implementation

Despite the continuing security threat, India's defence industry struggles to keep up with multiple security challenges and expanding strategic interests. India occupied the top arms importer position for over a decade till 2013. Between 2004–2008 and 2009–2013, India's share of the volume of international arms imports increased from 7% to 14% (SIPRI, 2014).

Since 2014, Saudi Arabia with a 12% share in the global arm imports has been topping the list followed by India with a share of 9.5%. Indian arms imports fell to 24% between 2009–2013 and 2014–2018. This has been partly due to delays in deliveries of fighter jets and submarines produced under licence from Russian and French original equipment manufacturers. Some analysts believe that this is because of India's focus on developing the indigenous defence industry. However, defence experts caution against this view. The domestic defence production as a factor in the arms import reduction will be significant only if India stops importing a particular weapon system because it was being manufactured locally under the 'Make in India' initiative.

Another noticeable trend in India's defence industry is the diversification of India's arms acquisition sources. Russian arms products continue to dominate India's armoury, estimated to be more than 70%, though there has been a consistent decline in India's arms import from Russia falling 42% between 2009–2013 and 76% in the years between 2014–2018. Between 2014 and 2018, India's arms import origins shifted to the United States, France and Israel (*The Hindustan Times*, 2019), with the United States becoming India's top arms supplier (Rossiter and Cannon, 2019; Sharma, 2013). American defence giants such as Lockheed Martin and Boeing have been exploring potential business partners in India, attracted by the low-cost, well-educated, English-speaking and technically sound workforce. The defence industry ties have also seen a robust strategic partnership of India with the United States, France and Israel (*India Today*, 2021).

Though relying on imports from first-tier arms-producing countries has enhanced India's defence capability, it has constrained indigenous research and development. Despite technology transfer and offset arrangements, India's defence industry continues to lag behind that of developed nations.

SIPRI report also shows that India's arms imports decreased by 33% between 2011–2015 and 2016–2020 (*Business Standard*, 2021). However, this drop seems to have been mainly due to its complex procurement processes, combined with attempts to reduce dependence on Russian arms.

For a long time, India's defence industry has been struggling to meet its demand and modernise despite this being the stated focus for more than a decade. Several factors contribute to these budgetary pressures, lack of clear-cut and long-term policy vision, bureaucratic hurdles, ignorance of military perspective in policymaking and limitations on research and development (Cohen and Gupta, 2010). Even the defence procurement process has been hindered by the lack of infrastructure and resources in the domestic procurement, and bureaucratic hurdles, resulting in friction and increased transaction costs in the Ministry of Defence's deals with foreign suppliers (Kundu, 2021). The excessive dominance of bureaucrats, foreign affairs personnel and politicians in defence planning has created a disconnect between the military capability and foreign policy goals, incompatibility between bureaucracy and military establishment resulted in a delayed defence policy that often lacked a clear-cut assessment of India's defence needs.

India's current military structure is inherited from British rule and is resistant to change without long-term policy effort (Pant, 2016). Currently, there is no sign of noteworthy systemic transformation. The Indian defence industry is marred by research and development works exceeding time frames and huge cost and time overruns in domestic production. The Indian government took a significant step in 2002 by opening the defence industry to private players by welcoming 100% private equity and 26% FDI. Since then, India has increased the FDI limit to 100%, allowing 74% through the automatic route and the remainder through the government route. Despite spending nearly 10% of its 2020 government budget on defence, India has only been able to attract a handful of foreign companies to set up manufacturing plants in India in partnership with an Indian company and has lagged behind other countries in attracting foreign investment, despite an attractive defence market.

India's defence industry business model, in which products are designed before potential buyers are found, creates uncertainty; national security concerns, particularly when complex technology is involved, and approval is time-consuming and uncertain. The government also encourages public sector procurement and promotes domestic production while also aiming to attract FDI from the US-based companies. The United States has the world's five largest arms manufacturers aiming to tap India's defence market. However, these are constrained by the US Arms Control Export Act 1976, which makes it difficult for them to share critical technologies. These factors hamper FDI flow into India's defence sector (Choudhury, 2021).

5. Conclusion

The term "military–industrial complex" was popularised by President Eisenhower to describe the nexus of legislators, businesses and government officials, as well as their powerful lobbying clout and emphasised the importance of defence industry as the leading contributor to US economic growth. The US MIC witnessed enhanced production of weapons and defence technologies, which was backed by increased military spending by the US federal government. During the first half of the twentieth century arms manufacturing in the United States shifted from public corporations to private firms. These businesses not only contributed to GDP growth but also created a large number of jobs.

In popular parlance, MIC has some unfavourable connotations since it is associated with an expansion of war outside US borders. In sharp contrast, India faces serious security challenges all along its land borders with China and Pakistan, an incipient threat from the Taliban in Afghanistan and Chinese intrusions into a number of areas in the Indian Ocean. India also has a major role to play in maintaining peace and security in the South and South-East Asian regions and, potentially, globally. Furthermore, except for its role in liberating Bangladesh from Pakistan in 1971, independent India has never engaged in wars on foreign soil. At the same time, India's industrial sector also needs urgent rejuvenation. Thus, the MIC takes on a different meaning in the current Indian context.

In India's case, the defence industry has the potential to take the lead, propelling India's economic growth and generating employment. India requires an MIC. The role of manufacturing in job creation has been significant. The 'Make in India' initiative is designed to create jobs. India needs a strong domestic manufacturing sector, which will protect it from international economic and political disruptions. This is important from a national security perspective where the risk of manufacturing incapability can make the country vulnerable. A country's over-reliance on imports and substantial manufacturing trade deficit further exposes a country's national security, which may occur due to exchange rate fluctuations, trade embargoes, supply chain disruptions, natural disasters, climate change or pandemics as evident during the COVID-19 outbreak. India is not immune to these disruptions given its weak manufacturing sector and over-reliance on defence imports.

Recently, steady progress has been made in the development of India's indigenous military industry, including exports. India's defence exports for 2019 entered in the global top 25 arms exporting nations. India is now exporting arms to 42 countries. Under the 'Make in India' programme launched in 2014, India set an export target in February 2020 of $5 billion annually within five years (Roche, 2020). India managed more than double value of its arms exports between FY2018 and FY2019. In 2021–2022, India's defence export touched the highest ever witnessing an increase of 54.1% over the year 2019–2020 (*The Economic Times*, 2022). India has upped its target even higher, with a $5 billion defence export target by 2025. India has a strong capability for producing weapons that, if correctly utilised, could make the nation a major player in the world arms market (Behera, 2022).

The recent developments in India's defence industry under the Modi government is a shift from the defence vs. development debate to a more inclusive policy of defence and development. However, India's goal of self-reliance in the defence sector and the development of defence sector as the lead sector will need much more government and private sector focus. Despite the emphasis on privatisation and public–private partnerships, the goal of producing 70% of defence products domestically is difficult. India needs to reinvent its military and manufacturing strategies in an integrated manner.

References

Aamir, A. (2020). China and Pakistan ink military MOU to counter US–India pact. *NIKKEI Asia*, 8 December. https://asia.nikkei.com/Politics/International-relations/China-and-Pakistan-ink-military-MOU-to-counter-US-India-pact. Accessed 12 January 2022.

Aleem, Z. (2017). Why "Made in China" could soon be a thing of the past. Vox, 27 February. http://www.vox.com/world/2017/2/27/14750198/china-wages-rising. Accessed 30 August 2021.

Ali, I., Zengerle, P., and Landay, J. (2021). Planes, guns, night-vision goggles: The Taliban's new U.S.-made war chest. *Reuters*, 20 August. https://www.reuters.com/business/aerospace-defense/planes-guns-night-vision-goggles-talibans-new-us-made-war-chest-2021-08-19/. Accessed 22 August 2021.

Banerjee, A. (2021). LAC: China's air defence at play, joint drill with Pak. *The Tribune*, 1 June. https://www.tribuneindia.com/news/nation/lac-chinas-air-defence-at-play-joint-drill-with-pak-261828. Accessed 2 June 2021.

Behera, L. K. (2022). Made in India: An aspiring brand in global arms bazaar. *Defense & Security Analysis*. Published ahead of print on 14 June 2022. DOI: 10.1080/14751798.2022.2084815. Accessed on 12 September 2022.

Bekkevold, J. I. and Kalyanaraman, S. (Eds.) (2021) *India's Great Power Politics Managing China's Rise*. Routledge, New Delhi.

Beckley, M. (2010). Economic development and military effectiveness. *Journal of Strategic Studies*, 33(1), 43–79.

Behuria, A. K. (2007). Fighting the Taliban: Pakistan at war with itself. *Australian Journal of International Affairs*, 61(4), 529–543.

Bloomfield, A. (2021). The India–China bilateral relationship: A 'serious and enduring rivalry'. *Journal of the Indian Ocean Region*, 17(1), 5–23.

Brecher, M. (1968). *India and World Politics: Krishna Menon's View of the World*. Oxford University Press, London.

Brewster, D. (2012). *India as an Asia Pacific Power*. Routledge, London.

Brewster, D. (2017). Silk roads and strings of pearls: The strategic geography of China's new pathways in the Indian Ocean. *Geopolitics*, 22(2), 269–291.

Business Standard. (2019). Only I can make India strong, superpower: Modi. 17 April. https://www.business-standard.com/article/news-ians/only-i-can-make-india-strong-superpower-modi-119041700287_1.html. Accessed 22 January 2022.

Business Standard. (2021). India's arms import dip by 33% between 2011–15 and 2016–20: Report. 15 March. https://www.business-standard.com/article/current-affairs/india-s-arms-import-dip-by-33-between-2011-15-and-2016-20-report-121031501067_1.html. Accessed 22 January 2022.

CGTN. (2017). Full text of President Xi's speech at opening of B&R Forum. 15 May. https://news.cgtn.com/news/3d59444f33677a4d/share_p.html. Accessed 12 March 2022.

Chinoy, S. (2021). CPEC: China's designs, Pakistan's ambivalence, and India's opposition. *The Hindustan Times*, 19 January. https://www.hindustantimes.com/opinion/cpec-china-s-designs-pakistan-s-ambivalence-and-india-s-opposition-101611066633406.html. Accessed 15 November 2022.

Choi, C. Q. (2014). $1 Trillion Trove of Rare Minerals Revealed Under Afghanistan. Live Science, 4 September. https://www.livescience.com/47682-rare-earth-minerals-found-under-afghanistan.html. Accessed 22 March 2022.

Choudhury, R. N. (2021). Big barriers on FDI in Indian defence. *East Asia Forum*, 19 August. https://www.eastasiaforum.org/2021/08/19/big-barriers-on-fdi-in-indian-defence/. Accessed 26 August 2021.

Ciorciari, J. D. (2011). India's approach to great-power status. *The Fletcher Forum of World Affairs*, *35*(1), 61–89.

Clary, C. and Narang, V. (2018/2019). India's counterforce temptations: Strategic dilemmas, doctrine, and capabilities. *International Security*, *43*(3), 7–52.

Clary, C. and Panda, A. (2017). Safer at sea? Pakistan's sea-based deterrent and nuclear weapons security. *Washington Quarterly*, *40*(3), 149–168.

Cohen, S. (2000). *India: Emerging Power*. Brookings Institution, Washington DC.

Cohen, S. and Gupta, S. D. (2012). *Arming without Aiming: India's Military Modernisation*. Brookings Institution Press, Washington DC.

Colley, C. K. and Suhas, P. H. (2021). India–China and their war-making capacities. *Journal of Asian Security and International Affairs*, *8*(1), 33–61.

Easterly, W. (2006). Reliving the 1950s: The big push, poverty traps, and takeoffs in economic development. *Journal of Economic Growth*, *2*(4), 289–318.

Ganguly, S. (2021). What the Taliban takeover means for India. Foreign Policy, 17 August. https://foreignpolicy.com/2021/08/17/afghanistan-taliban-takeover-india-security-terrorism/. Accessed 11 March 2022.

Gao, C. (2020). Here's how China made Pakistan into a military powerhouse. *National Interest*, 20, March. https://nationalinterest.org/blog/buzz/heres-how-china-made-pakistan-military-powerhouse-135137. Accessed 11 March 2022.

Grosman, D. (2021). China and the Taliban begin their romance. Foreign Policy, 21 July. https://foreignpolicy.com/2021/07/21/china-taliban-afghanistan-biden-troop-withdrawal-belt-road-geopolitics-strategy/. Accessed 11 March 2022.

Hirschman, A. O. (1958). *The Strategy of Economic Development*. Yale University Press, New Haven.

Hirschman, A. O. (1969). The strategy of economic development. In Agarwal, A. N. and Singh, S. P. (Eds.) *Accelerating Investment in Developing Economies* (pp. 45–56). Oxford University Press, London.

Horimoto, T. (2017). Explaining India's foreign policy: From dream to realisation of major power. *International Relations of the Asia-Pacific*, *17*(3), 463–496.

India Today. (2021). All about India-France strategic dialogue, 10 points. 7 January. https://www.indiatoday.in/india/story/all-about-india-france-strategic-dialogue-10-points-1756740-2021-01-07. Accessed 10 July 2021.

Jain, B. (2021). After Afghanistan, Pakistan eyeing more "aggressive tactics" in Jammu & Kashmir. *The Times of India*, 7 September. https://timesofindia.indiatimes.com/world/south-asia/after-afghanistan-pakistan-eyeing-more-aggressive-tactics-in-jammu-kashmir/articleshow/85990878.cms. Accessed 7 September 2021.

Jha, R. (2018). *Facets of India's Economy and Her Society: Current State and Future Prospects*, Vol. II. Palgrave Macmillan, Hampshire.

Jha, R. and Afrin, S. (2021). Structural transformation in South Asia: Does the pattern ensure growth momentum? *South Asia Economic Journal*, *22*(1), 7–28.

Kennedy, P. (1987). *The Rise and Fall of the Great Powers: Economic Change and Military Conflict from 1500 to 2000.* Random House, New York.

Khan, W. (2020). China and Pakistan conduct joint air drills — with eye on India. Nikkei Asia, 10 December. https://asia.nikkei.com/Politics/International-relations/Indo-Pacific/China-and-Pakistan-conduct-joint-air-drills-with-eye-on-India. Accessed 28 June 2021.

Korbel, J. (1954). *Danger in Kashmir.* Princeton University Press, New Jersey.

Krishnan, A. (2020). China, Pakistan to back each other's 'core interests' at the UN. *The Hindu*, 30 June. https://www.thehindu.com/news/international/china-pak-to-back-each-others-core-interests-at-un/article34283207.ece. Accessed 28 June 2021.

Kristensen, H. M., Norris, R. S., and Diamond, J. (2018). Pakistani nuclear forces, 2018. *Bulletin of the Atomic Scientists*, *74*(5), 348–358.

Kundu, O. (2021). Risks in defence procurement: India in the 21st century. *Defence and Peace Economics*, *32*(3), 343–361.

Ladwig III, W. C. (2010). India and military power projection will the land of Gandhi become a conventional great power? *Asian Survey*, *50*(6), 1162–1183.

Lee, K., Kim, J., and Ji, Y. (2021). In-regime manager: China's strategy against nuclear India. *International Area Studies Review*, *24*(2), 118–134.

Lemahieu, H. and Leng, A. (2021). Lowy Institute Asia power index: Key findings 2020. Lowy Institute. https://power.lowyinstitute.org/downloads/lowy-institute-2020-asia-power-index-key-findings-report.pdf. Accessed 10 August 2021.

Lintner, B. (2019). *The Costliest Pearl: China's Struggle for the Indian Ocean.* Oxford University Press, London.

Malik, M. (2011). *China and India: Great Power Rivals.* Lynne Rienner Publishers/First. Forum Press, Boulder and London.

Matsuyama, K. (1992). The market size, entrepreneurship, and the big push. *Journal of the Japanese and International Economies*, 6(4), 347–364.

Medcalf, R. (2012). Unselfish giants? Understanding China and India as security providers. *Australian Journal of International Affairs*, 66(5), 554–566.

Medcalf, R. (2020). *Contest for the Indo-Pacific: Why China Won't Map the Future?* La Trobe University Press, Melbourne.

Ministry of Finance, Government of India. (2017). *Economic Survey.*

Modi, N. (2013). Shri Narendra Modi addresses BJP Hunkar Rally at Patna, Bihar-Speech. 27 October. https://www.youtube.com/watch?v=j8ont7QjwS0. Accessed 22 June 2022.

Mohan, C. R. (2012). *Samudra Manthan: Sino-Indian Rivalry in the Indo-Pacific.* Carnegie Endowment for International Peace, Washington DC.

Murphy, K. M., Shleifer, A., and Vishny, R. W. (1989). Industrialisation and the big push. *Journal of Political Economy*, 97(5), 1003–1026.

Nehru, J. (2004 [1946]). *The Discovery of India.* Penguin Books, New Delhi.

Pande, A. (2018). *From Chanakya to Modi: Evolution of India's Foreign Policy.* Harpar Collins, Noida.

Pandit, R. (2021). India's weapon imports fell by 33% in last five years but remains world's second-largest arms importer. *The Times of India*, 16 March. https://timesofindia.indiatimes.com/india/indias-weapon-imports-fell-by-33-in-last-five-years-but-remains-worlds-second-largest-arms-importer/articleshow/81516403.cms. Accessed 26 July 2021.

Pant, H. (Ed.) (2016). *Handbook of Indian Defence Policy: Themes, Structures and Doctrines.* Routledge, New Delhi.

Pardesi, M. S. (2015). Is India a great power? Understanding great power status in contemporary international relations. *Asian Security*, 11(1), 1–30.

Pardesi, M. S. (2021). Explaining the asymmetry in the Sino-Indian strategic rivalry. *Australian Journal of International Affairs*, 75(3), 341–365.

Pasaribu, D. H. (2019). The Dutch disease, natural resource booms and policy adjustments: The case of Indonesia. Ph.D. Thesis, The Australian National University. December. https://www.researchgate.net/publication/341914282_The_Dutch_disease_natural_resource_booms_and_policy_adjustments_The_case_of_Indonesia. Accessed 30 July 2021.

Patranobis, S. (2018). Too close for comfort: China to build port in Myanmar, 3rd in India's vicinity. *The Hindustan Times*, 9 November. https://www.hindustantimes.com/india-news/china-myanmar-ink-deal-for-port-on-bay-of-bengal-third-in-india-s-vicinity/story-Lbm4IwOMuqrNvXGv4ewuYJ.html. Accessed 5 July 2021.

Paul, T. V. (2006). Why has the India–Pakistan rivalry been so enduring? Power asymmetry and an intractable conflict. *Security Studies*, *15*(4), 600–630.

Raghavan, S. (2019). The Security Dilemma and India–China Relations. *Asian Security*, *15*(1), 60–72.

Rajagopalan, R. P. (2021). The China–Pakistan partnership continues to Deepen. *The Diplomat*, 9 July. https://thediplomat.com/2021/07/the-china-pakistan-partnership-continues-to-deepen/. Accessed 28 June 2021.

Reuveny, R. and Thompson, W. R. (2001). Leading sectors, lead economies, and economic growth. *Review of International Political Economy*, *8*(4), 689–719.

Roche, E. (2020). India now exports defence products to 42 countries. *Mint*, 10 February. https://www.livemint.com/industry/manufacturing/india-now-exports-defence-products-to-42-countries-11581332398457.html. Accessed 26 February 2022.

Rogers, S. and Gentry, S. (2019). *Economic Development and Planning*. ED-Tech Press, UK; Higgins, B. 1954. Economic Development Doc. Control. 22 November. https://core.ac.uk/download/pdf/19879655.pdf. Accessed 19 July 2021.

Rosenstein-Rodan, P. (1943). Problems of industrialisation of Eastern and South-eastern Europe. *Economic Journal*, *53*(1), 202–211.

Rosenstein-Rodan, P. (1961). Notes on the theory of the 'big push'. In Ellis, H. and Wallich, H. (Eds.) *Economic Development for Latin America* (pp. 57–67). St. Martin's Press, New York.

Rossiter, A. and Cannon, B. J. (2019). Making arms in India? Examining New Delhi's renewed drive for defence-industrial indigenisation. *Defence Studies*, *19*(4), 353–372.

Roy, S. (2020). India pledges aid to rebuild Afghanistan, commits to projects worth $80 million. *The Indian Express*, 25 November. https://indianexpress.com/article/india/india-pledges-aid-to-rebuild-afghanistan-commits-to-projects-worth-80-million-7064393/. Accessed 14 June 2022.

Sachs, J. D. and Warner, A. M. (1999). The big push, natural resource booms and growth. *Journal of Development Economics*, *59*(1), 43–76.

Sagan, S. D. (2004). Nuclear dangers in South Asia. *Forum on Physics & Society*, *41*(6), 4–7.

Sagan, S. D. (Ed.) (2009). *Inside Nuclear South Asia*. Stanford University Press, Stanford.

Shao, G. (2019). China, the world's second largest defense spender, becomes a major arms exporter. CNBC, 26, September. https://www.cnbc.com/2019/09/27/china-a-top-defense-spender-becomes-major-arms-exporter.html. Accessed 22 June, 2022.

Sharma, A. (2012). The enduring conflict and the hidden risk of India–Pakistan war. *SAIS Review of International Affairs*, *32*(1), 129–142.

Sharma, A. (2013). US–India defence industry collaboration: Trends, challenges and prospects. *Maritime Affairs: Journal of the National Maritime Foundation of India*, 9(1), 129–147.

Sharma, A. (2017). *Indian Lobbying and Its Influence in US Decision Making: Post-Cold War.* Sage Publication, New Delhi.

Sharma, A. (2019). *India's Pursuit of Energy Security: Domestic Measures, Foreign Policy and Geopolitics.* Sage Publications, New Delhi.

SIPRI Fact Sheet. (2021). Trends in World Military Expenditure, 2020. April. https://sipri.org/sites/default/files/2021-04/fs_2104_milex_0.pdf. Accessed 12 January 2022.

Stockholm International Peace Research Institute. (2014). South Asia and the Gulf lead rising trend in arms imports, Russian exports grow, says SIPRI. 7 March. https://www.sipri.org/media/press-release/2014/south-asia-and-gulf-lead-rising-trend-arms-imports-russian-exports-grow-says-sipri. Accessed 22 June 2022.

Stockholm International Peace Research Institute. (2021). Global nuclear arsenals grow as states continue to modernise–New SIPRI Yearbook out now. 14 June. https://www.sipri.org/media/press-release/2021/global-nuclear-arsenals-grow-states-continue-modernise-new-sipri-yearbook-out-now. Accessed 22 June 2022.

Tellis, A. J. (2015). US–India Relations: The Struggle for an Enduring Partnership. In Malone, D. M., Mohan, C. R., and Raghavan, S. (Eds.) *The Oxford Handbook of Indian Foreign Policy* (pp. 482–494). Oxford University Press, Oxford.

The Economist. (2013). Can India become a great power? 30 March. https://www.economist.com/leaders/2013/03/30/can-india-become-a-great-power. Accessed 21 June 2022.

The Economic Times. (2019). India's defence exports more than double. 18 June. https://economictimes.indiatimes.com/news/defence/indias-defence-exports-more-than-double/articleshow/69835284.cms?from=mdr. Accessed 26 August, 2021.

The Economic Times. (2020). Our target is $5 billion of defence export in next five years: PM Narendra Modi. 5 February. https://economictimes.indiatimes.com/news/defence/our-target-is-5-billion-of-defence-export-in-next-five-years-pm-narendra-modi/articleshow/73958737.cms?from=mdr. Accessed 7 July 2022.

The Economic Times. (2021). Prepared to hold ground as long as it takes, potent collusive threat by Pakistan, China: Army Chief. 12 January. https://economictimes.indiatimes.com/news/defence/prepared-to-hold-ground-as-long-as-it-takes-potent-collusive-threat-by-pak-china-army-chief/articleshow/80236079.cms?from=mdr. Accessed 7 July 2022.

The Economic Times. (2022). India posts record Rs 13,000 crore worth defence exports in 2021–22. 8 July. https://economictimes.indiatimes.com/news/defence/india-posts-record-rs-13000-crore-worth-defence-exports-in-2021-22/articleshow/92752080.cms?utm_source=contentofinterest&utm_medium=text&utm_campaign=cppst. Accessed 29 July 2022.

The Global Times. (2018). China, Myanmar sign port deal after years of negotiations. 8 November. https://www.globaltimes.cn/content/1126664.shtml. Accessed 22 June 2022.

The Global Times. (2020). China, Pakistan hold joint naval exercises in the north Arabian Sea. 6 January. https://www.globaltimes.cn/content/1175924.shtml. Accessed 28 June 2022.

The Hindustan Times. (2019). After 10 years, India no longer world's top weapons importer. 12 March. https://www.hindustantimes.com/world-news/after-10-years-india-no-longer-world-s-top-weapons-importer/story-pYJwwbGo0JMZfuSOmJ9z9H.html. Accessed 10 May 2022.

The Indian Express. (2021). Threats for which military must be organised come from China, Pakistan: CDS. 5 March. https://indianexpress.com/article/india/threats-military-organised-come-from-china-pakistan-cds-7214775/. Accessed 30 June 2022.

The Times of India. (2017). China blocks another move to list Masood Azhar as global terrorist by the UN: Official. 7 November. https://timesofindia.indiatimes.com/india/china-again-blocks-move-to-list-masood-azhar-as-global-terrorist-by-the-un-official/articleshow/61460163.cms. Accessed 28 June 2022.

Trindade, V. (2005). The big push, industrialisation and international trade: The role of exports. *Journal of Development Economics*, 78(1), 22–48.

Vajpayee, A. B. (Prime Minister of India) (1998). Statement to parliament on nuclear tests in Pokhran. https://www.vifindia.org/sites/default/files/national-security-vol-1-issue-1-document-statement-to-parliament.pdf. Accessed 5 July, 2022.

Wang, Y. (2016). Offensive for defensive: The belt and road initiative and China's new grand strategy. *The Pacific Review*, 29(3), 455–463.

Wezeman, P. D., Fleurant, A., Kuimova, A., Tian, N., and Wezeman, S. T. (2019). Trends in International Arms Transfer. Stockholm International Peace Research Institute, March. https://www.sipri.org/sites/default/files/2019-03/fs_1903_at_2018.pdf. Accessed 12 June 2022.

Chapter 6

Conflicts and the Politicisation of Trade: Implications for Economic Cooperation in South Asia

Zahid Shahab Ahmed[*,†,§] **and Muhammad Jahanzaib**[‡,¶]

National Defense College, Abu Dhabi, UAE

†*Alfred Deakin Institute for Citizenship and Globalisation, Deakin University, Victoria, Australia*

‡*International Relations, International Islamic University, Islamabad, Pakistan*

§*zahid.ahmed@ndc.ac.ae*
¶*muhammad.phdir50@iiu.edu.pk*

Abstract

Despite regional cooperation through the South Asian Association for Regional Cooperation (SAARC) and sub-regional mechanisms, South Asia remains perhaps the least integrated region primarily characterised by conflicts than cooperation. Inter-state disputes, for instance between India and Pakistan, negatively influence South Asian regionalism and related matters such as economic cooperation. There are many occasions when bilateral tensions have led to the closure of borders, for instance this is the case of ongoing India–Pakistan relationship and previously happened when India closed its border with Nepal, and Pakistan with Afghanistan.

Consequently, the movement of goods, services and people have been severely impeded, leading to marginal economic cooperation in South Asia. Bilateral or regional agreements that aim to promote economic cooperation through free trade agreements often face obstacles and are frequently shelved or abandoned altogether. The persisting tensions between India and Pakistan further hinder regional cooperation. This has been witnessed in the case of SAARC becoming an ineffective regional organisation. This chapter examines how bilateral conflicts have influenced the politicisation of trade in South Asia by focusing on the dynamics of conflict and cooperation. By enhancing our understanding of these relationships, this chapter contributes to a better understanding of the relationship between conflicts and economic cooperation in South Asia.

Keywords: Conflicts, trade, South Asia, regional cooperation, economic cooperation.

1. Introduction

The South Asian region, home to over 1.9 billion people and a combined GDP ranking among the world's largest because of India's GDP (World Bank, 2023), is recognised for its significant economic potential. Given the region's shared cultural and historical ties, there have always been high expectations associated to the potential of regional cooperation. This was particularly the case when Bangladesh proposed a regional organisation in the early 1980s. The proposal was welcomed by other states and the South Asian Association for Regional Cooperation (SAARC) was founded in 1985 with the following seven member states: Bangladesh, Bhutan, India, Maldives, Nepal, Pakistan and Sri Lanka. According to Anbumozhi and Kalirajan (2020), cooperation can have many shapes and forms, such as policy coordination, shared infrastructure and inter-regional trade. In South Asia, there are some initiatives like SAARC and the Bay of Bengal Initiative for Multi-Sectoral Technical and Economic Cooperation (BIMSTEC). As it has been previously assessed, regional cooperation in South Asia is low compared to other regions like Southeast Asia (Ahmed, 2013; Asian Development Bank, 2023). There is no shortage of literature on factors that have contributed to the low level of regional cooperation in South Asia, but most authors believe that inter-state disputes are responsible for the lack of regional cooperation (Dash, 2008). The existing body of research on regional cooperation in South

Asia paints a complicated picture, coloured by political and religious influences, economic necessities, and security apprehensions (Kumar and Sharma, 2015). The presence of India and Pakistan, two nuclear-armed rivals, further intensifies these complexities, with their strained relations frequently overshadowing regional cooperation efforts (Yusuf, 2018). This is particularly the case of SAARC, which has failed to hold its summit, a meeting of heads of state, since 2014 because of tensions between India and Pakistan. Moreover, the politicisation of trade among South Asian countries serves as an additional barrier to potential cooperation (Bishwakarma and Hu, 2022). While bilateral trade routes have been disrupted regularly, India had accorded a most favoured nation status to Pakistan in 1996. Despite New Delhi's demands, Pakistan never reciprocated by according an MFN status to India. In the wake of bilateral tensions following a terrorist attack in the Indian-administered Kashmir in 2019, New Delhi decided to withdraw MFN status to Pakistan (*The Hindu*, 2019). The political issues, influenced by long-standing disputes, have been a major cause of India–Pakistan economic cooperation not meeting its potential. There have been significant fluctuations in bilateral trade that dropped from US$830.58 million in 2019–2020 to US$329.26 million in 2020–2021 (Kharsu, 2023). That mainly happened because of the heightened tensions following New Delhi's decision to revoke the special status of Jammu and Kashmir. In the first quarter of 2022, however, the bilateral trade increased to US$1.25 billion during April to December 2022 compared to US$516.36 million during 2021–2022 (Kharsu, 2023). While some level of bilateral trade is always ongoing, frequent fluctuations have been a major cause of the two countries not meeting the full potential of bilateral trade, estimated to be US$37 billion per annum by the World Bank (Basu, 2018, xvi). Even with a promising increase in bilateral trade in 2022, the two neighbours are far behind from meeting the actual potential of bilateral trade that requires depoliticisation of trade.

This chapter examines the above-mentioned challenges, investigating the impact of conflicts on the politicisation of trade and other facets of economic cooperation in South Asia. The chapter begins by examining the present state of economic cooperation in the region, exploring intra-regional trade patterns and evaluating the initiatives of SAARC and BIMSTEC. Subsequently, it focuses on the influence of conflicts on both bilateral and regional cooperation, citing recent historical events to underscore these conflicts' implications. In doing so, this analysis seeks to enhance understanding of the intricate dynamics between conflicts and regional economic cooperation in South Asia.

2. Regional Cooperation in South Asia

Since the 1980s, several regional bodies have been established to foster economic cooperation among the countries of South Asia. SAARC and BIMSTEC are two key examples of these regional bodies.

Established in 1985, SAARC comprises of eight South Asian nations, with the primary objective to accelerate economic and social development in member states through joint action in mutually agreed areas of cooperation (Bishwakarma and Zong-Shan, 2021). Afghanistan joined as SAARC's eighth member in 2007. Since its inception, SAARC has facilitated numerous initiatives in diverse fields, including trade, agriculture, rural development, science and technology, culture, health, population control, drug offences and terrorism (*Dawn News*, 2007). One of SAARC's flagship initiatives is the South Asian Free Trade Area (SAFTA), established in 2004 with the aim of reducing tariffs to enhance free trade among member countries (State Bank of Pakistan, n.d.). However, despite some initial progress, SAFTA's potential has been limited by non-tariff barriers, protectionist policies and political conflicts between member countries (Iqbal and Nawaz, 2017). BIMSTEC, established in 1997, brings together five nations from South Asia (Bangladesh, Bhutan, India, Nepal and Sri Lanka) and two from Southeast Asia (Myanmar and Thailand). While overlapping with SAARC and the Association of Southeast Asian Nations in terms of its mandate, BIMSTEC offers an alternative regional framework that bypasses the often-strained India–Pakistan relations that have hampered SAARC's progress (Ali and Medhekar, 2022). BIMSTEC focuses on 14 sectors of cooperation, including trade and investment, transport and communication, energy and technology, led by different member nations (Rahman and Grewal, 2017). While both SAARC and BIMSTEC have achieved varying degrees of success, their efficacy as vehicles for regional cooperation has been hindered by a host of issues, including political disagreements, security concerns and the lack of an enforcement mechanism for agreements. Nevertheless, they continue to be vital platforms for dialogue and cooperation in South Asia (Madhur, 2023).

Economic cooperation in South Asia is a crucial subject given the region's potential to reap substantial benefits from increased intra-regional trade and integration. According to Koyuncu (2022), the total trade of BIMSTEC countries with the world was estimated at around US$2.7 trillion. However, intra-regional trade accounted for just a fraction of this amount, estimated at approximately 5% of the total trade, compared to regions like the European Union or the Association of Southeast Asian Nations (ASEAN), where intra-regional trade forms a significant portion of the total trade, averaging around 60% and 25%, respectively (World Bank, 2023). The relatively low levels of intra-regional trade in South Asia can be attributed to a host of factors, including high tariff and non-tariff barriers, poor transport connectivity, political tensions and inadequate trade facilitation measures (ADB, 2023). Nevertheless, the potential for enhanced intra-regional trade is immense. Research from the Asian Development Bank (2023) suggests that with the removal of trade barriers and improved connectivity, intra-regional trade in South Asia could exceed billions of dollars (approximately US$100 billion) per annum, almost doubling the current figures. Despite these challenges, it is encouraging to note that South Asian countries have been engaging in policy initiatives to boost regional economic cooperation. Through regional bodies like SAARC and BIMSTEC, these countries have made attempts to foster regional integration and improve intra-regional trade, but the full potential of these initiatives is yet to be realised and more focused efforts are needed to overcome the challenges and harness the region's immense potential for economic cooperation.

SAARC and BIMSTEC have undertaken various initiatives to boost regional economic cooperation. One of the key initiatives under SAARC is SAFTA, which came into effect in 2006. SAFTA aimed to reduce customs duties on all traded goods to zero by the end of 2016, offering significant opportunities for increased trade within the region. However, despite initial enthusiasm, SAFTA has had limited success due to various factors such as the existence of sensitive lists (items exempted from tariff reduction), non-tariff barriers and a lack of effective dispute resolution mechanisms (Iqbal and Nawaz, 2017). Another SAARC initiative is the Agreement on Trade in Services, signed in 2010, which aims to liberalise the services sector within the region, but this has also failed to meet its targets (Kaur, Khorana and Kaur, 2020). In contrast, BIMSTEC, with its more sector-specific approach, has led several initiatives in sectors like trade, investment, transport and energy. The BIMSTEC Free Trade Agreement (FTA), under negotiation since 2004, aims to boost intra-regional trade by eliminating tariffs. However, it has faced delays due to unresolved issues around tariff reduction schedules, rules of origin and non-tariff barriers (Bhattacharjee, 2018). In terms of transportation, the BIMSTEC Motor Vehicle Agreement is an ambitious project that aims to enhance connectivity and foster economic development in the region, but its implementation has been delayed due to concerns related to regulatory and infrastructural issues (Palit and Tieri, 2019). Unlike SAARC however, BIMSTEC is not facing political challenges and therefore has more potential to expand economic cooperation involving countries from South and Southeast Asia.

3. Conflict and Cooperation

Understanding how conflicts affect regional cooperation is important for examining the complexities in South Asia. A significant body of literature has explored these dynamics, particularly focusing on the influence of disputes, disagreements and hostilities on collaborative efforts. One common observation in these studies is that conflicts, by instigating mistrust and hostility, create obstacles to cooperation (Ahmed, 2013; Putnam, 1988). Ongoing disputes often inhibit the ability of nations to trust each other and work together on shared goals. As Adler and Barnett (1998) argue, conflicts disrupt the establishment of 'security communities', where states engage in dependable expectations of peaceful change. A strand of literature further illustrates how conflicts can lead to the politicisation of economic interactions. Studies by Mansfield and Pollins (2001) and Gartzke and Li (2003) note that political tensions and hostilities can interfere with economic relationships, leading to scenarios where economic decisions become intertwined with political considerations. This has been identified as a significant issue in South Asia, where trade and other forms of economic cooperation have been affected by political disputes (Ahmed, 2013). Conflicts not only influence bilateral relations, but they also affect regional dynamics. The institutional framework of regional cooperation often gets hampered by conflicts among member states (Buzan and Waever, 2003). Kydd (2007) further notes that conflicts, by fostering an atmosphere of uncertainty and mistrust, can lead to a security dilemma where states engage in mutually detrimental defensive measures. The literature presents an intricate picture of how conflicts affect cooperation, emphasising the need for conflict resolution as a precondition for fruitful cooperation (Wallensteen, 2015). Applying these insights to South Asia reveals the multifaceted challenges to regional cooperation and provides a framework to explore potential pathways to conflict resolution and enhanced cooperation.

Some literature on regional cooperation in South Asia provides a nuanced understanding of the challenges and prospects faced by the region. It reveals how historical conflicts, political tensions and economic disparities have shaped inter-state relations and impeded cooperation in the region. A key observation made by numerous researchers is the persistent tensions between India and Pakistan overshadowing regional cooperation (Yusuf, 2018; Ahmed, 2013). Due to historical disputes and ongoing hostilities, these two nations have often been at odds, affecting the efficacy of regional platforms such as SAARC (Cohen, 2013). Another crucial aspect that the literature highlights is the politicisation of trade and economic cooperation. The preferential granting of MFN status or the imposition of trade sanctions has often been influenced more by political considerations than economic rationale (Iqbal and Nawaz, 2017). Furthermore, non-tariff barriers have often been used as instruments of political strategy, thus obstructing regional trade (Thomas and Marandu, 2017). However, the literature also points out certain positive strides. There have been some successful sub-regional efforts such as BIMSTEC, which offers an alternative cooperative framework that circumvents the Indo-Pak rivalry (Bhattacharjee, 2018). The organisation focuses on various sectors of cooperation, leading to some fruitful outcomes, particularly in areas like energy, transport and communication (Palit and Tieri, 2019).

Conflicts have long been a defining characteristic of South Asia's political landscape. The region, home to several diverse ethnic, religious and linguistic communities, has a complex history marked by territorial disputes, religious tensions, political disagreements and armed conflicts. The most prominent conflict in the region is the enduring rivalry between India and Pakistan, marked by three major wars, numerous border skirmishes and constant political tensions since their independence in 1947 (Cohen, 2013). The conflict over Jammu and Kashmir remains a persistent source of tension, with episodes of violence often derailing diplomatic relations and regional cooperation efforts. This has been particularly the case since India's revocation of Kashmir's special status in 2019. Pakistan continues to object to India's decision. On the other hand, India continues to criticise the inclusion of the disputed Jammu and Kashmir territory in Gilgit–Baltistan in the China–Pakistan Economic Corridor — a flagship project of China's Belt and Road Initiative. Also, New Delhi has been blaming Pakistan for cross-border terrorism and most recently such allegations have been responsible for not only further damaging bilateral relations but also regional cooperation via SAARC (Agarwal, 2022).

3.1. *Conflicts and economic cooperation*

Conflicts, regardless of their nature or location, tend to disrupt trade between countries. Often, physical infrastructure such as ports, roads and railways become inaccessible or are directly damaged during conflict, leading to reduced trade volumes. This disruption can be particularly damaging for perishable goods, which rely on swift transport. The closure or damage to trade routes also necessitates the use of alternative, often longer and more costly routes, which increase costs for businesses and consumers (Anderson, 2011). Conflicts often deter both domestic and foreign investments. Investors usually seek stability for their investments, and conflicts introduce a level of risk and uncertainty that can discourage investment. This can slow economic growth, particularly in developing economies, which rely heavily on foreign direct investment (FDI). A decrease in investment can also limit the potential for technology transfer and skills development, further impacting the long-term economic prospects of a region (Busse and Hefeker, 2007). Conflicts can impede infrastructure development, often a key aspect of economic cooperation. Infrastructure such as roads, bridges, ports and electricity grids can be directly damaged in conflicts, necessitating costly repairs or reconstruction. Additionally, the insecurity created by conflict can delay or prevent the implementation of new infrastructure projects, hindering economic development and cooperation (Collier, 1999). Conflicts can obstruct efforts towards regional integration. Tensions between countries can slow down or derail negotiations for regional agreements such as free trade agreements or customs unions. The lack of trust caused by conflict can also lead to countries imposing protectionist policies, which hinder the free flow of goods and services that is integral to economic integration (Mansfield and Reinhardt, 2003). Conflicts also lead to the diversion of resources from development to security concerns. Countries in conflict often allocate significant resources towards defence and security, which could otherwise be used for economic development. This diversion of resources perpetuates a cycle of low development and high conflict (Collier *et al.*, 2004).

As mentioned earlier, conflicts often result in disruptions to trade. For instance, the conflict between India and Pakistan has led to frequent trade blockades. When tensions escalate, borders are closed, and trade is severely affected. During these periods, imports and exports between the nations come to a standstill, leading to shortages of certain goods and causing economic strain. At the bilateral level, conflicts have resulted in trade disruptions and barriers. A significant manifestation of this is the frequent closure of borders between conflict-ridden states. For instance, the Wagah–Attari border crossing between India and Pakistan, a critical artery for bilateral trade, has seen sporadic closures due to political tensions, resulting in massive disruption of trade (Nayyar, 2019). The issue of MFN status has also been highly politicised in the region. Under World Trade Organization (WTO) rules, a country is expected to give MFN status to another country unless they both are part of a free trade agreement or are developing nations. India granted MFN status to Pakistan in 1996, but Pakistan has not reciprocated due to the ongoing conflict over Kashmir, further stunting bilateral trade opportunities (Iqbal and Nawaz, 2017).

Conflicts also deter bilateral investments. Political instability and uncertainty can discourage businesses from investing in neighbouring countries, stymieing opportunities for economic growth and development. This can be seen in the relatively low levels of FDI within South Asia compared to other regions (Rahman and Grewal, 2017). Bilateral conflicts can impede efforts to improve infrastructure connectivity, a key factor for facilitating trade. For example, disagreements over transit rights can hamper the development of regional transportation networks, affecting not just the conflicting countries but also landlocked nations that rely on these networks (Sahoo *et al.*, 2010). Conflicts among member states often obstruct the path towards greater regional economic integration. For instance, the tensions between India and Pakistan have consistently impeded the progress of SAARC and other regional economic cooperation initiatives (Agarwal, 2022). On a regional scale, conflicts have led to the postponement or cancellation of important regional summits, impacting the progress of regional cooperation initiatives. The SAARC summit is a key example. The 8th SAARC Summit, which was initially scheduled to be held in 1991 in Colombo, Sri Lanka, was indeed postponed due to tensions between India and Sri Lanka. The backdrop to this postponement was the ongoing Sri Lankan Civil War and the controversy surrounding the presence of the Indian Peace Keeping Force (IPKF) in Sri Lanka. The strained relationship between the two nations led to India's reluctance to attend the summit, resulting in its eventual postponement until 1992 (Sridharan, 1996). The 19th SAARC summit scheduled to be held in Islamabad in 2016 was cancelled after India, followed by Bangladesh, Bhutan and Afghanistan, pulled out citing an escalation of cross-border terror attacks. No subsequent SAARC summit has been held since then as of 2022, underscoring the hindrance conflicts have posed to regional cooperation (Agarwal, 2022). The inability to hold SAARC summits has obstructed decision-making on regional economic cooperation, as key decisions in SAARC are made through unanimity at the summit level. Furthermore, it has intensified calls for alternatives to SAARC, such as BIMSTEC, further fracturing regional cooperation. The impact of conflicts on SAARC serves as a stark reminder of the potential hindrances to regional cooperation in conflict-ridden areas (Bhattacharjee, 2018).

Trade patterns in South Asia indeed reveal a stronger orientation towards the outside world rather than intra-regionally. This trend is primarily due to the similarities in the structure of these economies, especially in terms of their agricultural sectors, which limit the potential for intra-regional trade under the traditional theory of comparative advantage (Nayyar, 2019). However, there are areas of significant potential for intra-regional trade that remain unexplored due to political constraints. A prime example is the automobile industry. India, with its well-established automobile manufacturing sector, could potentially be a significant supplier for countries like Pakistan. According to a study by the World Bank in 2021 (Kathuria, 2018), India's auto-parts could compete in terms of price and quality in the Pakistani market, potentially leading to substantial cost savings for Pakistan. Conflicts in South Asia have had a significant impact on bilateral cooperation, particularly in the domain of trade. Despite the economic potential, trade relations have often been marked by border closures, trade sanctions and the suspension of transport links (Nayyar, 2019). A vivid example of this is the aftermath of the Pulwama attack in 2019, when India imposed a 200% customs duty on Pakistani goods, effectively halting bilateral trade (News Desk, 2019). Conflicts have also disrupted bilateral cooperation between other countries in the region. For instance, tensions between Nepal and India led to the unofficial Indian blockade in 2015, which severely affected Nepal's economy (Karki, 2022). These examples demonstrate that political conflicts can cast a long shadow on economic relations in South Asia, posing significant challenges to bilateral cooperation and regional integration.

The most impactful bilateral conflict on regional cooperation is the India–Pakistan rivalry, which has frequently stalled the progress of SAARC. A key example is the continual postponement of the SAARC summits due to tensions between the two nations, hampering the decision-making process as SAARC operates on the principle of unanimity (Cohen, 2013). Furthermore, disagreements between India and Pakistan have often led to the failure of proposed regional initiatives such as the SAARC Motor Vehicle Agreement and SAARC Regional Airline Agreement (Palit and Tieri, 2019). The Indo-Pak conflict has also indirectly affected other bilateral relations within the region, resulting in a 'ripple effect' that hinders regional cooperation. For instance, Afghanistan's ties with Pakistan have been strained due to Afghanistan's then closeness to India, which had complicated regional dynamics (Yusuf, 2018). Furthermore, bilateral conflicts have often led to a spillover of tensions into regional platforms. For example, the 2015 border blockade between India and Nepal soured relations and affected their cooperation in regional forums (Karki, 2022).

Land trade between India and Pakistan has faced numerous restrictions due to ongoing political tensions. The Wagah–Attari border crossing, one of the few land routes between the two countries, has been intermittently closed during periods of escalated conflict, significantly disrupting trade. This lack of consistent access impacts sectors like agriculture, where the timely export of perishable goods is critical. Furthermore, this has led to indirect trade routes where goods are often routed through third countries like UAE and Singapore, escalating costs and causing inefficiencies (Nayyar, 2019).

Tensions between India and Pakistan have reached new heights in recent years. The political stance has prioritised national security over economic cooperation, resulting in a considerable reduction in bilateral economic activities (News Desk, 2019). In the wake of the Pulwama terror attack in February 2019, the Indian government made it clear that India would not engage in any dialogue with Pakistan until it took definitive action against terror groups operating from its soil. At the inauguration of the Kartarpur Corridor in November 2019, Prime Minister Modi stated, "The opening of Kartarpur Sahib Corridor before the 550th birth anniversary of Guru Nanak Devi Ji has brought us immense happiness…. May the Kartarpur Sahib Corridor prove to be a bridge of harmony and peace" (Modi, 2019a). Although this gesture was a positive development, the broader context of Indo-Pak relations remained marred by conflict and tension, affecting the potential for broader economic cooperation. Meanwhile, Pakistan has consistently emphasised dialogue as the only way forward. The then Pakistani Prime Minister Imran Khan, in his speech at the 75th United Nations General Assembly in September 2020, stated, "Peace and stability in South Asia was threatened by irresponsible policies of the Modi Government.... The only way forward was dialogue" (Khan, 2020). Despite this, the on-ground reality of cross-border terrorism and lack of trust between the nations continued to hinder meaningful progress in bilateral relations, including economic cooperation.

In August 2019, following the abrogation of Article 370 by the Indian government, which revoked the special status of Jammu and Kashmir, Prime Minister Modi said, "A new era has begun for the people of Jammu and Kashmir and Ladakh with the revocation of Article 370.... We want to build a new Kashmir, a powerful Kashmir" (Modi, 2019b). This move escalated tensions between India and Pakistan and had a significant impact on the already strained bilateral relations. In response to India's decision to abrogate Article 370, then Pakistani Prime Minister Imran Khan said in a public address, "We will fight it [the issue of Kashmir] at every forum. We're thinking how we can take it to International Court [ICJ] ... to the United Nations Security Council" (Khan, 2019). This reflected Pakistan's strategy of internationalising the Kashmir issue, which further complicated the prospects for peaceful resolution and meaningful bilateral or regional economic cooperation. Interestingly, a one-off exception to the stringent land trade restrictions was made when Pakistan allowed India's aid to Afghanistan to transit through its territory in late 2021. This decision, though isolated, suggested a potential thawing of relations and demonstrated the influence of regional dynamics on bilateral relations (Shahzad, 2021). The underlying lack of trust and unwillingness to engage with each other continues to hinder economic cooperation between India and Pakistan, underscoring the politicisation of trade in the region and the impact of conflict on economic activity.

Regional dynamics of South Asia continue to change because of state fragility facing some countries and external dynamics. After 20 years of the US-led NATO mission in Afghanistan, the Taliban took over in August 2021. Since then, Afghanistan has entered a new phase of instability as the new Islamic Emirate of Afghanistan has not been recognised by any state. While it still remains a member of SAARC, there will be no meaningful cooperation unless the new Taliban regime receives international legitimacy. While several states, including India and China, have found ways to cooperate with the Taliban, Pakistan's relationship deteriorates as the Taliban are harbouring anti-Pakistan terrorists of the Tehrik-e-Taliban Pakistan (Ahmed, 2022). Already bilateral hiccups have led to regular border closures and border skirmishes between Afghanistan and Pakistan (Ali and Yawar, 2023). Adding to this complexity in terms of evolving regional dynamics is China's increasing influence in the region. Through the Belt and Road Initiative (BRI), China has initiated major infrastructural projects across the region, including in Bangladesh, Maldives, Pakistan and Sri Lanka, and this worried India, which views South Asia as its sphere of influence. New Delhi is also against the China–Pakistan Economic Corridor that goes through the disputed Jammu and Kashmir territory in Gilgit–Baltistan (Ahmed and Sheikh, 2021).

4. Conclusion

South Asia, with its vast economic potential, has long been expected to experience substantial levels of regional cooperation. However, this vision remains largely unfulfilled via SAARC, as inter-member conflicts continue to dominate the region's landscape and the region is exposed to new geopolitical dynamics in the shape of the Taliban's takeover in Afghanistan and China's BRI. Despite efforts by organisations like SAARC and BIMSTEC, political disagreements, historical rivalries and security concerns have hindered the path to meaningful cooperation. This chapter examined the intricate dynamics between conflicts and regional economic cooperation in South Asia, with a particular focus on how conflicts have influenced the politicisation of trade. Bilateral conflicts between countries in the region have disrupted or closed vital trade routes, leading to reduced trade volumes and increased costs for businesses. Diplomatic tensions have also resulted in a decline in cross-border cooperation initiatives, with many regional agreements facing obstacles or being abandoned altogether.

SAARC and BIMSTEC, as platforms for fostering economic cooperation, have shown promise but have faced challenges due to unresolved bilateral conflicts, non-tariff barriers and a lack of enforcement mechanisms. India and Pakistan's long-standing rivalry has overshadowed the progress of SAARC and impacted regional cooperation efforts, while other bilateral conflicts have also affected regional dynamics. The low level of intra-regional trade compared to other regions is indicative of the barriers that persist within South Asia. However, the potential for enhanced economic cooperation is immense if these challenges can be effectively addressed. Trade liberalisation, policy dialogue, infrastructure development and harmonisation efforts under SAARC and BIMSTEC have yielded some positive outcomes, but more focused efforts are needed to overcome limitations and fully harness the region's economic potential.

To enhance regional economic integration in South Asia, a concerted effort towards conflict resolution and depoliticisation of trade is required. Regional organisations like SAARC and BIMSTEC are not suitable for this purpose as they are also victims of politicisation. Also, SAARC was created with the intention to avoid political issues. Hence, it is unlikely that SAARC or BIMSTEC will engage in any mediation. This role is the mandate of the United Nations that could push India and Pakistan to engage in dialogue to pave the way for more cooperation in South Asia.

Acknowledgements

The opinions expressed in this work are those of the author(s) and do not reflect the views of the National Defense College, or the United Arab Emirates government.

References

Adler, E. and Barnett, M. (Eds.). (1998). *Security Communities*. Cambridge University Press, Cambridge.

Agarwal, B. A. (2022, May 11). 7 Reasons why SAARC could not create a global influence and what it needs to do. India.com. https://www.india.com/opinion/7-reasons-why-saarc-could-not-create-a-global-influence-and-what-it-needs-to-do-5382863/.

Ahmed, Z. S. (2013). *Regionalism and Regional Security in South Asia: The Role of SAARC*. Routledge, Abingdon.

Ahmed, Z. S. (2022). The Taliban's takeover of Afghanistan and Pakistan's non-traditional security challenges. *Global Policy*, *13*(1), 125–131.

Ahmed, Z. S. and Sheikh, M. Z. H. (2021, September 15). Impact of China's belt and road initiative on regional stability in South Asia. *Journal of the Indian Ocean Region*, *17*(3), 271–288.

Ali, S. and Medhekar, A. (2022). The BIMSTEC free trade area. In *Handbook of Research on Economic and Political Implications of Green Trading and Energy Use* (pp. 97–116). IGI Global. DOI: 10.4018/978-1-7998-5774-7.ch006.

Ali, M. and Yawar, M. Y. (2023). Afghanistan-Pakistan border crossing reopens after talks to settle clashes. *Reuters*. https://www.reuters.com/world/asia-pacific/main-afghanistan-pakistan-border-crossing-reopens-after-nine-day-closure-source-2023-09-15/.

Anbumozhi, V. and Kalirajan, K. (2020). South Asia's economic integration with East Asia: An exploratory analysis with a focus on India. *Journal of Economic Integration*, 35(1), 91–116. DOI: 10.11130/jei.2020.35.1.91.

Anderson, J. E. (2011). The gravity model, annual review of economics. *Annual Reviews*, 3(1), 133–160.

Asian Development Bank. (2023). *Asian Economic Integration Report 2023*. http://dx.doi.org/10.22617/TCS230031-2.

Basu, K. (2018). Foreword. In Basu, K. (Ed.) *A Glass Half Full: The Promise of Regional Trade in South Asia* (pp. xv–xvi). The World Bank, Washington.

Bhattacharjee, J. (2018, January). SAARC vs BIMSTEC: The search for the ideal platform for regional cooperation (Issue No. 226). ORF Issue Brief No. 226. Observer Research Foundation. https://www.orfonline.org/wp-content/uploads/2018/01/ORF_Issue_Brief_226_BIMSTEC-SAARC.pdf.

Bishwakarma, J. K and Hu, Z. (2022). Problems and prospects for the South Asian Association for Regional Cooperation (SAARC). *Politics & Policy*, 50, 154–179. https://doi.org/10.1111/polp.12443.

Bishwakarma, R. and Zong-Shan, L. (2021). Problems and prospects for the South Asian Association for Regional Cooperation (SAARC). *Politics & Policy*, 49(3), 674–694. DOI: 10.1111/polp.12443.

Busse, M. and Hefeker, C. (2007). Political risk, institutions and foreign direct investment. *European Journal of Political Economy*, 23(2), 397–415.

Buzan, B. and Waever, O. (2003). *Regions and Powers: The Structure of International Security*. Cambridge University Press, Cambridge.

Cohen, S. P. (2013). *Shooting for a Century: The India–Pakistan Conundrum*. Brookings Institution Press, Washington.

Collier, P. (1999). On the economic consequences of civil war. *Oxford Economic Papers*, 51(1), 168–183.

Collier, P., Hoeffler, A., and Söderbom, M. (2004). On the duration of civil war. *Journal of Peace Research*, 41(3), 253–273.

Dash, K. C. (2008). *Regionalism in South Asia: Negotiating Cooperation, Institutional Structures*. Routledge, London.

Dawn News. (2007, April 4). Afghanistan inducted as 8th member: 14th SAARC summit begins. *Dawn News*. https://www.dawn.com/news/240651/afghanistan-inducted-as-8th-member14th-saarc-summit-begins.

Destradi, S. (2012). Regional powers and their strategies: Empire, hegemony, and leadership. *Review of International Studies*, *36*(4), 903–930.

Gartzke, E. and Li, Q. (2003). War, peace, and the invisible hand: Positive political externalities of economic globalisation. *International Studies Quarterly*, *47*(4), 561–586.

Iqbal, N. and Nawaz, S. (2017). Pakistan's bilateral trade under MFN and SAFTA: Do institutional and non-institutional arrangements matter? *The Pakistan Development Review*, *56*(1), 59–78. https://www.jstor.org/stable/44986516.

Karki, T. (2022, August 22). Political blackmailing: A case study of India's unofficial blockade on Nepal. SSRN. https://ssrn.com/abstract=4197326.

Kathuria, S. (Ed.). (2018). *A Glass Half Full: The Promise of Regional Trade in South Asia*. World Bank Publications, Washington.

Kaur, S., Khorana, S., and Kaur, M. (2020). Is there any potential in service trade of South Asia? *Foreign Trade Review*, *55*(3), 402–417. https://doi.org/10.1177/0015732520920469.

Khan, I. (2019). Public address on Article 370. Retrieved from the official Twitter account of Imran Khan.

Khan I. (2020, September 25). Statement by the Prime Minister of Pakistan H.E. Imran Khan to the seventy-fifth session of the UN General Assembly. Ministry of Foreign Affairs, Government of Pakistan. https://mofa.gov.pk/statement-by-the-prime-minister-of-pakistan-h-e-imran-khan-to-the-seventy-fifth-session-of-the-un-general-assembly-25-september-2020/.

Kharsu, S. M. (2023, September 4). India, Pakistan can step up direct trade. *The Hindu*. https://www.thehindubusinessline.com/opinion/india-pakistan-can-step-up-direct-trade/article67270663.ece.

Koyuncu, M. C. (2022, July 20). India's recent step: BIMSTEC. Ankara Center for Crisis and Policy Studies. https://www.ankasam.org/indias-recent-step-bimstec/?lang=en#_edn2.

Kumar, S. and Sharma, A. (2015). Regional cooperation in South Asia: Can prospects outweigh problems? CUTS International. Retrieved from https://cuts-citee.org/pdf/Regional_cooperation_in_South_Asia_Can_prospects_overweigh_problems.pdf.

Kydd, A. H. (2007). *Trust and Mistrust in International Relations*. Princeton University Press, Oxford.

Madhur, S. (2023). SAARC — time to change. *Indian Public Policy Review*, *17*(1), 35–48. https://doi.org/10.55763/ippr.2023.04.02.004.

Mansfield, E. D. and Pollins, B. M. (2001). The study of interdependence and conflict: Recent advances, open questions, and directions for future research. *Journal of Conflict Resolution*, *45*(6), 834–859.

Mansfield, E. D. and Reinhardt, E. (2003). Multilateral determinants of regionalism: The effects of GATT/WTO on the formation of preferential trading arrangements. *International Organisation, 57*(4), 829–862.

Modi, N. (2019a). Independence day speech. Retrieved from the official website of Prime Minister's Office, India.

Modi, N. (2019b). Speech at the inauguration of Kartarpur Corridor. Retrieved from the official Twitter account of Narendra Modi.

Nayyar, D. (2019). *Resurgent Asia: Diversity in Development*. Oxford University Press, Oxford.

News Desk. (2019, February 17). Post Pulwama attack: India raises import duty to 200% on Pakistani goods. *The Express Tribune*. https://tribune.com.pk/story/1912404/post-pulwama-attack-india-raises-import-duty-200-pakistani-goods.

Palit, A. and Tieri, S. (2019, September). BIMSTEC: Prospects for reconnecting the Bay of Bengal (Special Report Issue No. 3). Institute of South Asian Studies, Consortium of South Asian Think-Tanks, Konrad-Adenauer-Stiftung. https://www.isas.nus.edu.sg/wp-content/uploads/2019/10/Bimstec-Book-Full.pdf.

Putnam, R. D. (1988). Diplomacy and domestic politics: The logic of two-level games. *International Organisation, 42*(3), 427–460. https://www.jstor.org/stable/2706785.

Rahman, M. M. and Grewal, B. S. (2017). Foreign direct investment and international trade in BIMSTEC: Panel causality analysis. *Transnational Corporations Review, 9*(2), 97–112. DOI: 10.1080/19186444.2017.1326720.

Sahoo, P., Dash, R. K., and Nataraj, G. (2010). "Infrastructure development and economic growth in China". IDE Discussion Papers 261. Institute of Developing Economies, Japan External Trade Organisation (JETRO). https://ideas.repec.org/p/jet/dpaper/dpaper261.html.

Shahzad, A. (2021, November 23). Pakistan allows Indian aid transit to Afghanistan. *Reuters*. https://www.reuters.com/world/india/pakistan-allows-indian-aid-transit-afghanistan-2021-11-23/.

Sridharan, E. (1996). The origins, development and future of the South Asian Association for Regional Cooperation (SAARC). *Journal of Asian and African Studies, 31*(1–2), 139–160.

State Bank of Pakistan. (n.d.). Trade liberalisation between India and Pakistan. Retrieved from https://www.sbp.org.pk/publications/pak-india-trade/Chap_5.pdf.

The Hindu. (2019). India revokes most favoured nation status granted to Pakistan. February 15, 2019. https://www.thehindu.com/news/national/india-revokes-most-favoured-nation-status-to-pakistan/article26278480.ece.

Thomas, A. O. and Marandu, E. E. (2017). Rhetoric and realities of regional integration: Botswana SME perspectives on southern African trade. *South African Journal of Business Management*, 48(2), 75–86. https://doi.org/10.4102/sajbm.v48i2.30.

Wallensteen, P. (2018). *Understanding Conflict Resolution*. Sage, London.

World Bank. (2023). South Asia: Region at a glance. https://www.worldbank.org/en/region/sar.

Yusuf, M. (2018). *Brokering Peace in Nuclear Environments: U.S. Crisis Management in South Asia*. Stanford University Press, California.

© 2025 World Scientific Publishing Company
https://doi.org/10.1142/9789811298394_0007

Chapter 7

Implications of Trade Barriers and Their Effect on South Asian Countries

Deepika Dhingra[*,‡], **Rahul Mehriya**[†,§], **Hardik Sharma**[†,¶], **and Abhishek Kumar Singh**[†,∥]

[*]*BML Munjal University, Gurugram, Haryana, India*

[†]*Bennett University, Greater Noida, India*

[‡]*mithudhingra@gmail.com*
[§]*mehriya2728@gmail.com*
[¶]*hardik999988@gmail.com*
[∥]*7avi.cr7@gmail.com*

Abstract

This chapter examines the trade distortion due to tense relations between two largest South Asian countries and other various aspects of international trade and their implications. The chapter delves into the impact of human-made trade barriers such as subsidies, intellectual property rights, non-tariff barriers, exchange rate manipulation and trade agreements and their impact on international trade and economic development in developing countries in South Asia. Additionally, the chapter explores the effects of globalisation on income inequality and distributional effects, as well as the role of trade in the transmission of environmental and labour standards. This chapter presents a comprehensive analysis of the challenges and opportunities for South Asian countries in the global context.

Keywords: Gini Index, trade liberalisation, protectionism, trade ban, political hostilities.

1. Introduction

South Asian economies have been growing rapidly in recent years, but they still face several challenges in the global market, including trade barriers, subsidies, intellectual property rights, non-tariff barriers, exchange rate manipulation and trade agreements. These challenges can limit their ability to export goods and services to other countries and can impede their economic growth and development. Trade barriers are government policies that restrict the flow of goods and services between countries. They can include tariffs, quotas and other measures. South Asian economies often face higher tariffs and other barriers when exporting their goods and services to developing countries, which can make it more difficult for them to compete in international markets. For example, India has imposed tariffs on a wide range of goods from China, which has made it more expensive for Chinese exporters to sell their products in India. This has hurt the Chinese economy and has made it more difficult for China to achieve its economic development goals.

Subsidies are government payments to producers or exporters. They can distort the market and make it difficult for South Asian economies to compete with subsidised products from developed countries. For example, the European Union subsidises its agricultural sector, which makes it more difficult for South Asian economies to compete with European agricultural producers. This has hurt the economies of South Asian countries that rely on agriculture for a significant portion of their GDP. Intellectual property rights (IPRs) are legal protections for inventions, trademarks and creative works. Developed countries often have stronger IPR laws than South Asian countries, which can make it harder for South Asian economies to compete in industries that rely on IPRs, such as pharmaceuticals, software and entertainment. For example, the United States has strong IPR laws that protect pharmaceutical companies from competition from generic drug manufacturers in South Asian countries. This has made it more difficult for South Asian countries to access affordable medicines. Non-tariff barriers (NTBs) are a wide range of measures that restrict trade, such as technical standards, regulations and licensing requirements.

At the regional level, the economic cooperation among the South Asian countries is found to be very low. For example, Kumar (2019) reports that the intra-regional trade of South Asia stands at only 5.20%, which is substantially low as compared to the other trade blocs worldwide. They report that trade is heavily oriented towards extra-regional markets. The possible reasons are restricted regional trade policies and political differences (see Kumar, 2020). Trade agreements can benefit South Asian economies by increasing market access, reducing trade barriers and promoting investment. However, they can also have negative consequences, such as job losses in certain industries. For example, the South Asian Free Trade Area (SAFTA) has been credited with increasing trade between South Asian countries. However, it has also been blamed for job losses in certain industries in South Asian countries. Overall, the impact of trade barriers, subsidies, IPRs, NTBs, exchange rate manipulation and trade agreements on international trade and economic development in South Asian economies is complex and multifaceted. South Asian economies must carefully consider the potential impact of these policies and negotiate for fairer terms to achieve sustainable economic development.

Intraregional trade in South Asia remains one of the lowest in the world and accounts for about 5% of the region's total trade, compared with 50% in East Asia and the Pacific. Bangladesh's trade with South Asia is only 9% of its global trade. By reducing human-made trade barriers, trade within South Asia can grow three times, from $23 billion to $67 billion, says a new World Bank report. Bangladesh has the potential to more than double its trade with South Asian countries. Increased regional trade can accelerate Bangladesh's growth and create more jobs for men and women (see Kathuria, 2018; World Development Report on South Asia Economic Focus, 2021).

1.1. *Trade in South Asia: Empirical context*

The neoclassical economic literature emphasised trade as the engine of economic growth, hence provided a theoretical link between trade and economic growth. Recent studies, for example, Bandara and Yu (2003) examine the scope of SAFTA in the South Asian context. The results suggest that India will experience significant welfare gain, while small countries will gain only marginally. The findings further suggest that Bangladesh will lose out due to SAFTA. They find that bilateral trade arrangements benefit South Asian countries more than multilateral trade agreements such as SAFTA. Mamun and Nath (2004) also hold significant long- and short-run causal relations between export and economic growth in Bangladesh. This chapter offers a link between trade, economic growth and income inequality in Bangladesh. We find little evidence that trade affects income distribution or that income distribution affects growth or investment. Given the poor quality of data on inequality measures, there is room for further investigation. Sensitivity analysis with sample change period suggests that investment was significant during the post-independence period, which had a positive impact on trade liberalisation.

Siriwardana and Yang (2007) show that the FTA offers high scope for the expansion of trade between Bangladesh and India. This agreement will help Bangladesh to slow down the growing trade imbalance.

Bellamy (2014) emphasised that international trade promotes the human skills and technological base of the country through the import of innovations.

Hye and Lau (2015) examined the relationship between trade openness of physical and human capital on economic growth measured by the GDP growth rate in India using the ARDL model and other multivariate causality techniques. The results state that the trade openness index negatively affects economic growth in the long term, while the impact of physical and human capital is found to be positive. A study by Kumar (2020a) offers interesting results on the spillover of India's bilateral trade and economic growth on the economic growth rate of other countries in the region (Bangladesh, Sri Lanka, Nepal and Bhutan). The results highlight that India's imports from South Asian countries other than Pakistan have a significant positive impact on their economic growth rates. Kumar (2020b) provided facts about current and prospects, for regional trade integration in South Asia against the backdrop of multilateral trade agreements. The study applies the trade intensity index of the four largest South Asian countries (India, Bangladesh, Pakistan and Sri Lanka) for short and long estimates operate trade cointegration in an autoregressive multilateral framework. Kumar (2022) stressed that intra-regional trade significantly affects economic well-being measured by the gross domestic product per capita of the people of the region, which increases the need for higher regional trade openness.

After reviewing the literature on this topic, we found some of the gaps in the studies. Through our chapter, we are going to emphasise mainly the topics such as trade liberalisation policies, challenges faced during export and import, the role of exports and imports in developing nations, how South Asian countries will be benefited if regional trade is open, etc. The unique part of our chapter is that we did a graphical comparison among the South Asian countries in terms of challenges and opportunities, tariff rate, Gini Index (see World Bank, 2023; The World Inequality Lab, 2023) and more. We gain a great level of understanding by reading these research papers and we used that knowledge, added some new perspective to this topic and added data in a graphical form to make it more understandable.

2. Economic Cooperation in South Asia: Current State of Art

2.1. *India and Pakistan: A strain on both economies*

In August 2019, India revoked Article 370 of its constitution, which gave special status to the state of Jammu and Kashmir. In response, Pakistan imposed a trade ban on India. The ban has had a significant impact on the economies of both countries. India has been the largest market for Pakistani goods, and the ban has led to a decline in exports. Pakistan's exports to India fell by 25% in the first year after the ban was imposed. This has had a knock-on effect on the Pakistani economy, as it has led to job losses and a decline in tax revenue (see Kumar, 2020a).

India has also been affected by the trade ban. India imported goods worth $2 billion from Pakistan in 2018–2019. The ban has led to a shortage of these goods in India and has also pushed up prices. This has harmed Indian consumers and businesses. The trade ban has also had a political impact. The ban has further strained relations between India and Pakistan and has made it more difficult for the two countries to resolve their differences. The long-term impact of the trade ban is uncertain. The ban may be lifted in the future, but it is also possible that it will remain in place for some time. The impact of the ban will depend on some factors, including the political situation in the region and the economic conditions in both countries.

The trade ban is a complex issue with no easy solutions. It is important to consider the impact of the ban on both countries, as well as the political implications. The ban is a reminder of the challenges that India and Pakistan face in their relationship. However, it is also a reminder of the importance of dialogue and cooperation. In addition to the economic and political impacts, the trade ban has also had many social and environmental impacts. For example, the ban has led to job losses in both countries, which has hurt the livelihoods of many people. The ban has also led to a shortage of goods in India, which has pushed up prices and made it difficult for people to access essential items. Additionally, the ban has disrupted supply chains, which has harmed the environment. The trade ban is a significant challenge for both India and Pakistan. However, it is also an opportunity for the two countries to come together and find a mutually beneficial solution. By working together, India and Pakistan can overcome the challenges posed by the trade ban and build a more prosperous future for both their people.

The trade ban between India and Pakistan is a complex issue with far-reaching consequences. It has had a significant impact on the economies of both countries, as well as on the social and environmental sectors. The long-term impact of the ban is uncertain, but it will continue to be a major challenge for both countries. However, it is also an opportunity for India and Pakistan to come together and find a mutually beneficial solution. By working together, the two countries can overcome the challenges posed by the trade ban and build a more prosperous future for both their people.

2.2. *The cost of conflict: Political hostilities and the impact on trade*

South Asia is a region with a long history of political hostilities. These hostilities have had a significant impact on trade in the region, both directly and indirectly. One of the most direct impacts of political hostilities on trade in South Asia is the imposition of trade barriers. For example, India and Pakistan have a long history of trade disputes, and these disputes have led to the imposition of tariffs and other trade barriers on both sides. These trade barriers have made it more difficult for businesses in the two countries to trade with each other and have hurt the economies of both countries. Another direct impact of political hostilities on trade in South Asia is the disruption of supply chains. For example, the conflict in Kashmir has disrupted the transportation of goods between India and Pakistan, making it more difficult for businesses in the two countries to get the goods they need. This has been unfavourable for the economies of both countries and has also led to higher prices for consumers.

In addition to the direct impacts of political hostilities on trade, there are also some indirect impacts. For example, political instability can lead to uncertainty in the business environment, which can make businesses reluctant to invest in the region. This can harm trade, as it can lead to a decline in demand for goods and services. Political hostilities can also lead to a decline in tourism, which can also have an adverse impact on trade. For example, the conflict in Kashmir has led to a decline in tourism in the region, which has hurt the economies of both India and Pakistan. The impact of regional political hostilities on trade in South Asia is significant. Both direct and indirect impacts have been felt, and these impacts have hurt the economies of the region. It is important to address these issues to promote trade and economic development in South Asia.

2.3. *Challenges and opportunities*

Developing countries face several challenges in international trade, such as trade barriers, volatility in commodity prices and limited access to finance and technology. Addressing these challenges requires policy interventions at the national and international levels, focusing on export diversification, improving trade facilitation and enhancing competitiveness. On the other hand, opportunities exist for developing countries to capitalise on their comparative advantages, regional integration initiatives and engagement in GVCs. By leveraging these opportunities, developing countries can foster sustainable economic growth and development through international trade. For example, India, being the largest economy in South Asia, experienced substantial growth between 2012 and 2021. The GDP increased from $1.827 trillion in 2012 to $3.176 trillion in 2021, demonstrating consistent economic progress, except for a slight dip in 2020, likely due to the COVID-19 pandemic's impact on global economies. Pakistan's GDP has also shown growth from 2012 to 2021, rising from $224.38 billion to $348.26 billion. The growth has been relatively consistent, but the economy faced a setback in 2019 and 2020, possibly due to the pandemic and other domestic challenges (see World Development Report on South Asia Economic Focus, 2021).

On the other hand, Nepal's economy has grown steadily over the years, with its GDP increasing from $21.7 billion in 2012 to $36.29 billion in 2021. This growth signifies improvements in various sectors and a stronger economy over time. Afghanistan's GDP has been relatively unstable, with fluctuations observed throughout the period. The GDP peaked in 2014 at $20.55 billion but declined to $14.79 billion in 2021, indicating potential economic challenges or political instability affecting the nation's growth. Sri Lanka's economy expanded from $70.45 billion in 2012 to $88.93 billion in 2021. The GDP peaked in 2018 at $94.49

Table 1. Trade indicators of South Asian countries.

Country	Regional trade share (%)				
	1990	1998	2006	2016	Average 1990–2016
India	1.57	2.78	2.60	3.19	2.53
Pakistan	2.72	3.98	6.59	7.05	5.08
Sri Lanka	5.65	6.89	17.36	17.31	11.80
Bangladesh	5.98	12.42	9.21	9.65	9.32
Nepal	11.88	32.63	63.26	65.12	43.22
Bhutan	9.70	64.77	74.88	92.79	60.54
Trade Intensity Index for South Asia					
India	1.58	2.55	1.64	1.27	1.78
Pakistan	2.74	3.64	4.21	2.81	3.08
Sri Lanka	5.69	6.31	10.88	6.95	7.62
Bangladesh	6.03	11.38	5.70	3.87	6.79
Nepal	11.98	30.02	40.23	28.08	27.14
Bhutan	9.72	59.02	45.23	37.40	45.37

Source: The data is compiled by the author from World Development Indicators and Asian Development Bank Database.

billion but faced a downturn in 2019 and 2020, possibly due to the pandemic or other domestic factors. Similarly, the trade indicators of all South Asian countries are very low as shown in Table 1.

In the context of tariffs in the South Asia region, for example, India's tariff rates have fluctuated throughout the years, with rates varying between 4.88% and 7.33%. This suggests a relatively dynamic trade policy, with tariff adjustments made in response to various economic factors and trade agreements. Pakistan's weighted mean tariff rates have also experienced fluctuations, ranging from 8.67% to 10.2%. Similar to India, this suggests that Pakistan has been making adjustments to its trade policy based on domestic and international factors. Nepal's tariff rates have shown significant fluctuations, with rates ranging from 10.55% to 15.04%. The high tariff rates, especially in 2013, suggest a protectionist trade policy, possibly to safeguard domestic industries from external competition. The available data for Afghanistan is limited, but it shows tariff rates of 6.95% in 2011 and 2012 and 8.38% in 2016. The missing data makes it difficult to draw a comprehensive conclusion, but it seems that Afghanistan's trade policy has experienced some changes during this period. Sri Lanka's tariff rates have shown considerable fluctuations, ranging from 7.87% to 16.38%. The high tariff rate in 2017 indicates a protectionist trade policy in that year, possibly to defend domestic industries (for example, see Development Report on South Asia Economic Focus, 2021; Pratibha and Krishna, 2022; World Bank Database, 2022).

These challenges can limit their ability to export goods and services to other countries and can impede their economic growth and development.

- **Trade barriers:** Trade barriers include tariffs, quotas and other measures that restrict the flow of goods and services between countries. Developing countries often face higher tariffs and other barriers when exporting their goods and services to developing countries, which can make it more difficult for them to compete in international markets.
- **Intellectual property rights:** Intellectual property rights refer to legal protections for inventions, trademarks and creative works. Developed countries often have stronger intellectual property laws than developing countries, which can make it harder for developing countries to compete in industries that rely on intellectual property, such as pharmaceuticals, software and entertainment.
- **Non-tariff barriers:** Non-tariff barriers include a wide range of measures that restrict trade, such as technical standards, regulations and licensing requirements. These measures can be particularly challenging for developing countries, which may not have the resources or expertise to comply with complex regulations and standards.
- **Infrastructure:** Developing countries often lack the infrastructure necessary to compete in international markets. This includes transportation infrastructure, such as ports and roads, as well as information technology infrastructure, such as broadband internet access.
- **Limited access to finance:** Developing countries often face limited access to finance, which can make it more difficult for them to invest in the infrastructure and technology necessary to compete in international markets.
- **Unequal trading relationships:** Developing countries often face unequal trading relationships, in which developed countries have more bargaining power and can dictate terms that are unfavourable to developing countries.
- **Limited market access:** Developing countries often have limited market access due to protectionist policies in developed countries, which can make it difficult for them to expand their exports and enter new markets.

3. How South Asian Countries Will Be Benefited If Regional Trade Is Open?

The current regional trade volume of all South Asian countries is under 5% as shown in Figure 1. If regional trade between South Asian countries is open, it can have several potential benefits for the region. Here are some key benefits:

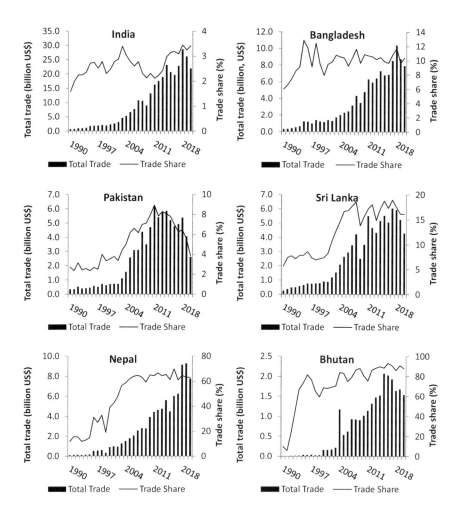

Figure 1.   Intra-regional trade of South Asian countries.
Source: Asian Development Bank Database.

1. **Economic growth:** Open regional trade can stimulate economic growth in South Asian countries. It allows the free flow of goods, services and investment, which can lead to increased production, job creation and overall economic development.
2. **Expanded market access:** Open trade promotes better market access for South Asian countries. By removing trade barriers such as tariffs, quotas and non-tariff barriers, businesses can more easily export their products to neighbouring countries. This expanded market access can help businesses diversify their customer base and increase their competitiveness.
3. **Trade diversification:** The openness of regional trade encourages South Asian countries to diversify their export markets. Dependence on a single market can be risky, but by exploring opportunities in the region, countries can reduce their dependence on external markets and reduce economic vulnerability.
4. **Investment and technology transfer:** Open regional trade can attract foreign direct investment (FDI) to South Asian countries. Increased investment flows can bring capital, technology, and expertise that can increase productivity and competitiveness in domestic industries. This can lead to the development of new industries, infrastructure projects and innovations.
5. **Lower costs:** Open trade promotes competition, which leads to lower costs for consumers. Access to cheaper inputs, intermediates and raw materials from neighbouring countries can lower production costs for businesses and make their products more affordable for consumers. This can improve living standards and increase the purchasing power of individuals.
6. **Enhanced regional cooperation:** Open trade can strengthen regional cooperation and promote political stability among South Asian countries. Increased economic interdependence fosters mutual understanding and cooperation, which can have positive spin-offs in other areas such as diplomacy, security and cultural exchanges.
7. **Poverty reduction:** Economic growth resulting from open regional trade has the potential to reduce poverty in South Asian countries. Job creation, income generation and improved living standards contribute to poverty alleviation and the well-being of the population.

It is worth noting that the realisation of these benefits requires effective implementation and cooperation between participating countries.

Addressing issues such as infrastructure gaps, harmonising trade regulations and resolving political disputes will be critical to fully reap the potential benefits of open regional trade in South Asia.

3.1. *Gini index in South Asia*

Gini index model is a widely used measure of income inequality within a population. Developed by Italian statistician and sociologist Corrado Gini in 1912, this index provides insight into the distribution of wealth and income among individuals in a society. We will discuss the methodology behind the Gini index, its interpretation and the limitations of using this model as a sole indicator of income inequality.

The Gini index, also known as the Gini coefficient, ranges from 0 to 1 (or 0–100 when expressed in percentage terms), where 0 represents perfect equality and 1 indicates perfect inequality. In a situation of perfect equality, every individual has the same income, while in a scenario of perfect inequality, one person possesses all the income and the rest have none.

The Gini index is derived from the Lorenz curve, a graphical representation of the cumulative share of income (or wealth) against the cumulative share of the population, ordered by income levels. To calculate the Gini index, we measure the area between the Lorenz curve and the 45-degree line of perfect equality, then divide this area by the total area under the line of perfect equality.

This Gini Index data of the South Asian countries help us understand income inequality trends in these countries over the selected years. India's Gini Index has fluctuated slightly between 34.6 and 35.9 during the observed years, suggesting a moderate level of income inequality that has remained relatively stable. Pakistan's Gini Index has varied between 28.8 and 31.3 during the observed years, indicating a lower level of income inequality compared to India. The trend has been relatively stable with small fluctuations. The only available data for Nepal is from 2010, with a Gini Index of 32.8. This suggests a moderate level of income inequality at that time, but we cannot determine any trends due to the lack of data. There is no available Gini Index data for Afghanistan, making it impossible to assess income inequality trends for this country. Sri Lanka's Gini Index has ranged from 36.1 to 39.3 during the observed years, suggesting a moderate to high level of income inequality. The index increased from 36.1 in 2009 to 39.3 in 2015 before decreasing to 37.7 in 2018, indicating fluctuations in income distribution (see Rama *et al.*, 2015; Hasell, 2023).

3.2. Aspects of international trade and its implications for developing countries: comparative advantage

Countries should specialise in producing goods and services where they have a lower opportunity cost relative to other nations. For example, India has a comparative advantage in information technology (IT) and business process outsourcing (BPO) due to its skilled labour force and low operating costs. In contrast, Sri Lanka and Bangladesh have advantages in the textile and apparel industries.

Implications: By utilising comparative advantage, South Asian countries can enhance their productivity, create jobs and foster economic growth. However, it is crucial to diversify their economies to minimise vulnerability to external shocks and ensure long-term stability.

Protectionism: Protective measures such as tariffs, import quotas and subsidies aim to safeguard domestic industries from foreign competition. For instance, India has historically employed protectionist policies in various sectors, including agriculture and manufacturing. Also, Pakistan has used protectionist measures in certain industries, such as the automotive sector, where high import duties are imposed on completely built-up (CBU) vehicles to promote local assembly and manufacturing.

Implications: While protectionism can help nurture infant industries, it can also lead to inefficiencies and hinder international trade. Reducing protectionist measures could open up new markets for South Asian countries, but it may also expose domestic industries to intense competition.

Trade liberalisation: Opening up markets and reducing trade barriers can foster economic growth by encouraging foreign investment, technology transfer and increased export opportunities. For example, India has gradually liberalised its economy since the 1990s, resulting in significant growth and development.

4. Conclusion

In conclusion, the effects of trade barriers on South Asian countries are multifaceted and have a significant impact on various aspects of their economies. It is essential to understand the impact of trade barriers, subsidies, intellectual property rights, non-tariff barriers, exchange rate manipulation and trade agreements on international trade and economic development in developing countries, especially in the South Asian region. Trade barriers such as tariffs and quotas restrict the flow of goods and services across borders and hinder international trade and economic growth. Developing countries in South Asia often face problems due to these barriers, as they limit their access to global markets and lead to higher costs for both exports and imports. Moreover, subsidies provided by developed countries to their domestic industry can distort the competitive environment and disadvantage producers from developing countries.

Intellectual property rights play a key role in international trade as they protect innovation and stimulate investment in research and development. However, strict intellectual property rights regimes can pose problems for developing countries as they limit their access to technology and stifle domestic innovation. Balancing intellectual property protection with access to affordable medicines and technologies remains a key issue. Non-tariff barriers such as technical standards and hygiene regulations can be used as covert protectionist measures to prevent developing countries from accessing the market. In addition, exchange rate manipulation can distort trade patterns and competitiveness, impacting the ability of South Asian countries to export and import goods and services. Trade agreements, on the other hand, offer developing countries opportunities to expand their market access and benefit from preferential trade arrangements. By reducing tariffs and addressing non-tariff barriers, these agreements can stimulate economic growth and promote regional integration. South Asian countries have recognised the importance of such agreements and have actively participated in regional initiatives such as the South Asian Free Trade Area (SAFTA) and bilateral trade agreements.

Trade liberalisation policies, including the removal or reduction of trade barriers, have the potential to accelerate economic development in developing countries. By promoting competition, facilitating access to foreign markets and promoting efficiency, trade liberalisation can increase productivity, attract foreign investment and increase the competitiveness of domestic industries. However, it is essential to implement these policies in a balanced way and to ensure that vulnerable sectors are sufficiently supported to cope with increased competition. Challenges facing the export of goods and services include inadequate infrastructure, limited access to finance, bureaucratic hurdles and lack of market information. Addressing these challenges through targeted policies and investments can help developing countries, including South Asian countries, diversify their export base, increase value-added production and integrate into global value chains.

Exports and imports play a key role in the economic development of developing countries, including those in South Asia. Exports generate foreign exchange earnings, stimulate employment and promote technology transfer. Meanwhile, imports provide access to basic raw materials, intermediate products and capital goods that are key to domestic production and industrial development. The Gini index model is used to measure income inequality within a country. Trade can have consequences for the distribution of income, with some industries and individuals benefiting more than others. It is important that policymakers address the potential inequalities arising from trade liberalisation and put measures in place to ensure inclusive growth.

International trade has both positive and negative consequences for developing countries. While it presents opportunities for economic growth, job creation and poverty reduction, it also presents challenges such as market volatility, fluctuating terms of trade and vulnerability to external shocks. Developing countries must adopt appropriate policies and strategies to maximise the benefits of international trade while mitigating its potential risks. In conclusion, trade barriers and their impact on South Asian countries have significant implications for international trade and economic development. Policymakers must address these barriers through trade liberalisation policies, facilitating export diversification and enhancing competitiveness. South Asian countries can thus harness the full potential of international trade to promote sustainable and sustainable development of the country.

References

Asian Development Bank Database. https://aric.adb.org/integrationindicators.

Hye, Q. M. A. and Lau W. Y. (2015). Trade openness and economic growth: Empirical evidence from India. *Journal of Business Economics and Management*, *16*(1), 188–205.

Joe, H. (2023). Measuring inequality: What is the Gini coefficient? Published online at OurWorldInData.org. Retrieved from: https://ourworldindata.org/what-is-the-gini-coefficient.

Kathuria, S. (2018). *A Glass Half Full: The Promise of Regional Trade in South Asia*. South Asia Development Forum, World Bank, Washington, DC.

Kumar, R. (2020a). India and South Asia: Geopolitics, regional trade and economic growth spillovers. *Journal of International Trade and Economic Development*, *29*(1), 69–88.

Kumar, R. (2020b). South Asia: Multilateral trade agreements and untapped regional trade integration. *International Journal of Finance and Economics*, *26*(2), 2891–2903.

Kumar, R. (2022). Policy challenges and testing the scope for regional trade integration — a case of South Asia. *Journal of Economic and Public Administration*. https://www.emerald.com/insight/content/doi/10.1108/JEAS-12-2021-0263/full/html.

Mamun, K. A. and Nath, H. K. (2004). Export-led growth in Bangladesh: A time series analysis. *Applied Economics Letters*, *12*(6), 361–364.

Pratibha, S. and Krishna, M. (2022). The effect of COVID-19 pandemic on economic growth and public debt: an analysis of India and the global economy. *Journal of Economic and Administrative Sciences*. DOI: 10.1108/JEAS-01-2022-0018.

Rama M., Li. Y., Mitra P. K., and Newman J. L. (2015). *Addressing Inequality in South Asia*. World Bank, Washington DC. https://documents1.worldbank.org/curated/en/878201468170975271/pdf/Addressing-inequality-in-South-Asia.pdf.

Sebastian Franco-Bedoya. (2022). Trade agreements in South Asia towards a successful story in the developing world. *Policy Research Working Paper*, 10211. World Bank, Washington, DC.

Siriwardana, M. and Yang, J. (2007). Effects of proposed free trade agreement between India and Bangladesh. *South Asian Economic Journal*, *8*(1), 21–38.

World Bank Database. (2022). http://databank.worldbank.org/data/source/worlddevelopment-indicators.

World Development Report on South Asia Economic Focus. (2021). https://www.worldbank.org/.

Chapter 8

External Debt Distress in Pakistan and India*

Shahida Wizarat

Dean CESD, IOBM, Karachi, Pakistan

drshahidawizarat@gmail.com

Abstract

Using panel data, I find a positive and significant relationship between military expenditure and external debt. One unit increase in military expenditure increases external debt by 8.4 units, which is significant at the 100% confidence level. GDP per capita has a negative and significant impact, the exchange rate has a positive but insignificant impact, while total reserves have a negative but insignificant impact on external debt. The value of $R2$ reflects that almost 85% of the variation in external debt has been explained by the model. The debt distress that has engulfed the sub-continent due to the import of arms, causing an increase in external indebtedness, decline in economic growth, loss of employment opportunities due to de-industrialisation and/or exporting jobs to armament producing countries, loss of development and increase in poverty with very adverse consequences on the socio-political fabric. We need to address the all-important question of how to bring peace to the sub-continent. Should Pakistan and India resolve their major

---

*I would like to thank Kamran Mahfooz for help with data collection and computations.

conflicts as European countries did prior to integrating their economies? In other words, should we emphasise geo-strategic option rather than geo-economics? Or should we emphasise geo-economics and postpone geo-strategic matters for some future date?

Keywords: Pakistan, India, debt distress, military expenditure, geo-strategic, geo-economic.

1. Introduction

A lot of interest on military spending and growth was generated with the publication of Benoit's (1973) paper, which stated that military spending increases economic growth in Third World countries. But Deger and Sen (1983) challenged Benoit's study. The differential approaches are better understood by applying differential models on which they are based. In the Keynesian model, increase in defence expenditure increases aggregate demand, causing an increase in output and employment. Therefore, defence expenditure increased economic growth (see for example, Benoit (1978), Kaldor (1976), Yildirim *et al.* (2005, 2006), Halicioglu (2003, 2004), Ando (2009), Atesoglu (2009)) Contrary to this, the neo-classical model predicts a negative impact of military spending on economic growth through crowding out of private investment, which reduces output and employment (Smith (1977, 1980a, 1980b, 1985), Rothschild (1977), Lim (1983), Deger and Smith (1983, 1985), Deger (1986), Knight *et al.* (1996), Roux (1996), Batchelor *et al.* (2000), Dunne and Skons (2011)).

Several studies on the impact of military spending on debt have been conducted for the sub-continent. For example, the study by Sheikh *et al.* (2017) explored the link between military spending, inequality and economic growth for Pakistan using GMM during 1972–2016. The authors use augmented Solow growth model with Harrod neutral technological change and report a positive relationship between military expenditure and growth, while inequality has a negative impact on growth. The study by Ajmair (2018) exploring the relationship between military spending and economic growth for Pakistan for the period 1990–2015 used the ARDL approach. A positive relationship between military spending and military personnel has a positive and significant impact on GDP only in the short run, but in the long run only the number of military persons has a positive impact on economic growth.

Abdul-Khalek *et al.* (2019) studied the impact of military spending on economic growth in India using time series data for the period 1980–2016. The authors do not find a causal relationship between military spending and economic growth in India. But there is evidence to support Granger causality from government spending and exports to economic growth. Moreover, in spite of the absence of military expenditure on growth, industrial development has been beneficial for development and economic growth through technological change and spillover effects.

In this study, I am attempting to explore how military expenditure is affecting the economies of Pakistan and India. This necessitates studying the impact of military spending on debt with very serious implications on the lives of 1.7 billion people who inhabit the sub-continent. Against this scenario, the following objectives will be pursued in the study. First, to study how military expenditure is affecting the economies of the two largest countries in the sub-continent, with particular emphasis on debt whose impact on growth, employment and inflation is severely affecting the lives of the people. My second objective is to explore the challenges to geo-economics and identify the benefits that could accrue by resolving conflicts.

Following this brief introduction, I go on to discuss the import of armaments, military expenditure as a % of GDP and total expenditure, external debt as a % of GDP and how these expenditures are pushing people into poverty during the period 1990–2021 in Section 2. In Section 3, I develop an econometric model to study the major determinants of external debt in Pakistan and India. The study is concluded and policy implications presented in Section 4.

2. Military Spending and External Debt in Pakistan and India

In an earlier study on five South Asian countries, Abbas and Wizarat (2017) investigated the long-term and short-term effects of military expenditure on external debt for the period 1991–2013. The authors found an increase in military expenditure by 1% of the GDP increases external debt by 1.607–1.999% of the GDP. The coefficient on GDP reveals a negative impact of 0.02%, while the exchange rate depreciation and foreign exchange reserves have a positive and significant impact. The study recommends South Asian economies to resolve their political differences and reduce military spending for achieving sustainable economic growth through debt reduction. This study was followed by Abbas *et al.* (2020) who explored social and economic determinants of external debt distress in the same South Asian countries from 1980 to 2018. The authors report large and increasing current account deficits, lowering gross capital formation, foreign direct investment and large military expenditures as the major causes. The socio-economic variables that increase external debt distress are an increase in life expectancy, while urbanisation reduces it.[1]

Narrowing our focus in this study, we turn to two largest and most populated South Asian countries, Pakistan and India, whose import of arms has turned the sub-continent into the most militarised zone in the region. With a total area spread over 4,083,358 sq. km and a combined population of almost 1.7 billion people, very unequal distribution of income and wealth and rampant poverty, the sub-continent is a bombshell waiting to explode. The countries are still grappling with British legacies, adamantly resisting the resolution of conflicts, giving rise to an arms race with the import of armaments, which have soared military expenditures, increased external indebtedness, with serious ramifications on economic growth, employment, income distribution, poverty and deteriorating standard of living of billions of people in the sub-continent.

Both Pakistan and India have been importing arms during the period 1990–2021 as can be seen from Table 1. The table and the accompanying Figures 1 and 2 show that a higher volume of import of armaments is helping to maintain high levels of military expenditures both as a percentage of GDP and total expenditure. In the case of Pakistan, military spending as a % of GDP was very high during the 1990s and has since experienced a decline except for the years 2018–2020. While military spending as a % of total expenditure was very high during the period 1990–2003, but started declining from 2004. In India, high arms imports fluctuated during the period 1990–2001, but from then onwards arms imports have maintained their high level, apart from occasional downturns. From 1988 onwards, it has borrowed heavily from the International Monetary Fund (IMF), as a result of which "the rate of growth of the economy has been adversely affected. The decline in growth rates is

---

[1] Some other studies for developing countries include: Azam and Feng (2017), Bacha (1990), and Benedict *et al.* (2014).

Table 1. Arms imports and military spending.

Year	Arms imports (SIPRI trend indicator values) in million dollars		Military spending (% of GDP)		Military spending (% of government expenditure)	
	IND	PAK	IND	PAK	IND	PAK
1990	2721	643	3.15	6.52	12.40	0
1991	1884	498	2.91	6.57	10.86	0
1992	1185	379	2.71	6.70	10.31	0
1993	737	1000	2.82	6.43	10.97	25.10
1994	884	890	2.67	5.92	10.35	27.40
1995	1479	366	2.58	5.82	10.50	27.21
1996	844	500	2.48	6.04	10.33	24.58
1997	1666	691	2.65	5.62	10.68	25.04
1998	753	699	2.73	5.42	10.66	23.45
1999	1211	874	2.96	5.19	11.64	23.98
2000	983	182	2.95	4.17	11.50	22.42
2001	1193	419	2.92	3.88	10.52	24.03
2002	2022	565	2.83	4.07	9.88	22.57
2003	2741	652	2.68	4.09	9.10	25.41
2004	2213	476	2.83	3.96	10.12	26.06
2005	1198	443	2.75	3.90	10.42	24.45
2006	1484	356	2.53	3.65	9.48	21.37
2007	2275	694	2.48	3.51	8.85	18.03
2008	1858	1070	2.63	3.46	8.89	16.13
2009	1863	1191	3.13	3.27	10.31	16.94
2010	2911	2205	2.89	3.42	9.86	16.83
2011	3598	1128	2.70	3.29	9.59	16.98
2012	4392	1014	2.62	3.48	9.27	16.09
2013	5381	1095	2.55	3.47	9.30	15.91
2014	3347	828	2.54	3.48	9.50	17.30
2015	3117	779	2.46	3.55	8.83	17.96
2016	3003	837	2.54	3.59	9.08	18.03
2017	2909	837	2.53	3.77	9.39	17.72
2018	1485	799	2.43	4.13	9.10	19.09
2019	3075	521	2.52	4.11	9.14	18.70
2020	2799	759	2.88	4.03	8.79	17.44
2021	2721	643	2.66	3.83	8.27	17.82

Source: World Development Indicators (WDI), World Bank.

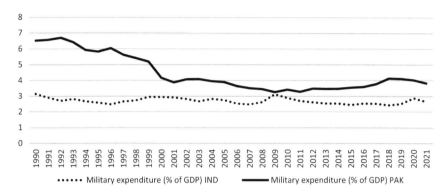

Figure 1. Military spending as a % of GDP.

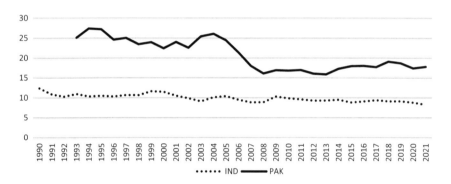

Figure 2. Military spending as a % of government spending.

having a decelerating effect on personal incomes, business profits and government revenues. Along with the closure of 5000 industrial units, downsizing and restructuring of State-Owned Enterprises (SOEs), decline in investments, migration of industrial units that have become non-viable due to escalation in their cost of production, are rendering millions unemployed".[2] The impact of the more recent IMF programme is, however, far more severe than was the case in the 1990s.[3]

There were two very severe consequences from IMF borrowing. First, it increased external debt as a % of GDP. Second, there was a

---
[2] Wizarat (2011).
[3] Wizarat (2022).

Table 2. External debt as a % of GDP.

Year	Ext debt % of GDP IND	PAK	Year	IND	PAK
1990	26.01	51.64	2006	16.97	27.27
1991	31.41	51.21	2007	16.77	27.76
1992	30.46	50.98	2008	18.94	29.3
1993	32.7	47.39	2009	19.1	33.7
1994	29.91	52.38	2010	17.33	35.63
1995	26.04	49.87	2011	18.34	30.31
1996	23.92	47.14	2012	21.48	28.38
1997	22.62	48.2	2013	23.01	25.99
1998	23.34	51.95	2014	22.44	26.27
1999	21.75	54.3	2015	22.76	25.36
2000	21.59	40.37	2016	19.85	23.93
2001	20.5	40.32	2017	19.29	27.02
2002	20.53	42.51	2018	19.28	27.86
2003	19.56	39.96	2019	19.81	33.62
2004	17.44	33.93	2020	21.18	38.51
2005	14.77	28.54	2021	19.29	37.45

Source: World Development Indicators (WDI), World Bank.

massive increase in poverty due to the closure of industries and the resulting employment losses, as well as cuts in government expenditures on health and education, which are mostly consumed by the poor. External debt as a % of GDP for Pakistan and India in Table 2 shows that India borrowed initially from the IMF, but has since pursued more prudent financial policies. That is why external debt as a % of GDP has been manageable in India. But frequent IMF programmes have taken their toll on Pakistan's economy, politics and the social fabric. Notice the very high rates during the 1990s with external debt as a % of GDP climaxing to 54% in 1999. Such a high percentage of external debt as a % of GDP has had a very damaging impact on Pakistan both on account of the harsh IMF conditionalities as well as the exit of large amounts of revenues to service debts.

In the 1990s, due to a decline in the growth rate, employment and per capita income poverty increased to 50% in Pakistan, but was as high as 85%

Table 3. Poverty headcounts — Pakistan and India.

Year	Poverty headcount ratio at $2.15 a day (2017 PPP)	
	IND	PAK
2004	39.9	20.2
2011	22.5	9.6
2015	18.7	5.1
2018	11.1	4.9

Source: World Development Indicators (WDI), World Bank.

in interior Sind according to the Asian Development Bank. Table 3 contains data on poverty for Pakistan and India in terms of the percentage of population living below the poverty line. The data reveals that since the 1990s the situation has improved considerably in Pakistan. But these data are only till 2018, when the current programme was signed with the IMF, which has made a major dent in the standards of living in Pakistan. This is mainly due to substantial increase in electricity, gas and petrol prices and increase in the lending rate to 22%, which is the highest in the world. These giving rise to massive increase in the Consumer Price Index (CPI), particularly prices of food items and utilities is making life unbearable for the people. Moreover, Table 3 reveals not only that the percentage of people living below the poverty line in India is much higher than Pakistan, but due to the large size of the Indian population, the number of people pushed into poverty is frightening. The table shows that 39.9% of the population in India was living below the poverty line in 2004. With a population of 1.136 billion in 2004 and 39.9% living below the poverty line means that more than 45 crore people were living below the poverty line in India in 2004.

3. Model Specification and Results

We formulated our external debt (ED) model in this section. Our main interest is to study how military expenditure by these two large Himalayan neighbours is affecting their external debt. Our dependent variable is therefore external debt as a percentage of GDP and is denoted by ED. And military expenditure as a percentage of GDP is the explanatory variable of interest. Another variable that affects external debt is the rate of exchange. The decline in the value of the currency increases the size of external debt in local currency, while an increase in the value of the currency reduces external debt and is denoted by ER. An increase in GDP per capita in US$ affects external debt through making external debts sustainable. While a decline in GDP per capita makes external debts unsustainable. We denote this variable by Y, while total reserves as a percentage of GDP is represented by TR. I used panel data containing two cross-sections for the period 1990–2021 for India and Pakistan to estimate equation (1) which is given below:

$$ED_{it} = \beta_{oi} + \beta_1 ME_{it} + \beta_2 ER_{it} + \beta_3 Y_{it} + \beta_4 TR_{it} + u_{it} \qquad (1)$$

where β_{oi} is the constant term, β_1, β_2, β_3 and β_4 are the coefficients, and u_{it} is the error term.

The results from estimating equation (1) are presented in Table 4. We find a positive and significant relationship between military spending and external debt. One-unit increase in military spending increases external debt by 8.4 units, which is significant at the 100% confidence level. GDP per capita has a negative and significant impact on external debt, which makes sense as an increase in GDP per capita through making revenues available will have a negative impact on external debt, while the exchange rate has a positive but insignificant impact on external debt. Total reserves have a negative but insignificant impact on external debt. The value of R^2 is high, reflecting that almost 85% of the variation in external debt has been explained by the model.

4. Recommendations and Conclusion

In this study, we have focused on the external debt distress of two largest South Asian economies, Pakistan and India, during 1990–2021. The failure to resolve outstanding disputes has pushed these countries to import huge quantities of armaments, increasing their external indebtedness with all its ugly manifestations. It has pushed several crore people into poverty by exporting the jobs promised to them at the time of elections as in India. In 2004, 39.9% of the population was living below the poverty line in India, which means more than 45 crore people were pushed into poverty. While Pakistan has been borrowing heavily from the IMF since 1988, resulting in decline in growth rates, de-industrialisation, rendering several lakh people unemployed, massive reduction in development expenditures, increasing the imbalance in the distribution of income and increase in poverty like

Table 4. External debt determinants Pakistan and India.

Variables	Dependent variable: ED Method: Panel least squares			
	Coefficients	Std. error	t-statistics	Prob.
C	4.015	2.5015	1.6050	0.1138
ME	8.4809	1.0893	7.7851*	0.0000
Y	−0.0047	−3.2602	3.2602**	0.0019
ER	0.0225	0.6436	0.6436	0.5223
TR	−206216.8	−0.8219	−0.8219	0.4144
R-squared				0.8475
F-statistic				81.999*
Prob. (F-statistic)				0.0000

Notes: *significant at the 100% confidence level.
**significant at the 98% confidence level.

never before. These giving rise to a massive social crisis in the form of kidnappings for ransom, burglaries, suicides, etc., and the political fallout has taken the country towards extreme polarisation and crisis. These are attributable both to the harsh conditionalities and a major chunk of resources exiting the economy to service debts. The external debt distress has given rise to several other distresses to more than 1.7 billion people who live in the sub-continent. Naively we keep looking towards big powers to resolve our problems, little realising that they are the major beneficiaries of the arms race in the sub-continent. They are most interested in wealth creation and bringing prosperity to their countries, rather than fulfilling their global leadership roles of making the world a better place. The civil society in Pakistan and India need to play their roles to pressurise their governments to resolve their outstanding disputes, especially the core issue of Jammu and Kashmir. This will help to remove the debt distress that has engulfed the sub-continent due to the import of arms, causing an increase in external indebtedness, decline in economic growth, loss of employment opportunities due to de-industrialisation and/or exporting jobs to armament producing countries, loss of development, increase in poverty with very adverse consequences on the socio-political fabric.

We need to address the all-important question of how to bring peace to the sub-continent. Should Pakistan and India resolve their major conflicts as European countries did prior to integrating their economies? In other words, should we emphasise geo-strategic rather than geo-economics? Or should we emphasise geo-economics and leave geo-strategic matters for some future date? This implies continuing with our present strategy of continuing to import arms, increasing our external indebtedness, giving rise to the various crises discussed earlier, but making some attempts at conflict resolution? Will the arms exporting countries greatly benefiting from continued import of their arms allow us to resolve our conflicts? The continued import of arms and the resulting external indebtedness causing growth, development, distributional, and social and political crises discussed earlier will continue to tear the socio-economic-political fabric of the sub-continent. Will the conflicts and the sufferings of those affected by the conflicts continue to some unknown future date? And in view of the attitude of the leadership to settle the conflicts unilaterally, will there be anything left to be settled while we are pursuing geo-economics?

References

Abbas, S. and Wizarat, S. (2018). Military expenditure and external debt in South Asia: A panel data analysis. *Peace Economics, Peace Science and Public Policy*, *24*(3), 1–7.

Abbas, S., Wizarat, S., and Mansoor, S. (2020). External debt distress in South Asia: Evidence from panel data analysis. *South Asian Journal of Macroeconomics and Public Finance*, *2*(9), 221–236.

Abdel-Khalek, G., Mazloum, M. G., and El Zeiny, M. R. M. (2020). Military expenditure and economic growth: The case of India. *Review of Economics and Political Science*, *5*(2), 116–135.

Ajmair, M., Hussain, K., Abbassi, F. A., and Gohar, M. (2018). The impact of military expenditure on economic growth of Pakistan. *Applied Economics and Finance*, *5*(2), 41–48.

Ando, S. (2009). The impact of defense expenditure on economic growth: Panel data analysis based on Feder model. *International Journal of Economic Policy Studies*, *4*(1), 141–154.

Atesoglu, H. S. (2009). Defense spending and aggregate output in the United States. *Defence and Peace Economics*, *20*(1), 21–26.

Azam, M. and Feng, Y. (2017). Does military expenditure increase external debt? Evidence from Asia. *Defence and Peace Economics*, *28*(5), 550–567.

Bacha, E. L. (1990). A three-gap model of foreign transfers and GDP growth rate in developing countries. *Journal of Development Economics*, *32*(3), 279–296.

Batchelor, P., Dunne, J. P., and Saal, D. S. (2000). Military spending and economic growth in South Africa. *Defense and Peace Economics*, *11*(4), 553–571.

Benedict, I., Ehikioya, I., and Asin, O. (2014). Determinants and sustainability of external debt in a deregulated economy: A co-integration analysis from Nigeria (1986–2010). *American International Journal of Contemporary Research*, *4*(6), 201–214.

Benoit, E. (1973). *Defense and Economic Growth in Developing Countries*. D.C. Health and Co., Lexington Books, Boston.

Benoit, E. (1978). Growth and defense in developing countries. *Economic Development and Cultural Change*, *26*(2), 271–280.

Deger, S. (1986). Economic development and defense expenditure. *Economic Development and Cultural Change*, *35*(1), 179–196.

Deger, S. and Sen, S. (1990). Military security and the economy: Defense expenditure in India and Pakistan. In Hartley, K. and Sandler, T. (Eds.) *The Economics of Defense Spending*. Routledge, London.

Deger, S. and Smith, R. (1983). Military expenditure and growth in less developed countries. *Journal of Conflict Resolution*, *27*(2), 335–353.

Deger, S. and Smith, R. (1985). Military expenditure and development: The economic linkages. *IDS Bulletin*, *16*(4), 49–54.

Dunne, P. and Skons, E. (2011). The changing military industrial complex. http://ideas.repec.org/p/uwe/wpaper/1104.htm.

Halicioglu, F. (2003). An econometrical analysis of effects of aggregate defense spending on aggregate output. *METU International Conference in Economics/VII*, Turkey, September.

Halicioglu, F. (2004). Defense spending and economic growth in Turkey: An empirical application of new macroeconomics theory. *Review of Middle East Economics and Finance*, *2*(3), 34–43.

Kaldor, M. (1976). The military in development. *World Development*, *4*(6), 459–482.

Knight, M., Loayza, N., and Villanueva, D. (1996). The peace dividend: Military spending cuts and economic growth. *Staff Papers — International Monetary Fund*, *43*(1), 1–37.

Lim, D. (1983). Another look at growth and defense in less developed countries. *Economic Development and Cultural Change*, *31*(2), 377–384.

Rothschild, W. K. (1973). Military expenditure, exports and growth. *Kyklos*, *26*(4), 804–815.

Roux, A. (1996). Defense expenditure and economic growth in South Africa. *Journal of Studies in Economics and Econometrics*, *20*(1), 19–34.

Tiruneh, M. W. (2004). An empirical investigation into the determinants of external indebtedness. *Prague Economic Papers*, *3*, 261–277.

Waheed, A. (2017). Determinants of external debt: A panel data analysis for oil and gas exporting and importing countries. *International Journal of Economics and Financial Issues*, 7(1), 234–240.

Wizarat, S. (2011). Chapter 16: Bypassing the IMF. *Fighting Imperialism Liberating Pakistan*. Centre for Research and Statistics (CRS), Karachi.

Wizarat, S. (2022, December). *Alternative to the IMF and Other Out of the Box Solutions*. Partridge Publishing, Singapore.

Wooldridge, J. M. (2010). *Econometric Analysis of Cross Section and Panel Data*. The MIT Press, USA.

World Development Indicators, *Various Issues*. World Bank, Washington DC.

Yildirim, J. and Ocal, N. (2006). Arms race and economic growth: The case of India and Pakistan. *Defence and Peace Economics*, 17(1), 37–45.

Yildirim, J., Sezgin, S., and Ocal, N. (2005). Military expenditure and economic growth in Middle Eastern countries: A dynamic panel data analysis. *Defence and Peace Economic*, 16(4), 283–295.

Part III

Bilateralism versus Multilateralism: Potential Trade Model in South Asia

Chapter 9

Regional Geopolitics and Economic Fallout of COVID-19: Policy Options for India

Rakesh Kumar

Deen Dayal Upadhyaya College, University of Delhi, New Delhi, India

saini_rakeshindia@yahoo.co.in

Abstract

This chapter presents the facts on policy challenges and lessons for India at the domestic and regional level to mitigate the economic toll caused by COVID-19. Amid the regional geopolitics coupled with potential constraints in South Asia, India has a limited scope for leveraging intraregional trade amid the COVID-19 crisis. For this purpose, the chapter emphasises the relevance of trade owing to the proposed India–Bangladesh Free Trade Agreement (FTA) in a wider perspective. The proposed econometric investigation suggests that the existing India–Bangladesh bilateral trade positively affects the economic growth rates of the two countries in the short run, and the economic growth rate of India in the long run as well. In current circumstances, it is high time India and Bangladesh leverage the bilateral trade for mutual benefits. India being the largest regional economy requires to engage Bangladesh through addressing the main concerns of the latter in taking forward the bilateral FTA.

Keywords: COVID-19, free trade agreement, bound testing, geopolitics, SAARC.

1. Introduction

The categorisation of the outbreak of COVID-19 as a pandemic by the World Health Organization (WHO) fuelled panic worldwide. The spread of the disease posed multifaceted economic threats to the world economy. The pandemic started at the end of December 2019 in the city of Wuhan of China, placing the entire city under effective quarantine. Soon after, the measures were extended for two more cities from Hubei province to curb the disease. The top five hardest-hit countries by the pandemic were the United States, India, Brazil, Russia and the UK with over 57 million cases and 1 million death tolls (See World Health Organisation Reports, 2021).

India remarkably contained the death toll due to COVID-19 because of early preventive measures involving the shutting down of educational institutions, commercial complexes and complete screening of international arrivals at all the airports. India, Pakistan, Bangladesh and Sri Lanka, and other smaller nations which are home to 1.8 billion people in South Asia, had so far reported comparatively smaller cases of infection and death toll of human lives. However, experts feared that they could be the next epicentre if strict preventive measures were not taken at full scale.

Acknowledging the crisis, the meeting of the leaders from the South Asia Association for Regional Cooperation (SAARC) through video conference at the initiative of Indian Prime Minister Narendra Modi highlighted the need for chalking out a coordinated strategy at the regional level. The regional leaders met after five years since the cancellation of the 19th SAARC meeting scheduled to be held in Pakistan in November 2016 after the boycott by India on the grounds of terrorist attacks on its military establishment (see Kumar, 2020b). In the meeting, the Emergency Fund aiming to cope-with the pandemic at the regional level was proposed, taking the total contribution worth $21.3 million coupled with other important decisions.

The economic fallout, however, was expected to be wide and far-reaching for India. India was believed to be the most affected country among the others in terms of its economy as its top trading partners like China, the United States, Japan and South Korea, including the European countries Germany, France, UK and Spain were under extensive lockdown. All eight countries had been the top trade partners for India, which serve as the destination of over 33.0% of total exports and source of over 32.0% of total imports. Given that, the external sector of India was under serious trouble until the resumption of normal economic activities in the trade partner countries. Therefore, India could feel it is high time to engage the South Asian countries as potential trade partners.

As of now, India serves as a source of over 61% of total trade for Nepal. Similarly, India is the source of 81% of total trade for Bhutan, hence the possibilities of further expansion of trade with the two countries are limited. India's trade with Pakistan, which is the second largest economy in South Asia, is under suspension. Similarly, the small consumer base of Sri Lanka and the Maldives and terrorism in Afghanistan are the main problems among the others, offering limited opportunities for India.

Given that, Bangladesh which is home to 161.4 million people, can be a potential trade partner for India under the current circumstances. As of now, India enjoys a dominant position and has a comparative advantage in trade at the intra- and inter-regional levels as compared to Bangladesh (see Islam, 2018). The two countries are in the final stage in finalising the bilateral agreement on the Comprehensive Economic Partnership Agreement covering the trade and services for mutual benefits. The study of Rahman *et al.* (2011) shows that the Indian market offers vast opportunities for exports from Bangladesh. Over the years, the number of products in the export basket of Bangladesh has increased, coupled with shifting the focus from the export of traditional products to the newer products. However, the growing role of China in Bangladesh's economy in recent years has posed potential challenges for Indian engagement with the former due to strained and uncertain political relations (see Sahoo, 2013).

The existing empirical study highlights that trade expansion between India and Bangladesh owing to the India–Bangladesh free trade agreement will benefit both countries in the long run. For example, Bandara and Yu (2003) explore the role of SAFTA in expanding trade in the South Asian region by utilising the global computable general equilibrium (GCE) model. The results show that India will get maximum economic welfare from SAFTA, while small countries will gain marginally. The study emphasises the bilateral trade agreements for maximum gain more than that of multilateral trade agreements like SAFTA. Another study, for example, by Siriwardana (2004) shows that the Indo-Sri Lanka Free Trade Agreement offers gains to both countries, Sri Lanka, on the other hand, will witness maximum economic gain if this trade agreement is extended to other SAARC nations. Similarly, Siriwardana and Yang (2007) show that the free trade agreement between India and Bangladesh tends to provide a high scope for expansion of trade between the two countries. This agreement will create gains for Bangladesh in the expansion of trade and a slowdown in the growing trade imbalance.

1.1. *COVID-19: Economic consequences*

The economic consequences caused by pandemic were apparent and posed serious socio-economic threats across the world. The fact that the virus had spread across the United States had further triggered the fear of economic uncertainty. The pandemic triggered the fear of recession worldwide, with the deceleration of the annual global growth rate of 2.9% during 2019, much lower than the earlier projection of 3.6% (see World Economic Outlook, 2020). The global economy was projected to contract sharply by 3% in 2020, much worse than the financial crisis of 2008–2009 caused by the US subprime crisis, the report added. The stalled lockdown to contain the virus means that the effect of COVID-19 would cause a slowdown in global production due to the closure of production centres in the United States and China as both countries account for over 20% of world exports. The immediate effect was the disruption in the global supply chain, which hampered the smooth supply of commodities and services. The cascading effects included job loss and contraction of allied economic activities including the service sector.

The impact of COVID-19 proved disastrous for the hospitability and tourism industry. The tourism industry witnessed the job loss of 50 million worldwide as per estimates of the World Tour and Travel Council. The outbreak of pandemic severely affected the demand for and supply of travel, as per the report of the UN World Tourism Organisation. The international tourists decelerated between 20% and 30% in 2020, which translates into a loss of between US$30 and US$50 billion in spending by international visitors, the report adds.

Translating the economic meltdown in growth numbers, the GDP growth rates are expected to decelerate about 0.5% for China and Japan, and about 0.4% for the United States, triggering the economic contagion as per the report of the United Nation Conference on Trade and Development (UNCTAD). For the first time since the great recession of the 1930s, the advanced economies, and emerging markets, and developing economies plunged into recession due to pandemic. For the FY 2020, the advanced economies were projected to experience a 5.4% contraction in output compared to emerging markets and developing economies excluding China with normal growth rate is expected to contract by 5.0% as per the World Economic Outlook (2020).

The oil-exporting countries, believed to be the worst hit in the current scenario, had witnessed a heavy shortfall in the demand for fuel due to lockdown across the world. The steep fall in crude oil price even below $20 within a month due to an oil price war between Saudi Arabia and Russia after the fallout of the OPEC+ agreement over production cut further worsened the trouble for oil-exporting countries. The high volatility in world equity markets triggered by prevalent economic despair wiped off the $9 trillion market capitalisation immediately after the outbreak of pandemic.

2. South Asia: An Overview

2.1. *Regional political economy*

Until that time, the South Asia region was the fastest-growing region among the different regions of the world, posting the highest growth in GDP in the last decades. The outbreak of COVID-19 had unprecedented consequences in terms of trade and human life for South Asia. South Asia witnessed a fall in growth rate to a range between 1.8% and 2.8% in 2020 depending upon the extent of lockdown across the region, a sharp decline from the earlier estimates of a regional growth rate of 6.3% (see World Bank Report on South Asia Economic Focus, 2020). It was noted that South Asia accounts for 2.54% and 3.38% in global exports and imports of goods and services, respectively. India, despite being the largest economy in South Asia, has regional trade under 5% because of high trade barriers. In fact, South Asia faces intraregional political differences, in addition to perceived and actual threats to national security, which pose major challenges hindering high economic integration.

The hostile relations between India and Pakistan have acted as the gravity for geopolitics in South Asia. Both countries have a troubling track record of conflicts caused by unresolved territorial disputes and proxy of terrorism. It has led the armed forces confrontations between India and Pakistan on many occasions since the independence in 1947. As a result, deeper trade ties among the countries from the region could not evolve till date. Pakistan, which was one of the major trade partners of India until the war of 1965 between the two countries, has reduced to US$2 billion of exports and source of US$495 million of imports for India as of now. Over the years, it has become difficult for any Indian government to engage Pakistan in meaningful dialogue to maintain peace in the region because of having a double-edged policy of talks and proxy terrorism simultaneously by the latter (see Misra, 2017). As of now, Pakistan has unilaterally suspended all its trade with India after the Indian action of revocation of Article 370 that grants an autonomous status to Jammu and Kashmir and 35A that provides special rights and privileges to the people of the state.

India on the other hand enjoys uninterrupted harmonious diplomatic trade relations with the other countries in the region. The trade volume of India with other South Asian countries is rising in the last decades; however, it is not as high as it should be (see Kumar, 2020b). After independence, South Asian countries directed their economic policies towards the goal of self-sufficiency through import substitutions rather than working on specialisation in the production of certain products based on the availability of resources. A rise in intraregional trade volume has been perceived as increasing dominance and dependency on India, rather than exploiting the potential opportunities that larger markets like India offers (see Kher, 2012). However, the rise of India as one of the emerging largest economies of the world with a GDP of US$2.40 trillion has motivated the neighbouring countries toward conducive engagement with India.

2.2. *Regional trade cooperation*

Acknowledging the benefits of intraregional trade, seven nations from South Asia (India, Bangladesh, Pakistan, Sri Lanka, Nepal, Bhutan and Maldives) formed the SAARC as a regional trade bloc in 1985 despite political differences. It was believed to be a top multilateral agreement for the promotion of regional cooperation in a wider perspective (see Kumar, 2020b). Under SAARC, the South Asian Preferential Trading Arrangement (SAPTA) was established in 1995 aiming to foster regional cooperation for the social and economic progress of the people. The policy arrangements were made consisting of preferential treatment through lower import tariffs on selected items across the product categories.

Further, a more comprehensive trade agreement — South Asia Free Trade Agreement (SAFTA) — initiated in January 2004, became fully operational with effect from January 2006. Under the agreement, India being the non-least developing country (NLDCs) was required to lower the tariff rates to 20% in the next two years, subsequently to the range of 0–5% through annual cuts till the end of 2013. While the least developing countries (LDCs) like Bangladesh, Maldives, Nepal, Bhutan and Afghanistan had additional three years time frame to reduce tariffs to 0–5% till the end of 2016. Despite decades passing since the creation of SAARC, it is far from achieving the desired objectives (see Kher, 2012). Further, in compliance to World Trade Organization (WTO), all the SAARC countries accord the Most Favoured Nation (MFN) status in a reciprocal way, except Pakistan, which has not given MFN status to India. Recently, India has revoked MFN status accorded to Pakistan after the latter was held responsible for a deadly suicide terrorist attack on the Central Reserve Police Force (CRPF) of India in Pulwama (Jammu amd Kashmir) in which 40 soldiers lost their lives (see *Economic Times*, 2019).

It is noted that India stands as the net exporter to South Asia with exports (imports) worth US$24.64 billion (US$4.6 billion) respectively in 2018. In terms of trade share, South Asia serves as a destination for over 7.65% of exports and a source of over 0.74% of imports for India. India's top exports include engineering products, which contribute about 33% followed by textiles and minerals, which contribute about 20% and 14% of total exports to South Asia, respectively. India serves as the top trading partner for Bhutan, as India is the destination for 90.7% of Bhutan's total exports and a source of 82% of Bhutan's total imports. Under the Indo-Bhutan Trade Agreements, free trade between the two countries takes place with no Basic Custom Duty on the imports from and exports to Bhutan. Similarly, India serves as the largest trade partner of Nepal, with a destination for 54.4% of Nepal's total exports and a source of 73.1% of Nepal's total imports. It is noted that the total trade volume of India with other countries from the region has grown in the last decades. This shows that India has maintained favourable trade relations in the region; however, Pakistan, which is the second largest economy in the region, maintains poor trade relations with India despite being accorded MFN status by the latter.

As per the recent report of the Ministry of Commerce and Industry, India (2018), Bangladesh stands as the largest trade partner for India from the region with US$9.82 billion trade volume accounting for a 1.21% trade share. Figure 1 shows that India's exports to and imports

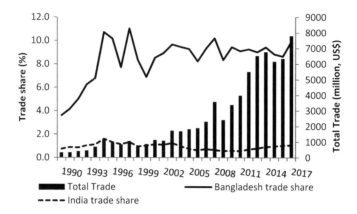

Figure 1. India–Bangladesh total trade volume and trade share.
Source: World Integrated Trade Solution, World Bank.

of goods and services from Bangladesh have grown manifold in the last decades due to pro-trade policies between the two countries. The top products in the export basket of India to Bangladesh are textiles and clothing (28.53% of total exports), transportation goods (13.77% of total exports), mechanical and electrical goods (10.77% of total exports), fuel (10.03% of total exports) and chemicals (9.13% of total exports) among the others, which accounts for 72.24% of total exports. While India's import basket includes textiles and clothing (60% of total imports), metals (9.88% of total imports), plastic and rubber (4.78% of total imports), transportation (4.45% of total imports) and food products (3.74% of total imports) amounting to 82.69% of total imports (see Table 1). The trade between the two countries has increased immensely in the last years; however, trade imbalance has not been just an economic issue for Bangladesh, it has generated visible political resonance affecting the political relations between the two countries (see Sikdar, 2006).

3. Data, Research Methods and Results

The proposed research employs a robust econometric procedure for testing the short- and long-run impact of India–Bangladesh bilateral trade shares on economic growth rates of the two countries. The

Table 1. India's total exports and imports (in US$, million), 2018.

Product group	Imports from Bangladesh	Total imports	Export to Bangladesh	Total exports
1. Animal products	23.03	240.26	50.15	10630.02
2. Chemicals	37.32	57955.76	798.16	44563.69
3. Food Products	40.44	3403.36	296.17	6798.52
4. Footwear	18.94	1007.33	12.07	3104.07
5. Fuels	0.08	205107.74	876.55	48563.41
6. Hides and Skins	32.33	1356.52	15.34	3287.31
7. Mach and Elec.	15.65	115462.32	941.87	32239.45
8. Metals	106.71	39812.18	705.73	26585.54
9. Minerals	15.94	10602.56	153.89	3901.81
10. Miscellaneous	4.71	19141.04	113.66	6380.75
11. Plastic or Rubber	51.66	23117.65	384.63	11027.41
12. Stone and Glass	2.03	83103.36	30.54	43121.35
13. Textiles and Clothing	647.84	8843.02	2493.00	37010.96
14. Transportation	48.09	17286.01	1203.74	24318.59
15. Vegetable	23.29	21542.05	579.27	18049.82
16. Wood	12.07	9964.45	84.58	2708.88
All products (1)–(16)	1080.15	617945.60	8739.35	322291.57

Source: World Integrated Trade Solution, World Bank.

sample data consists of the annual observations of sample variables for the period: 1990–2017, which are taken from the online databases of Asian Development Bank (ADB) and the World Bank. In addition, the study also uses two explanatory variables — gross capital formation (GCF) representing the physical investment and domestic credit to the private sector (CPS) representing the financial development for both countries — which are employed in the modelling. Both the variables are taken as the ratio of GDP (% of GDP), hence capturing the relative importance of domestic physical investment and financial development on the GDP growth rate of the respective country. The domestic credit to the private sector includes all credits to different sectors, which are extended by the financial sector consisting of monetary authorities, money banks and other financial corporations. The main consideration of selecting the sample period is the availability of the data of the sample variables for both countries. The long-run multivariate cointegration among the sample variables to be estimated is expressed as:

$$GDP_t = c_0 + c_1 TS_t + c_2 GCF_t + c_3 CPS_t + \varepsilon_t \quad (1)$$

where GDP_t is the GDP growth rate of the country, TS is the bilateral trade share, GCF_t is the gross capital formation, CPS_t is the domestic credit to private sector, and ε_t is the error term with zero mean and constant variance.

3.1. *Unit root test*

The application of econometric models requires testing the order of integration and stationary properties of sample variables. The sample variables with non-stationary tendency can generate biased and spurious results. To establish the order of integration, researchers principally use the augmented Dicky Fuller (ADF) test at the level and at the first difference of given variables. However, Perron (1989) proposes that stationary variables may produce spurious results if potential structural breaks are ignored in the data. Therefore, the potential impact of structural breaks should be robustly counted while determining the stationary property and order of integration of the variables. The structural breaks may occur when there is a shift in policy accounting substantial impact on the economic system in the country. ADF test takes the form of a unit root test as proposed by Perron (1989) if the known structural break is incorporated in the data. Perron (1989) proposed three different models for testing the order of integration and stationary property of variables with known structural breaks. These are (i) the crash model, if known structural break tends to occur in the intercept, (ii) the changing growth model if known structural break tends to occur in the slope and (iii) the crash-cum-growth model, if known structural breaks tend to occur in intercept and slope. The proposed study employs the following models, symbolically shown as:

Crash model:

$$\Delta y_t = \mu + \beta t + \theta DU_t + \alpha y_{t-1} + \sum_{i=1}^{k} c_i \Delta y_{t-i} + \varepsilon_t \quad (2)$$

Crash-cum-growth model:

$$\Delta y_t = \mu + \beta t + \theta DU_t + \alpha y_{t-1} + \gamma DT_t + \sum_{i=1}^{k} c_i \Delta y_{t-i} + \varepsilon_t \qquad (3)$$

where Δ is first difference operator, ε_t is error term, DU_t is dummy variable for a mean shift-break occurs at time TB, T is an index of time, DT_t is corresponding trend and shift in the variable, where

$$DU_t = \begin{cases} 1 & \text{if } t > TB \\ 0 & \text{otherwise} \end{cases}$$

and

$$DT_t = \begin{cases} t - TB & \text{if } t > TB \\ 0 & \text{otherwise} \end{cases}$$

The null hypothesis is tested as $\alpha = 0$, where the time series y_t contains a unit root with a drift without any structural break. While the alternative hypothesis proposes $\alpha < 0$, where time series y_t contains one-time break, which occurs at a known point of time. The proposed study considers the implementation of SAFTA as the structural break in the sample variables. This is because that all the South Asian countries have witnessed acceleration in trade after the implementation of SAFTA in the region (see Kumar, 2020a). The results of Perron (1989)'s unit root test for both the countries are shown in Table 2. It is noted that the null hypothesis for the non-stationary aspect is rejected at the first difference with the intercept, and with intercept and slope for both the countries. This shows that all the variables are stationary at first difference with significant structural breaks.

3.2. *Multivariate long-run cointegration*

We employ autoregressive distributed lag (ARDL) model as proposed by Pesaran and Shin (1999) and Pesaran *et al.* (2001) to test for the long-run cointegration among the sample variables and short and long-run impact of India–Bangladesh bilateral trade on the economic growth of two countries. The ARDL is more robust than the conventional procedures as proposed by Engle and Granger (1987) and Johansen (1988), hence the model provides more consistent results for small sample sizes. The model

Table 2. ADF test results.

	GDP	TS	GCF	CPS
ADF test at level with intercept				
India	−4.34**	−2.22	−0.15	0.88
	(0.025)	(0.500)	(0.500)	(0.500)
Bangladesh	−2.79	−3.19	−0.61	−0.61
	(0.100)	(0.100)	(0.500)	(0.500)
ADF test at level with intercept and slope				
India	−5.06***	−1.81	−0.13	−0.27
	(0.010)	(0.500)	(0.500)	(0.500)
Bangladesh	−5.25***	−3.20	−3.13	−3.13
	(0.010)	(0.100)	(0.400)	(0.100)
ADF test at first difference with intercept				
India	−5.44***	−5.64***	−5.60***	−4.87***
	(0.010)	(0.010)	(0.010)	(0.010)
Bangladesh	−7.35***	−5.34***	−4.21**	−4.21**
	(0.010)	(0.010)	(0.025)	(0.025)
ADF test at first difference with intercept and slope				
India	−4.45***	−5.74***	−5.57***	−4.25***
	(0.010)	(0.010)	(0.010)	(0.010)
Bangladesh	−7.46***	−5.68***	−4.21**	−4.21**
	(0.010)	(0.010)	(0.025)	(0.025)

Notes: probability values in bracket.
***,** denotes statistically significant at 1% and 5% level of significance.

is also suitable when dummy variables and different lag lengths for given variables have to be used in the system, which is not possible in the case of conventional techniques. The ARDL proposes the dependent variable as a function of its lagged values, and lagged and current values of independent variables. Equation (1) is parameterised in the ARDL model to be estimated, symbolically written as:

$$\Delta \text{GDP}_t = \alpha_0 + \lambda_1 \text{GDP}_{t-1} + \lambda_2 \text{TS}_{t-1} + \lambda_3 \text{GCF}_{t-1} + \lambda_4 \text{CPS}_{t-1}$$
$$+ \sum_{i=1}^{p} a_i \Delta \text{GDP}_{t-i} + \sum_{i=0}^{p} b_i \Delta \text{TS}_{t-i} + \sum_{i=0}^{p} c_i \Delta i_{t-i}$$
$$+ \sum_{i=0}^{p} d_i \Delta \text{CPS}_{t-i} + \gamma D + \varepsilon_t \qquad (4)$$

Here α_0 is constant, $\lambda_1 \ldots \lambda_4$ are long run multipliers, Δ is first difference operator, coefficients a_i, b_i, c_i and d_i represent the short run impact of explanatory variables on the dependent variable, and ε_t is error term.

Having found a confirmed structural break in bilateral trade due to the expansion of regional trade caused by SAFTA in South Asia, we introduce a dummy variable (D) in the model. The dummy variable has the value '0' before 2006 and '1' thereafter. The ARDL estimation involves two stages. The first stage is to establish the long-run cointegration among the variables as shown in equation (1). Having confirmed long-run cointegration, the second stage estimates the short- and long-run coefficients simultaneously with Error Correction Term (ECT). The first stage requires the variables to be integrated of order at level i.e. $I(0)$, at first difference i.e. $I(1)$, or mix order, while the second stage requires the variables to be integrated at first difference.

The ARDL model proposes the null hypothesis, i.e. $\lambda_1 = \lambda_2 = \lambda_3 = \lambda_4 = 0$, of non-significant long-run cointegration against the alternative hypothesis, i.e. $\lambda_1 \neq \lambda_2 \neq \lambda_3 \neq \lambda_4 \neq 0$, of significant cointegration, which exists among the variables. This hypothesis can be tested by estimating the F-statistic under the bound test, and subsequently comparing with bound critical values as proposed by Pesaran et al. (2001). If the F-statistic is higher than the upper bond of critical values, then the null hypothesis of non-significant long-run cointegration is rejected. If F-statistic is less than the lower bound of critical values, then the null hypothesis of non-significant long-run cointegration is accepted. Otherwise, the results are inconclusive.

Turning to the results of bound test for equation (1), the F-statistic for Bangladesh is F (GDP/TS, GCF, CPS) = 6.62, and for India is F (GDP/TS, GCF, CPS) = 10.82. The relevant upper bound critical value is 5.61 and lower bound critical value is 4.29 at a 1% level of significance. It is noted that the F-statistic for both the countries are found greater than the upper bound critical values, highlighting the null hypothesis of no long-run cointegration is rejected for both the countries. This shows that a significant long-run cointegration exists between the variables when the GDP is taken as the dependent variable. Therefore, we conclude that bilateral trade share, GCF, and CPS have a significant long-run impact on the economic growth rates of both countries. The results are consistent with existing studies that support the trade-led growth hypothesis for developing countries like India and Bangladesh (see Bandara and Yu, 2003; Siriwardana, 2004; Kumar, 2020b). The implication of the results is that the economic growth of India and Bangladesh have significant cointegration with bilateral trade in addition to financial development and physical infrastructure of both countries; hence both countries should leverage trade for mutual gains.

The best fit of models also requires to be examined, hence the proposed study conduct a CUSUM test for the stability of cocfficients as proposed by Pesaran *et al.* (2001). It is noted that the estimated coefficients fall within the bounds, which show that estimated coefficients are stable (see Appendix, Figure A1).

3.3. *Short- and long-run causality*

Having confirmed long-run cointegration, the next task is to estimate the coefficients for short and long-run causality for both the countries in the ECT framework as shown in equation (4). The ECT highlights the speed of adjustment in the dependent variable following the deviations of independent variables from the equilibrium position. In fact, it shows the joint impact of independent variables on the dependent variable simultaneously. The short- and long-run coefficients together with relevant diagnostic tests, when the GDP of Bangladesh is taken as a dependent variable are shown in Table 3. It shows that the net impact of bilateral trade share and gross capital formation are found positive in the short run on the economic growth of Bangladesh, while the short-run impact of domestic credit to the private sector is found negative.

The results for India are reported in Table 4. It shows that the impact of bilateral trade share is found significant positive in the short and long run on the economic growth of India. It is noted that coefficients of dummy variables for both the countries are found significant, highlighting the positive impact of trade expansion caused by SAFTA in South Asia on the economic growth rates of the two countries. The ECT coefficients for both countries are significantly negative and less than -1, showing the speed of recovery in GDP within the year following the deviations in bilateral trade, CPS and GFC (see Kumar, 2020a, 2020b). Further, the impact of CPS is found significantly negative for India and Bangladesh. It is noted that India has witnessed 4.8% GDP growth rate in 2019–20, the lowest reading in the last decades, because of a slowdown in domestic demand for credit in the wake of stress in the nonbanking financial sector. The results are consistent with the existing studies supporting the arguments of potential gains from the India–Bangladesh free trade agreement for both countries (see Bandara and Yu, 2003; Siriwardana and Yang, 2007; Kumar, 2020b).

Table 3. Short- and long-run causality for Bangladesh.

Long run causality		Short run causality	
TS	0.11		2.53***
	(0.308)	Constant	(0.000)
GCF	0.14		0.85***
	(0.186)	ΔGDP(−2)	(0.001)
CPS	−0.03		0.46***
	(0.396)	ΔGDP(−2)	(0.005)
			0.31***
		ΔTS	(0.001)
			−0.17**
		ΔTS(−1)	(0.032)
			1.16***
		ΔGCF	(0.000)
			−0.83***
		ΔGCF(−1)	(0.010)
			−0.02
		ΔCPS	(0.710)
			−0.16**
		ΔCPS(−1)	(0.038)
			−0.07
		ΔCPS(−2)	(0.282)
			2.14***
		D	(0.000)
R-square: 0.87.			
F-statistic: 8.57*** (0.000)			−1.63***
AIC: 1.17		ECT(−1)	(0.000)

Notes: Probability values in the parentheses.
***,** denotes statistically significant at 1% and 5% level of significance.

4. Conclusion and Implication

This chapter addresses the policy response for India in dealing with the economic fallout caused by COVID-19 at regional levels. Given the potential constraints at the regional level, India has limited options except for engaging Bangladesh for the expansion of bilateral trade through materialising the free trade agreement. India has enjoyed

Table 4. Short and long run causality for India.

Long run causality		Short run causality	
TS	5.72***		−12.74***
	(0.000)	Constant	(0.000)
GCF	0.21**		0.83***
	(0.011)	ΔGDP(−2)	(0.000)
CPS	0.03		0.25**
	(0.445)	ΔGDP(−2)	(0.053)
			1.36
		ΔTS	(0.407)
			−4.52***
		ΔTS(−1)	(0.009)
			−5.33***
		ΔTS(−2)	(0.002)
			−0.57***
		ΔCPS	(0.004)
			0.94**
		D	(0.050)
R-square: 0.88.			
F-statistic: 13.60*** (0.000)			−1.92***
AIC: 3.17		ECT(−1)	(0.000)

Notes: Probability values in the parentheses.
***,** denotes statistically significant at 1% and 5% level of significance.

harmonious diplomatic relations with Bangladesh since the latter came into existence in 1971. Hence, India should leverage the efforts for engaging Bangladesh for Comprehensive Economic Partnership. As of now, Bangladesh serves as the source of 1.6% of trade for India, while India serves as the source of 9.90% of trade for Bangladesh (see ADB Bank Database). This chapter employs a robust econometric procedure to investigate the potential impact of expanding trade on the economic growth of India and Bangladesh. The results report a significant long-run cointegration of GDP growth rate of two countries with the bilateral trade share. Further, the results highlight the short-run significant positive impact of bilateral trade shares on the economic growth rates of the two counties and the long-run impact on the economic growth rate of India.

The empirical results are highly insightful for policy implication, which points towards greater economic cooperation between India and Bangladesh for mutual benefits. Having diverse trade compositions, India requires the strengthening of economic engagement with Bangladesh in order to generate trade-led sustainable growth. As of now, the bilateral trade between the two countries is not at a level as high as it should be. Bangladesh needs to constructively work to become part of the production network of India in order to realise meaningful gains from the Comprehensive Economic Partnership. India, being the bigger economy in size, should address the main concerns of Bangladesh regarding the withdrawal of anti-dumping duty on jute products and removal of restrictions on the exports of farm products from India.

Appendix: Stability Testing of Coefficients

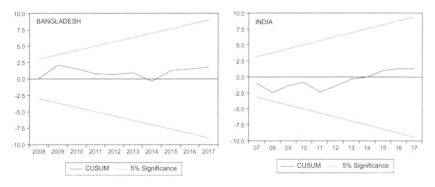

Figure A1. CUSUM test for stability of coefficients.

References

Asian Development Bank Database. https://aric.adb.org/integrationindicators.

Ding, D. and Masha, I. (2012). India's growth spillovers to South Asia. *IMF, Working Paper* 56, Washington, DC.

Economic Times. https://economictimes.indiatimes.com/news/politics-and-nation/no-longer-a-most-favoured-nation-will-that-hurt-pakistan/articleshow/68007834.cms?from=mdr.

Engle, R. F. and Granger, C. W. J. (1987). Cointegration and error correction representation: Estimation and testing. *Econometrica*, 55(2), 251–276.

Islam, A. M. (2018). Inter-and intra-industry trade relations between Bangladesh and India: Empirical results. *FIIB Business Review*, 7(4), 280–292.

Johansen, S. (1988). Statistical analysis of cointegrating vectors. *Journal of Economic Dynamics and Control*, 12(2&3), 231–254.

Kher, P. (2012). Political economy of regional integration in South Asia. *Background Paper on Regional Value Chain*, Paper No. 5, UNCTAD, Geneva.

Kumar, R. (2020a). Does trade interdependency lead linkages between stock markets? A case of South Asian countries. *International Journal of Emerging Markets*, 15(3), 490–506.

Kumar, R. (2020b). India & South Asia: Geopolitics, regional trade and economic growth spillovers. *Journal of International Trade and Economic Development*, 29(1), 69–88.

Ministry of Commerce and Industry. https://www.commerce.gov.in/.

Misra, A. (2007). An audit of the India-Pakistan peace process. *Australian Journal of International Affairs*, 61(4), 506–528.

Perron, P. (1989). The great crash, the oil price shock and the unit root hypothesis. *Econometrica*, 57, 1361–1401.

Pesaran, M. H., Shin, Y., and Smith, R. J. (2001). Bounds testing approaches to the analysis of level relationships. *Journal of Applied Econometrics*, 16(3), 289–326.

Rahman, M., Khan, T. I., Nabi, A., and Paul, T. K. (2011). Bangladesh's export opportunities in the Indian market: Addressing barriers and strategies for future. *South Asia Economic Journal*, 12(1), 117–141.

Sahoo, P. (2013). Economic relations with Bangladesh: China's ascent and India's decline. *South Asia Research*, 33(2), 123–139.

Sikdar, C. (2006). Prospects of bilateral trade between India and Bangladesh. *Foreign Trade Review*, 41(1), 27–45.

Siriwardana, M. (2004). An analysis of the impact of Indo-Lanka free trade agreement and its implications for free trade in South Asia. *Journal of Economic Integration*, 19(3), 568–589.

Siriwardana, M. and Yang, J. (2007). Effects of proposed free trade agreement between India and Bangladesh. *South Asian Economic Journal*, 8(1), 21–38.

UN World Tourism Organisation. https://www.unwto.org/tourism-covid-19.

United Nation Conference on Trade and Development (UNCTAD). https://unctad.org/en/PublicationsLibrary/gds_tdr2019_update_coronavirus.pdf.

World Bank. (2020). *South Asia Economic Focus, Spring 2020: The Cursed Blessing of Public Banks*. Washington, DC.

World Development Indicators. https://wits.worldbank.org/country-indicator.aspx?lang=en.

World Economic Outlook. https://www.imf.org/en/Publications/WEO/Issues/2020/04/14/weo-april-2020.

World Health Organisation Reports. https://www.who.int/emergencies/diseases/novel-coronavirus-2019.

Chapter 10

Institutional Setup and Export Performance: Evidence from South Asia

Suadat Hussain Wani[*,‡] and Effat Yasmin[†,§]

[*]*Indian Council of Social Science Research (ICSSR), New Delhi, India*

[†]*Department of Economics, University of Kashmir Hazartbal Srinagar, India*

[‡]*suadat.scholar@kashmiruniversity.net*

[§]*fgulwani@gmail.com*

Abstract

Using the augmented gravity model, the present study analyses bilateral exports between selected South Asian countries and their top trade partners. The panel data set between 1996 and 2020 is used and the Poisson pseudo-maximum likelihood (PPML) estimation technique is applied, accounting for heterogeneity, zero trade and endogeneity. The results confirm that regional trade agreements (RTAs) when supported by institutions play a significant role in the promotion of exports between participating nations. Further, trade integration between countries is positively impacted by the institutional framework. The main finding from this study is that RTAs reinforced by institutional framework play a significant role in advancement of trade between countries. Thus, these countries need to pay attention to infrastructural facilities to reduce trade costs. In addition, these member nations need to pay more attention to institutional reforms and increase regional trade cooperation among themselves.

Keywords: International trade, gravity model, institutional factors, regional trade agreement, panel data.

1. Introduction

The most common question that arises in policy circles is: do bilateral trade agreements (BTAs) and regional trade agreements (RTAs) increase trade? In the past decades, particularly from World War II, the number of BTAs and RTAs are continuously on the rise. However, empirical and theoretical evidence regarding the impact of these agreements remains inconclusive. The custom theory propounded by Viner (1950) concluded that regional integration could lead to a trade diversion or inefficient trade pattern by forcing customers to pay a higher price for items that can be imported from non-member countries at a lower price. Sorgho (2016) argues that imposition of tariff to protect the domestic firms could lead to inefficiency and make imports uncompetitive and adversely impact trade. However, many empirical studies (Frankel *et al.*, 1997; Hayakawa *et al.*, 2016) argue that regional integration could lead to trade creation, which may benefit both producers and consumers and improve trade pattern.

One school of thought (Clausing, 2001; Abrego *et al.*, 2005) that favours RTAs concluded that it can lead to trade creation. Another group of studies (Plummer, 2004; Pant and Sadhukhan, 2009) found that these agreements lead to both trade creation and diversion and their net effect cannot be determined or are ambiguous. Taking into consideration around seven RTAs, Carrere (2006) found that these RTAs indicate an increase in intra-regional trade coupled with reduction in imports from non-member countries. The study found trade diversion due to RTAs. However, there are many empirical studies (Baldwin and Venables, 1995; Head and Ries, 2004) that have shown that these agreements lead to enhancement of bilateral trade by increasing bargaining power of participating nations and promote the interests of favourable sectors. On the role of multilateral agreements and RTAs, Mujahid and Kalkuhl (2016) found that these agreements have significant positive impact on multilateral trade cooperation. Further RTAs are more effective than the membership of WTO in the facilitation of trade in food products among participating nations. Despite

Table 1. Intra-regional trade between different regions.

Region	Exports	Imports
East Asia and Pacific	50.87	50.99
Europe and Central Asia	69.55	66.58
Latin America and Caribbean	14.26	14.34
Middle East and North Africa	12.79	10.18
North America	30.1	18.45
Sub-Saharan Africa	26.1	16.72
South Asia	7.38	1.29
Trade in South Asia		
India	0.77	6.98
Pakistan	10.05	3.39
Bangladesh	1.91	14.18

Source: WITS, World Bank (2022).

contradictory views about the impact of these agreements as discussed above, the number of RTAs has continuously been on the rise in the past decades. The number of RTAs notified by the World Trade Organization was around 578 in August 2022.[1]

Given the role played by RTAs in other parts of the world in the enhancement of trade, South Asian countries[2] signed the South Asian Free Trade Area (SAFTA), which came into force in 2006, in addition to other BTAs to enhance trade (Akhter and Ghani, 2010). However, trade agreements have been more successful in Europe as compared to other regions of the world (Nawaz, 2020). Table 1 shows intra-regional trade among different regions. However, the picture is not encouraging in the case of South Asia as India, Pakistan and Bangladesh have a low volume of intra-regional trade.

Various studies (Hassan, 2001; Rahman *et al.*, 2006) show that SAFTA has been instrumental in increasing trade among South Asian countries. However, there are many other studies (Baysan *et al.*, 2006; Akhter and Ghani, 2010; Sultana and Asrat, 2014; Kathuria and Shahid, 2017; Abbas and Waheed, 2019) that have found SAFTA to be ineffective in increasing regional integration due to various reasons.

---

[1] http://rtais.wto.org/UI/Charts.aspx.
[2] India, Pakistan, Nepal, Bhutan, Bangladesh, Maldives and Afghanistan.

In light of these ambiguous results, recent literature (Gylfason *et al.*, 2015; Zhang *et al.*, 2020) has highlighted role of various institutions in promotion of BTA and RTA's between countries. With regard to South Asia, various studies (Kumar and Ahmed, 2015; Rynning, 2017; Wani and Mir, 2023) highlight factors that have restricted the progress of integration in this part of world. However, in the available literature, enough attention has not been paid to highlight the role of institutions in the regional integration of South Asia.

The present study contributes to the available literature in two ways. First, even though the number of empirical studies (Kumar and Ahmed, 2015; Wani and Mir, 2023) have highlighted various factors that obstruct the process of integration in South Asia, the role played by institutional factors have been ignored. This study provides new sights by applying an "interactive term of RTA and institutional setup", which highlights the role of institutions in making regional integration a success. Second, the present study attempts to address various econometric issues like multilateral resistance factors, endogeneity and heteroscedasticity by incorporating exporter-time, importer-time and country-pair fixed effect in the estimation technique.

In the section that follows, studies related to SAFTA and the role of institutions in trade cooperation are discussed. Section 3 presents the methodology, Section 4 highlights data description and discusses main findings and Section 5 concludes the study.

2. Review of Literature

As regards South Asia, various studies as discussed below argue that SAFTA has been instrumental in enhancing trade among member countries and can be beneficial for participating countries. Similarly, Hassan (2001) and Rahman *et al.* (2006) found opportunities for trade creation among the South Asian countries.

However, there are many other studies that have highlighted that SAFTA has been ineffective in enhancing regional integration due to various reasons. Baysan *et al.* (2006) argue that SAFTA has been ineffective due to small market size and high non-tariff restrictions in the region. According to Akhter and Ghani (2010), SAFTA may be beneficial for participating countries in the long term, but these countries were unable to reap the benefits of regional integration in the short run. Besides, Sultana and Asrat (2014) argue that high levels of protection, institutional factors and infrastructural hurdles have been the main reasons for the lower integration of these countries. In addition, Kathuria and Shahid (2017) concluded that political differences and weak regulatory frameworks negatively impact cooperation in this region. Besides, Rynning (2017) found that the exchange of ideas has not developed to the level to make regional cooperation successful. Finally, Abbas and Waheed (2019) argue that these countries need to revisit the RTA as SAFTA has been ineffective in creating trade opportunities.

Hassan *et al.* (2001) found a low magnitude of intra-trade among SAARC countries. Under the SAPTA framework, border trade needs to be liberalised and bilateral trade has to be strengthened through a separate set of concessions among these countries. Nag and Nandi (2006) concluded that there is positive trade complementarity between SAARC member countries. However, the current conditions of trade cooperation indicate contradictory results. This highlights the need for more integration among member countries for SAARC to be successful. Besides, Narayan (2010) argues that due to a lack of culture of cooperation, SAARC has been unable to achieve the expected outcomes as per the charter. Dembatapitiya and Weerahewa (2015) highlight that SAFTA has no significant impact on trade cooperation between member countries. However, BTAs significantly enhance trade between member countries and more bilateral trade agreements need to be signed. Muzaffar *et al.* (2017) has concluded that the time has come for prioritising development among member states to make regional cooperation a success story. Nawaz and Iqbal (2017) argue that due to non-institutional arrangements and less efficient institutions, SAFTA and Most Favoured Nation (MFN) prove to be ineffective. The study concludes that among member countries, trade agreements can contribute positively to trade cooperation only if they are reinforced by efficient institutions and a non-institutional framework. Gaurav and Bharti (2019) conclude that these nations need to reduce non-tariff barriers, ease rules of origin and make export basket complementary to boost regional trade. Bishwakarma and Hu (2022) argue that to make SAARC effective, it needs to be expanded and new members, particularly China, have to be made part of the group. The study highlights the paybacks of expansion in terms of trade, infrastructure and investment. Similarly, Shirazi and Iqbal (2022) emphasise the adoption of appropriate policy mechanism to enhance trade between member countries.

Studies (Francois and Manchin, 2013; De Mendonca, 2014) have shown that well-defined institutional setup enhances trade among the participating countries. Similarly, Naanwaan and Diarrossouba (2013) concluded that to enhance trade among countries, improvement in economic freedom index plays a positive role. Besides, Alhassan and Payaslioglu (2020) found that it is the economic institutions rather than political institutions that help to enhance trade cooperation among the member countries. In addition, Iqbal and Nawaz (2017) and Nawaz (2020) argue that for economic integration among countries, institutional setup plays an important role directly as well as indirectly. Similarly, Hou et al. (2021) found that institutional quality helps in the reduction of costs particularly related to trade of manufactured goods. Further, tariffs should be reduced and investments in transport facilities has to be increased to improve economic integration among countries.

3. Econometric Specification of Gravity Model

The gravity model is popularly known for its successful explanation of different types of flows like trade, tourism and migration. The model explains trade flow between set of countries as being proportional to their economic size, which is represented by GDP and inversely related to the geographical distance between them. The classical gravity model can be expressed as:

$$T_{ij} = G \frac{Y_i^\alpha * Y_j^\beta}{D_{ij}^\delta} \qquad (1)$$

where T_{ij} represents bilateral trade between country i and j, Y_i and Y_j denote national income of two countries, D_{ij} shows geographical distance, G is a constant and α, β, δ are parameters.

In addition to these variables, various other explanatory factors like GDP per capita, common border, common language, institutional factors and RTAs are included in the model. Thus, the linear form of equation (1) after adding these variables is:

$$\ln(E)_{ijt} = \alpha_0 + \alpha_1 \ln(Y_{it}) + \alpha_2 \ln(Y_{jt}) + \alpha_3 \ln(PCY_{it} - PCY_{jt}) \\ + \alpha_4 \ln(D_{ij}) + \alpha_5 (Contig_{ij}) + \alpha_6 (Comlang_{ij}) \\ + \beta_1 (RTA_{ijt}) + \beta_2 \ln(Inst_{it}) + \beta_3 \ln(Inst_{jt}) + \varepsilon_{ijt} \qquad (2)$$

where basic variables are same as in equation (1) and $(PCY_{it} - PCY_{jt})$, measures the difference in GDP per capita. The gravity model predicts that nations with different GDP per capita levels trade less as compared to nations who have similar GDP per capita levels. Similarly, $Contig_{ij}$ represents common border; $Comlang_{ij}$ shows common language; RTA_{ijt} represents regional trade agreement. Similarly, $Inst_{it}$ and $Inst_{jt}$ represent institutional factors in reporting and partner country.

Given the objectives of the study, using the data from WGI dataset, six dimensions are used to develop institutional quality index to analyse the role of institutions in regional cooperation. The dimensions used include political stability and absence of violence (PA), control of corruption (CC), rule of law (RL), government effectiveness (GE), regulatory quality (RQ) and voice and accountability (VA). The value of each dimension is between −2.5 and +2.5. The institutional quality index used in the present study is developed with a two-step procedure. First, following Raychaudhuri and Haldar (2009), each indicator is normalised within range between 0 and 1. Second, following Nawaz (2020) and Wani and Yasmin (2023), the below formula is used to form the final index:

$$INS_s = \frac{1}{6}\left(CC + GE + PA + RQ + RL + VA\right) * 100 \qquad (3)$$

The use of linear logarithmic form was popular in the empirical application of traditional gravity model. However, linear approach leads to biased results, which are inconsistent in the presence of heteroscedasticity (Silva and Tenreyro, 2006). Moreover, the logarithm operator applied to trade flow leads to the problem of zero trade flow[3] as the log of zero is undetermined. Among the possible alternative estimation techniques, Poisson pseudo-maximum likelihood method (PPML), as defined by Silva and Tenreyro (2006), is widely used. Given the nature of study and presence of zero trade flows as a dependent variable, the PPML estimator is preferred in the present analysis. Similarly, to account for all multilateral trade resistance as advocated by Anderson and van Wincoop (2003), both exporter-fixed effect (δ_{it}) and importer-fixed effect (μ_{jt}) are applied in line with Fally (2015). In addition, following Baier and Bergstrand (2007), the country-pair fixed effect (ρ_{ij}) is applied to tackle the issue of endogeneity not captured by the error term ε_{ijt}. In addition, to account for macroeconomic shocks, year-fixed effect (γ_t) is used. Taking all the

---

[3] For further detail, refer to Golovko and Sahin (2021).

above-mentioned issues into consideration, the extended gravity model that is to be estimated in the present study is as follows:

$$\begin{aligned}E_{ijt} = &\propto_0 + \propto_1 \ln(GDP_{it}) + \propto_2 \ln(GDP_{jt}) + \propto_3 \ln(PCGDP_{it} - PCGDP_{jt}) \\&+ \propto_4 \ln(Dis_{ij}) + \propto_5 (Contig_{ij}) + \propto_6 (Comlang_{ij}) + \beta_1(RTA_{ijt}) \\&+ \beta_2 \ln(Inst_{it}) + \beta_3 \ln(Inst_{jt}) + \theta_1(RTA_{ijt}) * \ln(Inst_{it}) \\&+ \theta_2(RTA_{ijt}) * \ln(Inst_{jt}) + \gamma_t + \delta_{It} + \mu_{jt} + \rho_{ij} + \varepsilon_{ijt}\end{aligned} \quad (4)$$

The coefficient $\theta_{1,2}$ captures impact of regional integration after interacting with institutions. This indicates that the marginal effect of regional integration on bilateral trade now explicitly depends on the value of institutions implying that

$\Delta \text{Log}(T_{ijt}) = \beta_1 + \theta_1 \log(Inst_{it})$ in case of reporter country only,

$\Delta \text{Log}(T_{ijt}) = \beta_1 + \theta_2 \log(Inst_{jt})$ in case of partner country only,

Further, it is the value of regional dummy variable that can also take two forms, $\frac{\partial \log(T_{ijt})}{\partial (ins)}(RTA_{ijt} = 1) = \beta + \theta$ and $\frac{\partial \log(T_{ijt})}{\partial (ins)}(RTA_{ijt} = 0) = \beta$; $\nabla \beta$ and $\nabla \theta$ capture the impact of institutions on bilateral trade. It is only after controlling institutional quality that the proposed equation is used to examine the impact of regional integration. If the results show that $\nabla \beta > 0$, it implies the positive impact of regional integration and institutions on bilateral trade.

4. Data Source

Table 2 shows the variables included in the proposed gravity model. The balance panel dataset from 1996 to 2020 that includes six countries from South Asia and top 10 trade partners[4] of the South Asian region are included in the present study. In addition to basic variables, institutional factors have been included in the model. The World Bank provides data for these indicators, which gives information about the governance

---

[4] Bangladesh, Bhutan, China, India, Hong Kong, Iran, Maldives, Myanmar, Nepal, Pakistan, Russia, Saudi Arabia, Singapore, Sri Lanka, Switzerland, UAE, USA.

Table 2. Variables and sources.

Variable	Definition	Source
Exports	Exports between selected countries	IMF
GDP (reporter)	Gross domestic product of reporting country	WDI
GDP (partner)	Gross Domestic Product of partner country	WDI
DGDP	Difference between GDP of partner countries	WDI
ECO_{ij}	Trade agreement when both are part of the agreement	WTO
ECO_i	Trade agreement when reporting country is part of the agreement	WTO
ECO_j	Trade agreement when only partner country is part of the agreement	WTO
GE	Government effectiveness	WGI
PS	Political Stability	WGI
VA	Voice and Accountability	WGI
CC	Control of corruption	WGI
ROL	Rule of law	WGI
RQ	Regulatory quality	WGI
DIS	Distance between country i and j	CEPII
Comlang_off	Dummy variable for common official language between countries	CEPII
Contig	Dummy variable for common border between partner countries	CEPII

performance of a particular country. The descriptive statistics of the included variables are presented in Table 3.

5. Empirical Analysis

The extended gravity model expressed in equation (4) is first estimated in five different specifications to examine the impact of different variables on bilateral export cooperation of South Asia as presented in Table 3. Second, the extended gravity model is estimated taking into consideration exporter-time, importer-time and country-pair fixed effect as presented in Table 5. The basic gravity model, which includes economic size and geographical

Table 3. Descriptive statistics.

Variables	Obs.	Mean	Standard deviation	Minimum value	Maximum value
Exports	9,961	3.62	2.17	0	4.81e+
GDP_i	11,025	25.35	2.37	19.92	30.69
GDP_j	11,024	25.14	2.52	19.92	30.69
PCGDPD	5,779	8.64	1.98	−1.94	11.42
Contig	11,025	0.12	0.32	0	1
Comlang	11,025	0.07	0.26	0	1
DIS	11,025	8.13	0.71	5.68	9.65
RTA	11,025	0.12	0.32	0	1
$Inst_i$	11,025	0.49	0.18	0.025	0.96
$Inst_j$	11,025	0.49	0.18	0.025	0.96
$Inst_i RTA$	11,025	0.056	0.16	0	0.96
$Inst_j RTA$	11,025	0.057	0.16	0	95.41

distance, is gradually extended to include the impact of border, language, trade agreements and institutional factors.

A look at the results (Table 4, column 6) indicates that it explains 87% of total changes in bilateral trade cooperation. Besides, the signs and size of coefficients are in line with the theoretical background. Koo et al. (1994) argued that the GDP of reporting and partner countries indicate their supply and demand capacity, respectively. A look at results indicate that coefficient of GDP is statistically significant and positive. The coefficient of GDP in the reporting country indicates that 1% increase in it leads to a 0.79% increase in trade. Similarly, the coefficient of partner countries indicates that 1% increase in GDP leads to 0.68% increase in trade. These findings are in line with the findings of Feenstra et al. (2001). Bougheas et al. (2000) who argue that an increase in income indicates a higher level of production and availability of more exportable goods in the reporting country. Similarly, a high level of income in the importing country means high purchasing power and more demand for both domestic and foreign goods. These results are in line with findings of Wani (2023) and Wani and Mir (2023).

The distance variable confirms the classical gravity model (Anderson and van Wincoop, 2003) as the coefficient is close to 1 in

Table 4. Results of basic and augmented gravity model.

Variables	1	2	3	4	5
GDPR	0.805***	0.791***	0.789***	0.792***	0.53***
	(0.02)	(0.02)	(0.02)	(0.02)	(0.02)
GDPP	0.671***	0.67***	0.673***	0.686***	0.603***
	(0.02)	(0.02)	(0.02)	(0.02)	(0.02)
lnDIS	−0.778***	−0.611***	−0.607***	−0.609***	−0.49***
	(0.05)	(0.06)	(0.06)	(0.06)	(0.08)
lnPCGDPD					0.12***
					(0.03)
Contig		0.402***	0.405***	0.435***	0.711***
		(0.09)	(0.09)	(0.09)	(0.09)
Comlang		0.881***	0.88***	0.866***	0.837***
		(0.06)	(0.07)	(0.06)	(0.07)
RTA	0.836***	0.443***	0.447***	0.252	0.428**
	(0.08)	(0.07)	(0.07)	(0.23)	(0.20)
Inst$_i$			−0.25	1.324**	2.697***
			(0.21)	(0.54)	(0.95)
Inst$_j$			0.223	1.063	0.247
			(0.19)	(0.72)	(0.50)
Inst$_i$RTA				0.139	−0.359
				(0.96)	(1.36)
Inst$_j$RTA				3.650***	1.608**
				(1.01)	(0.71)
Constant	−9.645***	−11.171***	−11.235***	−11.432***	−4.372***
	(0.83)	(0.95)	(0.96)	(0.99)	(0.79)
R-squared	0.644	0.699	0.693	0.718	0.879

Note: Standard errors in parentheses.
*$p < 0.10$, **$p < 0.05$, ***$p < 0.01$.

the basic model. However, the magnitude of coefficient decreases as the impact is distributed among other variables in the extended gravity model. These findings contradict the thesis that "distance is dead" due to increased integration around the world. Thus, it is clear that in spite of the rapid pace of globalisation, distance has maintained its significance as an explanatory variable of trade relations between countries.

In line with available literature, GDP per capita difference is used to examine either the Heckscher–Ohlin (H–O) or Linder hypothesis that dominates the trade between selected countries.

According to H–O theory, it is the availability of factors of production that countries gain comparative advantage and trade with other countries. This pattern mainly leads to inter-industry trade. The H–O theory is popular due to its explanation of inter-industry trade when different factors of production are available (Wang, 2006). However, with increase in integration, countries with same factors of production trade in intra-industry goods. The results (Table 4, model 5) indicate that the coefficient is statistically significant and has a positive sign. Thus, in the case of selected countries, H–O dominates Linder hypothesis, which indicates a high level of inter-industry as compared to intra-industry trade (Krugman, 1981).

Following Silva and Tenreyro (2006), the effect of change in variable x on variable y is calculated by $\{(e^{\alpha} - 1) * 100$, where α is the coefficient. The variable contig (common border) has a positive sign and is statistically significant, as common border enhances trade by $(e^{0.435} - 1) * 100 = 0.56\%$ as compared to countries where direct link is missing. Similarly, the variable Comlang (common language) among the participating countries increases trade by $(e^{0.866} - 1) * 100 = 0.87\%$ as compared to those countries who face language barrier in their trade relations. Similarly, trade policy liberalisation is expected to increase trade among countries. For this reason, RTA, which plays a leading role in trade cooperation between countries, is incorporated. The RTA indicates that member countries trade more by $(e^{0.252} - 1) * 100 = 0.47\%$ related to the countries who are not part of this agreement. Thus, it is beneficial for countries to be part of more BTAs and RTAs to increase cooperation with other countries of the world.

The primary variable of interest in this study is to examine the role of institutional factors in the integration of trade between selected countries. Given the available literature, it is expected that improvement in the role played by institutional factors may enhance bilateral trade cooperation between countries. The results in the present study indicate that only in the reporting country, institutional factors play a positive role in bilateral trade cooperation. The improvement in institutional quality by 1%, enhances trade by 1.324% (Table 4, model 4). In addition, the results show that institutional quality in the partner country is statistically insignificant though it has a positive sign. The positive sign of institutional factors indicates that improvement in institutional quality is expected to enhance bilateral trade cooperation. Finally, the use of interactive terms (RTA and institutional factors) indicates that improvement in institutional quality is expected to act as a supplement for regional cooperation. The RTA, which is supported by improvement in institutional quality, enhances trade more by 3.65% as compared to RTAs that do not get support from institutional factors.

In addition to the above discussed results, augmented gravity model is estimated taking into consideration export-fixed, import-fixed and year-fixed effect to check the robustness of results. Moreover, to check model misspecification, heteroscedasticity robust regression specification error test (RESET) is used for the PPML model as presented in Table 4. The results show that bilateral trade is expected to increase with an increase in the GDP of member countries. Similarly, bilateral trade is positively impacted by RTAs, which highlights the importance of these agreements to enhance cooperation between the member countries. The results as discussed above are same for all other variables.

In recent years, the association between trade cooperation and the role of institutional factors has gained prominence. Soeng and Cuyvers (2018) found that it is the domestic institutions that play a significant role in the export performance of Cambodia. Along the lines of these findings, the interaction term between institutions and RTA and the role of institutional factors was included in the present study. The results as presented in Table 5 indicate that $Inst_j$, which denote institutional factors in partner countries, have a positive sign and is statistically significant. These results indicate that institutions in the import country play a more important role in export promotion as compared to institutional factors in the export country. In addition, the interaction term between RTA and institutional setup ($Inst_j$RTA) has a positive sign and is statistically significant, which indicates the significance of institutional factors in the importing countries. Thus, from this discussion, it can be concluded that institutional setup, particularly in partner countries, plays a more significant role in export promotion.

Table 5. Augmented gravity model.

	(PPML)	(PPML)	(PPML)	(PPML)	(PPML)
lnGDPR	0.661***	0.869***	0.861***	0.861***	0.850***
	(0.02)	(0.02)	(0.02)	(0.02)	(0.02)
lnGDPP	0.732***	0.747***	0.738***	0.746***	0.742***
	(0.02)	(0.03)	(0.03)	(0.03)	(0.03)
lnGDPpc	0.125***				
	(0.03)				
lnDIS	−1.159***	−0.852***	−0.780***	−0.783***	−0.757***
	(0.08)	(0.06)	(0.06)	(0.06)	(0.06)
Contig		0.433***	0.260***	0.255***	0.247***
		(0.09)	(0.09)	(0.09)	(0.09)
Comlang		0.981***	0.876***	0.848***	0.834***
		(0.06)	(0.06)	(0.06)	(0.06)
RTA			0.513***	0.495***	
			(0.07)	(0.06)	
Inst$_i$				0.123	
				(0.18)	
Inst$_j$				0.613**	
				(0.26)	
Inst$_i$RTA					0.091
					(0.20)
Inst$_j$RTA					0.998***
					(0.20)
Constant	−5.115***	−13.714***	−13.969***	−14.556***	−14.046***
	(0.72)	(1.00)	(1.03)	(1.00)	(1.03)
Observations	5087	9960	9960	9960	9960
Pseudo R-sq	0.81	0.83	0.84	0.84	0.84
Wald chi2	4231.03	3738.81	4881.01	5508.04	5826.98
Fixed Effect					
Exporter-time	Yes	Yes	Yes	Yes	Yes
Importer-time	Yes	Yes	Yes	Yes	Yes
Year	Yes	Yes	Yes	Yes	Yes

Notes: Standard error in parentheses.
*$p < 0.10$, **$p < 0.05$, ***$p < 0.01$.

6. Conclusion

The present study examines bilateral export determinants of South Asian countries by applying the augmented gravity model. A comprehensive panel dataset of 19 countries from South Asia and their top trade partners is included to achieve the objectives of the study. To eliminate the problems related to the traditional gravity model, PPML estimation technique is used. In addition to basic gravity model, common language, common border, RTA, per capita income difference and institutional quality are included in the model. Further, an interactive term of institutional setup and RTA is also incorporated.

The results presented above provide a strong evidence in support of RTAs as they positively contribute to export promotion between countries. This highlights the significance of trade liberalisation in selected countries to increase the pace of economic development in the long run. In addition, the results provide ample evidence in support of institutional factors in partner countries. The institutional factors of partner countries play a more important role in export promotion of the reporting country. Furthermore, the interaction term of RTA and institutional setup also helps to promote export cooperation between these countries. Thus, these findings highlight that trade agreements accompanied by institutional reforms can be more effective as compared to trade agreements without support from the institutional setup of participating countries.

The results discussed above suggest that in order to lower trade costs, the governments in selected countries need to concentrate on vital infrastructural facilities. Furthermore, since institutions hold the key to leveraging trade agreements, these nations must prioritise institutional reforms in order to raise institutional standards and strengthen bilateral and regional economic cooperation. Thus in order to accomplish their goal of long-term economic growth, these nations must focus on enhancing the quality of their institutions and participate in additional trade agreements.

Acknowledgements

The author (Suadat Hussain Wani) is the awardee of the ICSSR Post-Doctoral Fellowship. This paper is largely an outcome of the Post-Doctoral Fellowship sponsored by the Indian Council of Social Science Research (ICSSR). However, the responsibility for the facts stated, opinions expressed, and the conclusions drawn are entirely of the author.

References

Abbas, S. and Waheed, A. (2019). Pakistan's global trade potential: A gravity model approach. *Global Business Review*, *20*(6), 1361–1371.

Abrego, L., Riezman, R., and Whalley, J. (2005). Computation and the theory of customs unions. *CESifo Economic Studies*, *51*(1), 117–132.

Akhter, N. and Ghani, E. (2010). Regional integration in South Asia: An analysis of trade flows using the gravity model. *The Pakistan Development Review*, *49*(2), 105–118.

Alhassan, A. and Payaslioglu, C. (2020). Institutions and bilateral trade in Africa: An application of Poisson's estimation with high-dimensional fixed effects to structural gravity model. *Applied Economics Letters*, *27*(16), 1357–1361.

Anderson, J. E. and Van Wincoop, E. (2003). Gravity with gravitas: A solution to the border puzzle. *American Economic Review*, *93*(1), 170–192.

Baldwin, R. E. and Venables, A. J. (1995). Regional economic integration. *Handbook of International Economics* (pp. 1597–1644), Vol. 3, Elsevier.

Baysan, T., Panagariya, A., and Pitigala, N. (2006). Preferential trading in South Asia. *World Bank Policy Research Working Paper*, (3813). World Bank, Washington.

Bishwakarma, J. K. and Hu, Z. (2022). Problems and prospects for the South Asian Association for Regional Cooperation (SAARC). *Politics & Policy*, *50*(1), 154–179.

Bougheas, S., Demetriades, P. O., and Mamuneas, T. P. (2000). Infrastructure, specialization, and economic growth. *Canadian Journal of Economics/Revue canadienne d'économique*, *33*(2), 506–522.

Carrere, C. (2006). Revisiting the effects of regional trade agreements on trade flows with proper specification of the gravity model. *European Economic Review*, *50*(2), 223–247.

Clausing, K. A. (2001). Trade creation and trade diversion in the Canada–United States free trade agreement. *Canadian Journal of Economics/Revue canadienne d'économique*, *34*(3), 677–696.

De Mendonça, T. G., Lirio, V. S., Braga, M. J., and Da Silva, O. M. (2014). Institutions and bilateral agricultural trade. *Procedia Economics and Finance*, *14*, 164–172.

Dembatapitiya, P. and Weerahewa, J. (2015). Effects of regional trading agreements on South Asian trade: A gravity model analysis. *Tropical Agricultural Research*, *26*(3), 468–485.

Feenstra, R. C., Markusen, J. R., and Rose, A. K. (2001). Using the gravity equation to differentiate among alternative theories of trade. *Canadian Journal of Economics/Revue canadienne d'économique*, *34*(2), 430–447.

Francois, J. and Manchin, M. (2013). Institutions, infrastructure, and trade. *World Development*, *46*, 165–175.

Frankel, J. A., Stein, E., and Wei, S. J. (1997). *Regional Trading Blocs in the World Economic System*. Peterson Institute for International Economics, Washington DC.

Gaurav, K. and Bharti, N. (2019). Has trade improved from SAPTA to SAFTA? Evidence from the gravity model. *International Journal of Business and Globalisation*, 23(4), 532–548.

Golovko, A. and Sahin, H. (2021). Analysis of international trade integration of Eurasian countries: Gravity model approach. *Eurasian Economic Review*, 11, 519–548.

Gylfason, T., Martínez-Zarzoso, I., and Wijkman, P. M. (2015). Free trade agreements, institutions and the exports of eastern partnership countries. *JCMS: Journal of Common Market Studies*, 53(6), 1214–1229.

Hassan, M. K., Mehanna, R. A., and Basher, S. A. (2001). Regional cooperation in trade, finance and investment among SAARC countries: The Bangladesh perspective. *Finance and Investment among SAARC Countries: The Bangladesh Perspective*. https://doi.org/10.2139/ssrn.3263379.

Hayakawa, K., Ito, T., and Kimura, F. (2016). Trade creation effects of regional trade agreements: Tariff reduction versus non-tariff barrier removal. *Review of Development Economics*, 20(1), 317–326.

Head, K. and Ries, J. (2004). Regionalism within multilateralism: The WTO trade policy review of Canada. *World Economy*, 27(9), 1377–1399.

Hou, Y., Wang, Y., and Xue, W. (2021). What explains trade costs? Institutional quality and other determinants. *Review of Development Economics*, 25(1), 478–499.

Iqbal, N. and Nawaz, S. (2017). Pakistan's bilateral trade under MFN and SAFTA: Do institutional and non-institutional arrangements matter? *The Pakistan Development Review*, 56(1), 59–78.

Kathuria, S. and Shahid, S. (2017). Boosting trade and prosperity in South Asia. *Regional Integration in South Asia: Essays in Honour of DR. M. Rahmatullah* (pp. 7–34). K.W. Publishers, New Delhi.

Koo, W. W., Karemera, D., and Taylor, R. (1994). A gravity model analysis of meat trade policies. *Agricultural Economics*, 10(1), 81–88.

Krugman, P. R. (1981). Intra industry specialization and the gains from trade. *Journal of Political Economy*, 89(5), 959–973.

Kumar, S. and Ahmed, S. (2015). Gravity model by panel data approach: An empirical application with implications for South Asian countries. *Foreign Trade Review*, 50(4), 233–249.

Mujahid, I. and Kalkuhl, M. (2016). Do trade agreements increase food trade? *The World Economy*, 39(11), 1812–1833.

Muzaffar, M., Jathol, I., and Yaseen, Z. (2017). SAARC: An evaluation of its achievements, failures, and compulsion for cooperation. *Global Political Review*, 2(1), 36–45.

Nag, B. and Nandi, A. (2006). Analysing India's trade dynamics vis-É-vis SAARC members using the gravity model. *South Asia Economic Journal*, *7*(1), 83–98.

Narayan, S. (2010). SAARC and South Asian economic integration. *The Emerging Dimensions of SAARC*, 32–50. DOI: 10.1017/UPO9788175968615.003.

Nawaz, S. (2015). Growth effects of institutions: A disaggregated analysis. *Economic Modelling*, *45*, 118–126.

Nawaz, S. (2020). Institutions, regional integration and bilateral trade in South Asia: PPML based evidence. *The Pakistan Development Review*, *59*(2), 221–241.

Rahman, M., Shadat, W. B., and Das, N. C. (2006). Trade potential in SAFTA: An application of augmented gravity model. *CPD Occasional Paper Series 61*, CPD, Dhaka.

Raychaudhuri, A. and Haldar, S. K. (2009). An investigation into the inter-district disparity in West Bengal, 1991–2005. *Economic and Political Weekly*, 258–263.

Shaikh, F. M., Syed, A. A. S. G., Shah, H., and Shah, A. A. (2012). Observing impact of SAFTA on Pakistan's economy by using CGE model. *Pakistan Journal of Commerce & Social Sciences*, *6*(1), 185–209.

Silva, J. S. and Tenreyro, S. (2006). The log of gravity. *The Review of Economics and statistics*, *88*(4), 641–658.

Soeng, R. and Cuyvers, L. (2018). Domestic institutions and export performance: Evidence for Cambodia. *The Journal of International Trade & Economic Development*, *27*(4), 389–408.

Sorgho, Z. (2016). RTAs' proliferation and trade-diversion effects: Evidence of the 'spaghetti bowl' phenomenon. *The World Economy*, *39*(2), 285–300.

Sultana, S. and Asrat, J. (2014). South Asian countries in regional integration perspective: A critical review. *Journal of Business and Technology (Dhaka)*, *9*(2), 43–59.

Viner, J. (1950). Full employment at whatever cost. *The Quarterly Journal of Economics*, *64*(3), 385–407.

Wani, S. H. (2023). Gravity model approach: An empirical application with implications for BRICS countries. *The Indian Economic Journal*. https://doi.org/10.1177/00194662221137267.

Wani, S. H. and Mir, M. A. (2023). Import determinants and potential markets of Pakistan: An application of PPML gravity model. *Studia Universitatis Vasile Goldiş Arad, Seria Ştiinţe Economice*, *33*(1), 57–73.

Zhang, Y., Liu, C., and Wang, T. (2020). Direct or indirect? The impact of political connections on export mode of Chinese private enterprises. *China Economic Review*, *61*, 101434.

Chapter 11

Can India's Export of Services Build Economic Partnerships in South Asia?

Sagnik Bagchi

*School of Business Management,
Narsee Monjee Institute of Management Studies,
V L Mehta Road, Vile Parle (W),
Mumbai, Maharashtra, India*

sagnik.bagchi@sbm.nmims.edu.in

Abstract

The magnitude of merchandise trade within South Asia has been much weaker than what their market sizes, cultural and geographical proximity offer. Some of the established factors responsible are poor connectivity, restrictive trade policies and lack of trust, among others. On the other hand, services are intangible in nature and there is more than one way to trade than the usual mode of merchandise trade. Due to these characteristic, services trade plausibly removes the shortcomings of merchandise trade, particularly in South Asia. *Can trade in services overcome the lacuna of merchandise trade*? Our results reveal that India's export share of services has been lower to its South Asian neighbours, but this occupies a significant portion in the import basket of the South Asian countries. In the service categories of Transport,

Travel, Telecommunications and Information Services, Financial Services and Personal Cultural and Recreation Services, India faces a high demand from its South Asian neighbours. The Government of India's efforts in shaping policies to allow educational institutes to set up offshore campuses, promoting courses of culture, yoga, ayurveda and medical tourism is just right to ensure that the South Asian economies remain connected to each other and subsequently build economic partnerships in the long run.

Keywords: Services trade, regional trade agreement, South Asia.

1. Introduction

Economic transaction within South Asia has been persistently low for a long time. Undoubtedly, there have been efforts by South Asian countries to improve economic relations with each other. To increase regional economic cooperation, South Asian member countries formed the South Asian Association of Regional Cooperation (SAARC) in 1985.[1] The objectives of SAARC are multifold and ranges from accelerating economic growth to contributing to building mutual trust. Subsequent deliberations of the SAARC secretariat led to the formation of the SAARC preferential trade agreement in 1993, but the outcome was not satisfactory. Subsequently, the South Asia Free Trade Area (SAFTA) was signed in 2004 and implemented in 2006. The main purpose of SAFTA was to reduce trade barriers within a decade and enhance economic activity. However, merchandise trade between SAFTA members continued to remain poor and they are well documented in several studies; see for instance Panagriya (2003), Banik and Gilbert (2010), Ding and Mishra (2012), Kumar (2021), Sinha and Sareen (2020), Mehndiratta and Nora (2022), among others. Altogether, this body of literature finds that despite countries lying in close geographical proximity, a trade agreement and having income similarity could not engage in high volume of trade. They point out that high tariff rates, poorer logistic support and low demand are

---

[1] The SAARC summit is held biennially, with the last being hosted in 2014 at Nepal. The 19th Summit to be hosted by Pakistan was boycotted by India along with support from Afghanistan, Bangladesh and Bhutan amidst bilateral tensions. After this, no other SAARC summit has been convened and the hopes of a multilateral regional economic cooperation came to a standstill.

the primary reasons behind low intra-regional trade.[2] Kaur *et al.* (2020) points out that amidst these deliberations in various summits about building economic partnership, countries have witnessed structural changes. The Service sector has become increasingly dominant in the GDP of the South Asian countries, and the performance of India in the service sector is remarkable. Recognising the increasing role of services in member countries, the 16th SAARC summit gave rise to signing of SAARC agreement of trade in services (SATIS) under a positive list approach and it became effective in November 2012.

In 2021–2022, the service sector's contribution to India's GDP was above 50% and it grew by 8.4% in 2022–2023 (PIB, 2022a, 2023). The Economic Survey of India (2022–2023) points out India is among the top 10 service exporting nations of the world and its share in world commercial services has been about 4% in 2021. More importantly, the report also stated that despite the global crisis caused by COVID-19, India's service sector export didn't take the beating that merchandise export did. In fact, India's account on trade in services enjoyed a surplus (PIB, 2022b). The World Investment Report prepared by UNCTAD in 2021–2022 reports that India is the seventh largest recipient of FDI, which includes US$7.1 billion FDI equity inflows in services. Other South Asian countries are no exception to this trend of services (see Table 1). These countries witnessed a shift from an agrarian economy to a more services-driven economy. The share of services in these economies of South Asia also contributes almost 50% of the GDP. On the other hand, the contribution from agriculture remained largely stable, but that of industry dipped by a considerable margin.

Kumar and Singh (2009) opine that India's large domestic market, human resources and aspirations for a global role endows it with a larger responsibility to increase regional cooperation. Kumar (2020) also points out that India need not only act as an engine of growth but needs to push forward SAARC engagement with political and diplomatic channels. Very recently in February 2023, the Managing Director of IMF remarked that India remains a relative bright spot in the global economy and is set to contribute 15% of global growth in 2023. In comparison, other South Asian countries such as Pakistan, Bangladesh and Sri Lanka are in talks for loans from various multilateral institutions to either bail them out from

---

[2] It is worth mentioning here that to improve connectivity in the East Asia region, The World Bank invests heavily in building environment-friendly transportation networks.

Table 1. Share of output (value added, as percentage of GDP).

Country	Agriculture, forestry and fishing				Industry				Services			
	2005	2010	2015	2021	2005	2010	2015	2021	2005	2010	2015	2021
AFG	31.11	26.21	20.63	33.48	26.81	21.15	22.12	15.59	39.01	48.88	53.24	46.51
PAK	22.96	23.28	23.82	22.67	19.92	19.72	19.09	18.80	51.39	52.84	52.16	52.11
NEP	33.82	33.18	26.52	21.32	16.47	14.20	13.16	11.72	45.83	46.40	50.54	52.58
BTN	20.20	14.78	14.44	19.19	36.92	43.81	42.49	34.20	39.13	37.31	38.62	43.99
BAN	18.57	17.00	14.78	11.63	23.30	24.96	26.83	33.32	52.88	53.50	53.71	51.30
SLK	11.82	9.05	8.22	8.70	30.19	27.78	29.54	29.79	57.99	53.01	54.21	55.11
MAL	7.73	5.63	5.56	5.27	11.73	9.43	10.68	8.94	69.57	77.69	72.33	73.25
IND	17.62	17.03	16.17	16.82	29.53	30.73	27.35	25.89	44.44	45.03	47.78	47.51
SA	18.35	17.51	16.70	16.70	27.91	29.16	26.37	25.94	46.11	46.48	48.95	48.53

Note: AFG: Afghanistan, PAK: Pakistan, NEP: Nepal, BTN: Bhutan, BAN: Bangladesh, SLK: Sri Lanka, MAU: Maldives, IND: India, SA: South Asia.
Source: World Development Indicators, The World Bank (2023).

their economic crisis and/or to meet economic restructuring. Our objective in this study is drawn from the motivation of what could be done to enable an increasing trend of intra-regional economic cooperation with South Asian countries. In other words, we intend to look into whether India's export of services to its South Asian neighbours can build regional economic partnerships.[3]

Our primary objective in this chapter is to discuss whether trade in services within South Asia led by India can act as an opportunity for the revival of geo-economic relationships. In spite of many cultural, linguistic, administrative and historical linkages, these countries could not enhance regional economic prosperity due to the above-discussed multitude of factors. In fact, Nalapat (2022) also observes that the nation-states are not in harmony with each other regarding the existing membership of countries and thereby are deficient in trust. We argue that services trade could act as a catalyst to regain trust among South Asian countries, which would subsequently have a cascading effect on trade in

---

[3]The CAGR of import of services computed using IMF's BoP data in the last decade (2010–2019) for Afghanistan, Bangladesh, Bhutan, Maldives, Nepal, Pakistan and Sri Lanka are 1.1%, 8%, 4.5%, 11.47%, 7.04%, 3.6% and 4%, respectively.

merchandise. Kathuria and Rizwan (2019) point out that in times of digital technology, trade is not restricted to the conventional methods. They argue that e-commerce strengthens commercial linkages in South Asia. In other words, services can be traded by different modes unlike the usual mode of merchandise trade. For instance, in the service category of travel where students or patients visit countries to study or for medical reasons, it fosters trust and economic cooperation between the participating countries.

1.1. *Trade in services: Theoretical conceptualisation*

Expansion of trade in services in the world can be largely attributed to the creation of General Agreement of Trade in Services (GATS) in the Uruguay round of 1995 and then the subsequent rounds of deliberations. The GATS agreement calls WTO members to eliminate restrictive trade practices in services and allows for bilateral, plurilateral or multilateral negotiations to enhance commitments by member countries. The agreement also laid special amendments to the Less Developed Countries so that they are given "maximum flexibility" in designing their trade policies in services. But what defines trade in service? For instance, watching a movie in an imported DVD is considered as trade in merchandise while watching a movie on Netflix is trade in services. Owing to its non-tangible nature of services, theoretical and empirical understanding of what services are is bit complex.

The interest in defining services grew manifold during the late 1970s and in 1980s, primarily because of the United States and other advanced economies; see Kravis (1983) for further details. These economies in those times advocated for liberalisation in trade of services across the world and wanted them to be included in the deliberations of the next rounds of multilateral trading negotiations. However, a conceptual clarity of what constitutes a service was not available. In fact, Sampson and Snape (1985) remark that during those early days, from an analytical perspective, trade in services was considered as the same as trade in goods.

Hill (1977) was one of the first to point out that services need to be distinct from goods, which otherwise was considered as trivial or "immaterial" goods. The author defines services as "… some change is brought about in the condition of some person or good …" and "… change is the result of activity of some other economic activity." Broadly, there are two types of services; *one that affects goods* and the *other that affects consumers*.

The producer of services that *changes* goods works on the goods belonging to the customer. Examples of them are transportation services, cleaning and maintenance services, among others. The producers of services affecting persons involves *changing* the physical and/or mental condition of the consumer. Passenger transportation, education services, entertainment and salon services are a few examples. The author, however, assumed that services are *non-storable*, as they have to be consumed at the same time they are produced. This restricted view was, however, pointed out by many scholars; see for instance Bhagwati (1984).

Bhagwati (1984) on the other hand, criticises the attempt to define services either from the consumption or production perspective. Rather, the author argues that as economies continuously experience structural and technical changes, services are produced through a "splintering process". Sometimes *services splinter off from goods* and *goods in turn also splinter off from services*. The former classification is categorised as the "progressive service industries" while the latter is classified as "unprogressive service industries". Bhagwati (1984) does not explicitly make it clear whether such disembodiment effects hold *irrespective* of whether providers and consumers of service require physical proximity or not.

One of the existing working classifications of services trade has its roots in the scholarly work of Sampson and Snape (1985). The authors argue that a way to distinguish trade in services from trade in goods is through how and where the services are produced. In other words, services can be traded internationally irrespective of physical proximity between the producer and the consumer (or receiver). The article classifies four categories of trade in services. First, transactions occur without any movement of factors of production and receiver of the service (e.g. consulting services, banking services). Second, transaction occurs due to the movement of the factors of production but not the receiver of service (e.g. construction teams visiting a particular site situated outside the country). Third, transactions where movement of the receiver of service occurs but not the provider (e.g. medical services). Fourth, transactions that require movements of both factors of production and the receiver of the service (e.g. some services occur in a third country). Apart from the first category, all other categories *cannot* be explained by trade theories where immobility of factors of production is considered. This deviation is the difference between trade in goods and trade in services.

Sapir and Winter (1994) further modified Samson and Snape's (1985) classification and eventually they were considered as the definition of services in the General Agreement of Trade in Services (GATS) framework developed in 1994. The GATS defines four modes of supply: (I) cross-border supply; (II) consumption abroad; (III) commercial presence and (IV) presence of natural persons through which trade in services can take place.[4] The measurement of trade in services encompassing these four modes is computed using two statistical domains: (i) Balance of Payments (BoP); and (ii) Foreign Affiliates Statistics (FATS).[5] Through BoP accounts, trade in services made in mode I, II and IV are captured and with mode III is accounted for via FATS.

The Extended Balance of Payments Services Classification (EBOPS) in 2002 is considered as the first step in creating a trade manual of services that contains both BoP and FATS domains. EBOPS-2002 classification extends the IMF's Balance of Payment, 5th Edition (BPM5) categories and also follows the FATS based upon System of National Accounts (1993). This classification has 11 service components and is considered to prepare the OECD-WTO Balanced Trade in Services (BaTIS) database for the period 1995–2012 encompassing 191 economies.[6] With the introduction of BPM6, EBOPS-2010 was created and it

---

[4] The first classification resorts to no requirement of movement of factors of production and consumers from their geographical territory. Examples of such transactions include consultancy service over the internet or telecommunication. The second classification considers the case where receivers of services move out of their geographical territory. Students studying in a foreign country and tourism are examples of the second category. The third kind classifies all those cases where supplier of service originates from a different country but establishes a legal entity in the consumer's geographical territory. A foreign bank providing service to the local customer is a case of the third category. The last case depicts those transactions where the seller of service temporary moves to the consumer's territory to sell.

[5] Data from BoP covers international service transaction between home and foreign countries while data of FATS compiles data of services transacted between individuals of the same country.

[6] The EBOPS-2002 service components are Transportation, Travel, Communication Services, Construction Services, Insurance Services, Financial Services, Computer and Information Services, Royalties and License Fees, Other business services, Personal, Cultural, and Recreational services, Government services, not included elsewhere.

has now 12 service components.[7] EBOPS-2010 is used to prepare two BaTIS database of 12 service components for 202 economies over the period 2005–2019 and 2005–2021. For more details on BaTIS databases prepared from EBOPS-2002 and EBOPS-2010, see Fortanier et al. (2017), Tajoli et al. (2021) and Liberatore and Wettstein (2021).[8] Alongside, there exists another database of WTO called Trade in Services by Mode of Supply (TISMOS). The database, however, covers data for 200 economies from 2005 to 2017 and is based on the EBOPS-2010 category.

In this chapter, we explore in detail the trend and pattern of bilateral trade in services between India and members of SAARC using the most comprehensive database on services available. We utilise the OECD-WTO prepared BaTIS database with EBOPS-2010 classification because they provide data at the bilateral service category-wise data encompassing a larger time frame. It is worth mentioning here that we will be considering the final balanced value data. This data reflects the reconciled bilateral trade flow, where exports equals imports. We believe our results have a promising case for policy suggestions, particularly as India plays a pivotal role in shaping up global politics. The United States and its allies emphasise India's success as a necessary strategy to restrain China from dominating the Indo-Pacific region. In fact, Ravi and Kapoor (2022) point out that in the recent past India's political closeness to the west is favourable and Pakistan's proximity to China is better than India. Amidst this existing geo-political landscape, one must rely on its neighbours who share not

---

[7]The EBOPS-2010 service components are Manufacturing services on physical inputs owned by others (SA), Maintenance and repair services not included elsewhere (SB), Transport (SC), Travel (SD), Construction (SE), Insurance and pension services (SF), Financial services (SG), Charges for the use of intellectual property not included elsewhere (SH), Telecommunications, computer and information services (SI), Other business services (SJ), Personal, cultural and recreational services (SK), Government goods and services not included elsewhere (SL). A detailed description of service categories can be found in the online annexes of Manual on Statistics of International Trade in Services (2010) published by UN.

[8]Furthermore, OECD claims that only about 63% of world trade in services is bilaterally specified, and the percentage is lower for the individual service categories. Therefore, the methodology used in this database considers all available official statistics and combines them with necessary estimation and adjustment to prepare a detailed matrix encompassing almost all countries of the world.

only a common boundary but cultural and common administrative linkages too.

The rest of the chapter is designed as follows. Section 2 discusses India's standing in the world in terms of export of services and South Asia's position in the import of services. Section 3 elaborates the bilateral trade in services between India and South Asian countries. Lastly, in Section 4 we discuss the outcomes of the study, limitations and policy recommendations.

2. India and South Asia in Services Trade

Over the period 2005–2021, the total service export of the world has increased annually by about 4.5%. About three-fifths of the total world export value is exported by 14 countries; see Table 2. Incidentally, these countries have at least 2% export share in the world. One could also find that none of the South Asian countries excepting India makes it into the list of top exporters. Among these 14 countries, we observe that the growth of export share in the world has been rapidly increasing for Ireland, Singapore, India, Hong Kong and China. Among the exporters of the world, India was ranked 19 in 2005 and 12 in 2020. It is also found that among the 12 service categories, the world has more exports in the service categories of "Other Business Services (SJ)", "Financial Services (SG)" and "Telecommunications, Computer, and Information Services (SI)"; see Figure 1. Table 3 lists the top exporter services category-wise. The dominant exporters are the United States, UK, Germany and China

Table 2. Exports by top countries in world: 2005–2021.

Countries	Share	Growth	Countries	Share	Growth
United States	15.33	0.59	Switzerland	2.95	−0.78
UK	7.56	−1.20	Spain	2.62	−2.70
Germany	6.04	−0.49	Singapore	2.62	3.53
France	4.73	−1.42	Italy	2.39	−3.25
Netherlands	3.94	0.03	Ireland	2.36	4.32
China	3.86	1.54	Hong Kong	2.34	1.39
Japan	3.11	−0.60	India	2.12	3.33

Note: Growth rates of export share over time were computed using semi-logarithmic regressions.
Source: OECD-WTO Balanced Trade in Services Database.

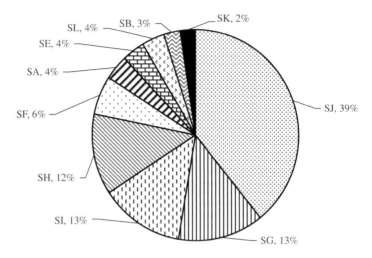

Figure 1. Median share of export value of world: 2005–2021.
Note: The nomenclature of service categories appears in footnote 7.
Source: OECD-WTO Balanced Trade in Services Dataset.

and at least one among them are present in all the service categories. In the service categories of SI and SJ, India is one of the leading exporters to the world while in other service categories India is not ranked higher but ahead of many developing economies. Having a high share in the most dominant service category places India certainly among the top exporters of the world.

On the other hand, in the case of imports too, we do not find emerging economies entering the top positions. Table 4 lists the median shares of the top countries. However, the annual growth rate of share has been falling for most countries. It is only China, Singapore and Hong Kong that have shown a positive growth in the share of imports. Also, when we computed the CAGR of import share of all countries for the period 2005–2021, we observe that it is the developing countries that mostly have a positive and a higher CAGR value. Due to space constraints, we do not report the values of all countries. However, we list the import share and annual growth rate of the share of imports for South Asian countries in Table 5. Bangladesh, Bhutan, Nepal and Maldives witnessed a higher growth rate in import share than other countries.

Table 3. Share of top exporters of world and India's share and rank.

Category	Top exporter to world				India's share and rank
	Rank 1	Rank 2	Rank 3	Rank 4	
SA	China (22.68%)	Germany (7.23%)	France (6.23%)	US (4.84%)	0.51%; 31
SB	US (23.61%)	Germany (9.77%)	Singapore (7.20%)	France (7.05%)	0.31%; 40
SC	Germany (6.62%)	UK (4.47%)	China (4.39%)	Singapore (4.32%)	1.35%; 23
SD	US (12.85%)	Spain (5.59%)	France (4.87%)	UK (4.46%)	1.27%, 21
SE	China (10.05%)	Japan (7.15%)	Korea (7.12%)	Germany (4.29%)	1.76%, 17
SF	Bermuda (14.49%)	UK (14.30%)	US (10.98%)	Germany (7.02%)	0.83%; 20
SG	US (26.99%)	UK (18.10%)	Luxembourg (7.98%)	Germany (5.73%)	0.70%; 21
SH	Netherlands (11.60%)	Japan (8.78%)	Switzerland (7.13%)	UK (5.86%)	0.20%; 26
SI	US (11.20%)	Ireland (9.99%)	India (8.24%)	UK (8.00%)	8.24%; 3
SJ	US (15.82%)	UK (10.41%)	Germany (7.83%)	France (6.11%)	3.10%; 7
SK	US (29.96%)	UK (11.55%)	France (4.69%)	Netherlands (4.20%)	1.31%; 14
SL	US (22.16%)	Germany (9.92%)	UK (4.57%)	France (4.00%)	0.45%; 40

Source: OECD-WTO Balanced Trade in Services Dataset.

In order to understand the position of South Asian countries in the world, we compute the median import value of the South Asian countries over the period 2005–2021 and their rank amidst the 202 countries across 12 different service categories; see Table 6. Undeniably, in most cases, the South Asian countries rank fairly low. However, in certain categories, their imports value is relatively sizeable in spite of having a lower rank in the world. In the service category of SA (Manufacturing services on physical inputs owned by others), it is only Sri Lanka that has a (median)

Table 4. Imports of top countries in world: 2005–2021.

Countries	Share	Growth	Countries	Share	Growth
US	11.94	−0.44	Japan	3.50	−1.63
Germany	6.78	−1.10	Ireland	2.81	4.61
UK	5.62	−1.27	Singapore	2.63	3.42
China	4.46	5.54	Italy	2.36	−3.19
France	3.93	−0.95	Canada	2.24	−1.17
Netherlands	3.66	0.06	Hong Kong	2.10	0.33
Switzerland	3.50	0.38	Belgium	2.04	−0.52

Note: Growth rates of import share over time were computed using semi-logarithmic regressions.
Source: OECD-WTO Balanced Trade in Services Database.

Table 5. Imports of South Asian countries in world: 2005–2021.

Countries	Share	Growth	Countries	Share	Growth
India	1.76	2.31	Bhutan	0.002	1.71
Pakistan	0.18	−2.09	Nepal	0.01	2.79
Sri Lanka	0.07	−0.8	Afghanistan	0.02	−0.87
Bangladesh	0.11	4.80	Maldives	0.01	4.29

Note: Growth rates of import share over time were computed using semi-logarithmic regressions.
Source: OECD-WTO Balanced Trade in Services Database.

import value worth US$100 million from the world. On the other hand, in the service category of SB (Maintenance & Repair Service) and SK (Personal, Cultural and Recreational Service), *no* South Asian country had reached the median value of US$100 million of import. While in the service category of SC (Transport), excepting Nepal and Bhutan, all other South Asian countries crossed the US$100 million figure mark. For the category of SD (Travel) too, excepting Bhutan, all other countries had imported at least US$100 million worth of services. In the category of SE (Construction) and SG (Financial services), it is only Bangladesh that imports a sizeable value each year. In the categories of SF (Insurance and Pension services), SH (Charges of use of intellectual property, n.i.e.) and SI (Telecommunication, Computer and Information Services) Pakistan and Sri Lanka were major importers. In the category of SH (Charges for the use of intellectual property n.i.e.), Pakistan, Bangladesh, Sri Lanka

Table 6. Median value of import and rank in world: 2005–2021.

Category	Pakistan	Bangladesh	Nepal	Bhutan	Sri Lanka	Afghanistan	Maldives
SA	World = 10.63	World = 0.39	World = 0.13	World = 0.03	World = 131.66	World = 0.21	World = 0.03
	Rank = 66	Rank = 158	Rank = 124	Rank = 132	Rank = 49	Rank = 174	Rank = 166
SB	World = 77.14	World = 52.94	World = 2.53	World = 0.05	World = 11.96	World = 9.36	World = 0.008
	Rank = 84	Rank = 71	Rank = 131	Rank = 176	Rank = 125	Rank = 134	Rank = 188
SC	World = 1562.19	World = 2043.1	World = 58.51	World = 1.07	World = 1487.27	World = 891.3	World = 113.34
	Rank = 67	Rank = 51	Rank = 157	Rank = 199	Rank = 85	Rank = 101	Rank = 162
SD	World = 3408.03	World = 281.91	World = 778.02	World = 65.87	World = 835.72	World = 111.84	World = 188.30
	Rank = 48	Rank = 119	Rank = 86	Rank = 176	Rank = 125	Rank = 171	Rank = 142
SE	World = 47.81	World = 1314.04	World = 1.91	World = 0.78	World = 8.84	World = 51.09	World = 1.10
	Rank = 100	Rank = 18	Rank = 133	Rank = 167	Rank = 141	Rank = 109	Rank = 160
SF	World = 191.31	World = 27.77	World = 2.52	World = 0.21	World = 120.38	World = 11.66	World = 53.21
	Rank = 71	Rank = 98	Rank = 158	Rank = 190	Rank = 86	Rank = 142	Rank = 95
SG	World = 140.91	World = 216.31	World = 0.46	World = 6.23	World = 72.71	World = 6.46	World = 23.09
	Rank = 81	Rank = 71	Rank = 170	Rank = 148	Rank = 116	Rank = 152	Rank = 129
SH	World = 340.01	World = 1.22	World = 0.0002	World = 0.01	World = 129	World = 0.48	World = 0.02
	Rank = 55	Rank = 137	Rank-178	Rank = 188	Rank = 91	Rank = 140	Rank = 157
SI	World = 359.58	World = 299.31	World = 2.88	World = 11.64	World = 190.18	World = 56.37	World = 52.72
	Rank:66	Rank = 76	Rank = 181	Rank = 160	Rank = 100	Rank = 137	Rank = 121
SJ	World = 1489.50	World = 654.32	World = 19.08	World = 12.72	World = 365.05	World = 182.47	World = 81.04
	Rank:66	Rank = 70	Rank = 158	Rank = 160	Rank = 100	Rank = 137	Rank = 121
SK	World = 77.52	World = 1.72	World = 0.12	World = 7.67	World = 26.01	World = 0.47	World = 0.70
	Rank = 55	Rank = 139	Rank = 151	Rank = 112	Rank = 103	Rank = 153	Rank = 150
SL	World = 889.10	World = 153.69	World = 13.70	World = 19.12	World = 67.55	World = 81.23	World = 20.06
	Rank = 24	Rank = 51	Rank = 131	Rank = 129	Rank = 103	Rank = 90	Rank = 118

Note: Values are reported in Million US$.
Source: OECD-WTO Balanced Trade in Services Dataset.

and Afghanistan import the most. Lastly, in the category of SL (Government goods and services), it is Pakistan and Bangladesh that import at least US$100 million worth of services.

3. India's Export and South Asia's Import

India has been exporting services to almost 200 countries each year. However, the share of service exports is concentrated only to a few countries. About three-fifths of total services is exported to only nine countries. Table 7 lists the countries to whom India's (median) export share is at least 1% over the period 2005–2021. There are 20 countries in that list and the aggregate (median) share is about 72%. None of the South Asian countries makes it into this list. In fact, the aggregate (median) share of India's export to South Asian countries over the period 2005–2021 is about 1.76%.

Table 8 lists the service category-wise India's top four export destinations along with concentration ratio of four countries' (median) export share. It is found that from the pool of South Asian countries only in the service category of SE, Bangladesh makes it to the top four export destination of India; while in all other cases none of them are in the top list. Also, the values of the concentration ratio indices reveal that excepting the service category of SA, all other service categories had relatively diversified export shares but export share to the South Asian countries are low. The median value and the SAGR of India's export to the world in each of the service categories are also reported in Table 8. The numbers indicate that India's export value has been increasing rapidly over the

Table 7. India's median export share to top countries: 2005–2021.

Countries	Share	Countries	Share	Countries	Share
USA	20.61	Hong Kong	2.82	Brazil	1.43
UK	8.26	Japan	2.69	Canada	1.21
Singapore	4.50	UAE	2.68	Ireland	1.91
Germany	4.20	South Korea	2.53	Italy	1.16
China	3.37	France	2.52	Thailand	1.13
Switzerland	3.15	Saudi Arabia	2.40	Chinese Taipei	1.08
Netherlands	3.00	Australia	1.78	*Total*	*71.79*

Source: OECD-WTO Balanced Trade in Services Database.

Table 8. Export profile of India: 2005–2021.

SA	SB	SC	SD
Hong Kong, France, Korea, United Kingdom	Germany, United States, France, Israel	China, United States, Singapore, Hong Kong	United States, United Kingdom, Australia, China
CR_4 = 62.80%	CR_4 = 34.18%	CR_4 = 28.85%	CR_4 = 34.88%
Median = 508.75	Median = 227.53	Median = 13607.22	Median = 14248.21
SAGR = 5.16	SAGR = 14.1	SAGR = 5.09	SAGR = 2.45
SE	**SF**	**SG**	**SH**
Japan, Bangladesh, Saudi Arabia, Kuwait	United States, United Kingdom, United Arab Emirates, Türkiye	United States, United Kingdom, Hong Kong, Singapore	United States, United Kingdom, Singapore, Switzerland
CR_4 = 39.59%	CR_4 = 34.97%	CR_4 = 47.02%	CR_4 = 45.29%
Median = 1658.35	Median = 1350.05	Median = 2618.17	Median = 675.83
SAGR = 7.38	SAGR = 6.26	SAGR = 6.87	SAGR = 14.12
SI	**SJ**	**SK**	**SL**
United States, United Kingdom, United Arab Emirates, Switzerland	United States, United Kingdom, Germany, Singapore	United States, United Kingdom, Switzerland, Singapore	Saudi Arabia, United States, United Kingdom, United Arab Emirates
CR_4 = 47.70%	CR_4 = 40.04%	CR_4 = 49.58%	CR_4 = 46.57%
Median = 32088.61	Median = 31194.62	Median = 882.02	Median = 705.63
SAGR = 9.32	SAGR = 9.36	SAGR = 10.29	SAGR = 3.06

Note: CR_4 are computed on median values on export share over the period 2005–2021. SAGR of export share over time was computed using semi-logarithmic regressions. Median values are in million dollars.
Source: OECD-WTO Balanced Trade in Services Dataset.

period 2005–2021 across all service categories and the value of export basket is significantly large.

What about India's export to South Asian countries across all the service categories? Does India's export basket contain a sizeable portion for the South Asian countries? Table 9 lists the median share of export by India to the South Asian countries for all the service categories. It is observed for all South Asian countries the median share of export across all service categories is meagre, but the export value has been increasing rapidly; see Figure 2. However, the growth rate of share has *not* improved

Table 9. Median share of service exports by India: 2005–2021.

Service category	Pakistan	Bangladesh	Nepal	Bhutan	Sri Lanka	Afghanistan	Maldives
SA	0.007	0.0000004	0.00001	0.000001	0.22	0	0
SB	1.72	0.06	0.003	0.002	0.007	0.05	0.000005
SC	0.84	1.93	0.05	0.001	0.65	0.35	0.03
SD	0.96	0.14	1.17	0.21	0.44	0.02	0.06
SE	0.03	9.33	0.01	0.0001	0.05	0.22	0.00001
SF	0.08	0.10	0.006	0.0008	0.39	0.03	0.12
SG	0.05	0.12	0.0004	0.05	0.09	0.008	0.01
SH	0.10	0.0005	0.0000002	0.0001	0.11	0.0009	0.00001
SI	0.11	0.26	0.004	0.02	0.20	0.07	0.04
SJ	0.10	0.30	0.01	0.01	0.17	0.06	0.02
SK	0.41	0.004	0.001	0.54	0.20	0.001	0.002
SL	0.55	0.47	0.08	0.36	0.16	0.17	0.02

Source: OECD-WTO Balanced Trade in Services Dataset.

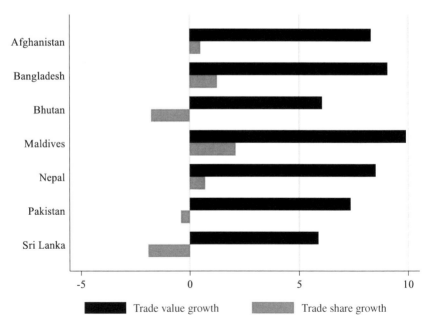

Figure 2. Growth rates of India's export value and share of services.
Source: OECD-WTO Balanced Trade in Services Dataset.

uniformly for all the countries of South Asia. Exports from India to Pakistan, Sri Lanka and Bhutan have seen a considerable decline over the years while others have increased.

Does India's export occupy less of the South Asian import basket? Though India's share of the export basket to South Asian countries is low, they make up a substantial share in the import basket of South Asian countries. Table 10 presents the list of top importers and their cumulative median share (CR_4) alongside India's rank in the country list of importers. In the service categories of SC, SD, SG, SI, SJ, SK India's exports occupy a significant portion of import share in all the South Asian countries. On the other hand, in the category of SA, none of the countries in South Asia imports significantly from India. In the categories of SB, SE, SF and SL not all countries uniformly import largely from India. For the category of SB, Pakistan, Bhutan and Afghanistan import highly from India while for SE the list of countries include Bangladesh, Nepal, Sri Lanka and Afghanistan. In the category of SF, it is only Afghanistan that is not a major importer from India. For the category of SH, it is only Bhutan who imports heavily from India. Lastly, in the category of SL, Bangladesh, Nepal and Bhutan have a high import share from India.

The low volume of exports by India to these South Asian countries prompt us to investigate trade restriction in services. We explore the services trade policy database jointly developed by World Bank and WTO to examine policy restrictiveness. It is a comprehensive database of trade policies and regulations applied by the importing economy. This database covers 68 economies and considers five major sectors that are further sub-divided into 23 sub-sectors and calculates Services Trade Restrictiveness Index (STRI). These five service sectors are: financial services, telecommunications, distribution, transportation and professional services.[9] The index assigns six distinct levels of restrictiveness scores (0–1) to each service category and to each mode of supply. Zero represents the situation where no restriction is imposed and one implies

---

[9]The sub-sectors are as follows: financial services (commercial banking, life insurance, non-life insurance, reinsurance), telecommunications services (fixed-line, mobile, Internet), distribution services (retail, wholesale), transportation (air freight domestic, air freight international, air passenger domestic, air passenger international, rail freight, road freight, maritime freight transport, maritime auxiliary services, maritime intermediation and other), professional services (accounting, auditing, legal services on foreign law, legal services on domestic law, legal advice and representation).

Table 10. Top importing countries and India's position: 2005–2021.

Category	Pakistan	Bangladesh	Nepal	Bhutan	Sri Lanka	Afghanistan	Maldives
SA	China, S. Korea, Romania, Ukraine $CR_4 = 62.48\%$ India's Share = 0.39 India's Rank = 26	Costa Rica, Malaysia, China, Paraguay $CR_4 = 89.85\%$ India's Share = 0 India's Rank = 0	Costa Rica, China, Tajikistan, Malaysia $CR_4 = 97.33\%$ India's Share = 0.06 India's Rank = 12	Costa Rica, China, Tajikistan, S. Korea $CR_4 = 99.94\%$ India's Share = 0.01 India's Rank = 5	China, Malaysia, Taipei, S. Korea $CR_4 = 57.37\%$ India's Share = 0.92 India's Rank = 17	Costa Rica, China Honduras, Malaysia $CR_4 = 99.98\%$ India's Share = 0 India's Rank = 0	Costa Rica, China, Netherlands, Malaysia $CR_4 = 100\%$ India's Share = 0 India's Rank = 0
SB	Singapore, US, UAE, UK $CR_4 = 30.42$ India's Share = 3.52 India's Rank = 5	Singapore, US, UK, Switzerland $CR_4 = 49.76\%$ India's Share = 0.4 India's Rank = 28	Singapore, US, Switzerland, Argentina $CR_4 = 48.37\%$ India's Share = 0.4 India's Rank = 21	India, Kosovo, Thailand, Mali $CR_4 = 18.93\%$ India's Share = 13.90 India's Rank = 1	US, Singapore, UK, Germany, $CR_4 = 51.68\%$ India's Share = 0.23 India's Rank = 31	US, UK, Singapore, Germany $CR_4 = 40.64\%$ India's Share = 1.3 India's Rank = 15	Singapore, US, Netherlands, UK $CR_4 = 52.14\%$ India's Share = 0.21 India's Rank = 25
SC	UAE, Singapore, India, China $CR_4 = 30.42$ India's Share = 7.61 India's Rank = 3	India, Singapore, UAE, US $CR_4 = 37.51\%$ India's Share = 12.88 India's Rank = 1	Singapore, India, China, US $CR_4 = 35.55\%$ India's Share = 10.78 India's Rank = 2	India, Liberia, Singapore, China $CR_4 = 35.84\%$ India's Share = 16.43 India's Rank = 1	Singapore, US, Hong Kong, India $CR_4 = 34.88\%$ India's Share = 6.11 India's Rank = 4	US, China, Turkey, UK $CR_4 = 31.03\%$ India's Share = 5.69 India's Rank = 5	Singapore, Netherlands, US, UK $CR_4 = 42.01\%$ India's Share = 2.92 India's Rank = 8

SD	UAE, China, UK, USA $CR_4 = 32.50$ India's Share = 4.04 India's Rank = 5	Australia, US, India, Thailand $CR_4 = 30.93\%$ India's Share = 7.07 India's Rank = 2	India, China, US, UK $CR_4 = 45.65\%$ India's Share = 22.09 India's Rank = 1	India, Singapore, China, Thailand $CR_4 = 61.61\%$ India's Share = 48.25 India's Rank = 1	US, Hong Kong, India, UK $CR_4 = 29.84\%$ India's Share = 7.40 India's Rank = 3	Turkey, US, China, UK $CR_4 = 33.12\%$ India's Share = 3.24 India's Rank = 7	US, Turkey, Hong Kong, China $CR_4 = 31.60\%$ India's Share = 4.67 India's Rank = 9
SE	China, UAE, S. Korea, UK $CR_4 = 49.37$ India's Share = 0.77 India's Rank = 15	China, India, Japan, Singapore $CR_4 = 44.24\%$ India's Share = 11.61 India's Rank = 2	China, India, S. Korea, Japan $CR_4 = 58.73\%$ India's Share = 15.49 India's Rank = 2	S. Arabia, UAE, Germany, Nigeria $CR_4 = 40.36\%$ India's Share = 0.32 India's Rank = 25	China, India, S. Korea, Singapore $CR_4 = 43.19\%$ India's Share = 13.36 India's Rank = 2	Turkey, China, India, Japan $CR_4 = 44.59\%$ India's Share = 6.29 India's Rank = 3	S. Arabia, Nigeria, Seychelles, Bahrain $CR_4 = 36.87\%$ India's Share = 0.01 India's Rank = 38
SF	UK, Singapore, UAE, US $CR_4 = 51.99$ India's Share = 0.37 India's Rank = 22	UK, Singapore, Barbados, China $CR_4 = 40.71\%$ India's Share = 5.04 India's Rank = 6	Barbados, UK, Hong Kong, UAE $CR_4 = 40.02\%$ India's Share = 3.26 India's Rank = 6	Barbados, India, UAE, Belarus $CR_4 = 59.91\%$ India's Share = 6.09 India's Rank = 2	UK, US, Singapore, Switzerland $CR_4 = 38.90\%$ India's Share = 4.56 India's Rank = 7	UK, US, Barbados, Switzerland $CR_4 = 47.98\%$ India's Share = 3.26 India's Rank = 7	Singapore, UK, Switzerland, US $CR_4 = 49.47\%$ India's Share = 3.10 India's Rank = 7

(Continued)

Table 10. (Continued)

Category	Pakistan	Bangladesh	Nepal	Bhutan	Sri Lanka	Afghanistan	Maldives
SG	US, UAE, UK, China $CR_4 = 52.12$ India's Share = 1.06 India's Rank = 12	US, Singapore, China, UK $CR_4 = 44\%$ India's Share = 1.73 India's Rank = 11	Luxembourg, UK, US, Singapore $CR_4 = 58.83\%$ India's Share = 2.43 India's Rank = 7	Singapore, India, Hong Kong, UK $CR_4 = 72.36\%$ India's Share = 20.98 India's Rank = 2	UK, US, Singapore, Luxembourg $CR_4 = 65.60\%$ India's Share = 3.53 India's Rank = 7	US, UK, Luxembourg, Switzerland $CR_4 = 73.74\%$ India's Share = 2.79 India's Rank = 9	Singapore, US, UK, Hong Kong $CR_4 = 63.21\%$ India's Share = 1.80 India's Rank = 8
SH	US, Japan, UK, Netherlands $CR_4 = 68.02$ India's Share = 0.22 India's Rank = 21	Paraguay, Cyprus, UAE, Antigua & Barbuda $CR_4 = 49.90\%$ India's Share = 0.24 India's Rank = 16	US, Japan, Netherlands, Switzerland $CR_4 = 66.67\%$ India's Share = 0.79 India's Rank = 15	India, Cyprus, US, Singapore $CR_4 = 20.85\%$ India's Share = 14.51 India's Rank = 1	US, Japan, Switzerland, UK $CR_4 = 64.75\%$ India's Share = 0.60 India's Rank = 15	US, UK, Luxembourg, Japan $CR_4 = 64.68\%$ India's Share = 0.54 India's Rank = 17	Paraguay, US, Netherlands, Singapore $CR_4 = 17.65\%$ India's Share = 0.15 India's Rank = 22
SI	UAE, Ireland, US, India $CR_4 = 68.02$ India's Share = 8.69 India's Rank = 4	India, US, Singapore, Hong Kong $CR_4 = 47.39\%$ India's Share = 30.83 India's Rank = 1	India, US, UK, Singapore $CR_4 = 63.03\%$ India's Share = 52.07 India's Rank = 1	India, Singapore, Sweden, UK $CR_4 = 80.55\%$ India's Share = 69.53 India's Rank = 1	India, Singapore, US, UK $CR_4 = 59.55\%$ India's Share = 41.75 India's Rank = 1	India, US, Sweden, UK $CR_4 = 65.37\%$ India's Share = 35.19 India's Rank = 1	Singapore, US, Netherlands, Ireland $CR_4 = 57.63\%$ India's Share = 26.81 India's Rank = 1

Can India's Export of Services Build Economic Partnerships in South Asia?   221

	1	2	3	4	5	6	7
SJ	US, UAE, UK, China CR_4 = 45.72 India's Share = 2.78 India's Rank = 7	India, US, Singapore, UK CR_4 = 44.53% India's Share = 15.83 India's Rank = 1	India, US, Singapore, UK CR_4 = 42.15% India's Share = 19.31 India's Rank = 1	India, Singapore, US, UK CR_4 = 68.24% India's Share = 49.56 India's Rank = 1	India, US, Singapore, UK CR_4 = 46.31% India's Share = 15.29 India's Rank = 1	US, UK, India, China CR_4 = 46.62% India's Share = 11.38 India's Rank = 3	Singapore, US, India, UK CR_4 = 43.52% India's Share = 7.81 India's Rank = 3
SK	US, UK, India, Luxembourg CR_4 = 65.48 India's Share = 5.19 India's Rank = 3	Antigua & Barbuda, UK, Dominica, Paraguay CR_4 = 31.90% India's Share = 2.49 India's Rank = 6	Luxembourg, US, India, Belarus CR_4 = 61.63% India's Share = 13.09 India's Rank = 3	India, US, UK, Singapore CR_4 = 79.13% India's Share = 62.74 India's Rank = 1	US, UK, India, Canada CR_4 = 54.40% India's Share = 7.92 India's Rank = 3	US, UK, Sweden, Cuba CR_4 = 43.68% India's Share = 3.21 India's Rank = 5	US, UK, Netherlands, Singapore CR_4 = 39.42% India's Share = 2.67 India's Rank = 7
SL	US, UAE, Kuwait, UK CR_4 = 30.64 India's Share = 0.39 India's Rank = 30	US, UAE, Germany, Greece CR_4 = 22.89% India's Share = 2.04 India's Rank = 13	US, Belgium, Germany, India CR_4 = 34% India's Share = 4.21 India's Rank = 4	US, S. Korea, Japan, Indonesia CR_4 = 27.15% India's Share = 13.50 India's Rank = 5	US, Germany, Belgium, Japan CR_4 = 47.54% India's Share = 1.74 India's Rank = 10	US, Germany, UK, Japan CR_4 = 53.49% India's Share = 1.41 India's Rank = 13	US, Netherlands, Germany, Japan CR_4 = 62.34% India's Share = 0.90 India's Rank = 16

Source: OECD-WTO Balanced Trade in Services Dataset.

Table 11. Level of trade restriction across service categories.

Service categories	Bangladesh	Sri Lanka	Pakistan
Distribution	Neither major nor minor restriction	Neither major nor minor restriction	Neither major nor minor restriction
Finance	Major restriction	Major restriction	Major restriction
Professionals	Major restriction	Major restriction	Neither major nor minor restriction
Telecommunications	Neither major nor minor restriction	Major restriction	Neither major nor minor restriction
Transport	Major restriction	Major restriction	Neither major nor minor restriction

Source: The World Bank and WTO.

full restriction by the importing country. Though not all countries of SAARC are covered in this database, it has data on Bangladesh, Sri Lanka, Pakistan and India, which are eventually the major players in South Asia.[10] More importantly, this data offers comparable STRI scores for the year 2016 and 2008 and thereby help us to explore the noticeable change in government policies. For further details on this database, see Borchert *et al.* (2019). Figure 3 plots the STRI scores for the years 2016 and 2008 across the five sectors.

The score points out that across these three economies there was hardly any paradigm shift observed in trade restrictive measures of 2008 and 2016. Bangladesh in the telecommunications services sector and Pakistan in the professional services sector are the only ones with observable shifts to a liberal trade policy. Furthermore, the database also categorises the STRI scores into six levels of restriction (0: No Restriction, 0.12–0.25: Minimal Transparency Issue, 0.25–0.5: Minor Restriction, 0.5–0.75: Major Restriction, 0.75–1: Closed) and we find that majority of service categories have a major restriction (see Table 11).

---

[10] We leave out India from this part of the analysis as the trade restrictive indices are based on imports. Our objective in this chapter is to explore how the other South Asian countries perform in the imports.

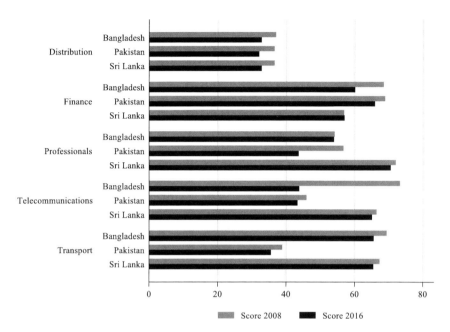

Figure 3. STRI scores in 2008 and 2016.
Source: The World Bank and WTO.

4. Conclusion

Can we build a regional economic partnership in South Asia? The short answer is *yes*. But how can it be done? To answer that, we at first summarise the main observations from the reported facts in the preceding sections. Services trade has been increasing rapidly across economies of the world. The major service categories that are traded in the world are Financial Services (SG), Charges for the Use for Intellectual Property (SH), Telecommunication and Information Services (SI) and Other Business Services (SL). India appears to be one of the top exporting nations of the world and it exports majorly services from the category of Telecommunication and Information Services (SI), Other Business Services (SJ) and Personal, Cultural and Recreational Services (SK). Furthermore, India has been receiving one of the highest FDI equity inflows in the world and aims to expand its trade in other service categories. On the other hand, imports of services by South Asian countries are meagre in terms of share in the world and value, but the annual growth of share is increasing. India's export share has been low to the South Asian countries, but the import share of these countries from India has been relatively high. We also observe that the service categories of SC, SD, SI, SG, SJ and SK made up a high share of the import basket of all South Asian countries from India. Alongside these categories, there were sporadic instances of South Asian countries importing in large numbers for the categories of SB, SE, SF and SL.

One also can find out from the facts reported above that the import value of South Asian countries is by itself low. Hence, these don't require a high export share of India. Therefore, low export share of India to South Asian countries in all the service categories must not be seen as a weak services trade between India and South Asian countries. It is also true that these countries do not solely depend on India for their services import, but they do reciprocate to India's expansion of exports in services. Nevertheless, India does also faces a strong competition from China and other European economies who seek to expand their trade relations with South Asian countries.

We also observe that India shares much cultural similarity with Bangladesh, Nepal, Pakistan, Bhutan and Sri Lanka and if these countries expand their import in the categories of Transport (SC), Travel (SD), Construction (SE), Insurance and Pension (SF), Financial Services (SG), Telecommunication and Information Services (SI), Personal, Cultural and Recreational (SK) with India, then the scope of economic partnership will expand. Also, the trading restrictions of major service categories need to be liberalised so that trade is expanded in this region.

For instance, India's higher education in IITs and IIMs and other Central Universities do cater to the demand for South Asian students. In fact, the University Grants Commission (UGC) under Ministry of Education of Government of India (GoI) has permitted opening up of offshore campuses. UGC too has initiated popularising language courses and other courses on culture, yoga and ayurveda, among others. On the other hand, in case of medical tourism, it has been observed that India offers a lower price for many common medical procedures than many countries in Asia. A report by Niti Aayog in 2021 on "Investment Opportunities in India's Healthcare Sector" points out that medical tourists in India have jumped by about 41% in between 2017 and 2019. Many of the tourists are from South Asian countries. In the context of insurance services, the much trusted Life Insurance Corporation of India has not only overseas offices but joint ventures with insurance companies in Sri Lanka and Nepal too. Needless to say, the Indian film industry has become increasingly popular for the non-Indian population in the South Asian region. These instances lead us to believe that South Asia has a huge demand for India's tourist destinations, health-care facilities, educational centres, Indian movies, constructional workers, pension funds, IT services, among others. Therefore, it is imperative for Governments of South Asian countries to develop policies that enhance regional trade in services and build long-term economic partnerships.

References

Banik, N. and Gilbert, J. (2010). Chapter 4: Regional integration and trade costs in South Asia. In Brooks, D. H. and Stone, S. F. (Ed.) *Trade Facilitation and Regional Cooperation in Asia*. Edward Elgar Publishing, Massachusetts, USA.

Bhagwati, J. N. (1984). Splintering and disembodiment of services and developing nations. *World Economy*, 7(2), 133–144.

Borchert, I., Gootiiz, B., Magdeleine, J., Marchetti, A. J., Mattoo, A., Rubio, E., and Shannon, E. (2019). Applied services trade policy a guide to the services trade policy database and the services trade restrictions index. *Staff Working Paper* ERSD-2019-14. WTO Economic Research and Statistics Division.

Ding, D. and Masha, I. (2012). India's growth spillovers to South Asia. *IMF Working Paper* 12/56. Washington DC, USA.

Fortanier, F., Liberatore, A., Maurer, A., Pilgrim, G., and Thomson, L. (2017). The OECD-WTO balance trade in services database (BaTIS). World Trade Organization, Geneva. https://www.wto.org/english/res_e/statis_e/daily_update_e/oecd-wto_batis_methodology.pdf.

Hill, T. P. (1977). On goods and services. *Review of Income and Wealth*, 23(4), 315–338.

Kathuria, S. and Rizwan, N. (2019). To strengthen regional trade, South Asia needs a multi-faceted approach. *World Bank Blogs*. https://blogs.worldbank.org/endpovertyinsouthasia/strengthen-regional-trade-south-asia-needs-multi-faceted-approach.

Kaur, S., Khorana, S., and Kaur, M. (2020). Is there any potential in service trade of South Asia? *Foreign Trade Review*, 55(3), 402–417.

Kravis, I. B. (1983). Services in the Domestic Economy and in World Transactions, NBER. https://www.nber.org/papers/w1124.

Kumar, R. (2020). India & South Asia: Geopolitics, regional trade and economic growth spillovers. *Journal of International Trade and Economic Development*, 29(1), 69–88.

Kumar, R. (2021). South Asia: Multilateral trade agreements and untapped regional trade integration. *International Journal of Finance and Economics*, 26(2), 2891–2903.

Kumar R. and Singh, M. (2009). India's role in South Asia trade and investment integration. *ADB Working Paper Series on Regional Economic Integration* No. 32. https://www.adb.org/sites/default/files/publication/28506/wp32-india-role-south-asia-trade.pdf.

Liberatore, A. and Wettstein (2021). The OECD-WTO balance trade in services database (BaTIS). World Trade Organization, Geneva. https://www.wto.org/english/res_e/statis_e/daily_update_e/oecd-wto_batis_methodology_bpm6.pdf.

Mehndiratta, S. and Nora, E. (2022). What will it take to connect the Bangladesh, Bhutan, India, Nepal (BBIN) sub-region? *World Bank Blogs*. https://blogs.worldbank.org/endpovertyinsouthasia/what-will-it-take-connect-bangladesh-bhutan-india-nepal-bbin-sub-region.

Nalapat, M. (2022). *Journey of a Nation: 75 Years of Foreign Policy*. Rupa Publications, New Delhi, India.

Panagariya, A. (2003). South Asia: Does preferential trade liberalisation make sense? *World Economy*, 26(9), 1279–1291.

Pollock, J. and Symon, D. (2023). Are China and India bound for another deadly border clash? *Chahtam House*. https://www.chathamhouse.org/publications/the-world-today/2023-06/are-china-and-india-bound-another-deadly-border-clash.

Press Information Bureau. (2022a). Services Contributed to 50% of GDP. https://pib.gov.in/PressReleasePage.aspx?PRID = 1793804.

Press Information Bureau. (2022b). India's External Sector Displays a Position of Strength in Spite of Global Headwinds. https://pib.gov.in/PressReleasePage.aspx?PRID = 1894926.

Press Information Bureau. (2023). Service Sector Grew at 8.4% (YoY) in FY 22. https://pib.gov.in/PressReleasePage.aspx?PRID = 1894897.

Ravi, S. and Kapoor, M. (2022). Quantifying India and its foreign relations through media monitoring. *TechTank, Brookings Institutions*. Available at https://www.brookings.edu/blog/techtank/2022/12/13/quantifying-india-and-its-foreign-relations-through-media-monitoring/.

Sampson, G. P. and Snape, R. H. (1985). Identifying the issues in trade in services. *World Economy*, 8(2), 171–182.

Sapir, A. and Winter, C. (1994). Service trade (No. 2013/8176). ULB–Universite Libre de Bruxelles.

Sinha, R. and Sareen, N. (2020). India's limited trade connectivity with South Asia. *Brookings Policy Brief*. Brookings Institution India Center, New Delhi, India.

Tajoli, L., Airoldi, F., and Piccardi, C. (2021).The network of international trade in services. *Applied Network Science*, 6(68). https://link.springer.com/article/10.1007/s41109-021-00407-1.

Chapter 12

Challenges for Regionalism in South Asia: The Role of Institutions and Human Development

Rashmi Arora

University of Bradford, Bradford, UK

r.arora6@bradford.ac.uk

Abstract

A large body of literature exists in the area of trade integration in various regions of the world (for instance, Mongelli *et al.*, 2005 for EU; Chen and Nory, 2011 for EU; Bouet *et al.*, 2017 for Africa, Athukorala and Yamashita, 2006 for East Asia; Bussiere *et al.*, 2005 for Central and Eastern European countries). However, not much literature is available on South Asian trade and economic integration. Intra-regional trade formed only 5% (in absolute terms $23 billion) of South Asia's total trade in comparison with the ASEAN region (25%) (World Bank). This is indeed perplexing as the countries within the region even though heterogeneous in terms of size and governed by different political ideologies, yet share similar cultural and historical closeness, high level of poverty and low level of human development (Arora and Ratnasari, 2014). Among the factors influencing low formal intra-regional trade are high trade barriers, high level of mistrust among the countries leading to several conflicts, especially between India and Pakistan. This chapter examines some of these issues and especially examines the association between low human development, institutional development and regional integration.

Keywords: South Asia, regional integration, human development, institutions.

1. Introduction

The South Asian region has over the years achieved rapid economic growth with rising per capita incomes over the years. The region's contribution to global GDP has increased from less than 5% in 2000 to more than 8% in 2019. Poverty too has declined significantly over the years. However, with the pandemic and current Russia–Ukraine war, the steady decline in poverty has been reversed, and as per the World Bank's estimate, about 58 million people in the region have additionally slipped into poverty (Mahler *et al.*, 2021). Regional trade integration in South Asia, which brings benefits in terms of reduction in poverty, inequality, increased competition and investment and promoting economic development, can help the countries to overcome the development issues (Salgado and Anand, 2023; Schiff and Winters, 2003; Martuscelli and Gasiorek, 2019).

International trade in Sustainable Development Goal (SDG) agenda, included in SDG targets 17.10, 17.11 and 17.12, is also well recognised as an engine for inclusive economic growth and poverty reduction and an important means for achieving the SDG goals. Further, other SDG targets SDG2, 2.B, SDG 8 (decent work and economic growth) and SDG 10 (reduced inequality) also cover international trade. Acknowledging South Asia as low in trade and economic integration, recently the World Bank has launched 'One South Asia' project with the objectives of promoting greater regional cooperation within the region, which in turn can lead to higher inclusive economic growth, climate change resilience, improved infrastructure, strengthened institutions and achievement of SDGs. The overall focus of the project is to 'enable regional connectivity, increasing climate resilience, and investing in human capital.'

However, it is well known that trade in the South Asian region is significantly below its potential. According to Kumar and George (2021), "about 67% of the estimated potential for trade between the subregional countries remains unexploited" (Kumar and George, 2021). The average level of trade costs between country pairs in South Asia is 85% higher than those in East Asia (Kathuria *et al.*, 2015). Not only the intra-regional trade within the region is low, but also intra-regional investment and global foreign direct investment, both inward and outward (Kathuria *et al.*, 2021). Considering the importance of trade, low engagement for South Asian countries in intra-regional trade is a cause of concern, especially as the countries are in close proximity to each other. Among the factors listed in influencing low formal intra-regional trade are high trade barriers, high level of mistrust among the countries leading to several conflicts especially between India and Pakistan and lack of political will (Arora and Ratnasiri, 2014).[1]

The urgency of regional trade has been emphasised by several studies and the current series of crises such as the pandemic, Russia–Ukraine war followed by the energy crisis and food insecurity has escalated the necessity of prioritising inter-regional trade among the countries in the region (Kathuria *et al.*, 2015, 2021, 2022).

Furthermore, these countries are not only low in trade integration but are also diverse in terms of institutional development and human development. Can these be factors behind poor integration within the region? Is there any relationship between these factors? Does regional trade integration take place only with sufficient levels of human development and developed institutions? The Human Development Index of all countries within the region is diverse ranging from low to high human development. For instance, for the year 2021 while Sri Lanka belongs to the category of high human development, Bangladesh, India and Nepal fall within medium human development group and Pakistan in the low human development group. Similarly institutional development is low in the region. For instance, in the 2023 index of economic freedom compiled by the Heritage Foundation, among 176 countries (where 1 is the highest), Bangladesh ranks 123, India 131, Sri Lanka 136, Nepal 142 and lowest is Pakistan at 152. Even within property rights, the score ranges from 29.0 in Pakistan to 51.6 in Sri Lanka (where 100 is maximum and lowest 1). In this chapter, we take a fresh look at the trends in inter-regional trade in South Asia and adopt an analytical methodological approach to examine the triangular relationship between trade integration in South Asia, institutional development and human development. The rest of the chapter is

---

[1] Kathuria *et al.* (2021) note that knowledge connectivity and intra-regional investment are other factors which could be impeding regional trade and investment.

organised as follows. Section 2 briefly develops the conceptual framework involving the three variables and also examines some of the empirical literature in this area. Section 3 provides a backdrop to the South Asian countries under consideration and lays down some stylised facts. The next section looks at the selected variables and discusses the core findings. Finally, Section 5 concludes the study.

2. Literature Review

2.1. *Conceptual framework*

The role of international trade in economic growth has been much discussed both in the theoretical and empirical literature. The evidence has, however, remained mixed with both positive as well as negative effects. The protagonists of trade argue that international trade leads to an increase in economic growth. Studies have also shown that regional integration leads to inclusive economic growth and helps in human development through four main channels of income, access to services, empowerment and sustainability (UNDP, 2011). Conceptually, this can be portrayed in Figure 1.

The channels through which human development and regional integration are related to each other (as shown in Figure 1) are through income, empowerment, sustainability and access to services. Income itself is closely related to employment (both in terms of quantity and quality)

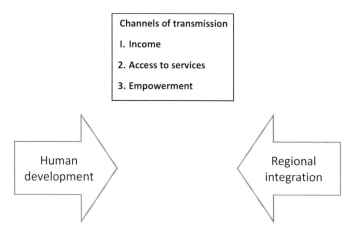

Figure 1. Relationship between regional integration and human development.
Source: Adapted from UNDP (2011).

and both are closely related to regional integration. However, even though theoretically, the relationship may be straightforward, empirically the impact of trade on economic growth is not so clear cut and may or may not lead to economic growth. It can create new jobs; however, it could also lead to increased investment in capital-intensive projects leading to loss of jobs or the so-called jobless growth (UNDP, 2011). Currently, focus has also moved to decent work implying that not just the quantity of employment, but also the quality matters. The differential impact of employment will also have an impact on human development. The distribution of income as a result of the above employment impacts will also influence human development.

The second channel through which regional integration can impact human development is through access to services, for example, education. Flexible regional mobility can enable individuals to take up opportunities relating to employment and education. This would, however, depend upon the whether the growth is inclusive and is more in the skilled sectors, rather than semi-skilled or unskilled sectors. A downside of the regional economic integration is a loss in tariff revenue for the governments. This may further create implications for government expenditure especially on social sectors and impact human development. This may also have gender implications as reduced government expenditures, particularly social expenditures may have negative impact on girls' school enrolment, child labour and human development.

The other two channels are empowerment and sustainability. Regional integration can also lead to empowerment in various aspects: such as through decent work; empowerment of women through increased employment opportunities leading to increased incomes, which further builds into increased access to nutrition, health and human development; youth empowerment through decline in crime and violence and empowerment through migration. Regional integration could also allow employment in trading countries. Also, regional integration could lead to more economic and political stability as countries get more integrated with each other and could strive to maintain stability. Regional integration, while on one hand, could lead to over exploitation of environment due to increased intra-regional trade, on the other hand, it could also create more awareness and adoption of best international practices leading to positive impact on human development (UNDP, 2011).

Institutional development too is strongly related to regional integration. New institutional approach argues that strong institutions are required for regional cooperation to take place as the institutions "act as the rules of the game and (*they*) link all actors and their action together" (Rattanasevee, 2014).

Regional trade could entail investment in capacity building and further reforms in the public sector. The greater trade and regional cooperation has a strong implication for the achievement of various SDG targets (UNCTAD, 2016). For instance, increased regional trade particularly that involving small and medium enterprises (SMEs) may help formalising the sector, thus supporting the SDG target 8.3. It can also lead to the development of new skill sets, knowledge spillovers, increased use of technology and greater human development. UNCTAD (2016) finds positive correlation between increased trade facilitation, GDP per capita and country's human and institutional development.

2.2. Empirical literature

A large body of empirical literature exists in the area of trade integration in various regions of the world (for instance Mongelli *et al.*, 2005 for EU; Chen and Novy, 2011 for EU; Bouet *et al.*, 2017 for Africa, Athukorala and Yamashita, 2006 for East Asia; Bussiere *et al.*, 2005 for Central and Eastern European countries). A number of studies have also examined regional trade integration in South Asia, or rather the lack of trade integration (Ahmed and Ghani, 2007; Kher, 2012; Aggarwal, 2008). Interestingly, the literature's scope on South Asia has recently widened from focusing only on regional trade integration to broader concepts such as regional cooperation in SDGs and climate change, regional investment and resilience.

Several studies have also shown that better institutional quality promotes higher trade among the countries (Than Le, 2009; Capannelli, 2011). For instance, Schönfelder and Wagner (2016) for European integration and its impact on institutional development, found that while prospective EU membership had a positive impact on institutional development, the institutional development loses momentum once the countries are part of the union. Mongelli *et al.* (2005) concentrated on European regional integration and institutional integration and found that the interaction between institutional integration and trade integration matters and the link is stronger from institutional integration to trade integration. Feng and Genna (2003) also found that the process of regional integration and domestic institutions reinforce each other. In the case of South Asia, Shah (2021) found that economic integration within the region increases economic growth and observed bidirectional causality between economic integration and democracy, regional integration and human capital, democracy and human capital and, democracy and labour. In other words, the study observed a relationship between economic integration and institutions. Rodrik and Subramaniam (2003) found that institutional quality is strongly and positively related to trade integration. Trade integration can also improve institutional quality.

Some studies, besides covering institutions and trade, also focus on their combined effect on human and economic development. Baliamoune-Lutz and Boko (2013) examine the relationship between institutions, trade, income and human development in the context of Sub-Saharan Africa. They also examine whether trade and institutions are linked to human development. Their findings show that trade and institutions do not impact human development. Their findings on the contrary show that income is the prime determinant of human development and also contributes to institutional development though with a threshold effect. In the case of the ASEAN region, Kumar (2017) examines the relationship between trade openness and human development. The study revealed significant relationship between trade openness and human development in the case of ASEAN countries.

3. Economies of South Asia

In this section, we briefly cover a few stylised facts on the countries in the South Asian region.[2] The countries within the region are quite similar in terms of culture, food, language to a certain extent, high level of poverty, yet they are heterogenous in terms of size, economy and political ideologies. Together, the selected countries in 2022 accounted for 4.3% of global

---

[2] Bose and Jalal (2022) argue that South Asia is more of a geographical construct. In the authors' own words, "South Asia is a more recent construction — only seven and half decades old — which today encompasses eight very diverse sovereign states of very different sizes ... The terms South Asia and India refer in the first instance to a vast geographical space stretching from the Himalayan Mountain ranges in the north to the Indian ocean in the South and from the valley of the Indus in the West to the plains of Brahmaputra in the east."

Table 1. Some socio-economic indicators of South Asia.

Year	Bangladesh	India	Nepal	Pakistan	Sri Lanka
Poverty headcount ratio at $2.15 a day (2017 PPP) (% of population)	13.5$	10.0*	8.2**	4.9@	1.0@@
GDP growth (annual %)	7.1	7.0	5.6	6.2	−7.8
GDP per capita (constant 2015 US$)	1785	2085	1083	1536	3988
Inflation, consumer prices (annual %)	7.7	6.7		19.9	49.7
Unemployment, total (% of total labour force) (modelled ILO estimate)	4.7	7.3	11.1	6.4	6.7
Population growth (annual %)	1.1	0.7	1.7	1.9	0.1
Population ages 15–64 (% of total population)	68.0	67.8	65.0	59.2	65.6

Notes: The data on poverty is for different years. Thus $ refers to year 2016, * data is for 2019, **refers to 2010; @ refers to 2018; @@ refers to data for 2020. All other data relates to the year 2022.
Source: World Bank Database.

output at current market prices, 97.8% of the total population in South Asia and 23.6% of the world's population.

Table 1 shows some social and economic indicators within the region. As can be seen from the table, the economic growth rate of countries in 2022 ranged from −7.8% in Sri Lanka to 7.1% in Bangladesh. The sharp decline in the case of Sri Lanka was due to the internal turmoil recently witnessed in the country. While almost all the countries in the study experienced a fall in growth rates in 2020, they recovered in the following year, though due to the impact of external factors the growth rates have remained sluggish. In 2023, the average growth rate in South Asia is expected to decline with growth expected to be lower in Pakistan, while in Sri Lanka the growth rate is expected to decline further by 4.3% on top of a decline of 7.8% in 2022. Rise in borrowing costs and high fiscal spending adjustments are expected to dampen India's growth rate at 6.3%. Similarly, lowering of growth projections is expected for Bangladesh too (World Bank, 2023). Figure 2 also shows trends in economic growth in the region. Population growth rate has declined in nearly all the countries in the region, and the countries are in the phase of demographic transition with more than 65% of the population in the working age group.

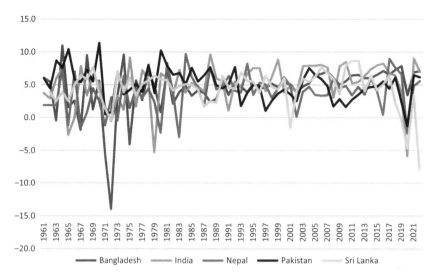

Figure 2. GDP growth (%) in South Asian countries.

Table 2. Share of different sectors in GDP (average 2018–2022).

Countries	Agriculture, forestry, and fishing, value added (% of GDP)	Industry (including construction), value added (% of GDP)	Services, value added (% of GDP)	Per capita GDP (5 yearly average)
Bangladesh	11.9	33.0	51.1	1616
India	17.1	25.5	48.6	1939
Nepal	21.8	12.4	52.3	1042
Pakistan	21.8	19.1	52.8	1463
Sri Lanka	8.1	29.5	55.8	4301

Source: World Bank Online Database.

The structure of economies is given in the Table 2. As can be observed, the share of services sector has increased in all the countries accompanied by a declining share of agriculture. The structural transformation picture shows that in all the countries (except India) within the region the share of services sector is more than 50% of GDP. For example, India's structural transformation has skipped the manufacturing sector and moved over to the service sector (termed as premature deindustrialisation by Lamba and Subramaniam, 2020). This has led to misallocation of resources with employment of skilled labour than unskilled labour.

Table 3. India's trade with different countries (% of total).

Regions	2017–2018 EX	2017–2018 IM	2018–2019 EX	2018–2019 IM	2019–2020 EX	2019–2020 IM	2020–2021 EX	2020–2021 IM	2021–2022 EX	2021–2022 IM
Trade with SAARC countries	7.61	0.69	7.68	0.85	7.00	0.81	7.57	0.86	8.11	0.89
Trade with other Asian developing countries excluding SAARC	25.34	34.95	25.20	34.15	23.63	34.59	26.26	38.42	22.89	35.67
Trade with OECD group countries	39.41	27.22	38.83	28.18	39.58	28.20	40.65	29.45	42.83	26.73

Note: EX and IM stands for exports and Imports respectively.
Source: Data from *RBI Handbook of Statistics on Indian Economy*.

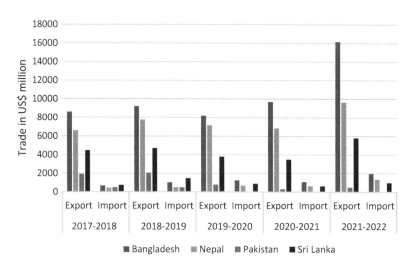

Figure 3. India's trade pattern within South Asia.

As mentioned earlier, although the countries geographically are in proximity with each other, and share a similar culture and history, yet trade among them is very low. A look at India's trade pattern with the countries in the region and beyond proves this point (Table 3).

Within the South Asian countries, India's trade (the largest economy within the region) with the neighbouring countries is shown in Figure 3.

4. Our Variables and Discussion

Our study includes five major countries in the region — Bangladesh, India, Nepal, Pakistan and Sri Lanka. We do not include other countries in the regions such as Bhutan and Afghanistan due to non-availability of time series data on some variables.

For institutional development, we consider World Bank Governance Indicators (WGI). The WGI include indicators for over 200 countries for the period 1996–2021 and covers six dimensions of governance — voice and accountability; political stability and absence of violence; government effectiveness, regulatory quality; rule of law; and control of corruption. The Appendix shows trends in multi-dimensional governance index in the South Asian countries.

We also consider UNDP's Human Development Index as an indicator of human development. The Human Development Index, constructed by UNDP, is built on three dimensions of long and healthy life, being knowledgeable and having decent standard of living. The health dimension is captured by life expectancy at birth, education (dimension of being knowledgeable) by mean years of schooling for adults aged 25 years or more and expected years of schooling for children of school entering age and finally, the third dimension of standard of living is measured by gross national income per capita.

Next, we consider Heritage Foundation's trade freedom data as a proxy indicator for regional integration.[3] The foundation has been constructing economic freedom index since 1995 and analyses the state of economic freedom in countries around the world. The 2023 index includes 184 countries and measures economic freedom based on 12 quantitative and qualitative factors grouped into four broad categories or pillars. These are rule of law, government size, regulatory efficiency and open markets. In the South Asian context, in the economic freedom index, Bangladesh, India, Nepal and Sri Lanka fall within the 'mostly unfree' category while Pakistan with an overall score of 49.4 ranks as a repressed economy. The reason behind choice of trade freedom as a proxy for regional integration is that it shows whether a country is open to international trade (whether

---

[3] Interestingly, Lombaerde and Langenhove (2005) argue that regional integration "can be seen as a multidimensional process that implies, next to economic cooperation, also dimensions of politics, diplomacy, security, culture, etc." In our study we however, refer to trade integration in economic terms only.

within the region or other parts of the world) and trade openness is reflected by the extent of tariff and non-tariff barriers. Trade freedom dimension is a composite measure of tariff and non-tariff barriers and the score is based on trade-weighted average tariff rate and qualitative measure of non-tariff barriers. The non-tariff barriers include quantity restrictions such as import quotas, voluntary export restraints, regulatory restrictions such as domestic content requirement, customs restrictions and direct government interventions.

Figure 4 shows trends in trade freedom index in the selected countries in South Asia. Due to limited data availability, we consider this data from 2010 onwards.

We then bring together the three variables — human development, institutional development and regional integration — in the context of selected South Asian countries and carry out a descriptive analysis. As the data from the Heritage Foundation shows, in terms of trade freedom (our proxy indicator for regional integration), the trade-weighted average tariff rate is 11.5% in Bangladesh. The non-tariff barriers also tend to be high in the country further impacting trade and investment. In the overall economic freedom index, the country with the score of 54.4 was ranked 123 in 2023. In India, the trade-weighted average tariff rate is 12.6% (higher than Bangladesh) and despite a large number of trade reforms since 1991, a

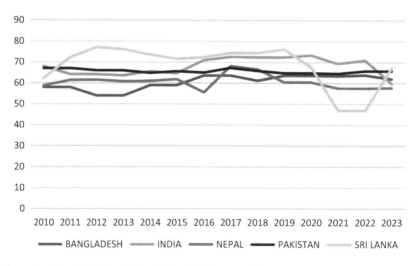

Figure 4. Trade freedom index of South Asian countries.

Source: Heritage Foundation.

significant number of 300 non-tariff barriers are still in force. The overall score of economic freedom of India was 52.9 with the ranking of 131 in the 2023 index. The trade-weighted average tariff rate is 13.6% in Nepal higher than other neighbouring countries. Pakistan's economic freedom score is 49.4, making its economy rank at 152, much lower compared to other South Asian counterparts. The trade-weighted average tariff rate, on the contrary, is lower at 9.6% in 2023. Sri Lanka's economic freedom at 52.2 leads to its ranking at 136 in the 2023 index. The trade-weighted average tariff rate is much lower at 6.4%, though extensive NTBs still persist.

We carried out Pearson's correlation to examine the association between the variables and the results are given below. These, however, should be treated with caution as these are only crude associations and may not accurately reflect the relationships. Also, the limited availability of data constrains us in carrying out further in-depth analysis. Nonetheless, the results are quite mixed and no definitive conclusions can be drawn. It does show that while HDI and trade freedom index (proxy for regional integration) are positively correlated in India and Bangladesh, in other countries the results are insignificant. Other studies too have found a positive relationship between globalisation, economic freedom and human development (Akhter, 2020). Reiter and Steensma (2010) also find a positive relationship between selective FDI flows and human development in developing countries.

We also find that regulatory quality is strongly and positively associated in India and Pakistan. Van der Marel and Shepherd (2013), in their study, find that restrictive regulations have a negative and significant impact on cross-border services trade, though there is some degree of cross-sectoral heterogeneity regarding the impact of regulations. Nagaraj and Zhang (2019) also observe a positive relationship between regulatory quality and financial openness and cost of capital. Among other findings, we observe that control of corruption and government effectiveness appear to be have a stronger and positive impact in India. Other studies have also noted that greater trade openness leads to decline in corruption, though other policy measures are equally crucial to control of corruption (Majeed, 2014; Sandholtz and Gray, 2003; Bryant and Javalgi, 2016). The dimension of rule of law which captures confidence in abiding by the rules includes contract enforcement, property rights, police, courts and control of violence and crime is positive and significant only in Bangladesh and is not bearing relationship with TFI in other countries. This finding, though in our case relevant only for Bangladesh, has been supported by other studies too such as Rigobon and Rodrik (2005).

Table 4. TFI correlation with other variables.

Country	Bangladesh	India	Nepal	Pakistan	Sri Lanka
Human development index	0.816**	0.727**	0.165	−0.575	−0.192
Regulatory quality	−0.093	0.832**	−0.099	0.604*	−0.457
Voice & Accountability	−0.791**	−0.609*	0.012	0.457	0.841**
Government effectiveness	0.280	0.714**	−0.165	−0.375	0.041
Political stability & absence of violence	0.662*	0.590*	0.054	−0.718**	0.765**
Rule of law	0.883**	−0.250	0.301	−0.232	0.491
Control of corruption	−0.279	0.854**	−0.085	−0.507	−0.098

Notes: *Correlation is significant at the 0.05 level (2-tailed).
**Correlation is significant at the 0.01 level (2-tailed).

5. Conclusion

This chapter examined briefly trends in regional integration in the South Asian countries. We examined specifically five major countries in the region — Bangladesh, India, Nepal, Pakistan and Sri Lanka. Findings showed that intra-regional trade is significantly low in the region. A number of factors have been listed as the reasons for low intra-regional trade including high trade barriers and high level of mistrust and conflict among the countries, especially India and Pakistan. Examining closely regional integration, human development and institutional development, we find that both human development and institutional development are low in the region and the triangular relationship among them yields mixed results. We may caution though that these are only crude associations and rigorous analysis is required to draw out firm policy implications.

Nonetheless, while the trade integration among the selected countries in South Asia has remained low, as was observed in the earlier discussions, recently the focus has moved on to developing greater regional cooperation among the South Asian countries with the objective of developing cooperation in climate change and inclusive economic growth. The World Bank (2023), in its latest policy stance, emphasised that "taking joint action can develop cross-border solutions to shared issues, strengthen regional institutions improve infrastructure and connectivity, and advance trade policy". This approach has been termed as 'One South

Asia' and the three-dimensional focus is on enabling regional connectivity, increase climate resilience and investment in human capital. Considering the significant mutual developmental benefits of trade integration including its impact on regional poverty, increased trade and regional cooperation is called for among the countries in South Asia.

Appendix: Trends in Multi-dimensional Governance Index in the South Asian Countries

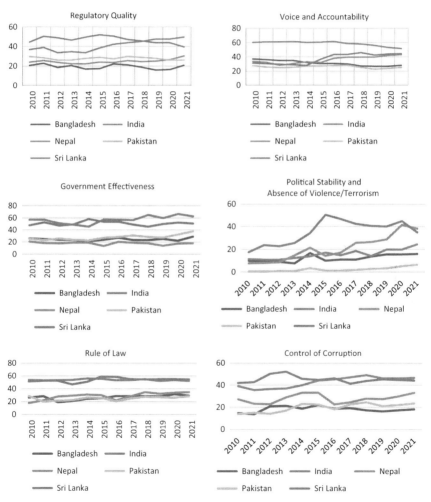

References

Aggarwal, A. (2008). Regional economic integration and FDI in South Asia — prospects and problems. http://www.eaber.org/node/22141.

Ahmed, S. and Ghani, E. (2007). *South Asia Growth and Regional Integration*. The World Bank.

Akhter, S. H. (2020). Is globalization what it's cracked up to be? Economic freedom, corruption, and human development. *Journal of World Business*, *39*(3), 283–295.

Arora, R.U. and Ratnasiri, S. (2014). Financial integration of South Asia: An exploratory study. *New Zealand Journal of Asian Studies*, *16*(1), 39–60.

Athukorala, P.-C. and Yamashita, N. (2006). Production fragmentation and trade integration: East Asia in a global context. *The North American Journal of Economics and Finance*, *17*(3), 233–256.

Baliamoune-Lutz, M. and Boko, S. H. (2013). Trade, institutions, income and human development in African countries. *Journal of African Economies*, *22*(2), 323–345. https://doi.org/10.1093/jae/ejs037.

Bouët, A., Cosnard, L., and Laborde, D. (2017). Measuring trade, integration in Africa. *Journal of Economic Integration*, *32*(4), 937–977.

Bose, S. and Jalal, A. (2022). *Modern South Asia: History, Culture, Political Economy*, 5th edn. Routledge.

Bryant, C. E. and Javalgi, R. G. (2016). Global economic integration in developing countries: The role of corruption and human capital investment. *Journal of Busienss Ethics, 136*, 437–450. https://doi.org/10.1007/s10551-014-2490-3.

Bussiere, M., Fidrmuc, J., and Schnatz, B. (2005). Trade integration of Central and Eastern European countries: Lessons from a gravity model (November 2005). *ECB Working Paper* No. 545. http://dx.doi.org/10.2139/ssrn.836424.

Capannelli, G. (2011). Institutions for economic and financial integration in Asia: Trends and prospects. *ADBI Working Paper* 308. Asian Development Bank Institute, Tokyo. http://www.adbi.org/workingpaper/2011/09/07/4689.economic.financial.integration.asia.trends.prospects/.

Chen, N. and Novy, D. (2011). Gravity, trade integration, and heterogeneity across industries. *Journal of International Economics*, *85*(2), 206–221.

De Lombaerde, P. and Van Langenhove, L. (2005). Indicators of regional integration: Methodological issues. *IIIS Discussion Paper* No. 64, March.

Estefania-Flores, J., Furceri, D., Hannan, S. A., Ostry, J. D., and Rose, A. K. (2022). A measurement of aggregate trade restrictions and their economic effects. *CEPR Discussion Paper* 16919, Center for Economic and Policy Research, Washington, DC.

Feng, Y. and Genna, G. M. (2003). Regional integration and domestic institutional homogeneity: a comparative analysis of regional integration in the

Americas, Pacific Asia and Western Europe. *Review of International Political Economy*, *10*(2), 278–309.

Furceri, D., Hannan, S. A., Ostry, J. D., and Rose, A. K. (2019). Macroeconomic consequences of tariffs. *IMF Working Paper* 19/009, International Monetary Fund, Washington, DC.

Kathuria, S. (2022). Is South Asia only a figment of the imagination? Far from it. Retrieved from https://sites.utu.fi/bre/is-south-asia-only-a-figment-of-the-imagination-far-from-it/.

Kathuria, S., Shahid, S., and Ferrantino, M. J. (2015). How has regional integration taken place in other regions? Lessons for South Asia. *SARConnect*, Issue No. 2. World Bank, Washington, DC. https://openknowledge.worldbank.org/entities/publication/eb75bdbd-f34a-54b4-b1b2-2ced35ca8669 License: CC BY 3.0 IGO.

Kathuria, S., Yatawara, R. A., and Xiao'ou Zhu. (2021). *Regional Investment Pioneers in South Asia: The Payoff of Knowing Your Neighbors*. World Bank, Washington, DC.

Kher, P. (2012). Political economy of regional integration in South Asia regional value chains *Background Paper*. Background Paper No. RVC5, UNCTAD.

Kumar, S. (2017). Trade and human development: Case of ASEAN. *Pacific Business Review International*, *9*(12), 48–57.

Kumar, N. and George, J. (2021). Leveraging regional cooperation for achieving the SDGS in South Asia. *South and South-West Asia Development Papers* 21-04, UNESCAP.

Le, T. (2009). Trade, remittances, institutions, and economic growth. *International Economic Journal*, *23*(3), 391–408. DOI: 10.1080/10168730903119443.

Martuscelli, A. and Gasiorek, M. (2019). Regional integration and poverty: A review of the transmission channels and the evidence. *Journal of Economic Surveys*, *33*(2), 431–457.

Majeed, M. T. (2014). Corruption and Trade. *Journal of Economic Integration*, *29*(4), 759–782.

Mahler, D. G., Yonzan, N., Lakner, C., Aguilar, R. A. C., and Wu, H. (2021). Updated estimates of the impact of COVID-19 on global poverty: Turning the corner on the pandemic in 2021? Retrieved from https://blogs.worldbank.org/opendata/updated-estimates-impact-covid-19-global-poverty-turning-corner-pandemic-2021.

Mongelli, F., Dorrucci, E., and Agur, I. (2005). What does European institutional integration tell us about trade integration? No. 40, *Occasional Paper Series*. European Central Bank.

Rattanasevee, P. (2014). Towards institutionalised regionalism: The role of institutions and prospects for institutionalisation in ASEAN. *Journal of the Korean Physical Society*, *3*(1), 556. https://doi.org/10.1186/2193-1801-3-556.

Rigobon, R. and Rodrik, D. (2005). Rule of law, democracy, openness, and income: Estimating the interrelationships. *The Economics of Transition and Institutional Change*, *13*(3), 533–564.

Rodrik, D., Subramanian, A., and Trebbi, F. (2002). Institutions rule: The primacy of institutions over geography and integration in economic development. *NBER Working Paper* 9305, October 2002. National Bureau of Economic Research, Cambridge, Massachusetts.

Salgado, R. and Anand, R. (2023). *South Asia's Path to Resilient Growth*. International Monetary Fund. https://www.imf.org/en/Publications/Books/Issues/2022/12/23/South-Asia-s-Path-to-Resilient-Growth-527427.

Sandholtz, W. and Gray, M. (2003). International integration and national corruption. *International Organization*, *57*(4), 761–800.

Schönfelder, N. and Wagner, H. (2016, September). Impact of European integration on institutional development. *Journal of Economic Integration*, *31*(3), 472–530. https://doi.org/10.11130/jei.2016.31.3.472.

Schiff, M. and Winters, L. (2003). *Regional Integration and Development*, No. 15172. World Bank, Washington DC.

Shah, M. I. (2021). Investigating the role of regional economic integration on growth: Fresh insights from South Asia. *Global Journal of Emerging Market Economies*, *13*(1). https://doi.org/10.1177/0974910120974800.

UNDP. (2011). *Regional Integration and Human Development: A Pathway for Africa*. United Nations Development Programme.

van der Marel, E. and Shepherd, B. (2013). Services trade, regulation and regional integration: Evidence from sectoral data. *The World Economy*, *36*(11), 1393–1405.

World Bank. (2023, April). Expanding opportunities: Toward inclusive growth. *South Asia, Economic Focus*. World Bank, Washington, DC. DOI: 10.1596/978-1-4648-1980-3.

Part IV

Rail and Road Connectivity: Scope for Regional Production Networks

Chapter 13

Trade Disruption and Shifting Trends in Trade Partners amid the Pandemic: A Case Study of South Asia

Mojtaba Hajian Heidary

Industrial Management, Allameh Tabatabai' University, Tehran, Iran

hajianheidary@atu.ac.ir

Abstract

In the aftermath of supply chain disruptions arising due to the COVID-19 pandemic, managers understood that in order to efficiently manage supply chains, they should analyse the decisions they make using a proper modelling approach. Especially as the global supply chains are more vulnerable to such a crisis. In this research, a system dynamics simulation model is presented based on a real case study in Iran. An international company that works with two partners based in the southern part of Asia is considered. Production, import and export and local demand are the most important components of the model in each zone and a free trade zone is also considered. A force majeure factor is considered as the disruption impact of the pandemic on the supply chain operations. The model was tested in different disruption scenarios. Simulation results showed that the flexibility of production capacity is an important way of avoiding the adverse impacts of such disruptions in the supply chain.

Keywords: Pandemic, South Asia, simulation, supply chain management, global supply chain.

1. Introduction

The recent COVID-19 pandemic has clearly shown to businesses that disruptions in the supply chain could be very destructive. Therefore, managers should pay more attention to investigating their supply chains in depth. After supply chains suffered severe disruption due to the pandemic, many studies have been conducted on the effect of disruption on the supply chain performance, which found that enterprises should reformulate their strategies to become more resilient, sustainable and collaborative with partners.

Cost reduction and productivity enhancement were two important drivers of supply chain strategies before the pandemic. The crisis brought about by the pandemic has forced companies to shift their focus to innovation, turn to new paradigms and also restructure efforts to ensure business continuity. Paying more attention to building more resilient and flexible supply chain is the main result of this shift. During the last year, supply chain managers have made transformational changes in the supply chain structure in response to the challenges of the crisis: improving efficiency, increasing inventories and improving their capabilities of digitalisation and risk management.

The other result of the pandemic is the emergence of new alliances between some global supply chain players. In certain industries, failures occurred as a result of the pandemic and also created critical links in the supply chain, which had led supply chain managers to co-develop partnerships between original equipment manufacturers (OEMs) and suppliers. As a result of increasing collaboration through sharing information and visibility, the adverse effects of disruptions have been decreased. Schmidt and Raman (2012) defined the disruption as 'an unplanned event that adversely affects a firm's normal operations'. Therefore, organisations and their managers should move closer to their suppliers and build more strong relationships to protect themselves against unforeseen disruption. Also, coordination efforts between global supply chain players are more important than local supply chains. Many strategic decisions have been made in the international supply chains. On the other hand, the existence of disruptions and various uncertainties in the supply, demand and import/export process have come complex in the decision-making process. In addition, the pandemic caused more complexities in the supply chains.

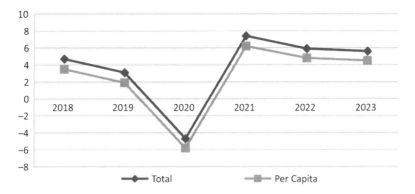

Figure 1. The GDP growth of south Asian countries amid the pandemic.
Source: World Economic Situation and Prospects (2022). www.un.org.

Asian countries, especially those in South Asia, were hit early by the pandemic. Figure 1 shows the South Asian GDP growth prepared by the UN. During the pandemic, GDP growth in South Asian countries decreased significantly and then recovered. This recovery, however, is still unstable and subjected to pandemic-related uncertainties and other risks.

Simulation is a powerful tool to model the uncertainty in supply chains. Particularly, system dynamics (SD) is a simulation approach that can model the strategic level problems and analyse them under different uncertainty scenarios. SD mainly focuses on the key ideas of a system described by interactions between variables, loops and causalities between variables (Currie *et al.*, 2018). Hence, we use this approach to model the trade disruption and shifting trends in the global supply chain. In addition, we consider the impact of the pandemic on the global supply chain by a pandemic severity factor in the model. In this chapter, we model the trade disruption and shifting trends in the global supply chain and the adverse effects of the pandemic on the common operations of the supply chain.

In general, there are many bilateral or regional contracts between Asian countries. Iran and China specifically have signed many free trade agreements or regional trade agreements with South Asian countries. If these contracts were connected on a map, the result would look like a spaghetti bowl. The growing number of agreements is called the spaghetti

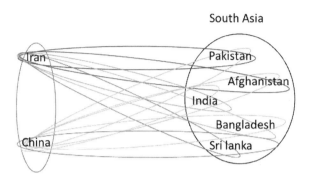

Figure 2. A schematic view of the contracts of free trade between Iran and China with South Asian countries.

bowl effect. The term spaghetti bowl effect was first introduced by Jagdish Bhagwati in 1995. Figure 2 depicts a schematic view of free trade contracts between Iran and China with South Asian countries.

By comparing the economic growth and trade in different South Asian countries, it can be concluded that there is a correlation between these variables. Countries with higher levels of GDP growth usually tend to have higher rates of growth in international trade (Aghion and Durlauf, 2005). One of the main requirements for trade is a powerful network of connectivity. Rails and roads are two important ways of transporting goods between the countries especially in South Asia, where these are the cheapest trade-related transportation modes. However, insufficient transport connectivity in the countries of South Asia have reduced the gains that could be made by trade (Chatterjee and Sing, 2020). On the other hand, geopolitical tensions in South Asia pose the main obstacle for integration between the countries. More integration between the South Asian countries will lead to better connectivity in trade and economic cooperation.

In this research, a model is presented to simulate a part of these contracts between Iran and South Asian countries using the system dynamics approach. The rest of the chapter is organised as follows: in Section 2, a literature review of SD is done. In Section 3, a short introduction to the SD approach is presented. The simulation modelling approach and case study description are explained in Section 4. Finally, numerical results of the simulation model along with discussions about the most important findings of the research are provided. In addition, concluding remarks are provided in the last section.

2. Literature Review

In this section, the relevant works in the literature are reviewed. The SD approach is a powerful technique to analyse the supply chain dynamics. Bhushi and Javalagi (2004) developed a SD model in a supply chain management problem and showed that the process of international supply chains is an important area of research that should be taken into account by the researchers. Sundarakani *et al.* (2010) analysed dynamics of the supply chain management in the global context using a system dynamics approach. They considered a four-echelon supply chain and their interactions in their model and also analysed different scenarios of economic conditions. The results of their analysis showed that information delays play an important role in the global context. Choi *et al.* (2012) investigated the disruption mechanism in an automobile manufacturer and asserted that in order to prevent the adverse effect of the disruptions, postponement strategy could be applied by the decision makers. Nedelciu *et al.* (2020) modelled a global phosphorus supply chain using a system dynamic approach. They divided the global network into eight sections. Social, economic and environmental dynamics are considered and analysed in their proposed model. The COVID-19 pandemic also had dramatic effects on the South Asian region. Rasul *et al.* (2021) investigated the existing and future impacts, risks and challenges of the pandemic on this region. They concluded that decreasing economic growth, increasing risk of macroeconomic instability and dwindling small and medium industries are the main problems arising from the pandemic.

Different simulation approaches have been developed in the literature to model the impact of the pandemic on the supply chain processes. Sinha *et al.* (2020) investigated the impact of the pandemic on supply chain operations and also checked different business scenarios in the pre- and post-pandemic situation. They proposed a force majeure coefficient in their model to consider the adverse impact of the pandemic. Wang *et al.* (2020) developed a SD model to predict the impact of distribution disruptions in the hog market in china. They demonstrated that delay is an important part of the model and also asserted that the disruptions occurred only for a short term. Hajian Heidary (2022) investigated a global supply chain considering disruptions caused by the pandemic. A simulation model is presented to analyse the adverse impacts of the recent pandemic on the operations of global supply chain. He concluded that more flexibility of the production process of supply chain is a key solution to solve the problems arising from the pandemic.

In addition, some of the researchers focused on the analysis of the supply chain operations in the South Asian region. Asgari and Hoque (2013) presented a system model to assess the performance of the ready-made garment supply chain in Bangladesh. Mareeh *et al.* (2022) investigated the sustainability and profitability measures in an oil supply chain case study in Malaysia using the simulation approach. Katrina and Moynihan (2009) studied local and regional disruptions due to force majeure conditions. Peng *et al.* (2014) proposed a new model to analyse different mechanisms of disruptions in disaster situations of a supply chain. Gu *et al.* (2014) surveyed risk management process in a reverse logistics system using the SD approach. They compared the impact of different kinds of supply disruption in their model. Gu and Gao (2017) studied the impact of production disruption in remanufacturing/manufacturing using a system dynamics model. Olivares-Aguila and Elmaghrebi (2021) introduced a framework for observing supply chain behaviours. They also examined different disruptions and their effects on the quality of services, profits and inventory levels. Zhu *et al.* (2021) presented a model to study the effects of SCI strategies with different dimensional focuses using the SD approach. They concluded that IT integration is the best practice to avoid disruptions in the supply chain. Zhang *et al.* (2023) used a system dynamics approach to develop a three-stage supply chain network. They explored mitigation measures for cash flow interruption during the pandemic. According to the literature review and to the best of our knowledge, there is no research that surveyed the supply chain considering the impact of the pandemic and free trade zone mechanism in the supply chain using the SD approach.

3. Methodology

In order to simulate the impact of the pandemic on the operations of supply chain, a system dynamics approach is used. The five main steps of the modelling and simulating of a system are: (1) problem articulation, (2) defining a dynamic hypothesis, (3) constructing relations between variables including causal loop diagram and stock and flow diagram, (4) testing the model and (5) policy evaluation. The decision-making process in the SD is done based on three steps: (1) "consequences", (2) "actions" and (3) "information loops" that connect the other parts (Sterman, 2000).

Forrester (2009) described the SD approach as the filling a glass (level variable) with water (rate variable). A feedback loop also is defined as the process of getting information about the level of water in the glass and water flowing into it if it is necessary. These loops play a key role in the model and it would have different effects on the behaviour of the model. The consequence could be defined as the amount of water in the glass. The action is also defined as closing or opening the water tap. Based on the framework developed by Sterman (2000) after implementing the two initial steps, the cause and effect diagram and stock and flow diagram are prepared. After this step, the model could be tested with simulation methods. The next step is to identify the feedbacks in the system and then developing a mental model and transforming it to a stock and flow diagram.

Consider a global supply chain consisting of three zones. As mentioned above, as the first step of the simulation approach proposed by Sterman (2000), problem articulation and dynamic hypothesis should be defined. Hence, the overall mechanism of the trade between the countries and also the basic loop of the model are depicted in the Figure 3.

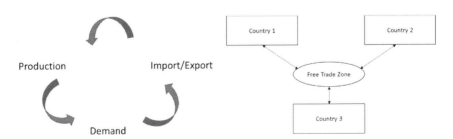

Figure 3. The main structure of the relationships in each zone (left) relationships between different zones of a global supply chain (right).

Table 1. Notations of variables and parameters of the model.

Stock variables	I_t (Inventory level); P_t (Price); B_t (Backlog); PC_t (Capacity of producer); FTZ (Free Trade Zone)
Rate variables	∂Q_t (Rate of production); $\partial(OR_t)$ (Rate of received orders); $\partial(CP_t)$ (Rate of change in price); $\partial(EX_t)$ (Rate of export); ∂S_t (Rate of supply); $\partial(OD_t)$ (Rate of delivered orders); $\partial(IM_t)$ (Rate of import)
Auxiliaries	IC_t (Importing cost); SG_t (Supply gap); DE_t (Production delay); EP_t (Exporting price); DSR_t (Ratio of Demand to supply); NI_t (Net income); ENI_t (Effect of net income); DD_t (Delivery delay); EI_t (Exporting Income); TAG_t (Time to adjust gap of production); D_t (Demand); SeI_t (Selling income); DPC_t (Desired production capacity); PDD_t (Perceived delivery delay); IP_t (Importing price); ES (Economic scale)
Parameters	ER (Exchange rate); IE (Income elasticity); NDD: (Normal delivery delay); Tar (Rate of Tariff); NoI (Normal income); PE (Price elasticity); TAC (Time to adjust capacity); MS (Market share); NoP (Normal price)

As depicted in the Figure 3, each zone consists of these subsystems: a subsystem for Production; a subsystem for Customer's Demand; and a subsystem for Import/Export.

As illustrated in the Figure 3, the local and global demand influence each other. Production has an effect on the demand and then local demand has an effect on the amount of import/export. We considered that in each period, import and export amounts are distributed uniformly. The pandemic condition is considered by an impact factor that influences the amounts of income, supply and imports.

In the next step of the simulation approach, based on Sterman (2000), relations between variables should be defined. Variables and parameters of the model are described in the Table 1.

The impact of the pandemic on the business conditions is defined as a coefficient in the model as a time-based trend. Time trend is defined based on Sinha et al. (2020). This function is named f_t. The formulas related to the free trade zone are adopted from Liu et al. (2021). The basic equations used in this model are described in Table 2.

Table 2. Equations of the model.

Variable	Formula	Variable	Formula
Q_t	$= O_t - (I_t - B_t)$	IP_t	$= P_t * ER * (1 + Tar)$
D_t	$= C(P_t)^{\varepsilon_p} (IN_t)^{\varepsilon_{IN}}$	EP_t	$= P_t/ER$
P_t	$= (D_t/S_t - 1) \times P_{t-1}$	IC_t	$= \partial(IM_t) * IP$
I_t	$= (O_t - S_t) + (IM_t - EX_t)$	EI_t	$= EP * \partial(EX_t)$
GEX_t	$= Ex_t \times Max(I_t - D_t, 0) \times Exch_t \times P_t$	SeI_t	$= NoI * f_t$
GIN_t	$= Im_t \times P_t \times (1 + Tar_t) \times Max(D_t - I_t, 0)/Exch_t$	NI_t	$= SeI_t + EI_t - IC_t$
SI_t	$= IN_t \times f_t$	DE_t	$= T/f_t$
NI_t	$= SI_t + GEX_t - GIN_t$	D_t	$= (D_0 * ((NoP/P_t)^{\wedge}PE)) * ((SeI_t/NoI)^{\wedge}IE)$
B_t	$= \int (Max(\partial(OR_t) - \partial(OD_t)) - \partial Q_t, 0)) \, dt$	DPC_t	$= D_t * 1.5$
I_t	$= \int (Max(\partial Q_t - \partial S_t, 0) + \partial(IM_t) - \partial(EX_t)) \, dt$	DD_t	$= B_t / \partial(OD_t)$
PC_t	$= \int \partial(CP_t)) \, dt$	FTZ	$= $ With lookup (Time, {[(0, 0) — (2035, 10)], (2000, 1), (2017, 1), (2035, 1)})
P_t	$= \int (Max(\partial(CP_t), NormalPrice) \, dt$	ES	$= (0.0144 \text{ total import and export trade}^{\wedge} 1.4)^{\wedge} (LN \text{ (scientific and technological innovation level } 0.971) + 1)$

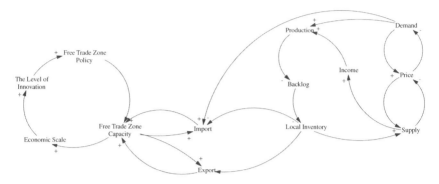

Figure 4. Casual loop diagram of basic relationships between the most important variables of the model.

The causal loop diagram of the main relations of the proposed model is depicted in the Figure 4. This structure is used in each zone of the global supply chain. Free trade zone is a common zone that serves different zones.

The stock and flow diagram of the proposed model is depicted in the Figure 5. The model consists of four subsystems. Three zones and a free trade zone are defined in this model. An international supply chain of a company based in Iran with a broad market including two countries from South Asia is considered to develop this model.

The structure of the model in three zones, including Iran, and two partners is the same as each other. Figure 6 depicts the main structure of a zone and Figure 7 also depicts the structure of the free trade zone.

Also, the free trade zone use tree is depicted in the Figure 8. This tree shows how the free trade zone is connected with other zones through import and export practices.

Structural and behavioural tests are usually employed to validate the models (Sterman, 2000). In this research, we used several tests including boundary adequacy test, dimensional consistency and parameter assessment in order to validate the structure of our model. Also, some tests were performed in order to validate the behaviour of our model including behaviour reproduction test and behaviour anomaly test. Structural tests showed the validity of the defined structure of the model. The results of behavioural tests showed that the behaviour of our model follows the expectations of the author's available knowledge regarding the effects of a pandemic on the supply chain.

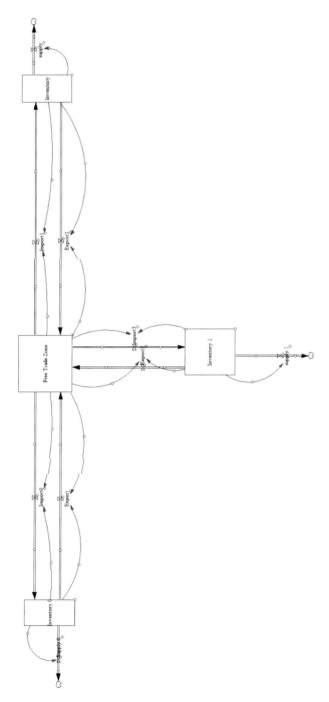

Figure 5. The main structure of the stock and flow diagram.

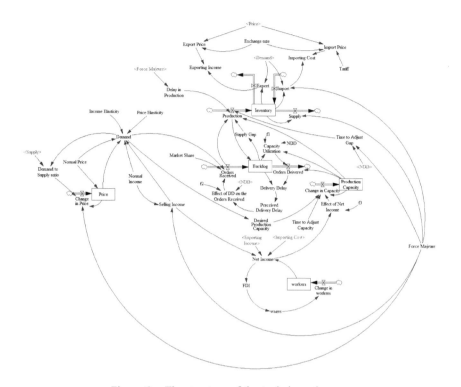

Figure 6. The structure of the trade in each zone.

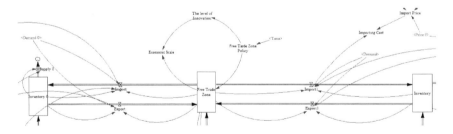

Figure 7. The structure of trade in the free trade zone and how it links with different zones.

4. Analysis of the Disruption Effects

The next steps in the simulation approach are to implement the model and test the model under different scenarios. In this section, implementation results of the scenarios are presented. The main source of disruption in this model is the force majeure factor representing the adverse effects of

Figure 8. Components of the global supply chain affected by the free trade zone.

a pandemic on the operations of supply chain. For simulation, a supply chain of dairy products is considered. An Iranian international company (zone 1) that works with partners in India and Bangladesh is taken as the case study in the model. We tested the model in different scenarios applying the force majeure factor. Three scenarios including pessimistic, optimistic and most likely are defined and results of the model are obtained separately. In the optimistic scenario, the effect of the pandemic on the operations of supply chain is low. In the most likely scenario, the effect of a pandemic on the supply chain operation is average. In the pessimistic scenario, the effect of pandemic on the supply chain operation is high. In this case, the partner in zone 2 is more reliable than the partner based in zone 3, but the capacity of the partner in zone 3 is higher than the partner based in zone 2.

Details of the outputs are presented in Table 3.

Based on the lessons learned from the pandemic, many firms decided to develop their capacities for local production, increase the flexibility of

Table 3. Outputs of the model in different scenarios of disruption.

Scenario of disruption	Change in the local demand	Zone 2				Zone 3			
		% of change in import	% change in export	% change in production	% change in the orders received	% of change in import	% change in export	% change in production	% change in the orders received
Optimistic	+10%	5.7	4.3	9.2	+5	8.8	7.3	9.5	+5
	+5%	5.2	4.3	7.4	+2.5	8.1	7.5	8.2	+2.5
	0%	4	4.3	4.1	0	7.6	7.7	7.5	0
	−5%	2.5	4.9	4.9	−2.5	6.9	7.9	7.4	−2.5
	−10%	1.2	4.9	5.7	−5	6.6	8.2	7.3	−5
Most likely	+10%	6.8	5.2	11.0	+7	10.6	8.8	11.4	+3
	+5%	5	5.2	8.9	+4	10.1	9	10.5	+1.5
	0%	4.8	5.2	4.9	0	9.1	9.2	9.0	0
	−5%	3	5.9	5.3	−4	8.5	9.5	8.9	−1.5
	−10%	1.4	5.9	6.8	−7	7.9	9.8	8.8	−3
Pessimistic	+10%	8.6	6.5	13.8	+10	13.2	11.0	14.3	0
	+5%	7	6.5	11.3	+5	12.2	11.4	12.5	0
	0%	6.0	6.5	6.2	0	11.4	11.6	11.3	0
	−5%	4	7.4	7.4	−5	10.7	11.9	11.1	0
	−10%	1.8	7.4	8.6	−10	9.9	12.3	11.0	0

their systems, decrease sourcing from uncertain suppliers and change their production strategies to minimise the on-hand inventory (Paul and Chowdhury, 2020). The results showed that in the pessimistic scenario, percentages of change in import, export and production are higher than the other scenarios.

Based on the results presented in Table 3, in the pessimistic scenario (worst case) more production capacity is very important. Hence, it could be concluded that in order to face the disruption, producers should expand their production capacities. On the other hand, in the pessimistic scenario, the company tends to acquire more supply from the more reliable partner.

Results showed that in the pessimistic scenario, most of the orders are received by the partner in zone 2. The reason is that the partner in zone 2 is more reliable than the partner based in zone 3. Finally, based on the results of this study, we suggest that in crisis conditions such as the pandemic, manufacturers must review the inventory levels and also safety stocks of the critical products every day. Also, longer contracts with the suppliers will reduce the risk of disruptions. In addition, redesigning of sourcing strategies is the other suggestion that would help the manufacturers to reduce the adverse effects of the disruptions on the supply chain.

Another result that we obtained from the numerical outputs of the model is that establishing a free zone brought resilience to the supply chain. The results of running the model without considering the free trade zone showed that the costs will increase by 20%, 30% and 50%, respectively, if we eliminate the free trade zone in optimistic, most likely and pessimistic scenarios.

These results would be more important in South Asia because of the inherent instabilities that exist in this region. Therefore, pessimistic scenarios such as the pandemic could occur in the future and because of the tensions in South Asia, the impact of such scenarios is more destructive in this region in contrast with other regions. Also, we can conclude that trade in South Asia needs more reliable partners from different countries inside and outside of the region.

5. Conclusions

The recent pandemic has caused many disruptions in supply chain operations. Many industries have been affected by the restrictions, especially those working globally. In this research, a model was presented to analyse the effects of pandemic on the supply chain. We used a simulation approach to model the stochastic supply chain. System dynamic as a simulation approach that is mainly used in the strategic level is used to model the supply chain. A force majeure factor is considered to model the adverse effect of the pandemic on supply chain operations. In order to analyse the proposed model, supply chain operation of an international company based in Iran that works with two partners in South Asia is modelled. A force majeure factor was considered in the model to formulate the effects of pandemic on the business conditions.

The proposed model is analysed in different scenarios of the adverse impacts of pandemic. Three scenarios including pessimistic, optimistic and most likely are defined and results of the model are obtained separately. The results showed that in the worst case of the pandemic impact, more production capacity is very important. Hence, it could be concluded that in order to face the disruption, producers should expand their production capacities. On the other hand, in the pessimistic scenario, the company tends more to shift to the more reliable partner. Additionally, a model is developed without considering free trade zone and results showed a significant role of free trade zones, especially in the pessimistic scenario.

The results of our simulations indicated that supply chains need well-designed strategies to respond to the crisis such as the recent pandemic. Considering reserved capacities of production and more flexible capacities are the most important strategies that could be considered in the global supply chain management. This research could be applied to any regional scenarios and could be modified for different severities of disruptions in the supply chain. As a suggestion for future researchers, examining different risk mitigation strategies in the supply chain could be a novel idea that could be done through a simulation approach. The application of sustainability-related strategies is another suggestion for future researchers.

5.1. Policy implication

The purpose of this research is to analyse a regional supply chain considering different uncertainties. This study contributes to the literature by developing a trade system between the countries through a free trade zone. This model is applied in a real case study in the South Asian region. This section briefly describes some suggested policies and their implications.

5.1.1. Longer contracts with suppliers

One of the main policies against the uncertainty in the supply chain is to develop longer contracts with suppliers. It could be very beneficial in different scenarios, but the existing fluctuations in the currency and tensions between countries are some of the obstacles that suppliers don't attach to these long-term contracts. Especially in the developing countries of the South Asia region, these kinds of contracts such as The South Asian Free Trade Agreement could be beneficial. The success of the agreement could be guaranteed if more connectivity between the countries could be established.

5.1.2. Reserving more buffers to control the impacts of the pandemic

Another important policy to cope with the uncertainties such as those that occurred during the pandemic is to reserve more buffers and inventories in the supply chain. Although it is a beneficial policy in different scenarios, costs of holding inventories play an important role in decision-making about this policy. It is worthwhile to note that most of the industries in the world, including the industries of South Asia, had suffered from lacking inventory during the pandemic.

5.1.3. Establishing more effective free trade zones

A free trade zone is a geographical area where products can be imported and handled without imposing some kinds of taxes or duties and play an important role in stabilising the supply chain. Especially during the pandemic, free trade zones helped the countries to facilitate the process of supply. The South Asian Free Trade Area is an important free trade zone in this region. Apart from increasing the number of free trade zones in South Asia, there is a need to improve the efficiency of the current zones and develop them to a higher level of performance.

References

Aghion, P. and Durlauf, S. (2005). *Handbook of Economic Growth*, 1st edn. Elsevier, North Holland.

Asgari, B. and Hoque, M. (2013). A system dynamics approach to supply chain performance analysis of the ready-made-garment industry in Bangladesh. *Ritsumeikan Journal of Asia Pacific Studies, 32,* 51–61.

Bhushi, U. M. and Javalagi, C. M. (2004). System dynamics application to supply chain management: A review, 2004. *IEEE International Engineering Management Conference, Singapore.*

Chatterjee, B. and Singh, S. (2020). Regional connectivity in South Asia: Role of the international road transports (TIR) convention, corridors of knowledge for peace and development. Sustainable Development Policy Institute. http://www.jstor.org/stable/resrep24374.20.

Choi, K., Narasimhan, R., and Kim, S. W. (2012). Postponement strategy for international transfer of products in a global supply chain: A system dynamics examination. *Journal of Operations Management, 30*(3), 167–179.

Forrester, J. W. (2009). Some basic concepts in system dynamics. Sloan School of Management, Massachusetts Institute of Technology, 17 p.

Gu, Q. and Gao, T. (2017). Production disruption management for R/M integrated supply chain using system dynamics methodology. *International Journal of Sustainable Engineering, 10*(1), 44–57.

Gu, Q. L., Tagaras, G., and Gao, T. G. (2014). Disruption risk management in reverse supply chain by using system dynamics. *Proceedings of the 2014 International Conference on Management Science and Management Innovation.* DOI: 10.2991/msmi-14.2014.89.

Hajian Heidary, M. (2022). The effect of COVID-19 pandemic on the global supply chain operations: A system dynamics approach. *Foreign Trade Review.* https://doi.org/10.1177/00157325211060932.

Schmidt, W. and Raman, A. (2012). When supply-chain disruptions matter. *Harvard Business School.* http://www.hbs.edu/faculty/Publication%20Files/13-00.

Liu, X., Wang, Z., and Cui, X. (2021). Scenario simulation of the impact of China's free-trade zone construction on regional sustainable development: A case study of the Pearl River delta urban agglomeration. *Sustainability,* 13. https://doi.org/10.3390/su13148083.

Mareeh, H. Y. S., Prabakusuma, A. S., Hussain, M. D., Patwary, A. K., Dedahujaev, A., and Aleryani, R. A. (2022). Sustainability and profitability of Malaysia crude palm oil supply chain management: system dynamics modelling approach. *Nankai Business Review International.* https://doi.org/10.1108/NBRI-01-2022-0003.

Moynihan, D. (2009). The response to Hurricane Katrina. https://irgc.org/wp-content/uploads/2018/09/Hurricane_Katrina_full_case_study_web.pdf.

Nedelciu, C. E., Ragnarsdottir, K. V., Schlyter, P., and Stjernquist, I. (2020). Global phosphorus supply chain dynamics: Assessing regional impact to 2050. *Global Food Security, 26,* 100426.

Olivares-Aguila, J. and Elmaghrebi, W. (2021). System dynamics modelling for supply chain disruptions. *International Journal of Production Research*, *59*(6), 1757–1775.

Paul, S. K. and Chowdhury, P. (2020). Strategies for managing the impacts of disruptions during COVID-19: An example of toilet paper. *Global Journal of Flexible Systems Management*, *21*, 283–293.

Peng, M., Peng, Y., and Chen, H. (2014). Post-seismic supply chain risk management: A system dynamics disruption analysis approach for inventory and logistics planning. *Computers & Operations Research*, *42*, 14–24.

Rasul, G., Nepal, A. K., Hussain, A., Maharjan, A., Joshi, S., Lama, A., *et al.* (2021). Socio-economic implications of COVID-19 pandemic in South Asia: Emerging risks and growing challenges. *Frontiers in Sociology*. https://www.frontiersin.org/articles/10.3389/fsoc.2021.629693/full.

Sinha, D., Bagodi, V., and Dey, D. (2020). The supply chain disruption framework post COVID-19: A system dynamics model. *Foreign Trade Review*, *55*(4), 511–534.

Sterman, J. (2000). *Business Dynamics: Systems Thinking and Modeling for a Complex World*. McGraw-Hill Education, USA.

Sundarakani, B., Vrat, P., and Kumar, P. (2010). Dynamic analysis of a global supply chain using system dynamics approach. *International Journal of Electronic Customer Relationship Management*, *4*(4), 340–358.

Zhang, X., Shi, Y., Zhang, P., Xu, F., and Jiang, C. (2023). System dynamics modeling and robustness analysis for capital-constrained supply chain under disruption. *Industrial Management & Data Systems*, *123*(2), 492–514.

Zhu, Q., Krikke, H., and Caniëls, M. C. J. (2021). The effects of different supply chain integration strategies on disruption recovery: A system dynamics study on the cheese industry. *Logistics*, *5*(2). https://doi.org/10.3390/logistics5020019.

Chapter 14

Supply Chain Network in South Asia

Karuna Chauhan*,‡ and Surender Kumar†,§

*SERD, Yamunanagar, India

†Jaipuria Institute of Management, Noida, India

‡karunachauhan.3@gmail.com
§surender.kumar@jaipuria.ac.in

Abstract

The supply chain network in South Asia is a vital component of global trade, facilitating the movement of goods and services from manufacturers to end-users. This intricate system involves various stakeholders, including manufacturers, suppliers, distributors, and logistics providers, collaborating to ensure the efficient production, transportation, and delivery of products. South Asia's burgeoning manufacturing sector, fueled by factors such as a large workforce, low labor costs, and strategic geographical location, positions the region as a pivotal hub for global production and distribution networks. Countries like India, Bangladesh, and Pakistan are emerging as significant players in global trade, supported by favourable government policies and participation in trade agreements. The dynamic nature of supply chain networks necessitates constant adaptation to evolving technology, trade patterns, and consumer demands. Ultimately, the supply chain network in South Asia underpins the region's economic growth and integration into the global marketplace.

Keywords: Supply chain network, South Asia, global trade, manufacturing sector, trade agreements.

1. Introduction

A supply chain network is a complex system that involves the movement of products or services from raw material suppliers to end-users. It consists of multiple parties, including manufacturers, suppliers, distributors, retailers and logistics providers, who are all involved in the production, transportation and delivery of goods or services to customers. The supply chain network is crucial for the functioning of any business as it impacts factors like cost, quality and customer satisfaction. Supply chain networks are highly dynamic and continuously evolving, with changes in technology, global trade patterns and customer expectations, leading to a constant need for adaptation (Christopher and Peck, 2004; Fawcett *et al.*, 2008 Chopra, and Meindl, 2016, Ketchen *et al.*, 2019).

The supply chain network in South Asia plays a vital role in the global trade of goods and services. South Asia is a region with a rapidly growing manufacturing sector, making it a hub for global production and distribution networks. The region has a large and diverse workforce, low labour costs and an abundance of raw materials, which are attractive to businesses looking to set up manufacturing facilities. Additionally, the region is strategically located at the crossroads of major global trade routes, making it a key transportation hub for the movement of goods across the world.

India, in particular, is emerging as a global manufacturing hub, with several multinational companies setting up their manufacturing facilities in the country (IBEF, 2022). The country's manufacturing sector has grown rapidly, driven by favourable government policies, a large and diverse workforce and improvements in infrastructure. In recent years, India has become a major exporter of a range of goods, including textiles, automobiles and pharmaceuticals.

Similarly, Bangladesh has become a major exporter of readymade garments, with the country's textile industry contributing significantly to the country's economy (*The Business Standard*, 2021). Pakistan, Sri Lanka and other countries in the region are also emerging as significant players in the global trade of goods and services (World Bank, 2021a).

The importance of the supply chain network in South Asia is also reflected in the region's participation in global trade agreements. For example, India is a member of several regional and multilateral trade agreements, including the South Asian Free Trade Area (SAFTA), the Asia-Pacific Trade Agreement (APTA) and the World Trade Organization (WTO). These agreements provide businesses in the region with access to markets in other parts of the world, making it easier for them to participate in global trade.

In summary, the supply chain network in South Asia is crucial for the region's economic growth and plays a significant role in the global trade of goods and services.

2. Overview of the Supply Chain Network in South Asia

The supply chain network in South Asia is diverse and includes a range of industries, such as textiles, agriculture, electronics and pharmaceuticals. The region's manufacturing sector is growing rapidly, making it a hub for global production and distribution networks. India is one of the largest manufacturing economies in South Asia, and the textile industry is one of the largest contributors to the country's economy. The industry accounts for around 5% of the country's GDP and 13% of its total exports (IBEF, 2022). Bangladesh is another major player in the textile industry and is the second-largest exporter of readymade garments in the world after China (*The Business Standard*, 2021).

The agriculture sector in South Asia is also a significant contributor to the region's economy. The region is home to some of the world's largest producers of rice, wheat and other grains. For example, India is the world's second-largest producer of wheat, and Pakistan is the world's fifth-largest producer of rice (World Bank, 2021b). The electronics industry in South Asia is also growing rapidly. India, in particular, is rapidly becoming a hub for electronics manufacturing, with several global tech companies establishing their manufacturing facilities in the country. The pharmaceutical industry is also growing in the region, with India being a leading producer of generic drugs (McKinsey & Company, 2019).

Despite the growth of various industries, the supply chain network in South Asia faces several challenges. These include inadequate transportation infrastructure, logistics and distribution challenges, regulatory barriers and technological limitations. The region's transportation infrastructure is often inadequate and underdeveloped, leading to long transit times and high transportation costs. Furthermore, regulatory barriers and customs procedures can be complex, leading to delays and additional costs.

In recent years, South Asia has seen the emergence of several innovative approaches to supply chain management. For example, blockchain technology is being used to increase transparency and efficiency in supply chain management, while advanced logistics systems are helping to optimise transportation and distribution networks.

3. Key Challenges in the Supply Chain Network in South Asia

South Asia is home to a vast and diverse range of supply chain networks. While the region offers significant opportunities for trade and growth, it also presents unique challenges that businesses and governments must navigate. Addressing these challenges requires a coordinated effort from governments, businesses and other stakeholders. Investment in road and rail infrastructure is critical to improving the efficiency and reliability of supply chain networks in South Asia. In addition, adoption of new technologies and best practices for supply chain management can help to optimise logistics operations and reduce costs (Mukherjee, 2017; Jayawardena and Liyanage, 2019; Farhan and Saleem, 2020). Finally, collaboration between businesses, governments and other stakeholders is essential for developing sustainable and effective solutions to the infrastructure challenges facing the region.

Here are some of the major challenges facing the supply chain networks in South Asia:

- **Infrastructure:** Poor infrastructure, including inadequate road networks, limited port capacity and insufficient transportation and storage facilities, creates bottlenecks and delays throughout the supply chain. This can increase lead times, raise costs and reduce efficiency.
- **Fragmentation:** The supply chain in South Asia is highly fragmented, with multiple intermediaries involved in the movement of goods from producers to consumers. This can result in longer lead times, higher costs and reduced visibility and control over the supply chain.
- **Lack of standardisation:** There is a lack of standardisation in terms of processes, documentation and technology across the supply chain in South Asia. This can result in errors, inefficiencies and delays.

- **Regulatory barriers:** Regulatory barriers, including complex customs procedures and inconsistent enforcement, can increase costs and create delays throughout the supply chain.
- **Political instability:** Political instability, including conflict and instability, can disrupt supply chain operations, leading to delays, damage to infrastructure and increased costs.
- **Limited access to finance:** Small and medium-sized enterprises (SMEs) in South Asia often struggle to access finance, which can limit their ability to invest in the supply chain and expand their operations.
- **Lack of transparency:** Lack of transparency and accountability in supply chain operations can lead to corruption, fraud, and unethical practices, which can damage the reputation of businesses and erode consumer trust.
- **Cultural and linguistic differences:** Cultural and linguistic differences can present communication challenges and make it difficult for businesses to establish trust and build relationships with suppliers and customers across the region.
- **Environmental concerns:** Environmental concerns such as air pollution, water scarcity and waste management are increasingly important considerations for businesses operating in South Asia. Supply chain networks must be designed with sustainability in mind to minimise negative impacts on the environment.

In summary, the challenges facing supply chain networks in South Asia are diverse and complex. Addressing these challenges requires collaboration between businesses, governments and other stakeholders to develop effective solutions that enable sustainable and inclusive economic growth in the region (World Bank, 2018, 2021b).

3.1. *Innovations and opportunities*

There are several innovative solutions that are currently being deployed in the supply chain networks in South Asia. Here are some of the latest innovations and opportunities in the region:

Digitalisation of supply chain: Digitalisation is increasingly becoming important in supply chain management in South Asia. With advancements in technology, supply chain participants in the region can leverage digital platforms to manage their inventory, track shipments and collaborate with suppliers, customers and logistics providers. Digitalisation can improve the efficiency, transparency and reliability of the supply chain network, as well as help to reduce costs. For example, Indian startup Locus provides an AI-powered logistics optimisation platform that has been used by companies like Delhivery and BigBasket to streamline their operations and reduce delivery times.

E-commerce: E-commerce is becoming increasingly popular in South Asia and is presenting opportunities for businesses to expand their reach and increase sales. Platforms like Amazon, Alibaba and Flipkart have established a significant presence in the region, and local startups are also emerging to cater to the growing demand for online shopping. The rise of e-commerce is driving investments in logistics infrastructure, such as warehouses and last-mile delivery systems, to improve the speed and efficiency of the delivery process.

Autonomous vehicles: Autonomous vehicles are being tested in several countries in South Asia to improve the efficiency of logistics operations. For example, Pakistani startup SaadWorks is developing an autonomous delivery robot that can navigate congested streets and deliver packages to customers. In India, autonomous drones are being used to deliver medical supplies to remote regions.

Blockchain: Blockchain technology is being explored in South Asia to enhance supply chain transparency and traceability. For example, Pakistani startup CIRCLE is using blockchain to create a transparent and secure supply chain for the textile industry, providing end-to-end visibility of the supply chain process and ensuring that all participants meet ethical and environmental standards.

Green supply chain: Green supply chain is gaining traction in South Asia as companies seek to reduce their carbon footprint and address environmental concerns. For example, Bangladeshi apparel manufacturer DBL Group has implemented a green supply chain system that includes rainwater harvesting, wastewater treatment and solar energy generation. Such initiatives are driving investments in sustainable infrastructure and creating opportunities for businesses to differentiate themselves in the market.

Overall, these innovations are providing opportunities for businesses to optimise their supply chain operations and improve their competitiveness in the region. These trends are expected to continue in the coming years as the region's economy continues to grow and evolve.

3.2. *Some cases of struggle and overcoming the challenges*

Here are some case studies that illustrate the challenges and opportunities in the supply chain network in South Asia:

Coca-Cola India: Coca-Cola India faced a supply chain disruption in 2014 due to a local water scarcity issue. The company responded by launching several water conservation and replenishment initiatives, such as rainwater harvesting, groundwater recharge and community water recharge. These initiatives not only helped Coca-Cola India overcome the water shortage challenge but also contributed to the sustainability of the local communities and the environment ("Coca-Cola India's supply chain: A 'thirst' for sustainability", *Supply Chain Management Review*).

Unilever Pakistan: Unilever Pakistan faced a challenge in 2012 when floods in the country caused significant damage to the company's supply chain. The company responded by establishing a disaster management plan and setting up a supply chain resilience team. These initiatives helped Unilever Pakistan quickly restore its supply chain and prevent a prolonged disruption to its operations ("Supply chain resilience: A case study from Unilever Pakistan", *Journal of Business Continuity & Emergency Planning*).

Walmart India: Walmart faced a challenge in 2018 when the Indian government implemented new regulations that restricted foreign-owned retailers from sourcing more than 25% of their inventory from a single supplier. This regulation created a challenge for Walmart, which had a significant portion of its inventory sourced from a single supplier. To overcome this challenge, Walmart India diversified its supplier base and expanded its product offerings. This not only helped Walmart comply with the regulation but also improved the company's supply chain resilience and competitiveness ("Walmart's supply chain diversification in India", *Supply Chain Brain*).

DHL Sri Lanka: DHL faced a challenge in 2019 when a series of terrorist attacks in the country disrupted its operations. The company responded by activating its crisis management plan and setting up a command centre to coordinate its activities. DHL also collaborated with local authorities to ensure the safety of its employees and the timely delivery of its shipments. These initiatives helped DHL quickly restore its operations and prevent a prolonged disruption to its customers ("DHL's response to the Sri Lankan terrorist attacks", *Supply Chain Management Review*).

These case studies illustrate the challenges and opportunities in the supply chain network in South Asia, such as supply chain disruptions, government regulations and crisis management. They also show how companies can overcome these challenges by adopting a proactive and resilient approach to their supply chain operations.

4. Potential for Growth and Development

The supply chain network in South Asia has enormous potential for growth and development but currently faces various challenges that hinder its expansion. Here are some key points and references to support this statement:

Challenges in the supply chain network: The supply chain network in South Asia faces various challenges, including inadequate infrastructure, inefficient logistics, complex regulations and lack of information technology systems (IT). These challenges affect the efficiency and effectiveness of the supply chain network and limit its growth potential (Asian Development Bank, 2017).

Potential for growth and development: Despite these challenges, the supply chain network in South Asia has enormous potential for growth and development, given the region's large and growing population, expanding middle class and improving business environment. South Asia can also leverage its strategic location to become a global hub for trade and commerce (World Bank, 2021b).

Opportunities for innovation: With the rise of digital technologies and e-commerce, there are opportunities for innovation in the supply chain network in South Asia. For example, the use of mobile applications, e-payment systems and real-time tracking can improve supply chain visibility and efficiency (McKinsey & Company, 2019).

Need for collaboration: To unlock the potential for growth and development in the supply chain network in South Asia, there is a need for collaboration between various stakeholders, including governments, businesses and civil society organisations. Collaboration can help to address the challenges facing the supply chain network and create an enabling environment for growth and development (International Finance Corporation, 2021).

Overall, while the supply chain network in South Asia faces significant challenges, there is enormous potential for growth and development. The region's strategic location, expanding middle class and opportunities for innovation provide a strong foundation for the supply chain network to become a global hub for trade and commerce. However, collaboration between various stakeholders is crucial to address the challenges and unlock the region's full potential.

References

Chopra, S. and Meindl, P. (2016). *Supply Chain Management: Strategy, Planning, and Operation.* Pearson Education, London, United Kingdom.

Christopher, M. and Peck, H. (2004). Building the resilient supply chain. *The International Journal of Logistics Management, 15*(2), 1–13.

Farhan, M. and Saleem, M. A. (2020). Challenges of supply chain management in South Asia: A review. *International Journal of Supply Chain Management, 9*(3), 226–235.

Fawcett, S. E., Magnan, G. M., and McCarter, M. W. (2008). Benefits, barriers, and bridges to effective supply chain management. *Supply Chain Management: An International Journal, 13*(1), 35–48.

https://www.businesstoday.in/current/economy-politics/how-ai-is-revolutionising-logisticsindustry-in-india/story/407326.html.

https://www.statista.com/topics/5265/e-commerce-in-india/.

https://gulfnews.com/world/asia/pakistan/startup-tests-autonomous-vehicle-for-deliveries-in-pakistan-1.79432722.

https://www.investindia.gov.in/team-india-blogs/blockchain-enabling-transparency-textile-supply-chain-pakistan.

https://www.thedailystar.net/business/news/dbl-group-implements-green-supply-chain-2043997.

Invest India. (2021). India's electronics industry. Retrieved from https://www.investindia.gov.in/sector/electronics-manufacturing.

India Brand Equity Foundation. (2022). India's textile industry. Retrieved from https://www.ibef.org/industry/textiles.aspx.

Jayawardena, C. and Liyanage, C. (2019). Key challenges in the South Asian logistics and supply chain industry. *International Journal of Supply Chain Management*, *8*(6), 98–109.

Ketchen Jr, D. J., Craighead, C. W., and Swinney, J. L. (2019). *Managing the Supply Chain: Concepts, Strategies, and Case Studies*. Business Expert Press.

McKinsey & Company. (2019). The pharmaceutical industry in South Asia. Retrieved from https://www.mckinsey.com/industries/pharmaceuticals-and-medical-products/our-insights/thepharmaceutical-industry-in-south-asia-opportunities-for-investment-and-growth.

Ministry of Commerce and Industry, Government of India. (2022). India's trade agreements. Retrieved from https://commerce.gov.in/trade-agreements-and-negotiations-india.

Mukherjee, K. (2017). Supply chain challenges in South Asia: An overview. *International Journal of Logistics Systems and Management*, *28*(3), 336–352.

Pakistan Embassy in Tokyo. (2022). 'Pakistan's manufacturing sector. Retrieved from https://www.pakistanembassytokyo.com/economy/manufacturing.htm.

Simchi-Levi, D., Kaminsky, P., and Simchi-Levi, E. (2008). *Designing and Managing the Supply Chain: Concepts, Strategies, and Case Studies*. McGraw-Hill Education, Boston, MA.

The Business Standard. (2021). Bangladesh's textile industry. Retrieved from https://tbsnews.net/bangladesh/apparel/bangladeshs-garment-industry-outlook-2021-189402.

World Bank. (2018). *South Asia's Infrastructure: A Continental Overview*. World Bank Group, Washington, DC.

World Bank. (2021a). Sri Lanka's export performance. Retrieved from https://www.worldbank.org/en/country/srilanka/brief/sri-lankas-export-performance.

World Bank. (2021b). South Asia's agriculture. Retrieved from https://www.worldbank.org/en/region/sar/brief/south-asia-agriculture.

Chapter 15

Enhancing Rail and Road Connectivity in South Asia: Challenges and Prospects

Manoj Chaudhary[*,‡] and Harjit Singh[†,§]

[*]Central Department of Management, Tribhuvan University, Kirtipur, Nepal

[†]Symbiosis Centre for Management Studies, Symbiosis International University, Pune, India

[‡]manoj86385@yahoo.com
[§]harjit.singh@scmsnoida.ac.in

Abstract

South Asia, a region with diverse cultures, histories and economies, has enormous economic growth and development potential. South Asia accounts for more than one-fifth of the global population and has a rich culture and enormous economic potential. However, the region's full economic growth and development potential has yet to be fully realised, largely due to inadequate rail and road connectivity. South Asian countries have realised the significance of improving transport networks to promote regional integration, trade and economic growth. This chapter explores the importance of rail and road connectivity in South Asia, the challenges faced and the transformative potential of an integrated transport network for the region's development and integration.

Keywords: South Asia, economic growth, regional trade, India, Nepal.

1. Introduction

South Asia, a region including India, Bangladesh, Nepal, Bhutan, Sri Lanka and the Maldives, is home to nearly a quarter of the world's population. Although South Asian nations' per capita GDP has steadily risen, its benefits do not reach the region's underprivileged people. Particularly, income in these South Asian nations rises for the wealthy but does not help the poor, creating disparity (Lin, 2020; Wang *et al.*, 2020). Despite its great potential, the region faces many challenges in achieving inclusive economic growth and development. Establishing and improving rail and road connections is an important factor that can pave the way for progress. Transport and communication systems via road, railway, waterway, air and fibre optic network are important means of physical connection. Connecting and facilitating traffic to ease the flow of people, goods and vehicles; improve the livelihoods of hard-to-reach areas; and promote trade and economic exchanges between countries. Research has shown that improved transportation infrastructure boosts productivity, competition and economic activity (Calderon and Serven, 2004; Sahoo and Sexena, 1999; Straub *et al.*, 2008). This is largely because it lowers the cost of getting from one place to another, which makes it easier to access markets.

Traffic and trade issues in South Asia mean that doing business with a counterparty in Brazil or Germany will cost an Indian company roughly 20–30% less than doing business with a counterparty in Nepal or Bangladesh. Greater economic growth and eradicating poverty in South Asia could result from decreased trade costs and improved connectivity. Countries also require well-designed land, river and seaports and integrated multimodal transport networks, such as roads, trains and interior waterways, for seamless connection. In order to maximise the advantages for nearby communities and enterprises, these multimodal corridors must be linked to regional, rural and local markets as well as logistics.

Additionally, by minimising time-consuming paperwork and clearance processes, digitising and automating customs and clearing procedures can support connection. Currently, transactions between Bangladesh and India require about 22 documents and 55 signatures. Competitive markets for transport services, updated border infrastructure and sophisticated risk management systems and standards are further actions that can support seamless transport connectivity — standardised assessment and improvement of cross-border inland roads. Additionally, integrated energy grids and digital connections present fresh opportunities to link South Asian countries for mutual benefit.

2. Empirical Context

In recent years, as South Asia has worked to overcome its infrastructure gaps and advance economic integration, the region has paid considerable attention to the effort to improve rail and road connections. In its attempts to improve transportation networks, South Asia, which is home to a wide variety of countries with varied levels of economic development, presents both difficulties and bright futures. In the context of economic growth, encouraging economic activity depends on establishing a strong transportation infrastructure that supports regional connections. The improvement of industrial and agricultural productivity is sparked by this investment in transportation infrastructure, which eventually results in an increase in aggregate supply, higher real income, lower costs of living and, as a result, a reduction in poverty (Wang *et al.*, 2020). Transport infrastructure plays a crucial role in boosting the economy, making it easier for people to access job opportunities and ensuring that everyone can access important services like healthcare and education. This helps reduce the gap between the rich and poor (Batool and Goldmann, 2020; Beria and Scholz, 2010; Rehman and Sohag, 2022). South Asian countries are also progressing in using their transport resources to achieve impressive annual growth.

Over the years, economic analysts have pointed out that South Asia's growth rates have masked the potential rigidity of the region's economy, leading to slow growth in the medium term. These significant economic challenges are that South Asian continues to be one of the least economically linked regions, with only 6% of the region's total commerce coming from within. Since intra-regional trade takes up about 50% of overall trade in other regions like East Asia and the Pacific, South Asia is one of the world's most separated regions. In Sub-Saharan Africa, intra-regional commerce makes up around 50% of total trade. Regional Trade: Government initiatives to establish open trade facilitation channels have resulted in a 22% improvement in regional trade over time. Bangladesh, Sri Lanka and Nepal are India's top export destinations in the area, while Myanmar, Sri Lanka and Bangladesh are its top import sources. India's neighbours have trade deficits with the country; Bangladesh has the largest at US$7.6 billion, followed by Nepal at US$6.8 billion.

Recently, South Asian nations have launched several initiatives across different scales to improve the effectiveness of their regional transportation and transit system. Nonetheless, they continue to confront various obstacles, both in terms of policy and procedures. These obstacles include transit agreements that lack effectiveness, common guarantee mechanisms and insufficient harmonisation procedures for transit, all of which constrain the growth potential. Previous research indicates insufficient attention has been paid to measures that facilitate trade and transport, particularly in customs efficiency, transport quality, the expense of international and domestic transportation, and associated border procedures.

India's major export markets in the South Asian region are Bangladesh, Nepal and Sri Lanka, which covers 3.38%, 2.28% and 1.37% of total export in 2021/2022 and decreased to 2.71%, 1.78% and 1.13% in 2022/2023, respectively. The overall export share of India to the South Asian region also saw a reduction, moving from 8.11% in 2021–2021 to 6.2% in 2022–2023. On the import side, India's imports from Bangladesh, Nepal and Sri Lanka exhibited similar fluctuations. In 2021–2022, imports from these countries accounted for 0.32%, 0.22% and 0.16% of the total, respectively. The total import share of India from the broader South Asian region also witnessed a decline, decreasing from 0.89% in 2021–2022 to 0.76% in 2022–2023. All neighbouring countries have trade deficits with India, with the highest being Bangladesh with a deficit of US$10.8 billion, followed by Nepal with US$7.2 billion, and Sri Lanka with US$4.03 billion in 2022–2023. The total trade surplus to India in South Asia was US$22.5 billion in 2022–2023 (Ministry of Commerce and Industry India, 2023).

South Asia's connectivity has to be strengthened through improved intra-regional trade. Such an initiative will assist in gaining access to new markets and luring foreign direct investment (FDI) into various industries by facilitating the movement of goods, services, people and expertise. The improvement in intra-regional trade is facilitated by the development of road networks, which enhances connectivity. In South Asian countries, the amount of roads they have differs from country to country. For example, Bangladesh has more roads even though only 31% of their roads are paved, and 61% live in rural areas without highways (Rehman and Norman, 2021; Zhang and Zhang, 2021).

2.1. *A case of India and Nepal*

Nepal and India have a special bond. These two nations are the most linked in the entire world. The system of open borders and the treatment accorded to nationals of one country living in another contribute to this situation. Every day, hundreds of thousands of people cross the border, particularly in the border regions between Nepal and India, for job, trade and economic reasons without passports or visa requirements. Additionally, thousands of border inhabitants wed across the border each year, enhancing the already idyllic relations between the two nations. Each polity has ensured a steady flow of individuals from one nation to another for hundreds of years.

India and Nepal's unrestricted border serves as a metaphor for continuous connectedness. If there is a good connection through infrastructure development and means of communication, trade and other economic activity between the two sides of the border can be enhanced even further. However, the region's postal, telephone, rail and road networks are the least developed. For many years, just the Janakpur–Jaynagar railway was utilised to connect Nepal and India, but more recently, its services have also been discontinued. The Indian government has helped the Nepali government construct Integrated Checkpoints (ICPs) at four crucial locations along the Nepal–India border, including Raxaul, India, in recognition of the advantages of an open border system — Sunauli (India), Birgunj (Nepal), Biratnagar (Nepal), Bhairahawa (Nepal), Jogbani (India) and Nepalgunj ((India)–Nepalgunj (Nepal) Road. In addition, the Indian government has agreed to build trans-railway railways connecting five locations along the Nepal–India border: Jaynagar to Bardibas, Jogbani to Biratnagar, Nautanwa to Bhairahawa, Rupaidiha to Nepalgunj and New Jalpaiguri to Kakarbhitta. Notably, work is being done on the Jaynagar–Bardibas railway, which would widen the track on 51 km of the line from Jaynagar to Bijalpura and extend it by 17 km to Bardibas. Similarly, work is being done on the 17.65 km Jogbani–Biratnagar railway between Jogbani and Biratnagar.

The development and modernisation of Nepal's infrastructure, particularly its highways and airports, has been significantly aided by India. India constructed the Tribhuvan highway in the middle of the 1950s when Kathmandu had no connections to other regions of the nation. 75% of the lengthiest east–west roadway in Nepal belongs to India. India's assistance to Nepal in building the Pokhara–Sunauli highway, which connects the western part of the highlands to Terai, is also crucial. Similarly, India was crucial in developing Nepal's regional airports and the Tribhuvan International Airport in Kathmandu. India's assistance to Nepal in constructing a fibre optic cable project along the East–West Corridor is also crucial. It is significant to remember that India funds all significant infrastructure and communication projects in Nepal through grants.

The possibility of increasing regional trade, as anticipated in the free trade agreement, is further hampered by the lack of comparative advantage in the region. Value chains and specialisation are important aspects of global trade. Compared to nations with high degrees of specialisation and similar products, countries with different comparative advantages and product specialisation will have more potential for mutual gain from trade. Most South Asian nations compete in their export markets for a small number of niche product categories, primarily textile exports. Due to its import policies, India primarily imports semi-finished goods, which its surrounding nations do not have a comparative advantage in. This demonstrates how little India imports from its neighbours.

In addition to being economically advantageous, increasing commerce in the South Asian region is crucial for India's integration into the world economy at a strategic level. In order to ensure that trade agreements are effective, a variety of non-tariff barriers in South Asia must be addressed, and governments' "sensitive lists" must be further reduced. In order to promote the removal of identified trade barriers, it is also necessary to adapt effective approaches from other regions to the South Asian context. Sub-Saharan Africa, for instance, has tackled non-tariff obstacles using a web-based system that consists of national monitoring committees in each nation to facilitate the removal of barriers. Stronger political will is required by India and its neighbours to address trade obstacles in the area, particularly in light of the COVID-19 issue's potential to lead to a wave of new protection measures.

The physical relationship directly impacts trade, investment and development. The better the trade, investment and development chances, the closer the connection. There are very few nations that are both wealthy and well-connected. Poor nations, on the other hand, fall behind in connectivity.

A nation can reach new markets for selling and importing goods because of connectivity. It enables the export of goods at greater prices and the import of goods at reduced costs. It helps the agricultural, industrial, commercial and service sectors to expand. Additionally, it boosts productivity, fosters innovation, opens up job opportunities and quickens the nation's socioeconomic development. It also boosts travel, airline, auto and other businesses.

To maximise the benefits of connecting with the outside world, there must be an impetus for developing connectivity in the country. Faced with this fact, Nepal has taken an important step in developing family connections. Much work has been done to develop links between rural and urban areas. Research shows that until the 1970s, Nepal had only 2,700 km of roads, stretching to 80,000 km. In the last 15 years alone, nearly 1,700 km of roads have been upgraded in all seasons. In addition, 164 trail bridges were built. Thus, domestic travel time has been reduced by 80%. In Nepal, the increased connectivity significantly boosted the country's Gross Domestic Product (GDP). During 2016–2017, Nepal's economic performance exhibited noteworthy growth, with the GDP growth rate soaring to 8.98%. This upturn was driven by a confluence of factors, including favourable monsoon conditions, an uptick in capital expenditure, adept energy management and investment in climate enhancements, encompassing overall supply chain dynamics (Economic Survey, 2017). However, in subsequent years, the GDP growth rate experienced a downward trajectory, dipping to 6.66% in 2019. The impact of the COVID-19 pandemic was particularly severe, leading to a sharp contraction, with the GDP growth rate plummeting to −2.37% in 2020. Nonetheless, there has been a subsequent resurgence in economic performance, with the GDP growth rate rebounding to 5.61% by 2022 (Asian Development Bank, 2022a).

3. The Need for Enhanced Connectivity

(a) Economic integration in fighting poverty and achieving economic growth

Improved rail and road connections will facilitate the flow of goods and services within and between South Asian countries. Currently, complex trade barriers and inadequate infrastructure impede trade in the region, making it costlier and more time-consuming than necessary. Improved connectivity will promote regional economic integration, making South Asia a more attractive destination for businesses and investors. South Asia is still home to a significant proportion of the world's impoverished population. Better transport infrastructure can stimulate economic activity in rural areas, create job opportunities and allow access to markets and services, reducing poverty and increasing prosperity for people in the region. Improved connectivity can boost economic growth by attracting investment, stimulating industrialisation and supporting job creation.

(b) **Tourism and cultural exchange**
South Asia is famous for its diverse cultural heritage, historical sites and breathtaking scenery. Better connectivity can facilitate increased tourism, allowing tourists to explore and experience the region's rich picture of traditions, festivals and natural wonders. This will promote cultural understanding and cooperation among South Asian countries. Indian Prime Minister Narendra Modi's recent visit to Lumbini, Lord Buddha's birthplace in Nepal, marked his fifth trip to Nepal and aimed to enhance cultural and religious ties, fostering Indo-Nepal relations amid evolving geopolitics and boosting religious tourism between the two nations. This visit signifies the strong cultural and religious bonds shared between India and Nepal, leveraging these connections for mutual benefit, particularly in tourism. Both countries have been collaborating on developing religious tourist circuits, and despite setbacks caused by the COVID-19 pandemic, they are working towards revitalising religious tourism (Basil, 2022). The Buddhist tourism circuit is important for East and Southeast Asia. It covers significant pilgrimage sites in India and Nepal, including Lumbini, Sarnath and Bodh Gaya. Connectivity is primarily by road, with an IRCTC Buddhist Circuit Train. India's Kushinagar International Airport and Nepal's Gautam Buddha International Airport aim to boost tourism. In 2018, Indian Prime Minister Modi and the Nepalese Prime Minister launched the India–Nepal Ramayana Circuit, connecting spiritual places related to Lord Rama. They inaugurated a bus service between Janakpur and Ayodhya, facilitating affordable pilgrimages and boosting Nepal's tourism. 15 destinations in India and Janakpur in Nepal are part of this circuit. Efforts also include yearly fairs in Ayodhya and Janakpur and a Rs. 100 crore development assistance for Janakpur. The Pashupatinath temple in Kathmandu and Varanasi's Pashupati Mahadev temple are vital pilgrimage sites. IRCTC initiated the Bharat Gaurav Tourist Train for the Ramayana circuit. The upcoming Ayodhya International Airport will further enhance connectivity in the circuit.

(c) **Trade facilitation**
Improved rail and road connections will lead to more efficient movement of goods and lower transport costs, thereby supporting increased trade in the region and with other global markets. Simplifying customs procedures, cutting non-tariff barriers and harmonising regulations can significantly improve economic cooperation and intra-regional trade. The World Trade Organisation's Trade Facilitation Agreement (TFA) provides a

framework to streamline cross-border trade processes. In April 2018, India and Nepal convened an Inter-Governmental Committee (IGC) Meeting to discuss trade, transit and cooperation — the meeting aimed to address trade imbalances and promote economic ties. Key decisions included reviewing the bilateral Treaty of Trade, amending the Treaty of Transit, improving border trade infrastructure, harmonising standards and establishing an India–Nepal Joint Business Forum. Preceding this, an Inter-Governmental Sub-Committee on Trade, Transit and Cooperation met at the Joint Secretary level.

(d) **Regional integration**
Better connectivity will strengthen people-to-people ties and cultural exchanges, increasing regional cooperation and mutual understanding. The Bay of Bengal Initiative for Multi-Sectoral Technical and Economic Cooperation (BIMSTEC) focuses on expanding trade and improving cooperation among member states. They aim to create a free trade area and remove trade barriers. Although progress has been made, there are differences in trade facilitation among member states. To address this, the BIMSTEC Trade Facilitation Strategic Framework 2030 was developed. It outlines a plan to enhance trade facilitation through infrastructure investment, capacity building and cooperation. The COVID-19 pandemic disrupted trade but also presents an opportunity to adopt new approaches as economies recover. BIMSTEC is committed to boosting trade and trade facilitation to ensure regional and global competitiveness (Asian Development Bank, 2022a).

(e) **Public–private partnership**
Private sector involvement in infrastructure development can accelerate projects and provide technical and financial expertise. Governments can create an enabling environment for private investment through well-structured public–private partnership (PPP) models. A United Nations-led discussion in Kathmandu in 2015 concluded that PPPs could be crucial in addressing South Asia's infrastructure needs, which require about $250 billion annually — the meeting aimed to share successful PPP experiences and build capacity for infrastructure development. Considering the substantial costs, ESCAP supports involving the private sector in infrastructure projects. The meeting involved government officials, policymakers and PPP experts from South and South-West Asia, leading to 30 policy recommendations for PPP development in the region (ESCAP, 2015).

4. Barriers to Rail and Road Connectivity

(i) **Geographical barriers**
Diverse landscapes, including rugged mountain ranges, dense forests and bodies of water, characterise South Asia. These geographical barriers have made developing effective rail and road infrastructure difficult, leading to isolated areas and limited cross-border connectivity.

(ii) **Limited cross-border coordination**
Political and historical disagreements have disrupted collaboration between South Asian countries, causing setbacks in cross-border infrastructure initiatives. To facilitate the seamless flow of goods and individuals across boundaries, it is essential to establish bilateral accords. The area grapples with political and geopolitical strains, which encompass historical contentions and territorial disagreements, and these strains can act as obstacles to cross-border infrastructure undertakings and cooperative efforts. A notable illustration of this is the enduring tensions between India and Pakistan, which have hampered endeavours to enhance road and rail connections between the two nations.

(iii) **Inadequate infrastructure**
Many countries in South Asia lack well-developed road and rail infrastructure. Existing infrastructure is often outdated and needs modernisation and expansion to accommodate the growing trade and transportation demands.

(iv) **Differing standards and regulations**
Different countries in South Asia have varying standards and regulations related to transportation, safety and environmental standards. Harmonising these standards can be a significant challenge.

(v) **Lack of regional cooperation**
Limited cooperation among South Asian countries on transportation projects and infrastructure development inhibits progress toward improving connectivity.

(vi) **Capital and investment**
Developing robust transport networks requires significant financial investments, which many countries in the region struggle to deliver.

In addition, attracting private investment is difficult due to perceived risks associated with political instability and uncertain regulatory framework.

5. Initiatives and Progress

(a) **Trans-Asian railway network**
The United Nations Economic and Social Commission for Asia and the Pacific (ESCAP) has launched the Trans-Asian Railway (TAR) project to connect South Asia with other regions through rail lines. TAR envisions better cross-border rail links, facilitating the movement of goods and passengers.

(b) **South Asian Association for Regional Cooperation (SAARC)**
SAARC member states emphasise the importance of regional connectivity. The SAARC Framework Agreement on Regulations for the Circulation of Passengers and Cargo is intended to facilitate road transport and resolve regulatory issues between Member States.

(c) **Sub-regional connectivity in South Asia**
Since 2010, the Asian Development Bank (ADB) has supported the South Asia Sub-regional Economic Cooperation (SASEC) programme to enhance regional transport connectivity in Bangladesh, Bhutan, India and Nepal. ADB has facilitated the planning and execution of vital projects under SAARC and BIMSTEC frameworks, focusing on transport corridors and railways. They have also endorsed projects like road connectivity in Bangladesh and Nepal and border infrastructure development in India, Bangladesh, Nepal and Bhutan to improve trade and regional cooperation.

(d) **Asian road network**
The South Asian countries are part of the Asia Highway Network, an initiative of ESCAP. The project aims to develop an integrated regional road network, improving connectivity and commerce.

(e) **Belt and Road Initiative (BRI) in China**
The object of both enthusiasm and prudence, the BRI has enabled the fundraising and construction of several infrastructure projects in South Asia. These initiatives, such as the China–Pakistan Economic Corridor

(CPEC) and the Bangladesh–China–India–Myanmar Corridor (BCIM), also aim to improve road and rail connectivity.

(f) **India–Nepal trade linkages**
Nepal plays a vital role in the BIMSTEC framework. A recent amendment to the Railway Services Agreement (RSA) between Nepal and India is significant. It allows authorised cargo train operators from India's public and private sectors to transport cargo to and from Nepal. This amendment covers various types of cargo and rolling stock. However, there are unresolved issues, such as expanding rail connectivity to more border points. Establishing direct rail links between Indian seaports and different parts of Nepal could greatly boost trade and industrialisation, fostering economic cooperation between the two nations. Further discussions on transit treaties are needed for Nepal's trade competitiveness.

6. Conclusion

Better rail and road connectivity in South Asia is vital for various reasons. Improved transportation infrastructure can stimulate economic growth, reduce poverty and promote regional integration. It can also enhance tourism, cultural exchanges and trade facilitation, increasing cooperation among South Asian countries.

However, several barriers hinder the progress of connectivity initiatives in the region. These include geographical challenges, political tensions, inadequate infrastructure, differing standards and limited regional cooperation. Additionally, securing the necessary capital and investment for infrastructure development remains a significant obstacle.

Despite these challenges, notable initiatives and progress in enhancing connectivity have been made. Projects like the Trans-Asian Railway Network, SAARC agreements and the Asian Road Network aim to improve regional transport links. Furthermore, China's Belt and Road Initiative (BRI) and India–Nepal trade linkages have the potential to contribute significantly to connectivity in South Asia.

In conclusion, while challenges exist, improving rail and road connectivity in South Asia remains crucial for economic growth, poverty reduction and regional cooperation. Addressing barriers and continuing collaborative efforts are essential to realising the full potential of the region's connectivity initiatives.

7. Policy Recommendations

Despite the benefit of closeness, South Asia's lack of regional connectedness has a long history of mistrust, violence and political change. Additionally, India's role as the region's "big brother" has discouraged its smaller neighbours from taking the lead. To foster trust and balance China's expanding connections with its neighbours, the policy must remove obstacles and promote greater connectivity in all sectors of India. To ensure mutual economic gains, countries in the region must acknowledge the potential and advantages of trade. The following recommendations are based on extensive trade and regional integration research in South Asia.

The realisation of robust rail and road connectivity in South Asia is a critical step towards harnessing the region's immense economic growth and integration potential. While challenges exist, initiatives like the Trans-Asian Railway, SAARC agreements, the Asian Highway Network and projects under the Belt and Road Initiative demonstrate the collective commitment to address these issues. Through coordinated efforts, increased funding and sustained cooperation, South Asia can overcome its connectivity challenges and emerge as a formidable player in the global economy.

As the post-COVID pandemic era begins, regional cooperation, especially for South Asian countries, is the way to go. Intra-regional commerce among South Asian countries accounts for only 5–6% of overall trade, or less than a third of its potential, making it one of the least integrated blocks. According to Cecile Fruman, Director of Regional Integration and Engagement for South Asia at the World Bank, intra-regional investments are considerably smaller, making up only 0.6% of global FDI coming into the region and 2.7% of global FDI leaving the region. Fruman has been making a concerted effort to increase connectivity with the nations in this region. She tells India Narrative in an interview that an increase in regional trade and investments would open up productivity improvements, job chances, and economic prospects.

References

Asian Development Bank. (2022a). Nepal's economy to modestly expand in FY2023. https://www.adb.org/news/nepal-economy-modestly-expand-fy2023.

Asian Development Bank. (2022b, December 23). BIMSTEC trade facilitation strategic framework 2030. https://www.adb.org/publications/bimstec-trade-facilitation-strategic-framework-2030.

Basil, A. K. (2022). Religious tourism: An opportunity to further Nepal–India ties. https://www.aidiaasia.org/research-article/religious-tourism-an-opportunity-to-further-nepal-india-ties.

Batool, I. and Goldmann, K. (2020). The role of public and private transport infrastructure capital in economic growth. Evidence from Pakistan. *Research in Transportation Economics.* https://doi.org/10.1016/j.retrec.2020.100886.

Beria, P. and Scholz, A. (2010). Strategies and pitfalls in the infrastructure development of airports: A comparison of Milan Malpensa and Berlin Brandenburg international airports. *Journal of Air Transport Management, 16*(2), 65–73. https://doi.org/ 10.1016/j.jairtraman.2009.10.004.

Calderon, C. A. and Serven, L. (2004). The effects of infrastructure development on growth and income distribution. *World Bank Policy Research Working Paper* No. WPS 3400. World Bank, Washington, DC.

ESCAP. (2015). Harnessing public–private partnerships to bridge infrastructure gaps in South Asia. https://www.unescap.org/news/harnessing-public–private-partnerships-bridge-infrastructure-gaps-south-asia.

ICIMOD. (2021, October 28). Regional Cooperation for Tourism Development: High-level dialogue on promoting India–Nepal cross-border tourism, trade, and industry. https://www.icimod.org/regional-cooperation-for-tourism-development-high-level-dialogue-on-promoting-india-nepal-cross-border-tourism-trade-and-industry/.

Lin, X. (2020). Multiple pathways of transportation investment to promote economic growth in China: A structural equation modelling perspective. *Transportation Letters, 12*(7), 471–482.

Rehman, F. U. and Noman, A. A. (2021). Does infrastructure promote exports and foreign direct investment in selected southeast Asian economies? An application of global infrastructure index. *Journal of Economic Studies, 48*(7), 1346–1370. https://doi.org/ 10.1108/JES-03-2020-0123.

Rehman, F. U. and Sohag, K. (2022). Does transport infrastructure spur export diversification and sophistication in the G-20 economies? An application of CSARDL. *Applied Economics Letters.* https://doi.org/10.1080/13504851.2022.2083554.

Sahoo, S. and Sexena, K. K. (1999). Infrastructure and economic development: Some empirical evidence. *Indian Economic Journal, 47*(2), 54–66.

Straub, S., Vellutini, C., and Walters, M. (2008). Infrastructure and economic growth in East Asia. *World Bank Policy Research Working Paper* No. 4589. World Bank, Washington, DC.

Wang, C., Lim, M. K., Zhang, X., Zhao, L., and Lee, P. T. W. (2020). Railway and road infrastructure in the belt and road initiative countries: Estimating the impact of transport infrastructure on economic growth. *Transportation Research Part A: Policy and Practice, 134,* 288–307. https://doi.org/10.1016/j.tra.2020.02.009.

Zhang, J. and Zhang, Y. (2021). The relationship between China's income inequality and transport infrastructure, economic growth, and carbon emissions. *Growth and Change, 52*(1), 243–264.

Part V

Resilient South Asian Economies amid Global Pandemic

Chapter 16

Financial Crises in South Asia Caused by COVID-19 Disruption

Muhammad Nadir Shabbir[*,‡], Kainat Iftikhar[†,§], and Tanveer Bagh[†,¶]

[*]School of International Trade and Economics,
Central University of Finance and Economics,
Beijing, China

[†]School of Finance, Central University of Finance and Economics,
Beijing, China

[‡]muhammadnadir948@gmail.com
[§]kainatiftikhar0298@gmail.com
[¶]baghtanveer@gmail.com

Abstract

An unprecedented and catastrophic COVID-19 pandemic threatened the lives of people everywhere. There has been a significant hit on the economic engine's ability to generate income and prosperity across the board. Countries in South Asia are likewise doing their best to deal with the effects of the pandemic. This chapter explores the scope of the pandemic, the actions taken by regional governments and potential next steps. All economic indices, predictions and growth trends were thrown off by the pandemic's impact on services, manufacturing, trade, supply chain and small enterprises in particular. In this chapter, we'll look at what countries have done to prepare for and respond to pandemics, as well as the possibilities that have arisen as a result of these crises.

Keywords: COVID-19, pandemic, South Asia, economy, job market, policy response.

1. Introduction

South Asia must now fight the COVID-19 pandemic for over two billion people. The extensive outbreak has hampered regional trade and finance. As suggested by the World Health Organization, the pandemic led to lockdowns, stay-at-home orders, community quarantines, travel restrictions and temporary company closures. The pandemic led to the closing of entire economic sectors, especially ones relying on human connection. Many people lost their employment as authorities forced such firms to close to prevent COVID-19. Unemployed workers reduced their expenditures. In 2020, COVID-19 outbreaks and lockdowns, mainly in Bangladesh and India, are predicted to affect regional output by 6.7% (Fu and Ls, 2021; Mathieu *et al.*, 2020; Ratna *et al.*, 2020).

Beginning in Nepal on 23 January 2020 and moving through Sri Lanka on 27 January, India on 30 January, Afghanistan on 24 February, Pakistan on 26 February, Bhutan on 6 March and the Maldives and Bangladesh on 7 March, tourists and students from Italy, the United States, China and Iran spread the disease throughout the South Asian region (ADB, 2020; Chalise and Pathak, 2020; IMF, 2020; WorldBank, 2020). New, perhaps more infectious COVID-19 variations are also on the horizon (Iqbal *et al.*, 2020; Sarkar *et al.*, 2020; *The Times of India*), The number of cases in Maldives and Bhutan has dropped to practically zero, as seen in Table 1. India experienced the most deaths, Bhutan the fewest. However, the delta variant's latest outbreak has harmed India's daily instances and deaths. India, Brazil and the United States are worst-hit. If COVID-19 cases rise, India and Pakistan may lock down and contain.

The impacted region suffered economic harm from World Health Organization lockdowns, stay-at-home orders, community quarantines, travel restrictions and temporary company closures. This closed huge parts of the economy, notably human-dependent ones. Many workers were fired when authorities used personal connections to shut down

Table 1. The situation of COVID-19 in South Asia May 2023.

Country	Total cases	Total deaths	Total recovered	Active cases	Total cases 1 (million)	Total deaths 1 (million)	Total tests
India	44,986,934	531,839	44,447,472	6,591	31,983	378	660,940
Pakistan	1,580,967	30,660	1,538,689	11,618	6,889	134	133,215
Bangladesh	2,038,539	29,446	1,998,448	10,645	12,142	175	90,862
Sri Lanka	672,380	16,868	655,461	51	31,164	782	300,619
Nepal	1,003,307	12,031	991,218	58	33,194	398	199,961
Bhutan	62,668	21	61,564	1,083	79,534	27	2,923,739
Afghanistan	220,559	7,912	196,378	16,269	5,412	194	30,819
Maldives	186,625	315	163,687	22,623	344,973	582	4,092,223

businesses to stop the spread of COVID-19. Jobless people also consume less. In 2020, COVID-19 breakouts and national lockdowns in Bangladesh, Pakistan and India are expected to reduce regional production by 6.7% (Fu and Ls, 2021).

Demand-side shocks on trade and production ties also decreased as a result of the lockdown, in addition to supply-side production and trade, business and holiday travel and domestic spending and investment. Governments in South Asia, like those in other regions, are employing fiscal and monetary tools to counteract fluctuations in aggregate demand. Manufacturing hub factories temporarily shut down, disrupting supply chains and reducing activity downstream, particularly in neighbouring countries. This affects AMS and supply chain workers. The administration cautiously took extra measures to deal with supply shocks because it was worried about the virus spreading. Governments supported non-shutdown industries that were hit by aggregate shocks.

As the COVID-19 pandemic quickly spread in China, most countries in South Asia limited or banned travel to and from China. As a result, businesses and the people who rely on them see an immediate and detrimental effect from the widespread cancellation of appointments within the tourism industry. This situation prompted the governments of South Asian nations to take action in support of their tourism and related businesses. Subsidies, tax exemptions, and loans were made available to the hospitality, transportation and retail industries. In addition, financial aid and subsidies were made available to those working in these fields.

2. Economic Growth Outlook

As COVID-19 spread in China, most South Asian countries cancelled flights and closed borders. Thus, tourism industry booking cancellations hurt firms and their customers. This crisis forced South Asian governments to provide tourist and ancillary industry aid. Hospitality, transportation and retail received subsidies, tax exemptions and loans. These professionals also received financial assistance and subsidies (Statista, 2020; worldometers.info, 2023; WTTC, 2020).

As shown in Table 2, South Asian governments cut their growth predictions but preserved most of their goals since they expected a minimal effect. By March 2020, the epidemic was shaking the region's underprepared health care systems. Business stopped due to government containment. The lockdown was likely to hurt exports, remittances, consumption, transportation and tourism, lowering growth predictions. We'll examine national forecasts.

2.1. *Afghanistan*

The country's top concerns are war, security and the precarious state of the peace process. Expectations for the underdeveloped economy's GDP growth were dampened by the pandemic. Due to the pandemic and security situation, the initial forecasts were reduced by 5.5%, and the second revision dropped them by further 8.5%. The drag-out on real GDP is forecast to decrease from −18.39% in January 2021 to −2.4% in 2022 and 1.3% in 2023.

2.2. *Bangladesh*

Before the pandemic, the country's economy ranked second in the region. COVID-19 lockdowns hurt the economy too. Growth predictions for July–June 2019–2020 were 2.0%. The second update in October 2019 factored in pandemic effects and lowered 2019/2020 forecasts to −5.2%. Fiscal 2020 and 2021 are expected to rebound with 6.9% and 7.1%, respectively. The expected growth rates for fiscal years 2022/23 and 2023/24 are 1.9% and 0.1% lower, respectively. Wage cuts or elimination may reduce private spending, increasing poverty.

Table 2. Market price Real GDP growth (%) in South Asia.

Country fiscal year		Real GDP growth at constant market prices (%)				Revision to forecast from October 2022 (%)	
		2021	2022	2023(f)	2024(f)	2023(f)	2024(f)
Calendar year basis							
South Asia region		8.2	5.9	5.6	5.9	−0.5	0.0
Maldives	January to December	41.7	12.3	6.6	5.3	−1.6	−2.8
Sri Lanka	January to December	3.5	−7.8	−4.3	1.2	−0.1	0.2
Afghanistan	January to December	−20.7	−2.4	1.3	0.4	−1.7	−3.9
Fiscal year basis		FY21/22	FY22/23(e)	FY23/24(f)	FY24/25(f)	FY23/24(f)	FY24/25(f)
India	April to March	9.1	6.9	6.3	6.4	−0.7	0.3
Fiscal year basis		FY20/21	FY21/22	FY22/23(e)	FY23/24(f)	FY22/23(f)	FY23/24(f)
Bangladesh	July to June	6.9	7.1	5.2	6.2	−0.9	0.0
Bhutan	July to June	−3.3	4.3	4.5	3.1	0.4	−0.6
Nepal	July to June	4.2	5.8	4.1	4.9	−1.0	0.0
Pakistan	July to June	5.7	6.0	0.4	2.0	−1.6	−1.2

2.3. Bhutan

Because of its dependence on and integration with its neighbour's economy, Bhutan's economy suffers. Before COVID-19, the country grew 5.5%. Tourism was hurt heavily by India's economic crisis. In March 2021, the GDP growth rate for fiscal year 2019/2020 was lowered down to 0.8% from 1.5%. GDP fell 3.3% in FY2020/2021 but rebounded 4.3% the following year. Early FY22/23 predictions indicate optimistic growth of 4.5%. The October 2022 updates cut FY2022/FY2023 predictions by 0.4% and 3.9%, respectively, and FY2024 projections by 0.6% and 1.2%. Thus, poverty reduction goals must be reassessed soon.

2.4. India

COVID-19 caused a nationwide lockdown of the region's major economy. Pandemic shocks and revenue losses will depress the economy. March 2021 lowered the 2020/21 fiscal year GDP drop from 9.6% to 8.5%. The FY2021/2022 GDP growth rate of 9.1% is actually greater. The initial GDP decrease projection for fiscal year (April–March) 2022/2023 was 2.2%, 6.9%, and 6.3% for FY23/24. According to October 2022 revisions, the pandemic's lasting effects will decrease economic growth to −0.7% in 2023/2024 and 0.3% in 2024/2025. Despite forecasts of a 1.1% rebound into the green zone in 2021, recent growth has been surprising due to financial uncertainty. Once the global economy steadied in late 2021, the export market and export-led industrial network were expected to grow.

2.5. Maldives

The baseline predictions predicted a 19.5% GDP drop, and the March 2021 update predicted 28%. Tourism-dependent industries suffered most. Early 2020 worldwide travel restrictions made the point clear. After removing the COVID restriction, the fiscal year 2021 growth rate was 41.7%, but it is expected to drop to 12.3% in 2022. Growth is expected to be 6.6% in 2023 and 5.3% in 2024. The relaxation of worldwide travel restrictions and global financial crises are expected to reduce GDP by 1.6% in 2023 and 2.8% in 2022. Since GDP was predicted to shrink, the October 2022 revision kept it in the red. GDP will rise 7.6% in 2021.

2.6. Nepal

Landlocked nations must trade with neighbours. As the pandemic expanded across the region, nominal GDP growth was lowered from 0.2% to 1.9% for the fiscal year (mid-July to mid-July). The latest predictions are far worse, with a 6.2% decline for 2019/2020 and 5.9% for 2020/21. In FY20/21, real growth was 4.2%, and in FY21/22, it was 5.8% (1.6% higher). Revenue growth will reach 4.1% in FY22/23 and 4.9% in FY23/24, −1.0% for FY22/23 and 0.0% for FY23/24, adjusted in October 2022. Nepal's tourism attractions and Everest climbing expeditions are also famous. Travelling and mobility restrictions in early 2020 halted all tourism operations, which will continue until COVID-19 and the world economy revive.

2.7. Pakistan

The country is an outlier because there was no nationwide lockdown and few COVID-19 deaths. The 2019/2020 fiscal year (July–June) GDP was expected to dip by 1.5%. Regional reductions of 3.9% and 2.5% in fiscal years 2019/2020 and 2020/2021 are comparable. However, the real growth in FY20/21 was 5.7% and in FY21/22, it was 6.0%. Due to COVID, unemployment, political uncertainty and global financial worries, the expected growth rate for 2022/23 has declined by 5.6% and for 2023/2024 by 0.4%. The October 2022 predictions show a poor −1.6% growth rate for FY22/23, which is anticipated to continue into FY23/24 at −1.2%. Pay cuts reduced economic activity and consumption. Political turmoil and governance issues will also cost the economy.

2.8. Sri Lanka

The country is an outlier because there was no nationwide lockdown and few COVID-19 deaths. The 2019/2020 fiscal year (July–June) GDP was expected to dip to 1.5%. Regional reductions of 3.9% and 2.5% in fiscal years 2019/2020 and 2020/2021 are comparable. However, FY20/21 real growth was 5.7% and FY21/22 was 6.0%. Due to COVID, unemployment, political uncertainty and global financial worries, the expected growth rate for 2022/23 has declined by 5.6% and for 2023/2024 by 0.4%. The October 2022 predictions show a poor −1.6 percentage point growth rate for FY22/23, which is anticipated to continue into FY23/24 at −1.2%. Pay cuts reduced economic activity and consumption. Political turmoil and governance issues will also cost the economy.

2.9. Result

The World Bank has given South Asia about US$31 billion since the global pandemic began in March 2020. After the health crises, we're ensuring a sustainable, varied and equitable resurrection.

- Social safety nets for more than 857 million people in South Asia were funded by 10 projects, which together contributed a total of US$2.73 billion. These funds allowed the neediest households to qualify for social assistance, which they used towards the purchase of necessities like food and medication.
- As a result of the US$2.5 billion that was invested in 15 different health programmes, more than 23,000 hospitals and other healthcare facilities were able to provide improved treatment for COVID-19 patients.
- The 24 education projects that are being funded by US$4.1 billion are providing benefits to tens of millions of students as well as their teachers. These activities include efforts to deal to school interruptions brought on by the COVID-19 pandemic, improve digitisation, boost access to remote learning and give training that is based on a person's specific requirements.
- The World Bank has made available more than $1 billion to assist with the distribution and procurement of vaccines in six South Asian countries. These countries are Bangladesh, Bhutan, Nepal, Pakistan and Sri Lanka. As many as 127 million doses have been purchased, 112 million doses have been delivered and 105.2 million doses have been utilised.

In addition to providing emergency assistance for South Asia's reaction to the crisis, we have maintained our attention on more long-term problems, such as climate change. Since March 2020, we have sent over US$10 billion of climate finance to the region, with 53% of that money going towards adaption activities. This is in addition to the emergency assistance that we have provided.

3. Financial Market Disruption

South Asian financial and commercial sectors felt the global lack of confidence induced by COVID-19 limitations. Business closures hit supply chains, tourism and small and medium-sized firms badly. The shutdowns increased debt default risk, undermining financial market and FDI credibility.

COVID-19 and global action have affected financial markets. Figure 1 shows that South Asian markets resemble global ones. Restrictions affect stock market performance. The Dow Jones Industrial Average fell 12.9% to 20,188.52. The 30-stock Dow fell more than 3,000 points in the last minutes of the session. The Nasdaq Composite plunged 12.3% to 6904.59, its worst day ever (Imbert, 2020), while the S&P 500 fell 12% to 2386.13, its lowest level since December 2018.

Indices for South Asia's four main stock markets — India, Pakistan, Bangladesh and Sri Lanka — are plunging dramatically. While the BSE SENSEX peaked at 42,273.87 in January 2020 and plummeted to 25,281 on 23 March 2020 due to the COVID-19, the KSE 100 recorded its lowest level ever on 25 March 2020, at 27,229. The DSE in Bangladesh

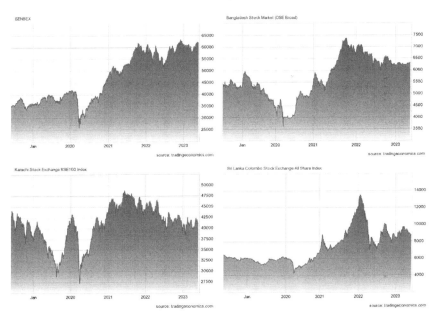

Figure 1. Indices of selected national stock markets.

touched an all-time low of 3604 on 18 March 2020, and the CSE in Sri Lanka hit 4248 on 12 May 2020. The market recovered quickly following the first shock.

UN estimates that 400 million people may become poor owing to the pandemic. Tourism, like other service sectors, is among the hardest hit. Most of the region has inflation, but Pakistan is seeing a rise, but at the worst of the epidemic, prices are falling again, which may be due to a drop in demand for fuel, electricity, transportation, etc. Figure 2 demonstrating the inflation rate during COVID-19.

Regional cases have decreased, boosting investor confidence and financial markets. The increase is due to COVID-19 containment and immunisation campaigns. Most governments use a 'smart lockdown', which doesn't entirely ban business. Monetary and fiscal policy improved performance. Most pandemic-affected nations are relieved that new infections have plummeted. India, where daily infections reached nearly a million, now has 30,000 (WHO, 2021). UNESCAP-SANEM South Asia CGE Model projections suggest 140 million job losses and 112.8 million Indians may be affected. Bangladesh would lose the second-most employment, behind Pakistan (11.7 million), Nepal (2.27 million) and Sri Lanka (0.92 million).

The unemployment rate in urban areas declined to 12.0% from a prior rate of 25.8%, while the rate in rural regions fell to 10.5% from a previous rate of 22.5%. It is not projected that the unemployment rates would become considerably worse in Pakistan, Bangladesh or Sri Lanka. As can

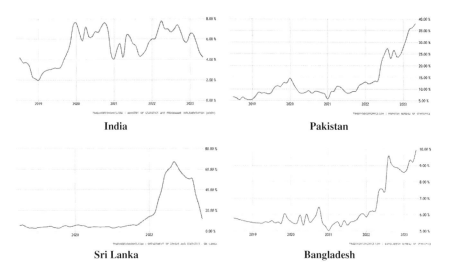

Figure 2. The rate of inflation during and after COVID-19.

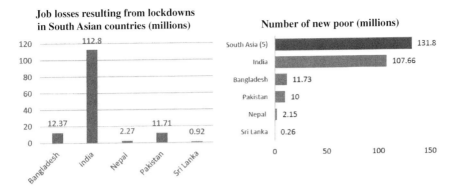

Figure 3. Job loss due to lockdown.

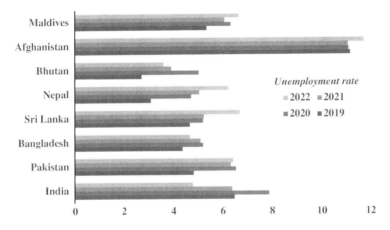

Figure 4. Pre and post COVID-19 unemployment rate.

be seen in Figures 3 and 4, this is going to have a considerable influence on the GDP of these countries.

3.1. *Travel and tourism*

According to the World Travel and Tourism Council, the industry has been expanding at a remarkable rate during the past few years. This industry is responsible for 330 million new jobs and the addition of US$8.9 trillion, or 10.3%, to the world's GDP. Exports in the travel and tourism industry totalled US$1.7 trillion (6.8% of the total) in 2016, while capital investment was US$ 948 billion (4.3%). 50 million jobs in the travel and tourist industry across Asia and the rest of the world have been threatened by the

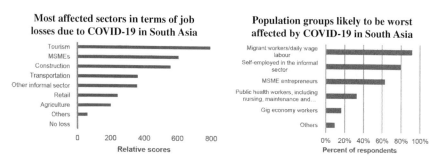

Figure 5. Most effected financial sectors by COVID-19.

COVID-19 pandemic, according to the World Travel and Tourist Council (Twining Ward & McComb, 2020; UNESCAP, 2020).

The COVID-19 outbreak is hurting tourism. COVID-19 may reduce worldwide tourist expenditure by US$8.1 trillion, and it may not recover to 2019 levels until 2024 (Binggeli *et al.*, 2021). Figure 4 shows that the epidemic might cost India US$43.4 billion and 9 million jobs. India's pandemic is accelerating. Tourism revenues in India fell from INR 182,810 million in February 2020 to INR 58,330 million in March 2020 as a result. Figure 5 shows the travel and tourism industry in the selected South Asian countries in 2019 and beyond.

3.2. *Market and Supply chain disruption*

Businesses have had more reason to disperse and delocalise production processes over the past three decades thanks to developments in information services, production technology, transport logistics and cross-border transactions. Emerging economies are adopting global supply networks that incorporate components from different nations. This pandemic revealed the world economy's vulnerabilities. A crisis in one place can quickly spread to another due to global supply chains.

Lockdowns in production and shipping can disrupt global supply lines and upset many nations. Government measures may interrupt the supply chain in addition to travel and mobility restrictions, demand declines and company halts. These actions may be taken to slow COVID-19 spread or to prevent food and medical shortages in the home market. Travel and mobility constraints cause immediate disruptions, but both worry about possible problems.

Governments must deliver life-sustaining items like medication and food while protecting supply chain workers in an unprecedented situation.

Protecting the diseased and weak is important, but so is protecting their customers. Despite the regional lockdown, governments are focusing on port and freight processing efficiency. Pakistan's food and medication supply lines were protected by smart lockdown. Governments have created social protection and food assistance programmes to keep low-income workers at home. Most South Asian economies are agriculturally dependent, thus logistics is the issue.

4. South Asian Governments' Reactions to the COVID-19 Pandemic

Short-term social aid and macroeconomic strategies to enhance economic activity and health care were implemented in South Asian countries in response to the pandemic. Income and cash transfers, assistance for the health sector, wage support and food vouchers have all been used by fiscal policy to aid the poor. Put off payments on rent, taxes and utilities to ease your budget. In order to maintain fluidity and stability in the financial sector, reserve requirements and monetary policy interest rates were lowered. South Asian central banks intervened in foreign exchange markets and increased liquidity for banks and non-bank financial intermediaries to stabilise currencies. Table 3 shows South Asian budgets. The UNESCAP COVID-19 stimulus tracker summarises South Asian countries' socioeconomic stimulus measures.

Bhutan received the most aid, while Sri Lanka received the least. Due to the uniqueness of national economies, fiscal packages expressed as a share of GDP cannot be compared. A massive disaster requires massive

Table 3. Fiscal spending due to COVID-19 as a share of GDP.

Country	Fiscal package as percentage of GDP
Bhutan	14
India	10
Bangladesh	3.5
Pakistan	3.1
Afghanistan	2
Sri Lanka	0.4

Table 4. The projected size of the fiscal stimulus needed to cushion South Asia's social and economic landscape, expressed as a percentage of the region's GDP.

Country	Economic revival	Social protection	Public health protection	Total
Bangladesh	5	3.5	2.5	11
India	7	4	3	14
Nepal	3.5	4	1.5	9
Pakistan	2	3	2	7
Sri Lanka	1	1	0.5	2.5

aid and incentives. The UNESCAP-SANEM Model replicates South Asian stimulus to reduce social and economic effects. Table 4 shows simulation results.

The simulations show that all South Asian nations except Sri Lanka would need massive stimulus packages of 7–14% of GDP, whereas Sri Lanka may only need 2.5%. Indian estimates show it requires 14% of GDP aid. Impact severity and India's starting conditions led to this high assessment. No price is too high to survive this historic pandemic. Financial assistance and debt reduction from the IMF will help member nations fight the pandemic.

4.1. *Conclusion*

The pandemic's economic impact is unprecedented in South Asia. Travel and business restrictions have caused a historic capital flow reversal, lowering emerging countries' revenue and level of living. Pakistan's high inflation rate due to unorganised sector employment losses caused its "real GDP growth rate" to drop. Slow nominal and real GDP growth in Afghanistan would also hurt. The Maldives' nominal GDP will fluctuate substantially due to the global tourism industry's restrictions, while its actual GDP will decline somewhat. South Asia has been affected by the economic crisis in Sri Lanka, the Pakistani floods, the global recession, the Ukraine conflict and the COVID-19 pandemic. South Asia is economically ailing, although some countries are doing better than others. India's large foreign reserves have helped exports and services recover faster than the global average. Tourism is boosting economic growth in

Nepal and Maldives. The epidemic and record-high commodities prices worsened Sri Lanka's financial problems and diminishing foreign reserves. Sri Lanka's greatest economic crisis may lower real GDP. Commodity prices have exacerbated Pakistan's external imbalances and reserves. The pandemic has reduced South Asian remittances.

COVID-19 would impact logistics because agriculture employs 60% of South Asia's workforce. The government created agricultural subsidies to keep farms running. The breakdown of the core raw material supply–demand chain affects all South Asian services and manufacturing sectors. Each country's administration is using a variety of immediate and long-term pandemic policies. Many auxiliary facilities support the service and manufacturing industries. South Asian governments used expansionary budgets and monetary stimulus to keep credit flowing. Short-term job programmes may aid unemployed people. Needs import and export require extra support to ensure on-time delivery. To boost domestic dependency, governments have invested in MSME sectors.

4.2. Policy recommendations

Migrant labourers' remittances boost South Asian GDP. After growing 6.1% in 2019, South Asian remittances are expected to drop 22% to US$109 billion in 2020 (The World Bank, 2020). The region grew 6.1% in 2019. Restrictions and lockdowns have hit the supply chain, travel and tourism and manufacturing sectors severely. The region's governments will likely develop new pandemic-fighting methods. Pakistan invented "smart lockdown" and used it to locate coronavirus hotspots and restrict them. Smart lockdown reduced viral propagation, allowing normal economic activity. This policy is lauded worldwide (*The Express Tribune*, 2020).

Traditional marketing, distribution and sales methods are disappearing. Most online businesses have grown and started selling online. E-commerce growth should reach 20% in 2020. In the second quarter, US retail e-commerce rose 44.5% year over year. Walmart's second-quarter e-commerce revenues increased 97% and Target's 273% (Davis, 2020). Asia has 49% of Internet users, Europe 16.8%, Africa 11% and North America 8.2% (Liedke, 2019).

COVID-19 regulations have made online shopping the most popular Internet activity. Figure 6 shows that Internet sales increased rapidly. Businesses can now extend their global market share because most

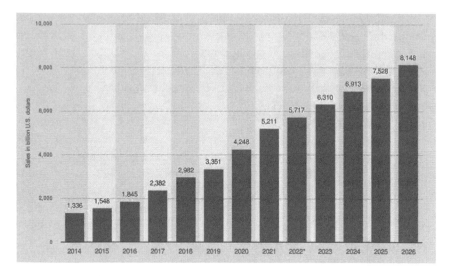

Figure 6. Online retail sales globally from 2014 to 2026 (in billions of US dollars).

countries are moving their economic activities to the Internet, especially in light of the COVID-19 pandemic. Online marketing, distribution and payment processing organisations will benefit from this. A large portion of South Asia's population lives in abysmal poverty. In this era of global restrictions, governments may offer e-commerce training to help small and medium-sized enterprises succeed. This will help businesses and enhance people's lives.

Asian governments should consider the following. First and foremost, we must vaccinate everyone. This will restore global financial activity and protect against the epidemic. To prevent another wave of dread from a new strain, governments should encourage everyone to get vaccinated. Second, governments should postpone all debt commitments to avoid enterprises from going bankrupt. This approach protects the nation's physical capital from the crisis. Third, they should keep an eye on how the pandemic is affecting the labour market and take measures to safeguard the industries, businesses and employees who are most vulnerable. The goal of social policy should be to shield those at the bottom from harm. The fourth strategy for dealing with demand shocks is to use fiscal, monetary and financial instruments. Many service and manufacturing enterprises will be able to survive the drastic decline thanks to this strategy. Finally, South Asian policymakers should consider the potential repercussions of various trade and taxation policy alternatives in order to ensure a steady supply of vital commodities.

References

ADB. (2020). ADB COVID-19 Policy Database: Policy Measures — South Asia. ADB. https://covid19policy.adb.org/policy-measures.

Binggeli, U., Constantin, M., and Pollack, E. (2021). COVID-19 Tourism Spend Recovery in Numbers. McKinsey & Company.

Chalise, H. N. and Pathak, K. P. (2020). Situation of COVID-19 pandemic in South Asia. *Journal of Health and Allied Sciences*, *10*(2), 11–14. https://doi.org/10.37107/jhas.184.

Davis, S. (2020). How Coronavirus (COVID-19) Is Impacting Ecommerce. ROI Revolution. https://roirevolution.com/blog/coronavirus-and-ecommerce/.

Fu, R. and Ls, Y. (2021). *Global Economic Prospects*, January 2021. World Bank, Washington, DC. http://hdl.handle.net/10986/34710.

Imbert, F. (2020). Dow drops nearly 3,000 points, as coronavirus collapse continues; Worst day since '87. *CNBC*. https://www.cnbc.com/2020/03/15/traders-await-futures-open-after-fed-cuts-rates-launches-easing-program.html.

IMF. (2020). Policy Responses to COVID19. IMF. https://www.imf.org/en/Topics/imf-and-covid19/Policy-Responses-to-COVID-19.

Iqbal, N., Khan, A., Gill, A. S., and Abbas, Q. (2020). Nexus between sustainable entrepreneurship and environmental pollution: Evidence from developing economy. *Environmental Science and Pollution Research International*, *27*(29), 36242–36253. https://doi.org/10.1007/s11356-020-09642-y.

Liedke, L. (2019). The Ultimate List of Online Business Statistics (2023). wpsforms. https://wpforms.com/the-ultimate-list-of-online-business-statistics/.

Mathieu, E., Ritchie, H., Rodés-Guirao, L., Appel, C., Giattino, C., Hasell, J., Macdonald, B., Dattani, S., Beltekian, D., Ortiz-Ospina, E., and Roser, M. (2020). Coronavirus pandemic (COVID-19). Our World in Data. https://ourworldindata.org/coronavirus.

Ratna, R., Kumar, N., Panda, S., and Kakarlapudi, K. (2020). COVID-19 and South Asia: National Strategies and Subregional Cooperation for Accelerating Inclusive, Sustainable and Resilient Recovery COVID-19 and South Asia: National Strategies and Subregional Cooperation for Accelerating Inclusive, Sustainable and Resilient Recovery.

Sarkar, A., Liu, G., Jin, Y., Xie, Z., and Zheng, Z.-J. (2020). Public health preparedness and responses to the coronavirus disease 2019 (COVID-19) pandemic in South Asia: A situation and policy analysis. *Global Health Journal*, *4*(4), 121–132. https://doi.org/10.1016/j.glohj.2020.11.003 (Special Issue on Global Responses to Covid-19 Pandemic: Challenges and Opportunities).

Statista. (2020). Retail e-Commerce Sales Worldwide from 2014 to 2023(in billion U.S. dollars). Statista. https://www.statista.com/statistics/379046/worldwide-retail-e-commerce-sales/.

The Express Tribune. (2020). Prime minister's 'smart lockdown' lauded globally. https://tribune.com.pk/story/2256498/prime-ministers-smart-lockdown-lauded-globally.

The Times of India. COVID new strain: Cause of origin and 4 symptoms to note, as per scientists. *The Times of India.* https://timesofindia.indiatimes.com/lifestyle/health-fitness/health-news/coronavirus-covid-new-strain-symptoms-cause-of-origin-and-4-symptoms-to-note-as-per-scientists/photostory/80232401.cms.

Twining Ward, L. and McComb, J. F. (2020). COVID-19 and Tourism in South Asia. https://doi.org/10.1596/34050.

UNESCAP. (2020). Policy Responses to COVID-19 in Asia and the Pacific. UNESCAP. https://www.unescap.org/covid19/policy-responses.

WHO. (2021). The Current COVID-19 Situation — Country Statistics. World Health Organization (WHO). https://www.who.int/countries/#I. https://covid19.who.int/.

WorldBank. (2020). World Bank Predicts Sharpest Decline of Remittances in Recent History. World Bank. https://www.worldbank.org/en/news/press-release/2020/04/22/world-bank-predicts-sharpest-decline-of-remittances-in-recent-history.

worldometers.info. (2023). COVID-19 Coronavirus Pandemic: Reported Cases and Deaths by Country, Territory, or Conveyance. worldometers.info. https://www.worldometers.info/coronavirus/#countries.

WTTC. (2020). Economic Impact Reports — Travel and Tourism Regional Performance Report 2019. Word Travel and Tourism Council. https://wttc.org/research/economic-impact.

Chapter 17

South Asia: A Case for Economic Diplomacy in Pre- and Post-Pandemic

Jitin Gambhir* and Ranu Kumar†

School of Management, Institute of Management Studies, Noida, India

*jitingambhir76855@gmail.com

†rksms13@gmail.com

Abstract

This chapter examines the opportunities and difficulties the pandemic presents for economic diplomacy in South Asian Nations. South Asian economies have been growing rapidly in recent years, but they still face several challenges regionally and globally. The human-made barriers and other actual and perceived threats on the part of national security are the prominent reasons for less cooperation at the regional level. South Asia is the least integrated region across the world. The threats of COVID-19 have offered potential opportunities for enhancing economic cooperation to mitigate the damage on the part of international trade. This chapter aims to explore the scope for economic diplomacy in the post-pandemic era, outlining its objectives, scope, methodologies and potential implications.

Keywords: Economic diplomacy, COVID-19, pandemic, trade, South Asia.

1. Introduction

The COVID-19 pandemic has brought about unprecedented challenges and disruptions to global economies, necessitating a re-evaluation of diplomatic strategies and priorities. As countries recover from the impact of the pandemic, economic diplomacy emerges as a crucial tool to revitalise economies, foster international cooperation and create sustainable growth (Ahmed, 2022). The global economy has been significantly impacted by the COVID-19 pandemic (Kamin and Kearns, 2021). The pandemic has caused widespread economic hardship, broken up supply chains and resulted in job losses (Gelderloos, 2022). Following the pandemic, nations are looking for strategies to rebuild their economies and spur economic expansion. Countries can use economic diplomacy as a key tool to advance their economic interests and accomplish their national objectives (Hwang, 2022). The pursuit of foreign investment, the negotiating of trade agreements and the promotion of exports are all examples of economic diplomacy (Lionnet, 2023). Economic diplomacy will be even more crucial in the post-pandemic era as nations work to rebuild their economies and spur economic growth (see Mishra, 2020; Gagnon *et al.*, 2022).

Economic diplomacy during the COVID-19 pandemic has presented both challenges and opportunities. On the one hand, the pandemic has disrupted global supply chains and made international trade more difficult (Broadbent, 2020; Kyte, 2020). It is now more difficult for countries to promote their exports and attract foreign investment as a result of this disruption. On the other hand, the pandemic has accelerated the global economy's digital transformation. This has opened up new avenues for countries to collaborate on issues such as digital trade and investment. Countries will need to adapt their economic diplomacy strategies to new challenges and opportunities in the post-pandemic era.

A recent report of the World Bank projected lower growth rates as compared against the earlier estimates. South Asian countries have witnessed lower investment flows, disruption in supply chains, a substantial increase in debt and over 60 million people are expected to be added to the poverty pool if economic activities are not resumed, the report adds (see World Bank Report on South Asia Economic Focus, 2021). Kumari and Bharti (2020) find that that trade facilitation, political corruption and financial development affect intra-regional trade costs of South Asia significantly. All the South Asian countries stand to gain from trade if trade barriers are overcome. Further, Kaur *et al.* (2020) show that trade complementarities exist in South Asia as Pakistan and Sri Lanka have a competitive advantage in Transport Services, while India has a competitive advantage in Computer and Information Services and Other Business Services. Maldives and Nepal enjoy competitiveness in travel-based services, while Bangladesh in Government Services.

A recent study by Kumar (2020) shows the significant spillovers of India's bilateral trade and economic growth on the economic growth rates of other countries such as Bangladesh, Sri Lanka, Nepal and Bhutan. The results highlight that the imports by India from other South Asian countries except Pakistan have a significant positive impact on their economic growth rates. In addition, Kumar (2021) highlights that long-run trade complementarities exist between the trade of Pakistan and Sri Lanka, while short-run trade complementarities exist between the trade of India and Bangladesh, and between the trade of India and Sri Lanka. Pakistan and Bangladesh are found to be close trade competitors in South Asia in the short run. The study supports the argument that if trade barriers are overcome it will lead to greater trade openness in the region.

The policy implications of the chapter are to offer how financial and trade integration of South Asian countries, both regionally and globally through the means of economic diplomacy. Sustainable regional development should be pursued by unlocking regional sources of growth like promotion of regional trade and lowering down the restrictions on capital flows, promoting people to people contact in the region through trade and tourism. The financial and trade integration and tourism should be seen as an opportunity to correct regional economic growth imbalances. Table 1, which highlights the selected economic indicators for South Asian countries, shows that they are at the lowest level of development when compared to other peer countries from the immediate neighbourhood.

1.1. *Scope of economic diplomacy*

- **Trade promotion:** Economic diplomacy promotes international trade by negotiating trade agreements, lowering trade barriers and promoting exports. It entails diplomatic efforts to address trade imbalances, protect intellectual property rights and ensure domestic industries have fair market access.
- **Foreign direct investment (FDI):** Economic diplomacy is important in attracting foreign direct investment. It involves diplomatic efforts to

highlight a country's investment opportunities, create favourable investment climates and provide potential investors with the necessary incentives and assurances.
- **Science, technology and innovation cooperation:** Cooperation in science, technology and innovation (STI) is critical to promoting economic development and growth in countries and regions around the world (Cheung, 2022). This collaboration entails nations sharing knowledge, expertise and resources to address global challenges and create new opportunities. STI cooperation can significantly contribute to improving economic sustainability, competitiveness and overall prosperity by leveraging the collective strengths of different economies. Science, technology and innovation cooperation in economic development is critical not only for individual countries, but also for addressing global challenges and achieving long-term growth. Nations can build stronger partnerships that leverage their respective strengths and contribute to the collective advancement of science, technology and innovation by sharing knowledge, resources and expertise.
- **Infrastructure development:** Through diplomatic engagement and collaboration, economic diplomacy promotes infrastructure development. It entails encouraging cross-border infrastructure projects, attracting international financing and facilitating public–private partnerships to fill infrastructure gaps.
- **Economic and financial governance:** Economic diplomacy addresses global economic and financial governance issues. It involves engagement in international organisations such as the International Monetary Fund (IMF), World Trade Organization (WTO) and World Bank to shape policies, regulations and standards that impact global economic stability and development.

1.2. *Methodology of economic diplomacy*

- **Bilateral and multilateral engagements:** Economic diplomacy entails bilateral and multilateral interactions to negotiate trade agreements, settle disputes and promote economic cooperation. Diplomatic channels such as diplomatic missions, embassies and trade delegations are used.

- **Economic intelligence:** Economic diplomacy gathers and analyses economic data, market trends and investment opportunities through the use of economic intelligence. It aids in identifying potential markets, assessing risks and developing effective economic strategies. The COVID-19 pandemic has had a significant impact on global foreign direct investment (FDI). The year 2020 saw the largest annual decline in FDI flows since 1990, with a 35% drop. Numerous factors, including the slowing economy, supply chain issues and uncertainty about the future, all contributed to this decline. As the world begins to recover from the pandemic, there is a growing interest in FDI as a means of stimulating economic growth and creating jobs. As a result, governments are looking for ways to attract FDI, and economic diplomacy is an important part of that effort.
- **Public–private partnerships:** Economic diplomacy encourages governments and the private sector to work together. It entails bringing together businesses, trade associations and chambers of commerce to promote trade, investment and economic cooperation. PPPs, or public–private partnerships, are an important component of economic diplomacy. PPPs enable governments to deliver public services more effectively and efficiently by leveraging the private sector's resources and expertise. PPPs take many forms, but they all share the same fundamental idea: combining the efforts of the public and private sectors to achieve a single goal. This can include anything from building infrastructure to providing social services. Foreign direct investment (FDI) can be successfully attracted through PPPs.
- **Investment growth:** PPPs can help attract FDI, or foreign direct investment. This is because foreign investors are more likely to invest in countries where the government is open to working with business.
- **Increased innovation:** PPPs can help to foster innovation. This is because the private sector innovates more frequently than the public sector.
- **Greater public–private cooperation:** Public–private partnerships (PPPs) can help to foster greater public–private cooperation. This is because they provide a platform for the public and private sectors to collaborate in order to achieve common goals.
- **Advocacy and lobbying:** Advocacy and lobbying efforts are used in economic diplomacy to influence policies and regulations in favour of a country's economic interests. It entails diplomatic engagement with

Table 1. Development indicators of South Asian countries.

Country	1990	2000	2010	2022
GDP growth (annual %)				
Bangladesh	5.62	5.29	5.57	7.10
Bhutan	10.38	3.36	11.95	NA
India	5.53	3.84	8.50	7.00
Nepal	4.64	6.20	4.82	5.61
Pakistan	4.46	4.26	1.61	6.19
Sri Lanka	6.40	6.00	8.02	−7.82
GDP per capita (current US$)				
Bangladesh	294.90	413.10	776.86	2688.30
Bhutan	515.30	722.83	2194.13	..
India	368.75	442.03	1350.63	2388.62
Nepal	184.92	223.71	589.17	1336.55
Pakistan	346.67	531.31	911.09	1596.66
Sri Lanka	466.90	869.75	2836.97	3354.38
Poverty headcount ratio at US$6.85 a day (2017 PPP) (% of population)				
Bangladesh	NA	93	89.4	83.1
Bhutan	NA	NA	NA	8.4
India	NA	NA	NA	NA
Nepal	NA	NA	80.4	NA
Pakistan	98	NA	90.4	NA
Sri Lanka	87.2	NA	NA	NA

Source: World Development Indicators.

foreign governments, international organisations and stakeholders in order to achieve specific economic goals.

1.3. *Potential implications of economic diplomacy*

The effective implementation of economic diplomacy in the post-pandemic era can lead to several potential implications:

- **Economic growth:** Economic diplomacy can help boost economic growth by increasing market access, attracting investment and

encouraging international collaboration. It can assist countries in recovering from the economic downturn caused by the pandemic and creating opportunities for long-term growth.
- **Strengthened diplomatic relationships:** Economic diplomacy fosters stronger diplomatic relationships by promoting economic cooperation and resolving trade disputes through dialogue and negotiation. It can help build trust, deepen partnerships and foster long-term diplomatic ties.
- **Geopolitical considerations:** Economic diplomacy is intertwined with geopolitical considerations. It can influence geopolitical dynamics by shaping economic alliances, regional integration and power balances. It can also mitigate conflicts and promote stability through economic interdependence.
- **Sustainable development:** Economic diplomacy can contribute to sustainable development by promoting environmentally friendly practices, encouraging technology transfer and supporting sustainable investment projects. It can help countries achieve their environmental and social goals while pursuing economic growth.

2. South Asia: A Case for Economic Diplomacy amid the Pandemic

South Asia is categorised as a region with a long history of political hostilities and other armed conflicts. The proxy terrorism and actual and perceived threats on the part of national securities have never led the countries from the region to come close. The trade in South Asia is under 5% as compared to other regional trade blocs such as ASEAN and the European Union. For example, Kumar (2021) reports that the intra-regional trade of South Asia stands under 5.20%, which is substantially lower as compared to the other trade blocs globally. The trade in the region is heavily directed towards extra-regional markets. The possible reasons are restricted regional trade policies and political differences (see Kumar, 2020).

The two largest economies from the South Asian region, India and Pakistan, have a long history of armed conflict. It has created the trust deficits at the governments and general public level between the two countries. This problem has created trade disputes, and these disputes have led to the imposition of tariffs and other trade barriers on both sides.

Political hostilities can also lead to a decline in tourism, which can also have an adverse impact on trade and economy as a whole. To overcome the regional imbalances, seven South Asian countries (India, Pakistan, Bangladesh, Sri Lanka, Nepal, Bhutan and Maldives) formed the South Asian Association for Regional Cooperation (SAARC) as a regional trading bloc in 1985 for the promotion of economic cooperation at the regional level. It was believed to be a major multilateral agreement despite political hostilities in the region (see Kumar, 2020).

Subsequently, SAARC countries agreed to create South Asia Free Trade Agreements (SAFTA) in January 2004, which finally became operational from January 2006. Under the agreement, the non-least developing countries (NLDCs) India, Pakistan and Sri Lanka were made to cut the tariffs to 20% in the first phase of the next two years; subsequently tariffs would be reduced to 0–5% in a series of annual cuts in the final five-year phase ending in 2013. On the other hand, the least developing countries (LDCs) which include Nepal, Bhutan, Bangladesh, Afghanistan and Maldives were required to reduce the tariffs to 30% from the existing level in the first two-year phase, and subsequently they would reduce tariffs to 0–5% in the next eight years phase ending in 2016 (see Kumar, 2020). India accounts for the largest share in the export and import of goods and services in the total trade volume of the South Asian region with the rest of the world. However, the regional trade share of India stands under 3% as shown in Table 2. Bhutan and Nepal account for the largest trade shares, which are 91.34%, and 61.02% respectively, as shown in Table 2. Services has a significant share in the gross domestic product (GDP) of all the South Asian countries. Table 3 highlights the value of total service exports of all the South Asian countries with the rest of the world.

Table 2. Regional trade share (%).

Country	1990	2000	2010	2017
Bangladesh	5.98	7.98	10.84	10.80
Bhutan	9.70	79.86	80.34	91.34
India	1.57	2.48	2.30	3.09
Nepal	11.88	38.66	65.02	61.02
Pakistan	2.72	3.55	7.98	6.25
Sri Lanka	5.65	7.51	17.32	18.95

Source: Asian Development Bank Database.

Table 3. Trade indicators of South Asian countries.

Country	1990	2000	2010	2022
Service exports (BoP, current US$, in million)				
Bangladesh	391.57	815.81	2445.06	8270.07
Bhutan	NA	NA	68.84	21.90
India	4624.86	16685.07	117068.31	309374.07
Nepal	204.36	505.93	670.94	1224.86
Pakistan	1429.29	1340.00	6575.00	7357.97
Sri Lanka	439.63	938.71	2474.19	NA
Service imports (BoP, current US$, in million)				
Bangladesh	700.45	1647.70	4389.17	12155.29
Bhutan	NA	NA	140.22	209.66
India	6089.55	19187.99	78912.97	176837.63
Nepal	167.34	199.95	869.66	1978.88
Pakistan	2072.86	2130.00	7173.00	10508.08
Sri Lanka	639.16	1621.45	3112.66	NA

Source: World Development Indicators.

2.1. *Regional economic diplomacy initiatives: A case of India*

In Afghanistan, India built vital roads, dams, electricity transmission lines and substations, schools and hospitals, etc. India's development assistance is estimated to be worth well over US$3 billion. The 2011 India–Afghanistan Strategic Partnership Agreement recommitted Indian assistance to help rebuild Afghanistan's infrastructure and institutions; education and technical assistance for capacity-building in many areas; encourage investment in Afghanistan; and provide duty-free access to the Indian market. Bilateral trade between the two countries is now worth US$1 billion. The projects across the country, which are undertaken by India, include Salma Dam, Zaranj–Delaram highway, Parliament and many more. India has contributed desks and benches for schools, and built solar panels in remote villages and Sulabh toilet blocks in Kabul. New Delhi has also played a role in building capacity, with vocational training institutes, scholarships to Afghan students, mentoring programmes in the civil service and training for doctors and others. India had concluded with Afghanistan an agreement for the construction of the Shahtoot Dam in Kabul district, which would provide safe drinking water to 2 million residents. India also announced the start of some 100 community development projects worth US$80 million. As Afghanistan continues to grapple with the extreme food crises, India has donated 10,000 metric tonnes of wheat to the landlocked country.

When Sri Lanka slid into its worst economic crisis in seven decades leading to deadly riots and alarming shortages of fuel, food and medicines earlier this year, its giant northern neighbour stepped into the breach. Between January and July this year, India provided about US$4 billion in emergency assistance to Sri Lanka. India provided about US$4 billion in rapid assistance between January and July, including credit lines, a currency swap arrangement and deferred import payments and sent a warship carrying essential drugs for the island's 22 million people. Now, as Sri Lanka closes in on a US$2.9 billion loan deal from the International Monetary Fund (IMF) and its economy stabilises, India is seeking to land ambitious long-term investments, with an eye on countering the influence of regional rival China, a government minister and three sources said.

The COVID-19 pandemic of unprecedented proportions has devastated almost all the countries and pervaded globally. However, various vaccines have been developed to achieve immunity against the virus and limit transmissibility. By 18 November 2021, 52.6% of the world population got the first dose of the COVID-19 vaccine. South Asia shares 15% of the fully vaccinated and 22.6% of the partially vaccinated population in the world. Out of them, 56.5% of South Asian Association Regional Cooperation (SAARC) regions, consisting of Pakistan, Afghanistan, Bangladesh, India, Sri Lanka, Nepal, Maldives and Bhutan, got the first shot of COVID-19 vaccine, whereas 30.5% were fully vaccinated. India has the highest percentage of vaccinated population of about 46.5% among the SAARC countries. Although South Asian countries have unstable multiple socio-economic factors, including poverty, overpopulation, low literacy about medical care and medical systems, etc., the increasing trend in vaccination status has been observed. The high percentage of health budgets of SAARC countries was utilised for purchasing COVID-19 vaccines. This report observes that South Asian countries have been significantly tackling the threats of COVID-19.

The Governments of Bhutan and Nepal are expediting the process to sign the bilateral trade agreement. The trade agreement aims to promote and strengthen trade and commerce. Bhutan and Nepal agreed to revise the list of goods for concessions. Both sides are committed to expediting the process and aim towards signing the trade agreement within the next three months. In the region, Bhutan has a trade agreement with India. It recently signed a trade agreement with Bangladesh in December 2021. Nepal has signed bilateral trade agreements and treaties with India, Bangladesh and Sri Lanka. Nepal also has a bilateral preferential treatment arrangement with India. Bhutan exports to Nepal include gypsum, coal, heavy equipment, boring machinery, juice and industrial equipment. Nepal is one of Bhutan's top four export destinations. Nepal exports to Bhutan include iron rods and alloy of aluminium, transformers, snacks, soap, furniture, woollen carpet, farm products, jute bags and cooking appliances. Bhutan ranks 20th among Nepal's export destinations.

India is constantly building and enhancing its border infrastructure with its neighbours. India has constructed efficient railway networks and other means of transportation systems with its friendly neighbouring countries like Nepal, Bhutan and Bangladesh. The India–Nepal Raxaul–Kathmandu cross-border railway project is one of the key projects nearing completion, which will facilitate rail connectivity between India and Nepal. Such an initiative will play a vital role in countering the Chinese influence on Nepal by increasing the cross-border trade for both the nations. Furthermore, the India–Bhutan relationship is being strengthened by a broad gauge line from Assam to Bhutan. This initiative aims to draw more tourists towards Bhutan. Another landmark connectivity achievement is India–Myanmar Trilateral Highway. This would link India with South-East Asia by land, and help in boosting trade, health, business, tourism and education between the nations. The biggest challenge is the security over the border, making the task difficult to achieve. Apart from the security terrorism, drugs, trafficking and other illegal issues further accelerate the issues among the nations for their cordial relations.

Over the years, the flow of patients and health care professionals along with the medical technology, funding and regulatory frameworks across the national border have increased the need for production and consumption of better health care services. For this purpose, medical tourism has gained significant response, with countries coming up with significant policies and providing convenience for its citizens. A significant change among the people has been the move towards the less economically developed nations due to economic treatment and lower cost of living in those countries as compared to well-advanced nations. The nationals of Bhutan and Nepal enjoy freedom of movement as per the treaty of peace and friendship in 1949 and 1950 between India and Bhutan and India and Nepal, respectively. Such key initiatives not only help in improving the relations with the neighbours but also aim to boost the medical facilities within the nations making it a lucrative attraction for trade and commerce in years to come.

3. Conclusion

As countries seek to revive and strengthen their economies in the post-pandemic era, economic diplomacy has become increasingly important. Trade promotion, foreign direct investment, technology cooperation, infrastructure development and economic governance are all examples of economic diplomacy. Economic diplomacy can have significant implications, including economic growth, strengthened diplomatic relationships, geopolitical considerations and sustainable development by utilising methodologies such as bilateral engagements, economic intelligence and public–private partnerships. Economic diplomacy is an important tool for promoting economic recovery, resilience and international cooperation as countries navigate the complex global landscape.

References

Ahmed, D. (2022). COVID-19 pandemic recovery: Putting youth of Pakistan at the forefront. In Haroon, U. T., Niazi, I., and Aneel, S. S. (Eds.) *Beyond the Pandemic: Leaving No One Behind* (pp. 187–202). Sustainable Development Policy Institute. http://www.jstor.org/stable/resrep46221.20.

Asian Development Bank Database. https://aric.adb.org/integrationindicators.

Broadbent, M. (2020). Covid-19 Demand Shock and Preparedness Response: Securing Medical Supply Chains: The Trusted Trade Partner Network. Center for Strategic and International Studies (CSIS). http://www.jstor.org/stable/resrep27598y.

Cheung, T. M. (2022). Innovation-centered development. In *Innovate to Dominate: The Rise of the Chinese Techno-Security State* (pp. 17–50). Cornell University Press, Ithaca, NY. http://www.jstor.org/stable/10.7591/j.ctv20pxxmn.7.

Gagnon, J., Kamin, S. B., and Kearns, J. (2022). The Impact of the COVID-19 Pandemic on Global GDP Growth. American Enterprise Institute. http://www.jstor.org/stable/resrep45457.

Gelderloos, P. (2022). The solutions are already here. *The Solutions Are Already Here: Strategies for Ecological Revolution from Below* (pp. 88–145). Pluto Press London (UK). https://doi.org/10.2307/j.ctv28vb1wq.7.

Hwang, I. (2022). The 1976 March 1 incident: A transnational human rights issue and a US-ROK diplomatic quandary. In *Human Rights and Transnational Democracy in South Korea* (pp. 119–147). University of Pennsylvania Press, Philadelphia, PA. http://www.jstor.org/stable/j.ctv1q6bngx.10.

Kamin, S. B. and Kearns, J. (2021). The Impact of the COVID-19 Pandemic on Global Industrial Production. American Enterprise Institute. http://www.jstor.org/stable/resrep45458.

Kaur, S., Khorana, S., and Kaur, M. (2020). Is there any potential in service trade of South Asia? *Foreign Trade Review*, 55(3), 402–417.

Kumar, R. (2020). India & South Asia: Geopolitics, regional trade and economic growth spillovers. *Journal of International Trade and Economic Development*, 29(1), 69–88.

Kumar, R. (2021). South Asia: Multilateral trade agreements and untapped regional trade integration. *International Journal of Finance & Economics*, 26(2), 2891–2903.

Kumari, M. and Bharti, N. (2020). What drive trade costs? South Asia and beyond. *South Asia Economic Journal*, 21(2), 258–280.

Kyte, R. (2020). Great power, COVID-19, and our global future. *The Fletcher Forum of World Affairs*, 44(2), 5–10. https://www.jstor.org/stable/48599305.

Lionnet, P. (2023). Chinese foreign economic policy in a volatile world (1970–1978). *Finding a Path for China's Rise: The Socialist State and the World Economy, 1970–1978*, 1st edn. (pp. 283–400). Transcript Verlag Publishing Bielefeld, Germany. http://www.jstor.org/stable/j.ctv371c7vk.8.

Mishra, S. (2020). Pandemic geopolitics and India. *Indian Foreign Affairs Journal*, 15(2), 155–171. https://www.jstor.org/stable/48630172.

Rosário, A. T. (2023). Security in digital marketing: Challenges and opportunities. *Confronting Security and Privacy Challenges in Digital Marketing* (pp. 206–233).

World Bank Report on South Asia Economic Focus. (2021). https://www.worldbank.org/.

World Development Indicators. https://wits.worldbank.org/country-indicator.aspx?lang=en.

Chapter 18

Population Dynamics, Skill Heterogeneity and Globalisation: A General Equilibrium Analysis

Sushobhan Mahata[*,¶], Rohan Kanti Khan[†,‖],
Riddhi Sil[‡,**], Utsa Kar[§,††], and Purbita Nag[¶,‡‡]

[*]*Department of Economics, University of Calcutta, Kolkata, West Bengal, India*

[†]*Department of Applied Economics, Maulana Abul Kalam Azada University of Technology (MAKAUT), Kolkata, West Bengal, India*

[‡]*Indian Institute of Foreign Trade (IIFT), Kolkata, West Bengal, India*

[§]*Department of Economics, St. Xavier's College, Kolkata, West Bengal, India*

[¶]*sushobhanmahata@gmail.com*
[‖]*rohankantikhan@gmail.com*
[**]*silriddhi2000@gmail.com*
[††]*karutsa2002@gmail.com*
[‡‡]*purbita.nag2@gmail.com*

Abstract

In this chapter, we attempt to develop a discrete-dynamic general equilibrium model that examines how globalisation in terms of foreign capital investment is intertwined with the skill composition of the population and its dynamics. FDI is a major driving force of globalisation and has been associated with increased income disparity between skilled and unskilled workers. As a result, this influences household fertility choices on the one hand, as well as mortality rates on the other. We find that globalisation in terms of foreign capital investment has a disproportionate effect on demographic characteristics of the economy over time if general equilibrium interlinkage effects are carefully dealt with.

Keywords: Population overshooting, demographic transition, globalisation, general equilibrium.

1. Introduction

The world population increased from 1 billion in 1800 to around 8 billion in 2022. The world population is 2000 times the size of what it was 12,000 years ago. Throughout history, population growth and the scientific or industrial revolution have been accompanied by globalisation and trade. The United Nations World Population Prospect (2022) projected that the global population could grow to around 8.5 billion in 2030, 9.7 billion in 2050 and 10.4 billion in 2100. In 2022, the most populous region was Asia, where Eastern and South-Eastern Asia had 2.3 billion people (29% of the global population) and Central and Southern Asia had 2.1 billion (26% of the global population).[1] Specifically, China and India comprise most of the population in these two regions.

The advent of globalisation in the early 1990s led to a surge in international capital flows. The experience of the success of East Asian countries created a spotlight on the role of foreign capital flows in creating the extensive opportunity for economic prosperity. Due to the refinement in the investment environment in developing economies accompanied by a fall in real interest rates, there was a surge in foreign direct investment (FDI) to developing countries (see Calvo and Reinhart, 1996; Fernández-Arias and Montiel, 1996; Chaudhuri, 2014). According to UNCTAD (2022), the FDI flows in developing economies increased from US$33,608 million in

---

[1]For more details, see https://www.un.org/development/desa/pd/sites/www.un.org.development.desa.pd/files/wpp2022_summary_of_results.pdf.

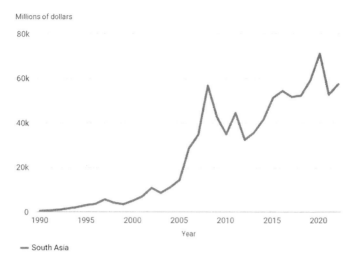

Figure 1. Foreign direct investment in developing economies (1990–2021).
Source: UNCTAD World Investment Report (2022).

1990 to US$836,571 million in 2021 (see Figure 1). Despite the highly adverse effect of the COVID-19 pandemic, the developing economies in Asia received 40% of the global foreign investment inflows. UNCTAD (2022) highlighted that the FDI flows to the developing economies in Asia rose by 19% to an all-time high of US$619 billion in 2021. The process of liberalisation in most South Asian countries started during the 1990s. The average growth rate of FDI in South Asian countries was 9.5% (World Investment Report, 2016; Chaudhury *et al.*, 2020). Since then, there has been an upward trend in FDI inflow in the South Asian economies (see Figure 1). Within South Asia, India had a major share of FDI inflow, which ranged between 75% and 85% of total FDI inflow in the entire South Asia. However, Bangladesh recorded the highest growth rate of foreign investment inflows (21%), followed by the Maldives (19%) and India (13%). This reveals that FDI has been a major source of financing since the 1990s for the South Asian economies.

Globalisation impacts the distribution of skilled and unskilled wages in the labour market. As a result, this influences household fertility choices on one hand, as well as mortality rates on the other besides influencing the skill distribution in the labour market. Globalisation is therefore bound to cause endogenous shocks in the path of demographic transition in an economy. For example, from Figures 2 and 3, we observe a downward trend in fertility rate and crude death rate for the South Asian nations in the

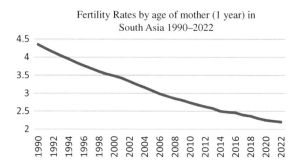

Figure 2. Fertility rates.
Source: UN World Population Data.

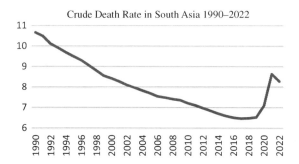

Figure 3. Crude death rates.
Source: UN World Population Data.

post-liberalisation period. Corroborating the two facts of an upward trend in FDI and a downward trend in mortality rate and fertility rate hints at an intertwining relationship between FDI and demographic transition. A two-way causal relationship exists between these two factors. Much of the existing literature had been dominated by analysis of the impact of population on FDI inflow, which includes inter alia Mitra and Abedin (2020), Crenshaw (1991), Higgins and Williamson (1996) and Aziz and Makkawi (2012). What remained ignored in the scholarship is the impact of FDI on demographic variables. In light of the fact that FDI is a major ingredient in the process of globalisation, some pertinent questions arise. What is the impact of an increase in foreign capital inflow on population dynamics? Could foreign investment account for population overshooting? What is the impact of foreign investment on the skill composition of the population? In order to address the questions at hand, this chapter develops a discrete-dynamic general equilibrium model that examines how globalisation and population overshooting are intertwined with the demographic transition. Given that FDI is a major driving force of globalisation, we analyse how foreign capital investment impacts the fertility choice of the household, mortality and skill composition of the population. This chapter places particular emphasis on the fertility choice of skilled and unskilled families. The theoretical framework to determine a family's fertility choice is motivated by the seminal work of Becker and Barro (1988), which examined fertility within an explicitly intergenerational model and emphasised the utility of altruistic parents as a result of having children and the utility of those children. Consequently, we derive certain short-run conditions which reflect overshooting of the population.

A few scholarly works that delve into the intricate realms of trade, globalisation and population dynamics are in order. There are two main strands of empirical literature on this aspect, one dealing with the effect of trade and globalisation on population growth, and the other dealing with how demographic characteristics influence foreign investment inflows. Asongu (2013) analyses the relationship between population growth and a broad range of investment dynamics using asymmetric panels from 38 countries with data from 1977 to 2007. They found a long-term positive causal relationship between population growth and exclusively public investment. The effect of international trade on birth rates had been studied in Doces (2011) for the time period 1960–2006. It uses a large sample of developed and developing countries where a time-series cross-section empirical analysis revealed an inverse and statistically significant association between international trade and birth rates. This implies that an increase in international trade lowers the demand for children and promotes a mortality revolution that begins earlier. Aziz and Makkawi (2012), using data from 56 African and Asian countries, found that a country's population would be positively related to FDI. Using a panel dataset of eight capital source countries and 38 capital host countries for the years 2001–2007, Narcisco (2011) examined the impact of ageing on foreign direct investments (FDI) and foreign portfolio investments (FPI) at a bilateral level. Interestingly, the study found that ageing leads to an increase in aggregate savings and capital demand, which attracts foreign investment. Alsan et al. (2006) employ data from a sample of 35 African countries for the year 1997–2017 to analyse the effect of population health on net FDI inflows in Africa. Their study found that increasing life expectancy by one year raises FDI inflow by 9%. Bhattacharya (2020) extends the work of Alsan et al. (2006) by exploring the causal effect of population longevity on attracting FDI flows to middle-income countries over a longer period and found that good health is not an end but a means to enable countries better integrate with the global markets.

There is a handful of theoretical literature that deals with the aspect of trade and population. Becker and Barro (1988) use an overlapping generation model to analyse the determinants of fertility in an open economy. Their study solved the equilibrium number of children from the marginal benefit from an extra child and child-rearing cost. They found that in an open economy setup, fertility is positively influenced by the world's long-term real interest rate, degree of family altruism towards children and an improvement in child survival probability, and negatively by technical progress. Haaparanta (2004) analysed how demographic decision depends on where people reside in terms of a migration model. The analysis of the paper reveals how high population growth and a high return to human capital lowers terms of trade as the economy opens to international trade. According to Galor and Mountford (2006), accelerated expansion of international trade during the second phase of the industrial revolution has been crucial to demographic transitions in different parts of the world. Interestingly, their results show that the gains from trade in industrial economies are channelled towards investment in human capital, while for developing economies the gains from trade are reflected in population growth. Lehmijoki and Palokangas (2007), using a family-optimisation model, found that trade liberalisation leads to an increase in income, which causes population growth in the short run, while in the long-run population growth decreases. This is because high income in the short run leads to capital accumulation, which in turn raises women's wages, thus making labour market participation more attractive than child-rearing.

Our departure from the extant literature is diverse. We intervene to provide a theoretical understanding of the empirically observed results. First, the extant literature is mostly limited to empirical analysis. Second, our analytical framework is a general equilibrium model that incorporates a multitude of cross-effects and sectoral interdependence in determining the effects of FDI inflow on population heterogeneity. Third, to the extent of our knowledge, we find that the majority of the empirical or theoretical works ignored the aspect of foreign investment in determining demographic decisions. However, foreign investment is a major aspect of the process of globalisation. Methodologically, using the Beckerian child preference approach, this chapter applies Jones' (1971) specific factor model for the first time to analyse population dynamics. The analysis of our household optimisation model brings out three main factors, viz., "the family income effect", "child's future prospect effect" and "direct rearing cost effect", which determine the demand for children in skilled and unskilled households. In addition to these, we derive another factor specific to skilled families, the "opportunity cost effect", which points to the labour income forgone by parents for child-rearing activities within households. In other words, this is the opportunity cost of child-rearing. Similar to Becker and Barro (1988), the optimum demand for children by families in our model is determined by the parity between marginal gain and the marginal cost of having an extra child. However, unlike Becker and Barro (1988), the marginal gain includes the child's future prospect effect, that is, the future discounted value of the child's labour market earning and the marginal cost includes the opportunity cost effect besides other factors. Interestingly, we find that an inflow of foreign capital leads to a spike in the total population in the short run only if for unskilled families the income effect and future prospect effect dominate the direct rearing cost effect, while the opposite for the skilled families. In the long run, however, this spike in population could not be sustained, thus flattening the population curve. Moreover, we find that in the short run, FDI inflow tends to skew population distribution towards unskilled individuals and away from those who are skilled. On the other hand, its long-run consequences are the opposite which moves in favour of the skilled population.

The remainder of the chapter is organised as follows. In Section 2, we provide a brief overview and discuss the working of the model. In Section 3, we model the unskilled and skilled family preferences for children to solve for the optimum number of children. The short-run and long-run general equilibrium analogue is developed in Section 4. The consequences of foreign capital inflow on the distribution of population and population dynamics are examined in Section 5. Finally, Section 6 concludes the chapter.

2. Description of the Model

The stylised economy comprises two heterogenous groups of families, where the families are differentiated according to the skill level of the household head (parents). Assuming that there are $\bar{L}$ number of unskilled families and $\bar{S}$ number of skilled families. Each family is composed of a parent and a child, and the number of children is determined by the family's fertility choice. The parents (male and female) are assumed to be one adult working member of the household, thus implying a unitary decision-making family.[2] Parents derive utility from consumption and children, however, are constrained by their labour income, the discounted present value of the child's future income and the cost of child-rearing. Each family type is endowed with one unit of labour hour. Besides skilled and unskilled labour, capital is the other factor of production, the supply of which is determined exogenously (denoted by $\bar{K}$). The production side of the economy closely resembles Jones (1971) 2×3 specific factor model, which is bifurcated into a high-skilled final good sector (sector 1) and a low-skilled final good sector (sector 2). The high-skilled sector (sector 1) produces an exportable output X_1 using skilled labour and capital. On the other hand, the low-skilled sector (sector 2) is an import-competing one that produces output X_2 using unskilled labour and capital. Therefore, the skilled and unskilled labours are sector-specific factors and earn the wage rate W_S and W_L, respectively. Capital, on the other hand, is a common factor that is mobile across the sectors and earns a competitive return r. The production technology exhibits constant returns to scale and diminishing returns to each factor. The economy resembles a small open developing economy, thus, prices of the traded goods are determined by the world market equilibrium conditions.

3. Family Fertility Choice

This section examines the optimising behaviour of unskilled and skilled households in order to determine the number of children. The first sub-section (Section 3.1) deals with the unskilled family and their decision on the number of children, while the latter sub-section (Section 3.2) deals with the decision-making of the representative skilled households. On one hand, both types of families perceive children as a source of satisfaction,

---

[2] Here it is assumed that male and female member together constitute a single unit in the family. This single unit chooses the number of children in an unitary framework. In an otherwise family bargaining model, the child preference is solved which hinges on the relative bargaining power of male and female in the family. However, we abstain from this bargaining approach and use a unitary approach instead. This assumption is in compliance with the objective of the model to determine the effects of globalisation on child preference by households.

akin to "consumption good". This is because the presence of a child brings joy and contentment to the family or household. On the other hand, children are also viewed as an "investment good", providing support to the family in old age and serving as a form of insurance in broader terms (children are treated as assets par excellence). They do not need to be bought, although there are costs to child-rearing and they embody income-earning possibilities, both now and in the future. However, opportunity costs of child-rearing differ sharply between families. The number of hours spent raising a child is significantly lower in the unskilled household since they spend most of their time earning a living. Parents in skilled households, however, can afford to sacrifice their labour hours to raise their children. As a consequence, they forego potential earnings in the labour market, which is their opportunity cost of child-rearing.

3.1. *The unskilled family*

We have assumed an unskilled household where parents are altruistic towards their children. Parents' preference is represented by a separable log-linear utility function defined by their family consumption and the number of children. Therefore, the utility function of the unskilled household is given by the following equation:

$$U_L = \log(C_L) + \beta_L \log(Z_L); \quad \beta_L > 0 \tag{1}$$

where C_L is the Hicks' composite lifetime consumption of the unskilled family and Z_L represents the number of children. While the family has the option to choose fertility (i.e. Z_L), however, it is possible that not all their children will survive. The survival rate of the children, represented by S_L defined as follows:

$$S_L = 1 - m_L(W_L); \quad m'_L < 0 \quad \text{and} \quad 0 < \delta_L < 1 \tag{2}$$

where the mortality rate m_L has a negative relationship with the unskilled wage W_L. A rise in the unskilled wage rate accentuates family income and raises health expenditures, resulting in a reduction in mortality rates.

The labour income of adult in the unskilled family is W_L. The present discounted value of the surviving children's future income children is given by $\delta_L W_L S_L Z_L$, where δ_L is the time discount factor (or, degree of patience).[3,4] The family bears the child-rearing cost of the amount $\phi S_L Z_L$, where, ϕ is the per unit child-rearing cost.[5] Therefore, the budget constraint of the unskilled household is represented by the following equation:

$$C_L = W_L + \delta_L W_L S_L Z_L - \phi S_L Z_L \qquad (3)$$

The household optimisation problem assumes the following form:

$$\begin{aligned} &\text{Max} \quad U_L = \log(C_L) + \beta_L \log(Z_L); \quad \beta_L > 0 \\ &\{C_L, Z_L\} \\ &\text{subject to:} \\ &C_L = W_L + \delta_L W_L S_L Z_L - \phi S_L Z_L \\ &S_L = 1 - m_L(W_L); \quad m'_L < 0; \quad 0 < \delta_L < 1 \end{aligned} \qquad (4)$$

The solution of equation (4) leads to the following lemma:

Lemma 1. *Household optimisation leading to an interior solution $Z_L(W_L, S_L) > 0$ is guaranteed by the condition $\delta_L W_L < \phi$.*

Proof. Substituting equation (2) in equation (1) and taking the derivative with respect to Z_L leads to the following *first-order necessary condition* (FONC) to obtain an interior solution:

$$\frac{dU_L}{dZ_L} = \left(\frac{\delta_L W_L S_L - \phi S_L}{C_L} \right) + \frac{\beta_L}{Z_L} = 0 \qquad (5)$$

---

[3] The interpretation of δ_L as degree of patience implies that a higher value of δ_L implies a greater weightage to the surviving children future labour income. In the extreme case of $\delta_L = 0$, the family does not care about their children's future income and as δ_L approaches towards 1 the households become more patient about the future earning potential of their children.

[4] This model assumes that children born into families with unskilled (skilled) parents inevitably acquire low (high) skills themselves, thus becoming unskilled (skilled) workers in the future. Therefore, the skill levels of parents are believed to be directly inherited by their children, leaving no room for skill advancement opportunities. The impact of parent's education/skill level on child's education has been analysed by Davis-Kean *et al.* (2021), Chevalier (2004), Erola *et al.* (2016), and Chevalier *et al.* (2013) among many others.

[5] The child-rearing cost refers to the expenses associated with raising and caring for a child. Child-rearing costs include essentials like food, clothing, healthcare, education, childcare services, etc. Although these costs may depend on the family and individual preferences.

The first-order condition requires the necessary condition, $\delta_L W_L < \phi$ in order to obtain a strictly positive solution.

The *second-order sufficient condition* (SOSC) for optimisation is as follows:

$$\frac{d^2 U_L}{d Z_L^2} = -\left(\frac{\delta_L W_L S_L - \phi S_L}{C_L}\right)^2 - \frac{\beta_L}{(Z_L)^2} < 0 \qquad (6)$$

The solution of equation (5) yields the following optimal value of the number of desired children by unskilled families:

$$Z_L(W_L, S_L) = \frac{\beta_L W_L}{(1+\beta_L) S_L (\phi - \delta_L W_L)} > 0 \qquad (7)$$

Lemma 2. (i) Z_L rises with an increase in δ_L and (ii) with an increase in W_L the effect on Z_L is positive provided $\left\{\frac{1}{W_L} + \frac{\delta_L}{(\phi - \delta_L W_L)}\right\} \geq (\leq) \frac{|m'_L|}{S_L}$.

Proof. Taking log on both sides of equation (7) and differentiating with respect δ_L and W_L, the following properties can be derived.

$$\text{(i)} \quad \frac{\partial Z_L}{\partial \delta_L} = \frac{Z_L W_L}{(\phi - \delta_L W_L)} > 0$$

$$\text{(ii)} \quad \frac{\partial Z_L}{\partial W_L} = Z_L \left[\frac{1}{W_L} + \frac{m'_L}{S_L} + \frac{\delta_L}{(\phi - \delta_L W_L)}\right]$$

where, $\frac{\partial Z_L}{\partial W_L} > (<) 0$ if $\left\{\frac{1}{W_L} + \frac{\delta_L}{(\phi - \delta_L W_L)}\right\} > (<) \frac{|m'_L|}{S_L}$

In what follows, we provide an intuitive explanation of the above properties and Lemma 2. With an increase in δ_L, parents in the current generation are more patient about their child's earnings in future. This may be due to the improved future prospect of the future period labour market. Given the view of a child as an investment good, therefore, this will cause a higher demand for children (Z_L rises). This is implied by Lemma 2(i). On the other hand, the impact of an increase in the unskilled wage (W_L) has three channels of impact. On one hand, an increase in W_L raises the income of the unskilled family, therefore, the parents can afford to have more children. This channel views a child as a consumption good and is termed as the *income effect*. On the other hand, a rise in the parent's earnings lowers the mortality rate, thereby raising the survival rate. Now, as more children survive, they can bring in more income to the households. This is termed as the *future prospect effect*. Thus, the demand for children increases. Nevertheless, the increase in survival rate also raises the cost of child-rearing, which leads to a decrease in the family preference for children. This can be termed as the *direct cost effect*. Thus, Z_L increases with an increase in W_L if the income effect and the future prospect effect dominate the direct cost effect, which is implied by the condition $\left\{\frac{1}{W_L} + \frac{\delta_L}{(\phi - \delta_L W_L)}\right\} > \frac{|m'_L|}{S_L}$. This proves Lemma 2(ii).

3.2. *The skilled family*

The parents in the skilled household are assumed to be altruistic towards their children. Analogous to the unskilled family, the skilled family has a log-linear additively separable utility function, which depends on their consumption, and the number of children. Given that each skilled family is endowed with 1 unit labour, the parent spends l_S fraction of time in the household for child-rearing activities, while $(1 - l_S)$ unit of time in the labour market. Parental time spent at home in nurturing their child will have a positive effect on the child's quality, which is denoted by $Z_S l_S$. Skilled households derive psychological satisfaction from their child's quality (or, spending time with them at home), which is reflected in the utility function with positive marginal utility.[6] Besides child quality, private consumption entails positive utility. The utility function of the skilled household takes the following form:

$$U_S = \log(C_S) + \beta_S \log(Z_S l_S); \quad \beta_S > 0 \qquad (8)$$

---

[6] Unlike the skilled families, low income parents are most likely to work in stressful, low-quality jobs that feature low pay, little autonomy, inflexible hours and few or no benefits. And low-income household's children whose parents are working are more likely to be placed in inadequate child care or to go unsupervised. Meanwhile, in the case of unskilled families, they must take their children with them to work, thereby depriving them of the attention necessary to improve the quality of the child. Consequently, there is no time for them to care for the child.

Here β_S is the degree of altruism, that is, a higher β_S implies more importance is given to utility from child quality. The lifetime consumption of the skilled household and the number of children is represented by C_S and Z_S, respectively. The survival rate of the children in the skilled household (S_S) is defined as follows:

$$S_S = 1 - m_S(W_S); \quad m'_S < 0 \text{ and } 0 < \delta_S < 1 \tag{9}$$

where m_S is the mortality rate of children. The parent in the skilled household works for l_S fraction of the time in the skilled labour market and earns the wage rate W_S. Therefore, the total income earned by the parent in the skilled household is $W_S(1 - l_S)$. Eventually, the children of a skilled family can earn wage rate W_S as adult. Hence, the discounted future potential income from the children will be $\delta_S W_S S_S Z_S$, where, δ_S is the patience factor and the cost of child-rearing is $\phi S_S Z_S$. The budget constraint of the skilled family is represented by the following equation:

$$C_S = W_S(1 - l_S) + \delta_S W_S S_S Z_S - \phi S_S Z_S \tag{10}$$

As a result of spending a fraction of their time raising children, the parent in this household forgoes some part of their labour income. This is the opportunity cost of child-rearing, which is represented as $W_S l_S$, reflected in the budget constraint in equation (10) as a negative term. Here it is interesting to note that there arise two effects with a rise in l_S. First, as l_S rises, the parents are spending more time with their children at home, which improves child quality, leading to a direct increase in their utility. Second, with an increase in l_S the opportunity cost of child-rearing rises.

Thus, the household optimisation problem of the skilled household assumes the following form:

$$\begin{aligned} &\text{Max} \quad U_S = \log(C_S) + \beta_S \log(Z_S l_S); \quad \beta_S > 0 \\ &\{C_S, Z_S, l_S\} \\ &\text{subject to:} \\ &C_S = W_S(1 - l_S) + \delta_S W_S S_S Z_S - \phi S_S Z_S \\ &S_S = 1 - m_S(W_S); \quad m'_S < 0; \quad 0 < \delta_S < 1 \end{aligned} \tag{11}$$

The above optimisation exercise leads to the following lemma.

Lemma 3. $\delta_S W_S < \phi$ and $(2\phi - \delta_S W_S) > \delta_S \phi$ leads to an optimal interior solution of $Z_S(\beta_S, W_S, \phi) > 0$ and $l_S(\beta_S, W_S, \phi) > 0$.

Proof. Substituting the value of C_S using the budget constraint in equations (9) and (10) into the utility function in equation (8), we have 2 choice variables i.e. Z_S and l_S.

On taking derivative w.r.t, l_S and Z_S, the following first-order necessary conditions for interior solutions are obtained:

$$\frac{\partial U_S}{\partial l_S} = \frac{(-W_S)}{W_S(1-l_S) + \delta_S W_S S_S Z_S - \phi S_S Z_S} + \frac{\beta_S}{l_S} = 0 \qquad (12)$$

$$\frac{\partial U_S}{\partial Z_S} = \frac{(\delta_S W_S - \phi) S_S}{W_S(1-l_S) + \delta_S W_S S_S Z_S - \phi S_S Z_S} + \frac{\beta_S}{Z_S} = 0 \qquad (13)$$

In order to satisfy the second-order condition, the following Hessian matrix has been derived:

$$|H| = \begin{vmatrix} \frac{\partial^2 U_S}{\partial l_S^2} & \frac{\partial^2 U_S}{\partial l_S \partial Z_S} \\ \frac{\partial^2 U_S}{\partial l_S \partial Z_S} & \frac{\partial^2 U_S}{\partial Z_S^2} \end{vmatrix}$$

where

$$\frac{\partial^2 U_S}{\partial l_S^2} = -\frac{(W_S)^2}{\{W_S(1-l_S) + \delta_S W_S S_S Z_S - \phi S_S Z_S\}^2} - \frac{\beta_S}{(l_S)^2} < 0$$

$$\frac{\partial^2 U_S}{\partial Z_S^2} = -\frac{\{(\delta_S W_S - \phi) S_S\}^2}{\{W_S(1-l_S) + \delta_S W_S S_S Z_S - \phi S_S Z_S\}^2} - \frac{\beta_S}{(Z_S)^2} < 0$$

$$\frac{\partial^2 U_S}{\partial l_S \partial Z_S} = \frac{\partial^2 U_S}{\partial Z_S \partial l_S} = \frac{(\delta_S W_S - \phi) S_S W_S}{\{W_S(1-l_S) + \delta_S W_S S_S Z_S - \phi S_S Z_S\}^2}$$

Population Dynamics, Skill Heterogeneity and Globalisation   341

The sufficient condition $\delta_S W_S < \phi$ satisfies the second-order condition (SOSC) for maximisation (i.e. $|H| > 0$).

Arranging equations (12) and (13) in the matrix form, we get:

$$\begin{bmatrix} (1+\beta_S)W_S & \beta_S S_S(\phi - \delta_S W_S) \\ \beta_S W_S & S_S\{2\phi - \delta_S W_S(1+\beta_S)\} \end{bmatrix} \begin{bmatrix} l_S \\ Z_S \end{bmatrix} = \begin{bmatrix} \beta_S W_S \\ \beta_S W_S \end{bmatrix}$$

Solving using Cramer's rule, the following optimal values of l_S and Z_S are obtained:

$$l_S = \frac{\beta_S W_S S_S \{(2\phi - \delta_S W_S) - \beta_S \phi\}}{\Delta} \tag{14}$$

$$Z_S = \frac{\beta_S (W_S)^2}{\Delta} \tag{15}$$

where, $\Delta = (1 + \beta_S)W_S S_S\{2\phi - \delta_S W_S(1 + \beta_S)\} - (\beta_S)^2 W_S S_S(\phi - \delta_S W_S)$

Lemma 4. *With an increase in W_S, l_S rises, while Z_S may rise or fall provided $\beta_S > (<) \beta_S^* = \frac{2+2\sqrt{3}}{2}$.*

Using equations (14) and (15) the following properties have been derived:

(iii) $\dfrac{\partial l_S}{\partial W_S} = \dfrac{(1-\beta_S)\phi(\beta_S)^2 \delta_S}{\{\phi(\beta_S)^2 + 2\beta_S W_S \delta_S - 2\beta_S \phi + \delta_S W_S - 2\phi\}^2} > 0$

(iv) $\dfrac{\partial Z_S}{\partial W_S} = \dfrac{-\phi \beta_S \{2(1+\beta_S) - (\beta_S)^2\}}{S_S \left[\begin{array}{c} \{(1+\beta_S)W_S S_S \{2\phi - \delta_S W_S(1+\beta_S)\}\}^2 \\ -(\beta_S)^2 W_S S_S(\phi - \delta_S W_S) \end{array} \right]}$

where $\dfrac{\partial Z_S}{\partial W_S} > (<) 0$ accordingly as $\beta_S > (<) \beta_S^* = \dfrac{2+2\sqrt{3}}{2}$.

The properties are logically explained as follows. The relation between wages in skilled households (W_S) and time spent looking after their child (l_S) as shown in equation (10) provides a surprising result.

Usually, as the wages of the skilled parents increase, the supply of labour should have increased thereby giving less time at home, but here in this equation (10), we get the opposite result. That is as the wages rise, they are willing to give more time to child care by staying home. According to this result, as the skilled wage rate rises, households are able to afford luxury by reducing their efforts on the backward-bending part of the labour supply curve. Alternatively, their income has increased so much that it has dominated their opportunity cost, resulting in an increase in the time they are able to spend with their children. The impact of the increase in the skilled wage has three channels of impact. On one hand, an increase in the W_S raises the income of the skilled family; hence, the parents can afford to have more children (*income effect*). On the other hand, a rise in the parent's earnings lowers the mortality rate, thereby raising the survival rate. Now, as more children survive, they can bring in more income to the households, which raises the demand for children (*the future prospect effect*). However, an increase in survival rate also raises the cost of child-rearing, which leads to a decrease in the family choice for children which is the *direct cost effect*. Another round of effect involves the opportunity cost of child-rearing. The rise in the skilled wage rate raises the opportunity cost of child-rearing since parents spending more time in child care implies absence in the labour market and hence, loss in income. This can be termed as the *opportunity cost effect*. Z_S decreases with a rise in W_S if the opportunity cost effect and the direct cost effect dominate the income effect and future prospect effect, which is implied by the condition $\{(\beta_S)^2 - 2\beta_S - 2\} < 0$ or $\beta_S < \beta_S^* = \frac{2+2\sqrt{3}}{2}$. This proves Lemma 4.

4. The General Equilibrium Analogue

In this section, we construct the general equilibrium analogue (GE, henceforth) of the representative economy to examine both short- and long-run effects of globalisation on population dynamics. For our model to incorporate dynamics, we use the superscript t (as a superscript) to denote short-run analysis and the notation $t + j$ to denote long-run analysis, where $j > 0$ is the transition time taken for children to add into the adult labour force. In what follows, we analyse the short-run GE in Section 4.1 followed by the long-run GE in Section 4.2.

4.1. Short-run model specification

The profit-maximising conditions of the high-skilled (sector 1) and the low-skilled sector (sector 2) are given by the following two equations:

$$W_S^t a_{S1}^t + r^t a_{K1}^t = P_1^t \tag{16}$$

$$W_L^t a_{L2}^t + r^t a_{K2}^t = P_2^t \tag{17}$$

where $a_{\upsilon\varsigma}^t$ represent the factor coefficient, or, input (υ)-output (ς) and are functions of factor price ratio such that $\dfrac{\partial a_{\upsilon 1}^t(W_S/r)}{\partial (W_S/r)} < (>)0$ as $\upsilon = S$ (or, K) and $\dfrac{\partial a_{\upsilon 1}^t(W_L/r)}{\partial (W_L/r)} < (>)0$ as $\upsilon = L$ (or, K), respectively.

The full-employment conditions of skilled labour $(\bar{S}^t)$, unskilled labour $(\bar{L}^t)$ and capital $(\bar{K}^t)$ are represented by the following equations, respectively:

$$a_{S1}^t X_1^t = \bar{S}^t \{1 - l_S^t(W_S^t)\}; \quad \frac{\partial l_S^t}{\partial W_S^t} > 0 \tag{18}$$

$$a_{L2}^t X_2^t = \bar{L}^t \tag{19}$$

$$a_{K1}^t X_1^t + a_{K2}^t X_2^t = \bar{K}_D^t + \bar{K}_F^t \tag{20}$$

Substituting equations (18) and (19) in equation (20) yields the following expression:

$$\frac{a_{K1}^t \bar{S}^t \{1 - l_S^t(W_S^t)\}}{a_{S1}^t} + \frac{a_{K2}^t \bar{L}^t}{a_{L2}^t} = \bar{K}_D^t + \bar{K}_F^t \tag{20.1}$$

Given the total number of skilled families $\bar{S}^t$, each skilled labour spends l_S^t amount of time in child-rearing and the remaining fraction of hours in the labour market. Therefore, the total availability of skilled labour endowment in sector 1 is given by $\bar{S}^t(1 - l_S^t)$. However, unskilled families supply 1 unit of labour inelastically, thus, the total availability of unskilled labour in sector 2 is $\bar{L}^t$. The total availability of the mobile factor capital, which is used in sector 1 and sector 2 is $\left(\bar{K}_D^t + \bar{K}_F^t\right)$, where the domestic capital stock is given by $\bar{K}_D^t$ and the foreign capital investment is given by $\bar{K}_F^t$.

In this general equilibrium system, there are five main endogenous variables, W_S^t, r^t, W_L^t, X_1^t and X_2^t with the same number of independent equations (i.e. equations (16)–(20)). The determination of the general equilibrium system is as follows. Equations (18) and (19) solve for the values of X_1^t and X_2^t in terms of W_S^t, W_L^t and r^t. On substituting these values in equation (20), the expression boils down to equation (20.1) in terms of W_S^t, W_L^t and r^t. Finally, solving equations (16), (17) and (20.1) simultaneously, we get the final equilibrium values of the three-factor prices. Following the solution of the factor prices, all the values of endogenous variables and the factor coefficients are determined. Non-reversibility of factor-intensity ranking ensures the stability of the general equilibrium model. This completes the determination of general equilibrium values and description of the working of the model.

4.2. *Long-run model specification*

In the long run (i.e. in the time period $t+j$), the endowment equations of skilled and unskilled labour boil down to the following equations, respectively:

$$a_{S1}^{t+j} X_1^{t+j} = \bar{S}\left\{1 - l_S^{t+j}\left(W_S^{t+j}\right)\right\}\left[1 + Z_S^t\left\{1 - m_S^t\left(W_S^t\right)\right\}\right] \quad (21)$$

$$a_{L2}^{t+j} X_2^{t+j} = \bar{L}\left[1 + Z_L^t\left\{1 - m_L^t\left(W_L^t\right)\right\}\right] \quad (22)$$

The children of skilled and unskilled families in period t becomes adult labour in the period $t+j$. The adult labour in this period $t+j$ has the analogous preference (in terms of utility function) as their parent in period t. The number of surviving children in period t in the skilled and unskilled family is given by $Z_S^t\left\{1 - m_S^t\left(W_S^t\right)\right\}$ and $Z_L^t\left\{1 - m_L^t\left(W_L^t\right)\right\}$, respectively. Therefore, these surviving children in period t adds to the labour market in period $t+j$. The right-hand side of equations (21) and (22) represent the aggregate labour supply of each type in period $t+j$. The rest of the equations (16), (17) and (20) remain unchanged, however, the variables appear with superscript $t+j$.

5. Globalisation and Demographic Dynamics: The Role of Foreign Capital Inflow

Foreign capital inflows can have significant implications for globalisation both in the short run and long run. In our model, foreign capital inflow is captured in terms of an increase in the supply of foreign capital $\bar{K}_F^t$ in equation (20). We begin by examining the short-run consequences of its effects on population dynamics. It follows from Jones (1971) 2 × 3 specific-factor model that an increase in the endowment of the mobile factor raises the output of both sectors. Therefore, an increase in $\bar{K}_F^t$ leads to an expansion of both the high-skilled sector (sector 1) and low-skilled sector (sector 2) which is evident from equation (20). The expansion of both sectors raises the demand for both skilled and unskilled workers. Therefore, the factor prices of skilled and unskilled labour, i.e. W_S^t and W_L^t rises to equilibrate the labour market. On the other hand, the increase in the supply of capital lowers the return to capital r^t. The rise in wages of both skilled and unskilled labour improves the survival rate of the children for both the families as mortality rate decreases. For unskilled families, the rise in the unskilled wage rate has three effects namely, the *income effect*, the *future prospect effect* and the *direct cost effect*. It follows from Lemma 2 that the income effect and future prospect effect dominate the direct cost effect, resulting in an increase in children in unskilled families. On the other hand, for skilled families, the rise in the skilled wage rate generates four effects, viz., *income effect, future prospect effect, direct cost effect* and the *opportunity cost effect*. From Lemma 4, we find that the direct cost effect and the opportunity cost effect dominate the income effect and the future prospect effect, thus the demand for children falls in the skilled family. Since the number of skilled and unskilled workers in the initial period t is exogenously determined, the variation in the number of children contributes to the dynamic of the population structure. Thus, with a rise in Z_L^t the unskilled labour population increases and with a fall in Z_S^t the skilled labour population decreases. As a result, the distribution of the population in the short run gets skewed towards unskilled population and away from skilled ones. This leads to the following propositions.[7]

---

[7]The mathematical derivation and the logical explanations of $\frac{\partial Z_L^t}{\partial W_L^t} > 0$ and $\frac{\partial Z_S^t}{\partial W_S^t} < 0$ have been derived in Sections 3.1 and 3.2, respectively.

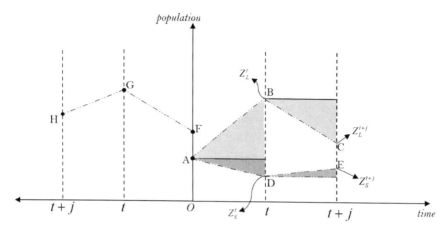

Figure 4. Population dynamics due to FDI inflow.

Proposition 1. *In the short run, a rise in foreign capital inflows results in an increase in the unskilled population and a decrease in the skilled population, while the mortality rate declines for both types of population.*

Corollary 1. *Population in the economy overshoots if the rise in children in unskilled families outnumber the fall in children in skilled families.*

In Figure 4, the geometric illustration depicts the change in population composition and total population dynamics as a result of foreign capital inflow. The right-hand side panel comprising points A–E shows the change in the skill composition of the population, while the left-hand side panel comprising points F, G and H shows the total population transition. Consider point A to be the initial point where the total population of skilled and unskilled are equal at time period O, such that $\bar{L} = \bar{S}$ and $Z_S^O = Z_L^O = 0$. As there is FDI inflow, we find from Proposition 1 that the unskilled population rises from the initial point A to point B, while the skilled population falls from A to D. Note that the magnitude of the rise in unskilled population labelled by dotted line AB is steeper than the magnitude of fall in skilled population labelled by dotted line AD. Thus, the area spanned by AB is larger in magnitude than the area spanned by AD, which implies that the former effect dominates the latter. This causes a spike in total population from point F to G (see left panel) at the time period t.

We now turn our attention to the long-run effects of foreign capital inflow. The children born in period t are now added to the labour force in period $t+j$. It follows from the short-run analysis that there was a rise in Z_L^t and a fall in mortality rate (m_L), therefore, in the long run, the unskilled labour supply increases (see R.H.S of equation (22)). The excess supply of unskilled labour, in the long run, is absorbed in sector 2 at a lower equilibrium wage rate, thus W_L^{t+j} falls. This, in turn, leads to an expansion of sector 2, i.e. X_2 increases (see L.H.S. of equation (22)). On the other hand, in the short-run Z_S^t decreases, therefore, in the $t+j$ th period, the skilled labour supply falls. This leads to an increase in the skilled wage rate W_S^{t+j}. Besides this, the fall in mortality rate (m_S^t) in the short-run, leads to an increase in the skilled labour supply in the period $(t+j)$ which causes a fall in W_S^{t+j}. Thus, there are two opposite effects. First, a fall in skilled labour supply due to a fall in fertility (Z_S^t) in the short run. Second, a rise in skilled labour supply due to a fall in the mortality rate. If the former effect dominates the latter, the skilled wage rate in the long run (W_S^{t+j}) falls. Thus, we find that both W_L^{t+j} and W_S^{t+j} are lower relative to their short-run values. It follows from Lemmas 2 and 4 (see properties (ii) and (iv)) that there will be a fall in Z_L^{t+j} and a rise in Z_S^{t+j} besides a rise in both m_L^{t+j} and m_S^{t+j}. The following proposition is immediate.

Proposition 2. *Over the long run, the population skews toward skilled families relative to its unskilled counterpart, while the mortality rate increases.*

Geometrically, in Figure 4, this is demonstrated by a fall in the unskilled population from point B to point C and a rise in the skilled population from point D to E. However, the line connecting BC is steeper than the line DE which implies that the fall in the unskilled population dominates the rise in the skilled population. Thus, the total population falls from point G to point H in period $t+j$. This leads to the following corollary:

Corollary 2. *The initial population overshooting in the short run may be reversed in the long run provided a fall in Z_L^{t+j} dominates a rise in Z_S^{t+j}.*

Corollary 2 implies that the short-run effects of population overshooting may not be sustained in the long run without any external policy interventions. It is therefore possible that the initial spike in total population (marked by point G) gets flattened as the economy traverses to the long-run situation (marked by point H). Furthermore, the initial population composition, which was dominated by unskilled workers and a relatively small number of skilled workers, changes over time to one with a large number of skilled workers.

6. Conclusion

This chapter examines a developing economy using a discrete dynamic household-optimisation model followed by a general equilibrium framework. The number of children, in this model, is a normal good in preferences and wealth. There has been a number of empirical studies and a few theoretical explanations on the impact of globalisation due to trade liberalisation; however, no theoretical explanation has been provided so far in terms of a formal structure for the impact of FDI inflow on globalisation. This chapter attempted to fill the theoretical space in the literature by providing an analytically tractable model that can explain the consequences of foreign capital investment on globalisation in short-run and long-run framework. It is found that inflow of foreign capital increases total population only when the income effect and future prospects effect dominate the direct rearing cost effect for unskilled families, while it is the opposite for skilled families. This population spike, however, may not be sustained in the long run, causing the population to flatten. Additionally, we find that inflows of FDI tend to skew population distribution towards unskilled individuals. Its long-run consequences are the opposite, which moves in favour of the skilled population. Therefore, globalisation in terms of foreign capital investment has a disproportionate effect on the demographic characteristics of an economy over time. Thus, a great deal of caution should be exercised when a general equilibrium model is used to draw conclusion about population dynamics of an economy.

Acknowledgement

The authors are grateful to the editors for providing this opportunity to research this relatively less-discussed theoretical aspect of the impact of globalisation on population dynamics. Riddhi Sil is, in particular, grateful to Dr Ranajoy Bhattacharyya (IIFT, Kolkata) for his insightful comments and suggestions on the earlier draft of the paper. The authors are also grateful to Dr Oindrila Dey and Dr Duke Ghosh for their thought provoking questions and comments. However, the usual disclaimer applies.

References

Aslan, S., Kandiş, H., Akgun, M., Cakır, Z., Inandı, T., and Görgüner, M. (2006). The effect of nebulized NaHCO 3 treatment on "RADS" due to chlorine gas inhalation. *Inhalation Toxicology*, *18*(11), 895–900.

Asongu, S. A. (2013). How would population growth affect investment in the future? Asymmetric panel causality evidence for Africa. *African Development Review*, *25*(1), 14–29.

Aziz, A. and Makkawi, B. (2012). Relationship between foreign direct investment and country population. *International Journal of Business and Management*, *7*(8), 63–70.

Bhattacharjee, A. (2023). Does population longevity attract foreign direct investments in developing countries? *Global Business Review*, *24*(2), 393–410.

Calvo, S. and Reinhart, C. (1996). Capital flows to Latin America: Is there evidence of contagion effects? In Calvo, G., Goldstein, M., and Hochreiter, E. (Eds.) *Private Capital Flows Markets after the Mexican Crisis*. Institute for International Economics/Austrian National Bank, Washington, DC/Vienna.

Chaudhuri, S. and Mukhopadhyay, U. (2014). Foreign direct investment in developing countries. *A Theoretical Evaluation*. DOI: 10.1007/978-81-322-1898-2.

Chaudhury, S., Nanda, N., and Tyagi, B. (2020). Impact of FDI on economic growth in South Asia: Does nature of FDI matters? *Review of Market Integration*, *12*(1–2), 51–69.

Chevalier, A. (2004). Parental education and child's education: A natural experiment. https://docs.iza.org/dp1153.pdf.

Chevalier, A., Harmon, C., and Walker, I. (2013). The impact of parental income and education on the schooling of their children. *IZA Journal of Labor Economics*, *2*(1), 1–22.

Crenshaw, E. (1991). Foreign investment as a dependent variable: Determinants of foreign investment and capital penetration in developing nations, 1967–1978. *Social Forces*, *69*(4), 1169–1182.

Davis-Kean, P. E., Tighe, L. A., and Waters, N. E. (2021). The role of parent educational attainment in parenting and children's development. *Current Directions in Psychological Science*. https://doi.org/10.1177/0963721421993116.

Doces, J. A. (2011). Globalization and population: International trade and the demographic transition. *International Interactions*, *37*(2), 127–146.

Erola, J., Jalonen, S., and Lehti, H. (2016). Parental education, class and income over early life course and children's achievement. *Research in Social Stratification and Mobility*, *44*, 33–43. https://doi.org/10.1016/j.rssm.2016.01.003.

Fernández-Arias, E. and Montiel, P. J. (1996). The surge in capital inflows to developing countries: An analytical overview. *The World Bank Economic*

Review. Reprinted in Milner, C. (Ed.) (1997) *Developing and Newly Industrializing Countries.* The Globalization of the World Economy. Edward Elgar, London.

Galor, O. and Mountford, A. (2006). Trade and the great divergence: The family connection. *American Economic Review*, *96*(2), 299–303.

Haaparanta, P. (2004). International trade, resource curse and demographic transition. *HECER Discussion Paper* No. 11. University of Helsinki, Helsinki.

Higgins, M. J. and Williamson, J. G. (1996). Asian demography and foreign capital dependence. *NBER Working Papers* 5560. National Bureau of Economic Research, Cambridge, MA. http://dx.doi.org/10.2139/ssrn.1702995.

Lehmijoki, U. and Palokangas, T. (2009). Population growth overshooting and trade in developing countries. *Journal of Population Economics*, *22*, 43–56.

Mitra, R. and Abedin, M. T. (2021). Population ageing and FDI inflows in OECD countries: A dynamic panel cointegration analysis. *Applied Economics Letters*, *28*(13), 1071–1075.

Narciso, A. (2010). The impact of population ageing on international capital flows. https://ideas.repec.org/p/pra/mprapa/26457.html.

Roser, M., Ritchie, H., Ortiz-Ospina, E., and Rodes-Guirao, L. (2019). World population growth. Retrieved from https://ourworldindata.org/world-population-growth.

UN Population Division Data Portal. https://population.un.org/dataportal/home.

United Nations Conference on Trade and Development (UNCTAD). (2016). World Investment Report.

UNCTAD. (2022). Trade and Development Report. Retrieved from https://unctad.org/tdr2022.

Index

A

accelerated expansion, 332
advance trade policy, 240
Afghanistan, 30
AMS, 297
Article 370, 94
artificial intelligence (AI), 24, 35
ASEAN Free Trade Area (AFTA), 16
ASEAN region, 233
Asian Development Bank (ADB), 12, 41, 119, 156, 287
Asia-Pacific Trade Agreement (APTA), 269
Association of Southeast Asian Nations (ASEAN), 7, 86, 119
augmented Dicky Fuller (ADF), 174
autoregressive distributed lag (ARDL), 175

B

B2B, 34
Bangladesh, 5, 7, 27
Bay of Bengal Initiative for Multi-Sectoral Technical and Economic Cooperation (BIMSTEC), 80, 116, 285
Belt and Road Initiative (BRI), 12, 288
Bhutan, 5, 15, 27, 67
bilateral export cooperation, 191
bilateral level, 331
bilateral trade agreement, 12, 184, 315, 321–322
bilateral trade routes, 117
BIMSTEC countries, 42
border blockade, 125
Brazil, 94
Buddhism, 27, 30, 74
Buddhist circuit, 75
Buddhist religious circuit, 74
Buddhist tourism, 75
business environment, 138
business process outsourcing (BPO), 145

C

cascading effect, 204
Central Reserve Police Force (CRPF), 171
Char Dham Yatra, 29, 73
chatbot, 35
China, 94
classical gravity model, 192

Cold Start Doctrine (CSD), 92
comparative advantage, 282
competitive advantage, 315
completely built-up (CBU), 145
Consumer Price Index (CPI), 156
corporate social responsibility (CSR), 33
COVID-19, 5, 17, 39, 49
cross-border inland roads, 279
cross-cultural, 75
crowdsourcing, 31
cultural influence, 92
cultural preservation, 73
custom theory, 184

D
debt reduction, 152
defence industry, 92
defence sector, 87
developing economies, 169
diplomatic influence, 92
diversity, 25
DVD, 205

E
Economic and Social Commission for Asia and the Pacific (ESCAP), 287
economic cooperation, 118, 205
economic corridor, 127
economic crisis, 322
economic development, 122
economic development goals, 134
economic diplomacy, 314
economic governance, 324
economic growth, 141, 151
Electronic Travel Authorization, 31
equitable resurrection, 302
Error Correction Term (ECT), 177
European countries, 159
European regional integration, 232
European Union, 119, 134, 319

exchange rate manipulation, 134
expansion of trade, 167
external debt distress, 158
external debt (ED), 156
external security, 91

F
FDI regulations, 91
financial and trade integration, 315
financial assistance and subsidies, 298
foreign direct investment (FDI), 143, 280, 317, 331
foreign portfolio investments (FPI), 331
foreign tourists, 58
France, 94
Free Trade Agreement (FTA), 119

G
General Agreement of Trade in Services (GATS), 205
general equilibrium model, 348
generalised method of moments (GMM), 57
geo-economic relationships, 204
Germany, 94
Gini index model, 144
global computable general equilibrium (GCE), 167
global crisis, 203
global economy, 90
globalisation, 51, 329
Global Value Chains (GVC), 89
Government of India (GoI), 32, 224
government regulations and crisis management, 274
gross capital formation (GCF), 173
gross domestic product (GDP), 6, 12, 116

H
Heritage tourist circuits, 71
Hinduism, 27

human development, 231
Human Development Index, 229

I
import, 212
India, 5, 27, 60, 74, 89
India–Afghanistan Strategic Partnership Agreement, 321
India–Nepal Joint Business Forum, 285
Indian Peace Keeping Force (IPKF), 124
India's economic crisis, 300
Indo-Bhutan Trade Agreements, 171
Indonesia, 94
industrial economies, 332
information technology (IT), 24, 39
intellectual property rights (IPRs), 134, 141
Inter-Governmental Committee (IGC), 285
International Monetary Fund (IMF), 155, 316
international trade, 332
inter-regional levels, 167
inter-regional tourism, 51
intra-regional trade, 7, 170, 229, 280

J
Jainism, 27
Japan, 94
Jyotirlingams trip, 29

K
Kargil, 92
Keynesian model, 150
Korea, 94

L
least developed country (LDC), 90, 171, 320
less developing countries, 205
LLC test, 58

M
macroeconomic strategies, 307
Make in India, 87
Maldives, 6, 49
market equilibrium conditions, 334
Middle East, 36
military expenditure, 151
military–industrial complex (MIC), 87
Most Favoured Nation (MFN), 117, 187
MSME, 87
multilateral, 184
multilateral agreement, 170
multilateral interactions, 316
Myanmar, 42, 74

N
Nankana Sahib, 29
NATO, 126
natural resources, 27
negotiate trade agreements, 316
Nepal, 5, 74
NGOs, 40
Niti Aayog, 224
non-least developing countries (NLDCs), 171, 320
non-resident Indians (NRIs), 33
Non-tariff barriers (NTBs), 134
non-tariff obstacles, 282
North America Free Trade Agreement (NAFTA), 16

O
One South Asia, 240
OPEC+ agreement, 169
original equipment manufacturers (OEMs), 248

P
Pakistan, 5
Pakistan-occupied Kashmir (POK), 96
pandemic, 40, 166

peace, 73
pilgrimages, 75
Poisson pseudo-maximum likelihood method (PPML), 189
political and geopolitical strains, 286
political hostilities, 138
political leadership, 90
Political turmoil, 301
private sectors, 52
public–private partnership (PPP), 285, 317

R
Railway Services Agreement (RSA), 288
recession, 168
regional cooperation, 121, 125
regional dynamics, 126
regional economic integration, 283
regional economic partnerships, 204
regional integration, 122, 231
regional level, 135
regional stability, 73
regional trade, 229
Regional Trade Agreements (RTA), 15, 184
regional trade integration, 228
regional trade policies, 135
regression specification error test (RESET), 195
religious tourism, 10, 23, 25, 29, 36, 66
repercussions, 311
resilience, 92
risk mitigation, 262
Russia, 94

S
SAARC agreement of trade in services (SATIS), 203
Saudi Arabia, 87
Shakti Peeths, 29

shock, 304
Siddh Peeths, 29
Sikhism, 27
simulation approach, 258
small and medium enterprises (SMEs), 232
socioeconomic development, 282
South Asia, 29, 44
South Asia Economic, 169
South Asia Economic Focus, 314
South Asia Free Trade Agreements (SAFTA), 5, 7, 263, 320
South Asian Association for Regional Cooperation (SAARC), 5, 24, 116, 166, 202, 322
South Asian countries, 2, 137, 211, 249, 283, 286, 314, 329
South Asian economies, 52, 134, 151
South Asian financial, 303
South Asian Free Trade Area (SAFTA), 118, 135, 202, 263, 269
South Asian nations, 278, 282
South Asian policymakers, 310
South Asian Preferential Trading Arrangement (SAPTA), 170
South Asian region, 251
South Asia Sub-regional Economic Cooperation (SASEC), 41, 287
Spain, 94
Sri Lanka, 5, 7, 27
stochastic supply chain, 262
strategic outreach, 91
supply chain management, 251
sustainability and profitability, 252
sustainable and collaborative, 248
sustainable development goal (SDG), 228
sustainable economic growth, 139
sustainable growth, 314
sustainable infrastructure, 272
Sustainable regional development, 315
system dynamics (SD), 249, 262

Index

T
total service export, 209
tourism industry, 9
tourist circuit, 69
touristic mobility, 25
trade barriers, 134
trade cointegration, 136
trade creation and diversion, 184
trade disruption, 11
trade expansion, 167
Trade Facilitation Agreement (TFA), 284
trade liberalisation, 348

Trans-Asian Railway (TAR), 287
tribal, 70

U
UK, 91
UNESCAP-SANEM, 304
UNESCO, 71, 78
United Nation Conference on Trade and Development (UNCTAD), 168, 329
United Nations Alliance of Civilizations (UNAOC), 41
United Nations World Tourism Organization (UNWTO), 26
United States, 91, 94
University Grants Commission (UGC), 224

V
Vietnam, 89

W
Wildlife, 71
World Bank, 117, 302, 314
World Development Indicators, 6
World Economic Forum, 55
World Economic Outlook, 169
World Health Organization (WHO), 166, 296
World Investment Report, 203
World Tour and Travel Council Report, 9
World Trade Organization (WTO), 269, 316

Printed in the United States
by Baker & Taylor Publisher Services